KU-284-410

ROYAL HISTORICAL SOCIETY
GUIDES AND HANDBOOKS
No. 6

HANDBOOK OF ORIENTAL HISTORY

HANDBOOK OF ORIENTAL HISTORY

BY

MEMBERS OF THE
DEPARTMENT OF ORIENTAL HISTORY,
SCHOOL OF ORIENTAL AND
AFRICAN STUDIES,
UNIVERSITY OF LONDON

EDITED BY

C. H. PHILIPS, M.A., PH.D.

PROFESSOR OF ORIENTAL HISTORY
IN THE UNIVERSITY OF LONDON

LONDON
OFFICES OF THE ROYAL HISTORICAL SOCIETY
96 CHEYNE WALK, S.W.10
1951

Made and Printed in Great Britain by Butler & Tanner Ltd., Frome and London

TABLE OF CONTENTS

SECTION IV

CHINA

By O. P. N. B. Van der Sprenkel, B.Sc.

Lecturer in the History of the Far East, School of Oriental and African Studies

SECTION V

JAPAN

By W. G. Beasley, B.A., Ph.D.

Lecturer in the History of the Far East, School of Oriental and African Studies

PREFACE

AS the interdependence of the countries of the world increases, the realization grows that the histories of all peoples form a common heritage. European political activities and the spread of western ideas and technology in the Orient have long since convinced the peoples of Asia of this fact; and daily the nations of the West are becoming more aware of the significance for them of the study and understanding of the languages and cultures of the East.

Even so, obvious difficulties confront those general readers and historians of the West who come to study Oriental history. Among other things the strangeness of Oriental personal and place names, the transliteration and pronunciation of Oriental languages, the meanings of the main political, economic, social and religious terms and the unfamiliar systems of dating used in Oriental lands, constitute formidable problems. Clearly such readers need a companion to Oriental historical studies, which will both identify these problems and give guidance through the more important difficulties. This *Handbook* seeks to perform these functions through the range of Oriental history from ancient to modern times and across the whole field of Asia from the Near to the Far East. We have not included the pre-Islamic Near East.

No living person possesses, or indeed is likely to possess, an adequate knowledge of all the main languages and historical problems of these areas. A co-operative method is therefore inevitable and indeed is desirable. At the same time, to achieve a unity of conception and treatment each area and its problems are considered under the same broad headings.

Especially in compiling our lists of dynasties and rulers, we have gratefully to acknowledge the use that has been made of the following works: *The Cambridge History of India*, vols. iii and iv (Cambridge, 1937); G. Coedes, *Les états hindouisés d'Indochine et d'Indonésie* (F. de Boccara: Paris, 1948); G. E. Harvey, *History of Burma from the earliest times to 1824* (Longmans, Green & Co.: 1925); N. J. Krom, *Hindoe-Javaansche Geschiedenis* (The Hague, 1926); S. Lane Poole, *The Mohammadan Dynasties* (London, 1894); R. C. Majumdar, H. C. Raychaudhuri and K. Datta, *An Advanced History of India* (Macmillan & Co.: London, 1946); B. H. M. Vlekke, *Nusantara* (Harvard University Press: Cambridge, Mass., 1944); E. de Zambaur, *Manuel de généalogie et de chronologie pour l'histoire de l'Islam* (2 vols. Hanover, 1927). We are particularly indebted for permission to include the following: the list of the kings of Champa from Georges Maspero, *Le royaume de Champa* (Les Éditions G. van Oest: Paris et Bruxelles, 1928); the list of the kings of Bengal from the above-cited *Advanced History of India*; the list of the kings of Khāndesh from the third volume of the *Cambridge History of India*; the list of early sovereigns of Japan from R. K. Reischauer, *Early Japanese History* (2 vols. Princeton

University Press, 1937). In the section on China, the comparative table of initials and finals is adapted from an article, 'Chinesisch', by W. Simon in M. Heepe, *Lautzeichen und ihre Anwendung in Verdschiedenen Sprachgebieten* (Berlin, 1928); in describing the pronunciation of Chinese use has been made of a leaflet by Mrs. Hope Wright published by Probsthain & Co., London; and the comparative table of the Wade and G. R. systems is adapted from W. Simon, *A Beginners' Chinese-English Dictionary of the National Language* (Lund Humphries & Co.: London, 1947).

We have been extricated from numerous difficulties and given helpful advice by many of our colleagues, and especially by Dr. L. D. Barnett, Dr. A. L. Basham, Mr. C. C. Brown, Professor G. Coedes, Mr. F. J. Daniels, Professor H. A. R. Gibb, Miss Eugénie Henderson, Mr. P. J. Honey, Mr. A. Master, Dr. Reginald Le May, Dr. Nur-ul Hasan, The Rev. H. S. O'Neill, Mr. E. G. Pulleyblank, Professor W. Simon, Miss Judith Stead, the late Professor J. A. Stewart, Sir Richard O. Winstedt and Professor P. Wittek. To one and all of them we are deeply indebted. We also owe much to the general assistance given by Miss June Bridges. In the somewhat difficult process of preparing this work for the press, Mr. Philip Grierson has contributed greatly, and only those who have enjoyed his advice, his kindly patience and his forbearance, will appreciate how much he has eased my task.

C. H. PHILIPS.

SCHOOL OF ORIENTAL
AND AFRICAN STUDIES,
5 *April* 1950.

SECTION I

THE NEAR AND MIDDLE EAST

1. The romanization of words.
2. The Arabo-Islamic name.
3. Note on place-names.
4. Select glossary.
5. Calendars and systems of dating; with comparative tables of A.H. and A.D. dates.
6. Dynasties and rulers.

   (i) Orthodox Caliphs. (ii) Umayyad Caliphs. (iii) ʻAbbāsid Caliphs. (iv) Umayyads of Cordova. (v) Fāṭimid Caliphs. (via) Baḥrī Mamlūks. (vi*b*) Burjī Mamlūks. (vii) Seljūqs. (viii) Ottoman Sultāns. (ix) Mongols of Persia. (x) Shāhs of Persia. (xi) The line of Muḥammad ʻAlī in Egypt. (xii) Kings of Iraq. (xiii) Presidents of Syria. (xiv) Presidents of the Lebanon. (xv) Presidents of Turkey. (xvi) French High Commissioners in Syria-Lebanon. (xvii) British High Commissioners for Palestine and Transjordan.

I. THE ROMANIZATION OF WORDS

One of the main difficulties encountered by the non-specialist reader of oriental history is the bewildering profusion of transcriptions found in European books on oriental subjects. Arabic itself is used over a vast area. With additional letters, the Arabic script is also used for Persian, Urdu, Malay and other languages spoken by Muslims, and was until recently used for Turkish, both Ottoman and Eastern. The same words, names and even letters will be pronounced differently by a Moor, an Egyptian, an Iraqi, a Turk, a Persian or an Indian. They will be heard and transcribed differently by an Englishman, a Frenchman, a German, a Russian or an Italian. So the Arabic word meaning a river valley is written 'wadi' by Englishmen in the Near East and 'oued' by Frenchmen in North Africa. The founder of Islam is variously written Muhammed, Muḥammad, Mohammed, Mahommed, Mohamed, Mahomet, Mehemet, and in medieval texts even Mahound, Mahowne and Machomet. His book is called the Koran, Kuran, Qur'ān or Alcoran. An early Arab governor of Iraq is Hajjaj in England, Hadjdjadj in France, and was for a time Hadschdschadsch in Germany.

There exist scientific systems of transliteration whereby each letter of the original is rendered in the Latin script, but unfortunately there are several of these in use. The following notes are based on the system commonly used by British orientalists, and the most frequently encountered divergences noted. The phonetic values given are approximate.

Consonants

c̲h̲ As in English *church*. Sometimes written *ç* or *č*, also *tch* (French) and *tsch* (German). Used in Persian and Turkish but not in Arabic.

ḍ Arabic emphatic *d*. In some Arabic dialects and in most other Muslim languages it is usually pronounced as *z*; e.g. Qāḍī, Persian and Indian Qazi ('judge').

d̲h̲ As English *th* in *the*. Sometimes transliterated *ḏ*. Other Muslim languages render *z*. Arabic dialects render *d* or *z*.

g̲h̲ A strongly guttural *g*, similar in sound to the γ in Modern Greek. Sometimes transliterated *ġ* or *g̨*. In Turkish the sound is often much weaker, and is written *ğ*: e.g. oğlu or og̲h̲lu. *Gh* is sometimes used to render the Persian pronunciation of *q* (*q.v.*).

ḥ Slightly stronger than *h*, though not as strong as *k̲h̲* (*q.v.*). The distinction between *ḥ* and *h* is usually ignored in non-scientific transcription.

j As English *j* in *John*. French writers usually use *dj*, Germans use *dsch* or *ǧ*. In Egypt the Arabic *j* is pronounced as a hard *g*, and is often given this value in transcriptions:

e.g. Jamāl, Jemal, Djemal, Ğemal, Dschemal, Gemal. (*J* in German works usually represents *y*.)

kh As *ch* in Scottish *loch*. Also written *ḫ*, and *ch*, especially in Germany. In Turkish it is pronounced as an ordinary *h*, and is sometimes so transcribed: e.g. Khalil, Chalil, Ḫalil, Halil.

q A guttural *k*, pronounced further back in the throat. Often transcribed *ḳ* or simply *k*. The Persians pronounce it as *gh* (*q.v.*), the Turks as ordinary *k*: e.g. waqf, waḳf, wakf. In pure Turkish words *q* is used for *k* in the Arabic script to indicate hard vowels, e.g. Qara for Kara.

ṣ Arabic emphatic *s*, also rendered *ç* in French. Not distinguished in languages other than Arabic: e.g. Ṣaliḥ, Çaleh, Saleh.

sh As in English *ship*. Sometimes written *š* and *ş*, also *ch* (French), *sch* (German), *sci* (Italian) and *x* (Spanish): e.g. Sharīf, Šarif, Cherif, Scharif, etc.

ṭ Arabic emphatic *t*. The distinction between this and *t* is usually ignored in other languages.

th As English *th* in *through*. Often transcribed *ṯ*. Persian, Turkish and colloquial Arabic usually sound it as *s*, occasionally as *t*: e.g. Thābit, Ṯabit, Tabit, Sabit.

w Arabic value as in English. French writers often render it *ou*: e.g. Kairouan for Qairawān. Persian and Turkish sound it as *v*: e.g. Wālī, Vali. In Persian *Khwā* the *w* is silent and often ignored in transcription, while the *ā* may become an *o*, e.g. Khwārazm, Khārazm, Khorazm.

ẓ Arabic emphatic *z*. The distinction between this and *z* is usually ignored in Persian and Turkish and in non-scientific transcriptions. Occasionally rendered *dh* and *d* (dialectal values): e.g. Ḥāfiẓ, Hafiz, Hafidh, Hafid.

zh As French *j* or English *s* in *pleasure*. Sometimes written *ž*. A Persian sound, not used in Arabic, rare in Turkish.

' Glottal stop, as in Cockney '*li'l bo'ls*'. Usually omitted at the beginning or end of a word.

' A guttural sound with no English equivalent. In non-scientific transcriptions it is usually confused with the foregoing or ignored altogether. It is not sounded in Persian or Turkish: e.g. 'Alī, 'Ali, Ali.

The following peculiarities of the new official Turkish romanized script should be noted:

c As *j* in *John*.
ç As *ch in church*.
ğ As *gh*.
j As *zh*.
ş As *sh*.

Vowels

The Arabic script only indicates three short vowels, three long vowels and two diphthongs, as follows:

a As in English *hat*, and often rendered ***e***: e.g. balad, beled, emir, amir; with emphatics or gutturals usually pronounced as *u* in *but*: e.g. Khalīfa, Baghdād.

i As in English *bit*. In Persian often rendered *e*: e.g. jihād, jehād.

u As in English *good*. Often pronounced and written *o*: e.g. Muḥammad, Mohammad.

In Arabic dialects, particularly those of North Africa, unaccented short vowels are often omitted altogether, and long vowels shortened: e.g. Oued for Wādī, bled for balad, etc.

ā Long *a*, variously pronounced as in *sand*, *dart* and *hall*. The last is commonest in Persian and Indian usage, and is often written *au* or *aw*: e.g. Imām, Imaum.

ī As *ee* in *feet*. In early books often rendered *ee*. In Indian usage the Persian *ī* is often replaced by *ê*: e.g. Shêr (for Shīr), Pêshwā (for Pīshwā).

ū As *oo* in *boot*. Early English writers often wrote *oo*. The French transcription *ou* is often met in English books: e.g. Maḥmūd, Mahmood, Mahmoud.

ai Pronounced in classical Arabic as English *i* in *hide*, in colloquial Arabic and other Muslim languages as *a* in *take*. Variously transcribed as *ai*, *ay*, *ei*, *ey*, and *ê*: e.g. sheikh, shaikh, shaykh, etc.

aw Pronounced in classical Arabic as English *ow* in *town*, in colloquial Arabic and in Persian as in *grow*, in Turkish as *ov* or *ev* in *shovel* or *never*. Variously rendered *aw*, *ew*, *au*, *ô*, *av*, *ev*: e.g. Tawfiq, Taufiq, Tevfik, etc.

Turkish and Persian use the vowels *e* and *o*, which have no proper equivalents in the Arabic script. Turkish also has three additional vowels, as follows:

i̊ Similar in sound to English *e* in *butter*, but may be stressed. It is also rendered *y*, *ou*, *u*. In the new official Turkish script it is represented by the undotted *ı*.

ö As in German, or French *eu*. It is often thus transcribed.

ü As in German, or French *u*. It is often thus transcribed.

The Arabic Article

Many Arabic names are preceded by the definite article *al*, usually written without a capital and joined to the following word by a hyphen: e.g. al-Ḥasan, al-ʻAlamain. The article is often rendered as *el*, and appears frequently as *il*, or *ul* in genitive compounds (see below) where its vowel is determined by the case of the preceding word.

Certain letters at the beginning of a word assimilate the *l* of the article. These are *d*, *ḍ*, *dh*, *n*, *r*, *s*, *ṣ*, *sh*, *t*, *ṭ*, *th*, *z*, *ẓ*. Thus ar-Raḥmān (for al-Raḥmān), an-Nāṣir (for al-Ṇāṣir). This rule is often ignored in transcription.

Genitive Compounds

Many Arabic names and titles are in fact genitive compounds, like 'Slave of the Merciful', 'Pillar of the Faith', etc. Possession is normally indicated in Arabic by placing the possessor immediately after the thing possessed. The former usually takes the article, the latter never: thus—'Abd ('slave') and Majīd ('glorious') give 'Abd al-Majīd ('Slave of the Glorious'); 'Imād ('pillar') and Dawla ('State') give 'Imād ad-Dawla ('Pillar of the State').

In classical Arabic the first component takes a final vowel, varying according to the case (*u* nominative, *i* genitive, *a* accusative). The vowel of the following article is elided with this. Thus, a strict transliteration would be 'Abdu'l-Majīd (nom.), 'Abdi'l-Majīd (gen.), 'Abda'l-Majīd (acc.). This system is sometimes used, though that given above is commoner, as it avoids the need to confuse the European reader with irrelevant Arabic grammatical points.

In non-scientific transcriptions the article of the second word is often reduced to an enclitic of the first: e.g. Abdul Majid. Frequently the whole is written as one word, as Salaheddin (for Ṣalāḥ ad-Dīn), Asadullah (for Asad Allah), etc. The vowel of the article in these transcriptions varies considerably, depending on case and more particularly on dialect. In Persian, Turkish and colloquial Arabic all three case vowels are reduced to a single neutral vowel. In Indian transcription the nominative is commonly maintained; e.g. Fariduddin.

In the Persian genitive compound possessor and thing possessed are separated by the particle *i*, the latter preceding: e.g. Kūh i Nūr ('Mountain of Light'), Qaiṣar i Hind ('Emperor of India'). In the Turkish genitive compound the thing possessed comes second, and takes a suffix, *i*, *ỉ*, *u*, or *ü*, according to the vowels of the word to which it is attached; e.g. Bustanjỉ Bas̲h̲ỉ, 'Head of the Gardeners' (from bustanjỉ, 'gardener', and bas̲h̲, 'head'). If the word ends in a vowel, the letter *s* is inserted between the final letter of the word and the suffixed letter; e.g.: Yenic̲h̲eriler Ag̲h̲asỉ, 'the Agha of the Janissaries'.

Plurals

The regular Arabic plural is formed by adding to the singular *ūn* (masculine, nominative), *īn* (masculine, accusative and genitive), or *āt* (feminine, all cases). Only the last two are used in colloquial Arabic; e.g. fallāḥūn, fellahin, fellāḥāt (peasants). There are also many irregular ways of forming the plural; e.g. Waqf (Awqāf), S̲h̲aik̲h̲ (S̲h̲uyūk̲h̲).

The ending *-ain* indicates the dual, e.g. al-'Alamain.

The Persian plural is formed by adding *hā*, or in some cases *ān*, to the singular. The former is commoner in modern Persian.

The Turkish plural is formed by adding *ler* or *lar* to the singular.

Gender

The Arabic feminine ending is *at*, usually reduced to *a*, then sometimes transcribed *ah*. e.g. Dawlat, Dawla, Dawlah, and in Turkish Devlet.

Neither Persian nor Turkish words vary for gender.

2. THE ARABO-ISLAMIC NAME

Until very recently, surnames in the European sense of the word were almost unknown in the Muslim Near East, and they are still rare. The Arabo-Islamic name is normally made up as follows.

(1) The *Ism* or *'Alam*, the personal name. This is usually Arab, and may be of several types, of which the following are the commonest:

(*a*) Biblical names in their Koranic forms, such as Hārūn (Aaron), Ibrāhīm (Abraham), Sulaimān (Solomon), Idrīs (Enoch), etc.

(*b*) Other Arab names, largely pre-Islamic in origin, most of them being Arabic adjectives or substantives with a definite meaning: e.g. Aḥmad, 'Alī, Ḥasan, Ḥusain, Muḥammad, 'Uthman, etc. Some of these are often to be found with the Arabic definite article, e.g. al-Ḥasan, al-'Abbās, etc.

(*c*) Compound names, usually consisting of '*Abd* (' slave ') followed by Allah (' God ') or by one of the ninety-nine divine attributes; e.g. 'Abd al-'Azīz, ' Slave of the Mighty ', 'Abd al-Majīd, ' Slave of the Glorious ', 'Abd al-Karīm, ' Slave of the Generous ', etc. Other compounds with Allah are also used: Ni'mat Allah, ' Grace of God ', Hibat Allah, ' Gift of God ', etc. Among the Arabic-speaking Christians such compounds as 'Abd al-Masīḥ, ' Slave of Christ ', will also be found.

Non-Arab Muslims also use a certain number of non-Arab names, such as Persian names drawn from old Iranian history and legend (e.g. Jamshīd, Rustam, Khusraw), and Turkish names (e.g. Arslan, Tughrul, Timur, Qilij Arslan, Büri, Kurbuga). In recent times the nationalist movements in Persia and Turkey have increased the tendency to use national instead of Arab names.

(2) The *Kunya*, usually a name compounded with *Abū* (' father of ') or *Umm* (' mother of '), *Abū* being frequently written Bou in North Africa. Thus Abū Mūsā 'Alī = 'Alī, the father of Mūsa, Abū Isḥāq Ibrāhīm = Ibrāhīm, the father of Isḥāq, Umm Aḥmad, the mother of Aḥmad.

The *Kunya* is not necessarily real. It may be metaphorical, referring to some desired quality; e.g. Abū'l-Barakāt, ' father of blessings ', Abū'l-Faḍl, ' father of merit ', Abū'l-Khair, ' father of good '. Sometimes it is a nickname, based on some personal characteristic; e.g. Abū'd-Dawānīq, ' father of farthings ', a name given to the 'Abbāsid Caliph al-Manṣūr, noted for his meanness, and Abū Naḍḍāra, ' father of spectacles ', the soubriquet of a well-known Egyptian journalist of the 19th century. Even when followed by a name *Abū* does not necessarily refer to a real person. The *Kunya* may express the hope for a son and the intention of giving him a certain name. Many *Kunyas* are automatically attached to certain names (*Ism*) by custom, often based on Biblical or historic precedent. Thus a man called Ibrāhīm might be given the *Kunya* Abū Isḥāq, Isḥāq might be called Abū Ya'qūb, etc. The *Kunya* always precedes the proper name.

(3) The *Nasab* or pedigree, a list of ancestors, each name being introduced by the word *ibn*, 'son of'. This is also written *bin* and *ben*, and is often abbreviated to *b*. The feminine is *bint*. Oriental writers may quote as many generations as they feel to be necessary, and in extreme cases will go all the way back to Adam. The usual practice is to give one or two; e.g. 'Alī b. Muḥammad b. Aḥmad = 'Alī, son of Muḥammad, son of Aḥmad. It is not uncommon for one of the ancestors in the list to be mentioned by a name other than his *Ism*; e.g. 'Alī b. Abī Ṭālib = 'Alī, the son of Abū Ṭālib (the father of Ṭālib).

In Persian the word *ibn* is usually omitted, and replaced by the particle *i* (also written *e*); e.g. Ḥasan i Sabbāḥ = Ḥasan, son of Sabbāḥ. In the Muslim lands generally at the present time, with the exception of Morocco, *ibn* is no longer used, and the name and father's name are simply juxtaposed; e.g. Aḥmad 'Alī = Aḥmad, son of 'Alī. The Persians, followed by the Turks, often use the *Zāde* (son), added as a suffix to the father's name or title, which is placed before the *Ism*; e.g. Qāḍīzāde, 'son of a judge', Kemālpāshāzāde, 'son of Kemāl Pasha'. The Turkish word *oghlu* is also used in the same way; e.g. Mikhaloghlu, 'son of Mikhal', Baydu oghlu, 'son of Baydu'. Many of these names in *Zāde* and *Oghlu* have become surnames of a sort, borne by whole families and referring to a common ancestor rather than to an immediate progenitor; e.g. Köprülüzāde, a name borne by a family claiming descent from the famous Ottoman wazirs. In the same way the Arabic *ibn* may sometimes refer to an ancestor rather than a parent, and be used as a kind of surname. Such for example are Ibn Khaldūn, Ibn Baṭṭūṭa, Ibn Sīnā (the Avicenna of the schoolmen).

(4) The *Laqab*, an honorific or descriptive epithet, sometimes a nickname, often a title. In its original and simplest form it is a descriptive nickname usually referring to a physical quality; e.g. aṭ-Ṭawīl, 'the tall', al-A'war, 'the one-eyed', al-Aṭrash, 'the deaf'. At a later date Persian and Turkish *laqabs* are encountered, as well as Arabic; e.g. Jehāngīr, 'world-seizer', Yildirim, 'Thunderbolt'. *Laqabs* of a different character were adopted as throne-names by the 'Abbāsid Caliphs of Baghdad, and after them by most other Muslim rulers. As examples we may quote ar-Rashīd, 'the rightly guided', al-Mutawakkil 'ala Allah, 'who entrusts himself to God'. *Laqabs* of honour were also given as titles to princes, statesmen, generals and high officers of state generally. These are usually compounds with *Dīn* ('faith') or *Dawla* ('State'); e.g. Badr ad-Dīn, 'full moon of the Faith', Jalāl ad-Dīn, 'Majesty of the Faith', Sirāj ad-Dawla, 'Lamp of the State', Nāṣir ad-Dawla, 'Defender of the State'. Similar compounds may be formed with *Mulk*, 'Kingdom', as Niẓām al-Mulk, 'Order of the Kingdom'; with *Islām*, as Saif al-Islām, 'Sword of Islam', etc. Many persons are known principally by their *laqabs*, e.g. Saladin (= Ṣalāḥ ad-Dīn). In the course of time many of these *laqabs* ceased to be titles borne only by ruling princes and their officers, and became little more than personal names used by all and sundry.

(5) The *Nisba*, an adjective, usually derived from the place of birth, origin or residence, sometimes from the sect, tribe or family,

occasionally from a trade or profession. A man may thus have several *nisbas*, as al-Qurashī al-Hāshimī al-Baghdādī aṣ-Ṣairafī, 'of the tribe of Quraish, of the house of Hāshim, of the city of Baghdad, the moneychanger'. In Arabic the *Nisba* is almost always preceded by the definite article, and ends in *ī*. Among the Turks the place-*Nisba*, with the ending *li* (or *lu*), is normally placed at the beginning of a name; e.g. Izmirli 'Alī Riḍā, 'the Smyrniot Ali Riza'. The *Nisba* may be arbitrarily handed down from father to son, though its original relevance is lost.

These are the main possible components of an Islamic name. There are others, the most important of which is the *Takhalluṣ*, or pen-name adopted by a poet, e.g. Firdawsī, the Paradisiac. A person may be mentioned by one or more of these components, or by all of them. The Arab author of the *Damascus Chronicle* of the Crusades, for example, is referred to as Abū Ya'lā Ḥamza b. Asad b. 'Alī b. Muḥammad at-Tamīmī ad-Dimashqī al-'Amīd ibn al-Qalānisī, i.e. 'the father of Ya'lā, Ḥamza the son of Asad the son of 'Alī the son of Muḥammad, of the tribe of Tamīm, of the city of Damascus, the Chief (of the Chancery), the son of the hatter'.

None of these components strictly speaking amounts to a surname, though in practice the *Nasab*, *Laqab* or *Nisba* is sometimes so used. Its use, however, is optional and arbitrary.

In the contemporary Orient the custom is to use two names, the first of which is the personal name, the second being usually the father's name. It may, however, be equally the name of a grandparent or remoter ancestor, or a second personal name adopted by choice or given in the family, at school, in the army, etc., or one of the above-mentioned categories. The use of surnames is spreading among the upper classes, and the introduction of compulsory registration in several oriental countries will accelerate their adoption. In Turkey the adoption of surnames was imposed by law in 1928.

Bibliography

G. Gabrieli. *Onomasticon Arabicum.* Rome, 1915.

3. NOTE ON PLACE-NAMES

The following glossary contains the commonest words occurring in place-names. The letters A, P, T, indicate Arabic, Persian and Turkish respectively. A hyphen (-) before a term indicates that it is suffixed. The spellings given are those most frequently found in modern maps.

-ābād	P. Town or inhabited place
Ada	T. Island
'Ain	A. Spring
Ak	T. White
Baḥr	A. Sea
Bait	A. House
Balad	A. Town or village
Bi'r	A. Well
Boğaz, Boghaz	T. Straits, pass
Burun	T. Cape
Dağ, Dagh	T. Mountain
Dār	A. House
Darya	P. Sea or river
Dasht	P. Desert
Deir	A. Convent or monastery
Deniz	T. Sea
Derbend	P. Pass
Dere	T. Valley
Dih	P. Village
Eski	T. Old
Göl	T. Lake
Hisar	AT. Castle
Irmak	T. River
-istān	P. Ending indicating the name of a country or province
Jabal, Jebel	A. Mountain
Jazīra	A. Island, peninsula
Jisr	A. Bridge
Kafr	A. Village
Kara	T. Black
Khan	P. Caravanserai
Kızıl	T. Red
Khirbet	A. Ruin
Köprü	T. Bridge
Körfez	T. Bay or gulf
Köy	T. Village
Kūh	P. Mountain
Liman	T. Port
Maḥalle	TA. Quarter
Marj, Merj	A. Meadow
Mersa	A. Anchorage
Meydan	TP. Place or square
Nahr.	A. River
Orman	T. Forest
Oued	French North African spelling of *Wadi*
Qanṭara	A. Bridge
Qaryat	A. Village or small town
Qaṣr	A. Castle
Qurn	A. Peak
Rās	A. Cape or headland
Rūd	P. River
Şehir, Shahr, Shehir	P. T. Town
Sīdī	A. Title of a local saint (see Glossary)
Su	T. Water
Tel	A. Mound
Tepe	T. Hillock
Wādī	A. River-valley or dry watercourse
Yeni	T. New
Yeşil, Yeshil	T. Green

4. SELECT GLOSSARY

'ĀDA (ADET). A legal term for customary as distinct from *Sharī'a* law.

AGHA (AĞA). A title borne by numerous Ottoman officers of medium grade and by a few of senior grade, the most important of whom was the Agha or Commander-in-Chief of the Janissaries. Commanders of the *Ojaqs* (*q.v.*) were also called *Agha*. In late Ottoman times *agha* was the title used by officers up to the rank of lieutenant-colonel who were unable to read and write, in place of *Efendi* (*q.v.*). If they overcame this disability they were granted the title of *Efendi* by decree. The title *agha* was abolished when the constitution was introduced, but remained in popular use in Turkey as the general mode of address or reference for illiterates.

In addition to the foregoing, the term was also applied to the eunuchs of the imperial palace, the chief of whom, the *Kizlar Aghasi*, was a person of great consequence.

'AJEMIOGHLAN (ACEMOĞLAN). 'Foreign youth'—the Christian children levied for the janissaries or the palace service.

ALTUN (ALTÎN). A Turkish word meaning gold, applied generally to Ottoman gold coins. The first Ottoman gold pieces were minted in the 15th century, in imitation of the western ducat. Their weight was in the neighbourhood of 53 gr. They were sometimes known as *Fîndîklî*. A second gold sequin, of only 40 gr., was introduced in the early 18th century. It was known as the *Zer-Maḥbūb* ('beloved gold'). By 1839 its weight had dwindled to 25 gr., and it was finally suppressed by the currency reforms of 1844 and replaced by the Ottoman gold pound of 100 piastres (*q.v.*).

'ĀMIL. An Arabic term applied to the financial administrator of a province under the Caliphate. It was also occasionally used in the Ottoman Empire for tax-collectors. Cf. India Glossary, p. 58.

AMĪN (EMIN). An Arabic word originally meaning a trustworthy person. In Ottoman usage it was applied to the directors of certain government departments, both central and local, and sometimes to city governors, e.g. Defter Amīni, director of the cadaster, Gümrük Amīni, customs house director, Shehremini, the governor of Istanbul. Cf. India Glossary, p. 58.

AMĪR (EMIR). An Arabic title originally meaning 'commander', now usually translated 'prince'. *Amīr al-Mu'minīn*, 'Commander of the Faithful', was one of the earliest titles of the Caliphs. From 'Abbāsid times onward the title *amīr* was used by the virtually independent princes who ruled in many of the provinces of the Islamic Empire under the nominal suzerainty of the Caliphs, and eventually also, in the form *amīr al-umarā*, 'amīr of amīrs' by the Mayors of the Palace, who were the real rulers of the capital.

In the Arabic-speaking countries at the present time the

title is used primarily for princes of the reigning houses. It is also used as a hereditary title by certain families, especially in Syria-Lebanon. In Sa'ūdī Arabia it is given to governors of provinces, to certain chiefs of tribes, and even to the headmen of certain important villages. It was until 1946 used as a title of sovereignty by the ruler of Transjordan, and is still so used by some of the Arab rulers of south-east Arabia.

ANṢĀR. An Arabic word meaning 'helpers', the term applied to those citizens of Medina who rallied to Muhammad after his flight to that city from Mecca.

ARAB. A term first encountered in Assyrian inscriptions of the 9th century B.C., where it is used to describe the nomads of the north Arabian desert. It is used in a similar sense in Persian cuneiform and Biblical texts. In Greco-Roman usage it was extended to include all the peoples of the Arabian peninsula. In the earliest Arabic texts, traces of both meanings are found, the word being applied sometimes to the nomads as distinct from the town-dwellers, more often to all the Arabic-speaking peoples of the peninsula and the Syrian and Iraqi borders. After the Arab conquests it was applied to their descendants in the occupied provinces, and ultimately to all the conquered peoples, from Morocco to the borders of Persia, who adopted the Arabic language. In Arabic the term is still used in certain contexts to distinguish the allegedly pure nomadic Arabs from the arabized sedentary populations of the former conquered provinces of the Caliphate.

In cultural terms the adjective Arab or Arabic is often used to describe the whole complex civilization of the Caliphate, the main language of which was Arabic, though its creators were of many different faiths and nationalities.

'ARAQ. An alcoholic drink, made from palm-leaves, grapes or dates, and usually flavoured with aniseed. It is also known as *'Araqī*, and in Turkey as *Rakı*.

ARDABB. A measure of capacity of varying value, usually subdivided into 6 *waiba* each of 4 *rub'a*. The term is also applied to the area of land sown with an *Ardabb* of grain. In modern Egypt the *Ardabb* has been standardized at 197·7 litres.

'ASKARĪ. An Arabic word meaning a soldier, i.e. a member of the *'Askar*, army, possibly from the Latin *exercitus*. It is now usually used to describe the African native troops of the colonial powers.

ASPER. A term of Greek origin used in the later Middle Ages for the silver coins of the Byzantine Empire and the Empire of Trebizond. It subsequently designated the Turkish *Aqche*, the small silver coin which was the basic unit of Ottoman currency until the 17th century, when it was superseded by the *para* (*q.v.*). Its weight declined from its original 15 gr. to 2 gr. at the time of its disappearance in the 17th century.

ASSASSIN. The occidental form of the Arabic *ḥashīshī*, hashish-addict, the term applied to a heretical Islamic sect who in the 11th, 12th and 13th centuries conducted a reign of terror and assassination from their strongholds in the Persian and Syrian mountains. Their chief was the famous 'Old Man of the Mountain'.

ATABEG. A Turkish title meaning Father-Prince, originally given to the tutors or guardians of Seljūq princes. From this it developed into a general title of high rank and occasionally even of sovereignty in the Seljūq succession states. In Mamlūk Egypt it was applied to the commander-in-chief of the troops.

BADAWĪ (BEDOUIN). An Arabic word meaning desert-dweller, but used only of nomads of Arab speech. The common European form is Bedouin, presumably from the Arabic plural.

BAILO. An Italian term applied to the Venetian envoys to the Sublime Porte.

BAIRĀM. An Ottoman term applied to the two chief festivals of the Muslim year. The lesser *Bairām* (called *'Īd al-Fiṭr* by the Arabs) marks the end of the fast of Ramaḍān. The greater *Bairām,* also called *Qurbān Bairām* (*'Īd al-Aḍḥā* in Arabic), is the feast of sacrifice associated with the annual pilgrimage to Mecca.

BAKHSHĪSH. A Persian word meaning a gift, used all over the Near and Middle East to describe any 'gift', tip or bribe, from the beggar's alms to the pasha's *douceur.*

BASHAW. An early English spelling of *Pasha* (*q.v.*).

BASHĪ BOZUK. A Turkish term sometimes applied to the floating population of Istanbul, usually given to the irregular and undisciplined volunteer forces who sometimes followed the Ottoman armies into battle. An attempt to turn them into a regular force was abandoned after the war of 1877–8.

BASHKĀTIB. An Ottoman term for a chief secretary.

BAZĀR. See *Sūq.*

BEDEL. See *Jizya.*

BERĀT. An Ottoman rescript, usually of practical content, such as a grant of a fief or an office, an exequatur for a foreign consul, etc. Later the term was also applied to the patents given by the European consuls to their dragomans where these were of Ottoman nationality.

BESHLIK. An Ottoman five-para piece. See *Para.*

BEY (BEG). A Turkish title, originally meaning a noble or lesser prince, subordinate to a *Khān* (*q.v.*), later any person exercising authority. It is still used in the ex-Ottoman Arab countries to designate persons of eminence, in place of the more usual *Efendi* (*q.v.*). In Egypt it is a title conferred by the king, and is also allowed as courtesy title to the sons of pashas. In Tunisia it is the title of the reigning prince. In Turkey it has been officially replaced by *Bay,* an allegedly purer Turkish form, which is now the formal word for Mr., and precedes the name, European fashion, instead of following it.

BEYLERBEY. 'Bey of Beys', an Ottoman title formerly given to the governors of a province (*Eyālet*), consisting of several Sanjaq. Later replaced by Vali (*q.v.*).

BEZISTAN. A public market, more especially the great enclosed market in the centre of Istanbul.

BINBASHĪ. A major in the Ottoman service. The term was

retained in some of the Ottoman succession states and means in Turkish 'commander of a thousand'.

BÖLÜK BASHÎ. A captain in the corps of Janissaries.

BUHĀR. A synonym for *Qinṭār* (*q.v.*).

BURNUS. An Arabic word meaning a kind of hood worn by the nomadic Arabs.

BOSTANJÎ. A gardener, in European usage usually restricted to the gardeners of the Ottoman palace. The chief gardener was called the *Bostanjî-Bashî*, and was a functionary of fairly high standing.

BUYURULDU. An Ottoman decree, issued by a senior official of the central government or more especially by a provincial governor.

CALIPH. An Arabic word meaning deputy, adopted as title by the successors of Muḥammad in the headship of the Muslim community. In classical times the term denoted the supreme sovereign of the Islamic Empire, uniting in himself both the religious and the temporal powers. With the growth of a purely secular power under the Amirs and the Sultans (*q.v.*), the power and prestige of the Caliphs declined, and they became little more than figureheads, exercising some religious authority as titular heads of Islam, but bereft of all real power. After the extinction of the 'Abbāsid Caliphate at the hands of the Mongols in A.D. 1258, a line of puppet Caliphs, descended from an 'Abbāsid refugee from Baghdad, was maintained until A.D. 1517, as purely nominal religious pontiffs, by the Mamlūk sultans of Egypt. They were accorded only limited recognition by other Muslim rulers, many of whom began to assume for themselves the titles and prerogatives formerly peculiar to the Caliphate, as adjuncts of their secular authority. Among these rulers were the Ottoman sultans, whose claims to the Caliphate, reinforced after their conquest of the Mamlūk dominions in A.D. 1517 and the reputed transfer to them of the authority of the Cairo 'Abbāsids, secured some limited recognition outside the Ottoman Empire. The pan-Islamic policy of Sulṭān 'Abd al-Ḥamīd II (1876–1909) led to a reassertion of these claims, which had some effect in the Muslim world, especially in India. The Ottoman Caliphate, however, never won general acceptance, and was finally abolished in 1924.

CAPHAR. See *Khafara*.

CAPITULATIONS. From the Latin *capitula*, 'chapters', the term applied in Ottoman times to the privileges accorded by Muslim rulers to Christian states whereby the subjects of the latter were authorized to reside and trade in the Muslim dominions without being subjected to the disabilities imposed on their non-Muslim subjects. The first capitulations were granted to France in A.D. 1535 and to many other European countries in the years that followed. The term was also applied to similar rights conceded by the shahs of Persia. With the progressive decline of the Muslim states of the Middle East, the Capitulations came to confer privileges far exceeding those originally intended, and including exemption from local jurisdiction and taxation, the subjects of the Capitulatory powers being answerable only to their own consular courts. These extra-territorial rights were bitterly resented by the rising nationalist movements. The Capitulations were abolished in Turkey by the Treaty of Lausanne of 1923, in Syria and Palestine by the mandatory powers, in Iraq by international agreement in 1923, in Persia in 1928. In Egypt, where the Ottoman Capitulations had been recognized by the autonomous rulers of the house of Muḥammad 'Alī, they were retained and indeed considerably extended as a result of the growth of European investment in the country. After a lengthy agitation they were finally abolished by international agreement after the Conference of Montreux in 1937.

CASBA. A fortress or citadel, from the Arabic *Qaṣaba,* which includes this among its many meanings.

C͟HA'US͟H (CHAVUSH). A Turkish word meaning usher, applied to the corps of messengers in the Ottoman court, who might also be sent as ambassadors, and finally to N.C.O.s in the Ottoman forces. The *C͟ha'us͟h-bas͟hî,* the chief of the corps of *cha'ushes* attached to the Divan, was vice-president of the Grand Vizier's court, and an important court functionary.

C͟HORBAJÎ (ÇORBACI). An Ottoman term for a village notable. In former times it was also used as a title for Janissary officers, and often as a mode of address for Christians.

CID. A Spanish form of *Sayyid* (*q.v.*).

CRUSE. An early European form of Piastre (*q.v.*), from the Arabic *Qurūs͟h.*

DAIR (DEIR). A Christian convent or monastery in the Arab lands.

DĀNAQ. One-sixth of a *dirham* (*q.v.*).

DEFTERDĀR. An official keeper of records of income and expenditure for a department, a province or a state. In the Ottoman Empire the Minister of Finance was formerly known as the *Defterdār,* and his office as the *defterk͟hāne.*

DEY. A word of Turkish origin, meaning maternal uncle. It was used as title by the rulers, under Ottoman suzerainty, of Tunisia (until 1705) and Algeria (until 1830).

DIHQĀN. The rural aristocrats of pre-Islamic Persia. Under the early Arab Caliphate the *Dihqāns* retained many of their social and economic privileges and were absorbed into the revenue-collecting and governmental apparatus of the new state. They were later depressed to the level of the peasantry.

DĪNĀR. The unit of gold currency under the Caliphate, based on the Byzantine solidus and deriving its name from the Latin *denarius,* which was conceived of as meaning 'money' in a generic sense and 'gold coin' *par excellence.* The standard weight of the *dīnār* was 66 gr. The term passed out of use during the 13th and 14th centuries. It has been revived in modern Iraq as the name of the main unit of currency. The Iraqi *dīnār* equals £1 sterling, and consists of 1,000 *fils.*

DIRHAM. An Arabic corruption of the Greek *drachma,* used to describe the unit of silver currency, inherited from the Sāsānid Empire and current in the eastern provinces of the Caliphate. The standard weight varied in the neighbourhood of 2·97 gm.

The relation of the *dirham* to the *dīnār* (*q.v.*) fluctuated with the prices of the metals, though frequent attempts were made to establish a set rate of exchange, in the neighbourhood of 1 : 20. The two terms fell into disuse at about the same time, though the *dirham* remained in use as a weight for many centuries.

DĪWĀN (DIVAN). An Arabic word of Persian origin, first used for the public registers of Muslim warriors and pensioners in the days of the Arab conquests. Under the Caliphate the term was extended to government departments generally. The Ottoman Dīwān (State Council) was presided over by the Sultan, or, later, by the Grand Vizier. The collected works of an Arabic, Persian or Turkish poet are also known as his *Dīwān*. See India Glossary, p. 63.

DHIMMI. An Arabic word denoting a member of one of the 'protected' religions, i.e. the non-Muslim religions tolerated by the Muslim state in accordance with the Holy Law, on payment of certain taxes and on acceptance of an inferior social status.

DHOW. A European term of unknown origin applied to Arab sailing vessels, especially in the Red Sea and Indian Ocean. The commonest type is that known to the Arabs as Ghurāb ('crow').

DÖNÜM (DUNAM). A Turkish measure of area, of about 1,000 square yards. The metric *dönüm* or *dunam* now used in Palestine is of 1,000 square metres = 0·247 acres.

DRAGOMAN. A europeanized form of the Arabic word *Tarjumān*, an interpreter or translator. Both the Sublime Porte and the foreign embassies maintained dragomans, who were often of considerable importance in diplomatic negotiations.

EFENDI (EFFENDI). A Byzantine word meaning Lord, used by the Turks also to describe men of religious learning, then literate persons generally, as against *agha*, used for illiterates. In the Arab lands of the Near East, other than Iraq, and most of Arabia, it is now the normal word for Mr. It is applied more particularly to the educated landowning, professional and official classes.

EMIN. A Turkish form of *Amīn* (*q.v.*).

EMIR. See *Amīr*.

EVKAF. See *Waqf*.

EYĀLET. A term used by the Turks before the reforms in place of *vilāyet* (*q.v.*).

FALLĀḤ (FELLAH). An Arabic word, possibly of Aramaic origin, meaning a peasant. The common European form is *fellah* (plural *fellahin*).

FAQĪH. A doctor of the *Sharī'a*, or Holy Law. The *Faqīhs* are the canon lawyers of Islam.

FATWĀ. A ruling on a disputed point of Islamic law, issued by a *Muftī* (*q.v.*).

FEDDAN. An Egyptian measure of area, equal to 1·038 acres.

FEZ. A red cap, named after the city in Morocco, where it was first manufactured. It was introduced into Turkey in the early 19th century in place of the turban for non-ecclesiastical functionaries, and in course of time became general among the lay population of the country. It was abolished from Turkey in 1928, but is still worn in Egypt, Palestine and Syria, where it is known as the *Tarbūsh*.

FIQH. The Islamic science of jurisprudence, including the whole complex of religious, ritual, civil, criminal and public law. The Sunnī Muslims recognize four orthodox schools of *Fiqh*: Ḥanafī (founded by Abū Ḥanīfa, *ob.* 767); Ḥanbalī (founded by Aḥmad ibn Ḥanbal, *ob.* 855); Mālikī (founded by Mālik ibn Anas, *ob.* 795); Shāfiʿī (founded by Muḥammad ash-Shāfiʿī, *ob.* 820). There are four recognized sources of Muslim law: Qur'ān, Hadīth (*q.v.*), Ijmāʿ (the consensus of the learned) and Qiyās (reasoning by analogy).

FIRMAN (FERMĀN). An Ottoman or Persian imperial rescript, diploma or letter patent.

FRANK. A term first applied by the medieval Arabs to the peoples of western Europe, and ultimately used all over the Near East for all non-Balkan Europeans. It is also encountered in the forms *Frangi*, *Franji*, *Firengi*, etc.

FUNDUQ. An inn, storehouse or exchange for visiting merchants, applied more particularly to the Levantine establishments of European merchants from the time of the Crusades onward. It is also encountered in the forms Fondic, Fondique, Fondouc, Fonduc and Fondaco.

GAVUR (GIAUR, GIAOUR). A Turkish word of uncertain origin, meaning a non-Muslim, and more especially a Christian.

GHAFĪR. A watchman or escort. See *Khafara*.

GHĀZĪ (GAZI). An Arabic word originally meaning one who undertakes or leads a *Ghazwa* (= *Razzia*), later given as a title of honour to men who distinguished themselves in the war against the infidel. In late medieval times certain 'orders' of frontier fighters in Anatolia and elsewhere were called *Ghāzīs*. The title was conferred on Mustafa Kemal by the Turkish Republic in recognition of his victories in the war of independence.

GHULĀM. A young slave or *Mamlūk* (*q.v.*), corresponding roughly to a page or equerry in the medieval West. Pl. Ghilmān.

GOUM. A military formation of North African tribesmen, usually in the French colonial army. The word is derived from the Arabic *Qawm*, people, group or troop.

ḤABBA. A measure of weight, usually for precious metals. It is equal to one-sixtieth of a *dirham* (*q.v.*).

HADĪTH. A tradition of the sayings or practice of the Prophet. The corpus of *hadīth* forms one of the main sources of Muslim law.

ḤĀJJ. An Arabic title (Turkish and Persian forms *Ḥajjī*), assumed by persons who have performed the pilgrimage to the holy places of Islam. They are entitled to wear a green band around their headgear.

ḤANAFĪ. See *Fiqh*.

ḤANBALĪ. See *Fiqh*.

HAREM. A Turkish form of the Arabic *Ḥarām*, forbidden. The women's quarters of a Muslim house.

Hashimite. A descendent of Hāshim, the great-grandfather of the Prophet. In medieval times the term was applied more particularly to members of the house of ʿAbbās; in modern times it is used of the former ruling house of the Ḥijāz and its surviving branches in Iraq and Transjordan.

Hatti Humayun. Another spelling of *Khaṭṭ i Humāyūn*. See *Khaṭṭ i Sharīf*.

Hatti Sharif. Another spelling of *Khaṭṭ i Sharīf* (*q.v.*).

Hegira. A common European corruption of *Hijra* (*q.v.*).

Hekim Bashī. The chief physician of the Ottoman Sultan or the Shah of Persia.

High Commissioner. This term has been used in the Near East (*a*) for the British resident in Egypt between the occupation and the formal recognition of Egyptian independence in 1922, after which he was renamed ambassador; (*b*) for the British and French governors of the mandated territories of Iraq, Palestine and Syria.

Hijra. The 'flight' or migration of Muḥammad from Mecca to Medina, in A.D. 622, according to most accounts on 20 September. The Muslim era begins, not as is often supposed with the *Hijra*, but at the beginning of the Arab year in which the *Hijra* took place, i.e. on 16 July 622.

Horsetails. See *Tugh*.

Il-Khān. The title adopted by the Mongol rulers of Persia.

Iltizām. A term used in the Ottoman Empire for state lands, the taxes of which were farmed out to individuals. The holder of an *Iltizām*, called *Multazim*, levied the *Kharāj* (*q.v.*) from the peasants, and paid a fixed tax to the government. The term was also used loosely for any farming of state revenues.

Imām. An Arabic word used to describe the leader in prayer, also extended to denote the leader of the whole community of Islam. In the latter sense it was also one of the titles of the Caliphs. It was used more particularly by the Shīʿa opposition for their own pretenders to the Caliphate, and in Shīʿa parlance connoted a more extensive spiritual authority. This was never exercised by the Sunni Caliphs, whose authority was always religious rather than spiritual.

For some centuries *Imām* has been the usual title of the rulers of the Yemen.

Iqṭāʿ. A kind of feudal grant given by Muslim rulers. The *Iqṭāʿ* was of two main types, the first a grant of public lands to an individual, subject to taxes or tithes, the second a grant of the revenues of lands in lieu of payments from the public treasury. The extent of an *Iqṭāʿ* might vary from a few fields to a whole province granted as fief to a governor. In later times the *Iqṭāʿ* was in effect either a form of tax-farming or a military fief.

Irade. A written or oral order of an Ottoman sultan.

Janissary. The commonest English form of the Turkish *Yeni-Cheri*, 'new soldiers', the term applied to the Ottoman infantry, first recruited among Christian prisoners, then by the *Devshirme*, or periodic levy of young men among the non-

Muslim subject populations of the Empire. This method passed out of use in the 17th century, after which the Janissaries became a closed corps.

JARĪB. A measure of capacity, of varying value. It is a multiple of the *Qafīz* (*q.v.*).

JIHĀD. The holy war for Islam against infidel states—a collective duty imposed on the Muslim community by the Holy Law.

JIZYA. Originally a general term for the collective tribute paid by the conquered provinces to the Arab conquerors, later specialized to mean the poll-tax paid by the *D͟himmis* (*q.v.*). The term was used in the Ottoman Empire in this sense alongside the more usual *K͟harāj* (*q.v.*) until 1855, when the poll-tax was abolished by decree and replaced by a tax for exemption from military service, called *Bedel*.

JUND. An Arabic word meaning army, also used in early Islamic times for the administrative area occupied by a *Jund* in the period of the conquests and corresponding to a Byzantine *theme*. The province of Syria, for example, was divided into the *Junds* of Filasṭīn (capital Ramla), Urdunn (capital Tiberias), Damascus, Ḥims, and, later, Qinnasrīn. At a later date the term was used for the permanent paid forces of the sovereign, as distinct from the volunteer and vassal contingents. After the 10th century the *Jund* usually consisted of mamlūks.

KA'BA. An Arabic word meaning a building in cubic form, usually applied to the Sacred Shrine in Mecca, containing the Black Stone, a meteorite regarded as holy by the Arabs since pre-Islamic times.

KADI. See *Qāḍī*.

KĀFIR. An Arabic word meaning an infidel, i.e. a non-Muslim.

KAPUDAN PASHA. The supreme commander of the Ottoman fleets, until the 19th century.

KARAKOL. An Ottoman police station, also for some purposes the administrative centre of a village or quarter.

KĀTIB. A secretary.

KAVVAS. From the Arabic *Qawwās*, an archer. The term was applied in the Ottoman Empire to soldiers attached as personal bodyguards to high dignitaries and especially to ministers, diplomats, etc.

KÂYA (KYAHYA, KAHYA, etc.). A word of Persian origin, meaning steward or bailiff. In the Ottoman Empire the *Kâya Bey* was formerly the steward of the Grand Vizier's establishment, and in effect the Minister of Home Affairs. The title *Kâya* was also borne by a number of other Ottoman functionaries, notably the *K͟hazine Kâyasî*, or Keeper of the Sultan's Privy Purse, as well as by certain army commanders.

KAZA. A Turkish form of the Arabic *Qaḍā*, jurisdiction. The *Kaza* was an Ottoman administrative district, a sub-unit of a *Sanjaq* (*q.v.*). Before the reforms the chief personage of the *Kaza* was the *Qāḍī* (*q.v.*) or judge, whose functions extended beyond purely judicial matters to include most civil, municipal and other administrative affairs. The reforms restricted the *Qāḍī* to his judicial duties, and entrusted the civil administration of the *Kaza* to an official known as the *Qā'immaqām* (or *Kaymakam*) (*q.v.*).

KAZI'ASKER. An Ottoman title of Arabic origin, meaning military judge. The *Kaziasker* was at first a military judge appointed for a campaign. Later, the two *Kaziaskers* of Rumili and Anatolia were in effect the two vice-chancellors, in order, of the Ottoman Empire, presiding over the supreme court of law and, under the *Shaikh al-Islām* (*q.v.*), over the entire judiciary of the Empire.

KEVUTSA. A modern Hebrew term for a Jewish collective agricultural settlement in Palestine.

KHAFĀRA. An Arabic word meaning protection, and hence protection or escort tax. The term is used from late medieval times onward for the taxes levied on sedentary populations and travellers for protection against Bedouins and robbers. It is frequently encountered in the European travellers, with a wide variety of spellings, among which we may note *Caphar, caffare, capharre, gaffare.* The modern word *ghafīr*, a watchman or escort, is from the same root.

KHAMSĪN. An Arabic word meaning fifty, used to describe the hot wind from the desert.

KHĀN. (*a*) A Turkish princely title, in origin a contraction of *Khāqān* (*q.v.*). Its extensive use dates from the Mongol period, when it was adopted by members of the house of Jenghiz and later also by others exercising sovereign authority. In post-Mongol Persia its importance declined steadily. Under the Safavids the *Khān* was the governor of a province, and in modern Persia the word is the accepted equivalent of Mr.

(*b*) A large building for the accommodation of travellers and their wares. Also called *Karvānsarāy*.

KHĀQĀN. An old Turkish title of sovereignty, usually denoting supremacy over a group of tribes or territories. A *Khāqān* would rule over several beys. The title was also used by the Ottoman sultans, as well as the more usual Khān.

KHARĀJ. At first, like *Jizya* (*q.v.*), a general term for tribute, later specialized under the Caliphate to mean land-tax as opposed to poll-tax. In Ottoman usage it was also applied to the poll-tax levied on non-Muslims.

KHĀRIJITE. A member of a half-religious, half-political opposition movement that flourished under the early Caliphate. It survives only among small groups in Oman, Zanzibar and southern Algeria.

KHĀṢṢ (HASS, HAS). An Ottoman crown domain, usually given as appanage to princes and provincial governors.

KHAṬĪB. See *Khuṭba*.

KHAṬṬ I HUMAYUN. See *Khaṭṭ i Sharīf*.

KHAṬṬ I SHARĪF. *Khaṭṭ* is an Arabic word meaning writing. A *Khaṭṭ i Sharīf* ('noble writing') or a *Khaṭṭ i Humāyūn* ('imperial writing') is a *Firmān* (*q.v.*) bearing the Sultan's formula of command in his own hand.

KHĀTŪN. A Mongol title for empresses and other ladies of high rank. In post-Mongol times it is applied to ladies generally.

KHAZINEDĀR. An Ottoman intendant of the Treasury.

KHEDIVE A title of Persian origin, used by the autonomous Ottoman viceroys of Egypt. First used unofficially by Muḥammad 'Alī at the beginning of the 19th century, it was officially conferred by the Porte on his descendant Ismā'īl in 1867, and borne by him and his successors until 1914, when the last Khedive 'Abbās Ḥilmī was deposed and replaced by Ḥusain Kāmil with the title Sultan.

KHUṬBA. The Friday sermon in the mosque, given in early times as a political statement by the sovereign or the administrative head of the area, later as a purely religious ceremony by a preacher known as the *Khaṭīb*. Mention in the *Khuṭba* is one of the recognized marks of sovereignty in Islam.

KHWĀJA. A Persian title (pronounced *Khāja*) for civilian personalities, especially among the townsfolk and the learned. It was at times also applied to eunuchs. In Arabic (pronounced *Khawāja,* or, in Egypt, *Khawāga*), it is used as a title or form of address for native non-Muslims and more especially for Europeans. In Turkish (pronounced *Hojja*) it was the usual title for persons wearing the turban, i.e. members of the learned and ecclesiastical classes.

KIMIZ. (Also written *Kumiss*). Sour, fermented mare's milk. A common drink among nomadic Turks.

KİRBAJ. A rhinoceros-hide whip used in the Ottoman Empire and in some of the succession states for administrative purposes.

KONAK. A Turkish word meaning a halting-place and hence a villa, an inn, and often a government building.

KUFIC. An ornamental style of Arabic writing, named after the town of Kufa.

LEVANTINE. A term applied to the long-established resident European population of the Near East, more especially of the towns and seaports, to distinguish them from 'genuine' Europeans coming from Europe.

LIWĀ. An Arabic word meaning flag, sometimes used as a synonym of *Sanjaq* (*q.v.*) in the Ottoman Empire, and now the name of an administrative area in Iraq.

MADRASA. A school for Muslim learning, often, though not necessarily, attached to a mosque.

MAGHRIB. An Arabic word meaning west, applied generally to the Arabic-speaking countries of North Africa west of Egypt.

MAGHRIBĪ. A person from the *Maghrib* (*q.v.*).

MAHĀRĪ. A fast-riding dromedary. The members of camel corps are often referred to as *méharistes* in French.

MAHDĪ. An Arabic word meaning 'the Rightly Guided One', a messianic figure whose awaited return to earth will, according to popular Muslim belief, inaugurate an era of justice and equity. Many pretenders to this office have offered themselves during the centuries of Islamic history. The most notable in recent times was the celebrated Mahdī of the Sudan.

MAḤMAL. A palanquin that precedes the pilgrim caravan to Mecca. It is usually carried on a camel.

MAJLIS. An Arabic word meaning a council or assembly, used nowadays for the Persian and sometimes other parliaments.

MALIK. An Arabic word meaning king. It was not in classical times a title of sovereignty, but rather of high office under a sovereign. Its recent and modern use as an equivalent to 'king' is probably due to European influence. See India Glossary, p. 69.

MĀLIKĪ. See *Fiqh*.

MAMLŪK. An Arabic word meaning a slave, later restricted to white slaves and more particularly those used for military and administrative purposes. Many Mamlūks rose to high office, and Mamlūk dynasties ruled Egypt as an independent state from 1250 to 1517, and thereafter under Ottoman suzerainty until 1798. In the 16th and 17th centuries the Ottoman administration was largely of servile status in its higher ranks, officials being theoretically the slaves of the Sultan (*Kapı Kulu*, Slave of the Porte).

MANN. A measure of weight, of varying value. It is usually equal to two *raṭls* (*q.v.*).

MARABOUT. A French form of the Arabic *Murābiṭ*. The word originally meant frontiersman, and was used to describe the march warriors of Islam. In North Africa it later came to describe a holy man, who has achieved his standing either by asceticism and good works or by religious learning. The North African and Spanish dynasty of the Almoravids represents the same word in its original meaning. The coin known as the *Maravedi* (Arabic *Murābiṭī*) was originally struck by the Almoravid rulers of Spain, and acquired wide currency in North Africa and southern France as well as in Spain.

MARAVEDI. See *Marabout*.

MAUND. A common European spelling of *Mann* (*q.v.*).

MAWLĀ. An Arabic word, one of the meanings of which is client or freed slave. In early Islamic times *Mawlā* (plural *Mawālī*) was used to describe those Muslims who were not full members of an Arab tribe, i.e. the non-Arab converts to Islam, and those Arabs who for some reason had no proper tribal status. Another meaning of the word is 'lord' or 'master'. In this sense it has been used politically (e.g. in Morocco, where most of the sultans prefix the word *Mawlāy*, 'My Master', to their names), and religiously, for religious teachers and leaders, prominent mystics, etc. Spelt *Molla*, it is often used to describe the ecclesiastical classes as a whole in Persia. *Mawlawi* (= *Maulvi*) and *Mawlānā* ('Our Master') are sometimes used as titles by religious dignitaries.

MEJIDIYE. A Turkish decoration instituted by the Sultan 'Abd al-Majīd I (1839–61). Also a late Ottoman coin worth 20 piastres (*q.v.*).

MELCHITE. A term applied to the Greek Orthodox Christians of the Levant. It is derived from the Semitic root meaning 'king', and was first used by heretics to describe those whom they regarded as passive followers of the Byzantine state doctrine.

MIḤRĀB. A recess in the wall of a mosque, to show the direction of the *Qibla* (*q.v.*).

MILE. The basic measure of distance in the western, i.e. ex-Byzantine, provinces of the Caliphate. The Arab mile has been variously estimated, and was probably of rather more than 2,000 yards. It is usually subdivided into 4,000 cubits (*Dhirā'*) each of 24 digits (*Iṣba'*).

MILLET. A recognized religious community in the Ottoman Empire. Each *Millet* enjoyed a considerable measure of internal autonomy, under its own head and hierarchy and, in most matters, subject to its own laws and tribunals. In late Ottoman times the term acquired a national as well as a religious content.

MINARET. A Turkish form of the Arabic word *Manāra,* a light tower, used to describe the tower of a mosque, from which the call to prayer is given.

MINBAR. The pulpit of a mosque, used for giving the *Khuṭba* (*q.v.*).

MĪR. A Persian title, abbreviated from the Arabic *Amīr* (*q.v.*), to which it corresponds roughly in usage. It is also often used by poets and men of letters.

MIRALAY. An Ottoman colonel.

MĪRZĀ. A Persian title, shortened from *Mīrzāde,* son of a prince. Its use was extended in course of time to noblemen generally, and eventually came to correspond in Persia to that of *Efendi* (*q.v.*) in the Arab lands. In this sense it precedes the name. When used after the name, it retains the meaning of prince.

MISHĀRA. An Iraqi measure of area, equal to 0·617 acres.

MITHQĀL. A unit of weight, used more particularly for precious metals, based on the Byzantine solidus. (The *dīnār* (*q.v.*) weighs one *mithqāl.*) The relative weights of the *dirham* (*q.v.*) and the *mithqāl* are usually given as 7 : 10.

MIXED COURTS. This term usually refers to the special international courts set up in Egypt under the Capitulations (*q.v.*) régime to try cases between litigants of different nationalities. Their abolition was agreed upon in 1937.

MOSHAV. A Jewish smallholders' settlement in Palestine, organized on semi-co-operative lines.

MOZARAB. A Spanish term, from the Arabic *Musta'rib,* used to describe the Arabic-speaking Christians of Muslim Spain.

MU'ALLIM. An Arabic word meaning a teacher, often used as a form of address, especially among the non-Muslim minorities.

MUDD. A measure of capacity. See *Qafīz.*

MUDĪR. An Arabic word meaning director. In the late Ottoman administration the Mudīr was the official in charge of a *Nahiye* (*q.v.*). In Syria-Lebanon and Iraq the word is still used in this sense. In Egypt the Mudīr is the governor of a province (*Mudīrīya*).

MUEZZIN. The man who summons the faithful to prayer from the top of the minaret. He has no religious rank.

MUFTĪ. An Arabic word primarily meaning a jurisconsult, one competent to issue a *Fatwā* (*q.v.*; Turkish *Fetva*), i.e. an authoritative ruling on a disputed point of Sacred Law. In the Ottoman Empire it was the practice to appoint a *Muftī* to a province, district or city, who was in effect the chief authority in the area on all matters of Sacred Law and jurisdiction. One of his duties was to guide the *Qāḍīs* of his area. Appointments of this kind are still made in the Arab lands of the Near East.

MUḤĀFIẒ. An Ottoman term for the commandant of a fortress or a fortified town. In the republics of Syria and Lebanon the *Muḥāfiẓ* is the governor of a province (*Muḥāfaẓa*) corresponding to the former Ottoman *Sanjaq* (*q.v.*). In Egypt he is the governor of a special area outside the normal provincial units. These areas are Cairo, Alexandria, Damietta, Suez and the Canal Zone.

MUHĀJIR (plural MUHĀJIRŪN or MUHĀJIRĪN). An Arabic word meaning migrant. The term is used for those Meccans who accompanied Muḥammad on the *hijra* to Medina.

MUḤAṢṢĪL. An Ottoman revenue official, sometimes in charge of the revenues of a *Sanjaq* or *Vilayet,* sometimes of the collection of a specific tax. In later times he was known as a *Taḥṣīldār*. The earlier *Muḥaṣṣīl* was often the chief of a hierarchy of tax-farmers operating in a province.

MUḤTASIB. A magistrate in charge of markets, weights and measures, public morals, etc. The term survives in the Spanish *Almutacen.*

MUJTAHID. A Shī'ite divine, similar in status to a Sunni *Muftī* (*q.v.*) but exercising rather greater spiritual power.

MUKHTĀR. An Arabic word meaning chosen, used to describe the headman of a village after the Ottoman reforms. It is still so used in Arab Asia.

MULTAZIM. The holder of an *Iltizām* (*q.v.*).

MUQADDAM. An Arabic word meaning 'placed in front', used to describe one placed in command of a body of troops, a ship or a police unit.

MUQĀTA'A. A term used in Ottoman Syria for a feudal grant, the holder of which, the *Muqāta'ajī*, farmed the revenues of the area, sometimes from the governor or the chief tax-farmer of the province, sometimes from a local farmer of taxes.

MÜSELLEM. An Ottoman feudal soldier with certain immunities. The *müsellem* paid no money dues, but was bound to provide services for armies in transit, such as road-clearance, cartage, labour-service, etc.

At certain periods the title *Müsellem* was also used for administrative officials with authority to collect and spend public moneys.

MUSLIM. An Arabic word meaning 'one who surrenders himself to God', i.e. accepts Islam. It is sometimes spelt Moslem. A Persian form of the word, *Musulmān,* is also encountered in other Muslim languages.

MUTAṢARRIF. A late Ottoman term for the governor of a *Sanjaq* (*q.v.*). The term is still used for provincial governors in Iraq, the area governed being called a *Liwā*.

MÜTESELLIM. An Ottoman official appointed by a *Vali* or *Mutaṣar-*

rif to collect the revenues of a *Kaza*. The office was discontinued after the *Tanzimat* (*q.v.*).

NABĪL. A title given in modern Egypt to members of the royal house who are not princes in their own right.

NĀ'IB. An Arabic word meaning a deputy or delegate, used with a wide variety of meanings in Islamic lands. In the Ottoman administration the *Nā'ib* was a deputy or substitute of the *Qāḍī*, exercising his powers in the *Nahiye* (*q.v.*). See also India Glossary, p. 70.

NĀḤIYA (NAHIYE). An Ottoman administrative area, a sub-unit of a *Kaza* (*q.v.*). Until the reforms it was administered by a *Nā'ib* (*q.v.*), thereafter by a civil official known as a *Mudīr* (*q.v.*).

NISHANJI̊. An Ottoman secretary of state in charge of the Sultan's sign manual. In the early empire the *Nishanji̊* wielded considerable administrative and even legislative power.

NIẒĀM I JADĪD. An Ottoman term literally meaning new order. It was used to describe the new European style armies of the Ottoman reform period.

OGHLAN (OĞLAN). A Turkish word meaning a youth, especially a page or equerry. The term was also applied to certain light cavalry units, and in this sense passed into European usage in the form Uhlan.

OJAQ. A Turkish word meaning hearth, applied sometimes to a regiment of the Janissaries, sometimes to the whole corps. The three regencies of Algiers, Tunis and Tripoli were known as the Ojaqs of the Maghrib.

OKE. See *Uqqa*.

ORDU. A Turkish word meaning an army, sometimes used for the imperial camp in the army and for army camps generally. It has passed into European usage in the form horde.

PADISHAH. A Persian title, corresponding approximately to emperor, used by various Muslim sovereigns, especially the Ottoman sultans. It was also accorded to certain European monarchs, as a mark of honour, in Ottoman diplomatic usage.

PARA. An Ottoman silver coin, which came into circulation in the 17th century, replacing the *Aqche* or *asper* (*q.v.*) as the basic currency unit. Its original weight was 16 gr. (1·10 gm.), but it depreciated steadily until in 1843–4 it became a small copper coin, one-fortieth of a *piastre* (*q.v.*). A five-para piece was called a *Beshlik*.

PARASANG. The usual European form for the Perso-Arabic *Farsakh*, a measure of distance used in the provinces of the Caliphate east of the Euphrates. The Arabic authors regard it as equivalent to three Arab miles.

PASHA. A Turkish title of uncertain etymology, dating from the 13th century. It was formerly the highest title of honour in the Ottoman Empire, and although military in origin, was also given to civil and administrative personages. It was used more especially for the governors of provinces (*Pashalik*, *Eyalet* or *Vilayet*). The title has been abolished by the Turkish Republic, but is still conferred by the kings of Egypt and

Transjordan. It is not hereditary, and now carries no definite functions with it.

PASHALIK. An Ottoman province, later known as a *vilayet* (*q.v.*).

PIASTRE. The usual European term for the Ottoman *Kuru<u>sh</u>*, a silver coin which was based on the European groat or groschen, and first appeared in the 17th century, with a weight of 296 gr. The value of the piastre was fixed at 40 *paras* (*q.v.*). Like most Ottoman units of currency, the piastre depreciated steadily, and the currency reforms of 1843–4 reduced it to a small coin worth about twopence. At the present time the term *piastre* is used for the one-hundredth part of the Turkish, Syrian, Egyptian and, popularly, Palestinian pound.

QĀḌĪ. A judge in a court administering the Holy Law of Islam (*<u>Sh</u>arī'a, q.v.*). Until the reforms the Ottoman Qāḍī was not only a judge but also the chief local authority on almost all civil, administrative and municipal matters in the area of his jurisdiction (the *Qaḍā* or *Kaza*). Thereafter his powers were restricted to his judicial functions, and the remainder handed over to the *Qā'immaqām* (*q.v.*). The term will also be met in the forms *Kadi, Kazi, Qazi,* etc.

QAFĪZ. A measure of capacity, varying from 5 to 10 gallons (25 to 30 litres). The *Qafīz* normally consists of 12 *Sā'*, each of 4 *Mudd.*

QĀ'IMMAQĀM (KAYMAKAM). A Turco-Arabic word originally meaning *locum tenens,* at first used generally in that sense. After the Ottoman reforms, *Qā'immaqām* means the official governing a *Kaza* (*q.v.*). The term is still used in this sense in Syria, Lebanon and Iraq. The title was also borne by lieutenant-colonels in the Ottoman and later the Egyptian forces.

QAIṢARĪYA. An Arabic term of Byzantine origin, used in the Near East to describe an enclosed market or warehouse and in North Africa for a barracks.

QĀNŪN. A Turco-Arabic word of Greek origin, used to describe laws of non-<u>Sh</u>ar'ī origin, i.e. customary or secular law.

QIBLA. The direction towards which a Muslim turns in prayer, i.e. towards Mecca.

QINṬĀR. A measure of weight of varying value. It consists of a number of *Mann* (*q.v.*), ranging from under 100 to over 300. In modern Egypt the *Qinṭār* (often written *Cantar*) contains 1,200 *Ūqīya* and equals 99 lb. or 44·9 kg.

QĪRĀṬ. One twenty-fourth of a *dīnār* (*q.v.*) weight, and hence by extension a twenty-fourth part of any whole. The English word *carat* is derived from this.

RAMAḌĀN. The ninth month of the Muslim calendar, during which Muslims fast between sunrise and sunset. The Turkish and Persian pronunciation is *Ramazan*.

RAṬL. A unit of weight, varying greatly in value with time, place and the material weighed. In modern Egypt the *raṭl* is just under 1 lb. (11 *raṭls* = 10 lb. 12 oz.).

RAYAH (RI'ĀYĀ). A term applied to the peasantry, in late Ottoman times especially to the non-Muslim subjects.

RAZZIA. A French borrowing from the Arabic *<u>gh</u>azwa,* taken from North Africa in the 19th century. A Bedouin raid.

REDIF. A term applied in the Ottoman Empire to the army reserve.

REIS. A Turkish form of an Arabic word meaning chief or head, used in many compound titles. Following a personal name, it designates a Turkish admiral, e.g. Ali Reis.

REIS EFENDI. An Ottoman dignitary, directly under the Grand Vizier. Originally the head of the chancery of the Imperial *Divan* (*q.v.*), he later became in effect the Minister of Foreign Affairs. The office was suppressed in 1836.

RIFF. From the Arabic *rīf*, fertile land. It is used in European languages to describe the Moroccan coastlands and their inhabitants.

RIYĀL. A term generally applied in Muslim lands to the larger European silver coins, and more particularly, in the 18th and 19th centuries, to the Maria Theresa dollar. The official monetary unit in modern Persia is called the *Riyāl*, and is worth about $1\frac{1}{2}$*d*.

RŪZNĀME. A Persian word meaning a calendar, journal or daily record of events of any kind. In late Ottoman usage it was applied more particularly to the official chronicles kept by the *Rūznāmeji* or court historian.

SĀʿ. A measure of capacity. See *Qafīz*.

ṢADR AʿẒAM. The Ottoman title of the Grand Vizier. The term was also used with a similar sense in Persia. See *Wazīr*.

SAMBŪQ. A small sailing vessel, common in the Red Sea.

SANJAQ. A military administrative district of the Ottoman Empire, part of an *Eyālet*. The office in charge of a *Sanjaq* was called a *Sanjaq-Beyi*, and he was under the Beylerbey or Pasha of the province of which his *Sanjaq* was a part. With the *Tanzimat* it became a purely administrative area, ruled by a civil official called a *Mutaṣarrif* (*q.v.*). The *Sanjaq* might be part of a *vilayet* (*q.v.*), or might be independent, in which case it was sometimes called a *Mutaṣarriflik*. The term *Sanjaq* was abolished by the Turkish Republic.

SARACEN. A term applied in Greek, Latin and later in west European languages to the Arabs and eventually to the Muslim peoples of the Mediterranean countries generally. It is of disputed etymology, and may be derived from the Arabic *S̲h̲arqīyīn*, ' easterners ', or from the name of a Sinaitic tribe.

SARʿASKER. An Ottoman title, given to the Commander-in-Chief. The Serasker Pasha was the Minister of War.

SARAY (SERAIL, SERAGLIO). A Persian word meaning a palace, hence by extension the seat of government. The European limitation of the word to the women's quarters of the palace is not found in the Orient.

SARDĀR (SIRDAR, SERDAR). A Persian word, also used in other Muslim countries, meaning a military commander, and usually a commander-in-chief.

SAYYID. An Arabic word meaning ' Master ' or ' Lord ', for long used for descendants of Muḥammad in the line of Ḥusain, later used more extensively by Sunnīs. In Iraq it has now become the normal word for Mr. In the form *Sīdī* (for *Sayyidī*, ' my Master '), it is often applied to dervish saints and mystics.

A still further abbreviated form *Sī* is the usual word for Mr. in North Africa.

SCIMITAR. From the Persian *Shamshīr*, a kind of sword.

SEKBAN. A regiment of the Janissaries, originally in charge of the hunting dogs.

SERAIL. See *Saray*.

SHĀFI'Ī. See *Fiqh*.

SHĀH. A Persian word meaning king. It was sometimes used by lesser princes, and even as a personal name or a title. *Shāhanshāh* or *Shāhinshāh*, 'king of kings', is used as an equivalent for emperor.

SHĀHINSHĀH. See *Shāh*.

SHAIKH. An Arabic word meaning 'old man', used with a wide variety of meanings in Islamic lands. In the settled areas it usually denotes a religious dignitary, especially a graduate of a theological seminary. It is also applied to the heads of religious orders and fraternities and sometimes of craft-guilds. In Persia it is applied to the headman of a village. Among the Bedouin, the Shaikh is the head of the tribe. In eastern and south-eastern Arabia, the term is used as a hereditary title of sovereignty by the rulers of certain territories such as Kuwait and Masqat. Such territories are called Shaikhdoms. Other spellings include *Sheikh*, *Shaykh*.

SHAIKH AL-BALAD. 'Shaikh of the town', used in 18th-century Egypt to describe the local ruling families who competed, often successfully, with the Ottoman governors for the effective control of Egypt. Nowadays the term is used in Egypt for a village headman.

SHAIKH AL-ISLĀM. The 'Shaikh of Islam', a religious honorific title dating from the late 10th century, conferred on eminent theologians, canonists and mystics. It was later given more particularly to the *Muftī* of Istanbul, who was made head of the entire religious hierarchy of the Ottoman Empire, and became a person of very great power and influence.

SHAMSADĀR. The bearer of the ceremonial parasol, who often accompanied a Muslim monarch in medieval times.

SHARĪ'A. The Holy Law of Islām.

SHARĪF. An Arabic word meaning noble, used for the descendants of Muḥammad in the line of Ḥasan. It was until 1916 used as title by the hereditary local governors of Mecca. It is sometimes written *Sherīf*.

SHĪ'Ī. A follower of the Shī'a, the most important sect in Islām, which began as a legitimist group advocating the claims of 'Alī, the son-in-law of the Prophet, to the Caliphate, and rapidly developed into a religious movement differing on a number of points from orthodox Islam. The Shī'a split into a number of sub-sects, the most important of which at the present day is the *Ithnā'asharī* or 'Twelver' Shī'a, the dominant faith of Persia. Other groups are the Zaidīs, who flourish in the Yemen, and the Ismā'īlīs, who included the *Assassins* (*q.v.*).

SHROFF. A common English form of the Arabic *Ṣarrāf*, a banker.

SĪ. See *Sayyid.*
SĪDĪ. See *Sayyid.*
SIPĀHĪ. An Ottoman feudal cavalryman.
SOLDAN. An early European spelling of *Sulṭān* (*q.v.*).
SOPHI. A European corruption of *Ṣafawī,* the dynastic name of the family that ruled Persia from 1502 to 1736; used by the early travellers as title of the Shāh.
SUBAS͟HĪ. An Ottoman military title, given to officers exercising the functions of chief of police.
SUBLIME PORTE. The usual English translation of *Bāb i 'Ālī,* 'high gate', a term applied to the Ottoman Grand Vizierate and hence to the Ottoman Government generally.
ṢŪFĪ. A Muslim mystic, often a member of a mystic confraternity. See *Tarīqa.*
SULṬĀN. An Arabic word meaning rule, the use of which as a title dates from the 10th century. It was not, however, used until the 11th century with the special meaning of independent ruler of a definite territory. From then until the extinction of the Caliphate it denoted the supreme secular power as opposed to the supreme religious power embodied in the Caliph (*q.v.*). After the fall of the Caliphate it became the normal title of sovereignty among Muslim rulers. It is now going out of use, being replaced by king, but is still used by the rulers of Morocco and Zanzibar, as well as of a number of smaller states.
SUNNĪ. A Muslim belonging to the dominant majority group in Islam, usually called orthodox.
SŪQ. A market, usually enclosed and occupied by a single trade or craft. The usual form in Turkey and Persia is *Bazār* or *Pazar.*
TAḤṢĪLDĀR. An Ottoman revenue official (see *Muḥaṣṣīl*).
TANGA. A small silver coin, varying in weight from 20 to 35 gr., which formed the main unit of currency in the Mongol world from the end of the 14th century to the beginning of the 16th. It survived in central Asia until the 19th century, when *tangas* of about 50 gr. were minted by the central Asian amīrs and also by the Shāhs of Persia.
TANẒĪMĀT. The general term applied to the Ottoman administrative and governmental reforms of the period 1839–80.
ṬARĪQA. A *Ṣūfī* (*q.v.*) brotherhood or order, often associated with a craft-guild.
TEZKERE. A Turkish rendering of the Arabic *tadhkira,* used for any sort of certificate of identity, passport, ticket, etc.
TĪMĀR. An Ottoman military fief, more particularly one of the third and smallest category, i.e. with a revenue of less than 20,000 aspers.
TUG͟H. A crest or pennant of horse-tails, attached to a flagstaff as a badge of rank. Pashas of the highest rank were granted three tails.
TUG͟HRĀ. The sign manual of the Ottoman sultans, also used as a coat of arms.
'ULAMĀ. The Arabic plural of *'Ālim,* a scholar, more especially in

religious subjects. The term *'Ulamā* is loosely used to describe the whole Muslim ecclesiastical class.

ŪQĪYA. A unit of weight of varying value, sometimes given as 7 *mithqāls* (*q.v.*). In modern Egypt it is $\frac{1}{1200}$th part of a *Qinṭār* (*q.v.*).

UQQA (OKE). A unit of weight of varying value, usually containing between two and three *raṭls* (in modern Egypt 2·75). The modern Egyptian *Uqqa* = 2 lb. 11 oz. or 1·248 kg. In earlier times its value is sometimes given as 400 dirhams weight, sometimes as one-thirty-sixth of a *Qinṭār*.

'USHR. An Arabic word meaning tithe, a canonical tax levied on Muslims, and more or less equivalent to *Zakāt* (*q.v.*).

VA'AD LE'UMI. A modern Hebrew expression meaning National Council, an elected body at the head of the Jewish community in Palestine under the Mandate.

VALI (WĀLĪ). A Turkish title of Arabic origin, the governor of a province (*vilayet*) in the Ottoman Empire.

VALIDE. A Turkish form of the Arabic *wālida*, 'mother'. The title of the mother of the reigning sultan.

VILAYET. A Turkish form of the Arabic *Wilāya*. An Ottoman province, until the reforms of the 19th century, ruled by a Beylerbey and also called *Eyālet* or *Pashalik*. Later the *vilayet* became an administrative area governed by a *Vali* (*q.v.*).

WAFD. An Arabic word meaning delegation, the name of a political party originally formed to press the demand for Egyptian representation at the Paris Peace Conference, eventually the main instrument of Egyptian nationalism in the inter-war period.

WAHHĀBĪ. The name of a puritanical Islamic sect, founded in Arabia in the 18th century. It is now the dominant form of Islam in Sa'ūdī Arabia.

WAQF (plural AWQĀF). A pious endowment, usually of land, the revenues of which are assigned to a specific purpose. *Waqf* lands are in effect lands in mortmain, but the maker of the endowment could and often did reserve for himself and his heirs a usufructuary right in the property.

WAZĪR. An Arabic word of Persian origin, describing an officer who first appears under the early 'Abbāsids, as head of the chancery and chief executive of the administration under the Caliph. Under later Islamic dynasties the power and dignity of the office varied greatly. At times, as under the Seljūqs, the wazīr was effectively head of the administration. At others, he was a minor functionary of low rank. The Ottoman vizierate as a rule included high military command. The first vizier was called *vezir ā'ẓam* or *ṣadr a'zam*, usually translated Grand Vizier, with powers vastly exceeding those of his colleagues. He was supreme head for civil and military matters alike, presided over the Grand Divan and made almost all major decisions. During the 19th century he gradually dwindled into a prime minister, and his office ended with the Ottoman Empire. See also India Glossary, p. 78.

WEIGHTS AND MEASURES. The weights and measures of the Islamic

Near and Middle East are based on those current in pre-Islamic Arabia, together with the systems inherited from the Byzantine Empire and the older civilizations of the East. There is considerable diversity in the systems used, the individual measures varying in their values with time, place and material and even in their relation to one another. Notes on the main measures will be found under the following headings; *Ardabb, Buhār, Dirham, Ḥabba, Jarīb, Mann, Mile, Mithqāl, Parasang, Qafīz, Qinṭār, Qīrāt, Raṭl, Uqīya, Uqqa.*

YATAGHAN. A curved Turkish sabre.

YISHUV. A Modern Hebrew word meaning settlement, used to describe the Jewish community in Palestine.

YÜZBASHÎ. An army captain or naval lieutenant in the Ottoman service. The term was retained in some of the Ottoman succession states and means in Turkish a commander of a hundred.

ZAKĀT. A canonical tax levied on Muslims, usually consisting of a tithe (see *'Ushr*). In the earliest times it was in the nature of a capital levy for charitable purposes, but later developed into a tax on income, usually from land.

ZAPTIYE. A Turkish policeman.

ZI'ĀMET. An Ottoman military fief, with a minimum annual revenue of 20,000 aspers.

ZIKR (DHIKR). A religious ceremony in which mystical confraternities attempt to achieve ecstasy by dancing, singing and other means.

ZOUAVE. A French North African regiment, now consisting largely of French troops in Arab costume. The name is derived from *Zawāwa*, a Berber tribe of eastern Algeria.

Bibliography:

The Encyclopaedia of Islam. 4 vols. and Supplement. Leiden. 1913–1938.

For a classified and annotated bibliography of Islamic history, see:

J. Sauvaget. *Introduction à l'histoire de l'orient musulman.* Paris, 1943.

5. CALENDARS AND SYSTEMS OF DATING

The Muslim Calendar. The Muslim era is based on the Hijra, often misspelt Hegira. This was the migration of Muḥammad from Mecca to Medina, which took place in the Arab year beginning 16 July 622. The Muslim year is purely lunar, and has 354 days. It consists of the following months:

I	Muḥarram	30 days	VII	Rajab	30 days
II	Ṣafar	29 days	VIII	Sha'bān	29 days
III	Rabī' I	30 days	IX	Ramaḍān	30 days
IV	Rabī' II	28 days	X	Shawwāl	29 days
V	Jumāda I	30 days	XI	Dhu'l-Qa'da	30 days
VI	Jumāda II	29 days	XII	Dhu'l-Ḥijja	29 or 30 days

The months, being lunar, do not correspond to seasons, but may fall at any period in the solar year. There are roughly 103 *Hijrī* years to 100 Gregorian years.

The purely lunar character of the *Hijrī* era made it inconvenient for fiscal and administrative purposes, and Muslim governments from early times worked out a series of solar adaptations of the *Hijrī* year with Persian, Coptic, Julian and other months. The most important of these are the Turkish Financial Year and the Persian Solar Year.

The Turkish Financial Year (Maliye). An adaptation of earlier 'fiscal' calendars, combining the *Hijrī* era with a solar year, was introduced into the Ottoman revenue administration in A.D. 1789. This was a Julian year with most of the Syrian month names, used with a *Hijrī* era and a system of 'sliding' at intervals to bring the two eras into line.

The Persian Solar Year. Introduced in 1925, this is based on the *Hijra*, but is calculated in solar years, using an adaptation of the old Iranian month names, as follows:

Farvardīn	31 days each	Mehr	30 days each
Ordibehesht		Ābān	
Khordād		Āzōr	
Tīr		Dē	
Mordād		Bahman	
Shahrivar		Esfand	

To convert Persian solar years to Gregorian, add 622 to dates 1 Jan.–21 March, and 621 to dates 21 March–31 Dec. The 1st Farvardīn falls in the third week of March. This era is now used in Persia for all but purely religious purposes.

Bibliography

W. Haig. *Comparative Tables of Muhammadan and Christian Dates.* London, 1932.

S. H. Taqizadeh. 'Various Calendars and Eras used in the Countries of Islam', *Bulletin of the School of Oriental Studies,* ix (1938), 903–22; x (1940), 107–32.

F. Wüstenfeld. *Vergleichungstabellen der muhammedanischen und christlichen Zeitrechnungen.* 2nd edn, revised by E. Mahler. Leipzig, 1926.

COMPARATIVE TABLES OF A.H. AND A.D. DATES

The Hijrī year begins on the day of the month indicated

A.H.	A.D.		A.H.	A.D.		A.H.	A.D.	
1	622	16 July	61	680	1 Oct.	121	738	18 Dec.
2	623	5 July	62	681	20 Sept.	122	739	7 Dec.
3	624	24 June	63	682	10 Sept.	123	740	26 Nov.
4	625	13 June	64	683	30 Aug.	124	741	15 Nov.
5	626	2 June	65	684	18 Aug.	125	742	4 Nov.
6	627	23 May	66	685	8 Aug.	126	743	25 Oct.
7	628	11 May	67	686	28 July	127	744	13 Oct.
8	629	1 May	68	687	18 July	128	745	3 Oct.
9	630	20 April	69	688	6 July	129	746	22 Sept.
10	631	9 April	70	689	25 June	130	747	11 Sept.
11	632	29 March	71	690	15 June	131	748	31 Aug.
12	633	18 March	72	691	4 June	132	749	20 Aug.
13	634	7 March	73	692	23 May	133	750	9 Aug.
14	635	25 Feb.	74	693	13 May	134	751	30 July
15	636	14 Feb.	75	694	2 May	135	752	18 July
16	637	2 Feb.	76	695	21 April	136	753	7 July
17	638	23 Jan.	77	696	10 April	137	754	27 June
18	639	12 Jan.	78	697	30 March	138	755	16 June
19	640	2 Jan.	79	698	20 March	139	756	5 June
20	640	21 Dec.	80	699	9 March	140	757	25 May
21	641	10 Dec.	81	700	26 Feb.	141	758	14 May
22	642	30 Nov.	82	701	15 Feb.	142	759	4 May
23	643	19 Nov.	83	702	4 Feb.	143	760	22 April
24	644	7 Nov.	84	703	24 Jan.	144	761	11 April
25	645	28 Oct.	85	704	14 Jan.	145	762	1 April
26	646	17 Oct.	86	705	2 Jan.	146	763	21 March
27	647	7 Oct.	87	705	23 Dec.	147	764	10 March
28	648	25 Sept.	88	706	12 Dec.	148	765	27 Feb.
29	649	14 Sept.	89	707	1 Dec.	149	766	16 Feb.
30	650	4 Sept.	90	708	20 Nov.	150	767	6 Feb.
31	651	24 Aug.	91	709	9 Nov.	151	768	26 Jan.
32	652	12 Aug.	92	710	29 Oct.	152	769	14 Jan.
33	653	2 Aug.	93	711	19 Oct.	153	770	4 Jan.
34	654	22 July	94	712	7 Oct.	154	770	24 Dec.
35	655	11 July	95	713	26 Sept.	155	771	13 Dec.
36	656	30 June	96	714	16 Sept.	156	772	2 Dec.
37	657	19 June	97	715	5 Sept.	157	773	21 Nov.
38	658	9 June	98	716	25 Aug.	158	774	11 Nov.
39	659	29 May	99	717	14 Aug.	159	775	31 Oct.
40	660	17 May	100	718	3 Aug.	160	776	19 Oct.
41	661	7 May	101	719	24 July	161	777	9 Oct.
42	662	26 April	102	720	12 July	162	778	28 Sept.
43	663	15 April	103	721	1 July	163	779	17 Sept.
44	664	4 April	104	722	21 June	164	780	6 Sept.
45	665	24 March	105	723	10 June	165	781	26 Aug.
46	666	13 March	106	724	29 May	166	782	15 Aug.
47	667	3 March	107	725	19 May	167	783	5 Aug.
48	668	20 Feb.	108	726	8 May	168	784	24 July
49	669	9 Feb.	109	727	28 April	169	785	14 July
50	670	29 Jan.	110	728	16 April	170	786	3 July
51	671	18 Jan.	111	729	5 April	171	787	22 June
52	672	8 Jan.	112	730	20 March	172	788	11 June
53	672	27 Dec.	113	731	15 March	173	789	31 May
54	673	16 Dec.	114	732	3 March	174	790	20 May
55	674	6 Dec.	115	733	21 Feb.	175	791	10 May
56	675	25 Nov.	116	734	10 Feb.	176	792	28 April
57	676	14 Nov.	117	735	31 Jan.	177	793	18 April
58	677	3 Nov.	118	736	20 Jan.	178	794	7 April
59	678	23 Oct.	119	737	8 Jan.	179	795	27 March
60	679	13 Oct.	120	737	29 Dec.	180	796	16 March

A.H.	A.D.		A.H.	A.D.		A.H.	A.D.	
181	797	5 March	245	859	8 April	309	921	12 May
182	798	22 Feb.	246	860	28 March	310	922	1 May
183	799	12 Feb.	247	861	17 March	311	923	21 April
184	800	1 Feb.	248	862	7 March	312	924	9 April
185	801	20 Jan.	249	863	24 Feb.	313	925	29 March
186	802	10 Jan.	250	864	13 Feb.	314	926	19 March
187	802	30 Dec.	251	865	2 Feb.	315	927	8 March
188	803	20 Dec.	252	866	22 Jan.	316	928	25 Feb.
189	804	8 Dec.	253	867	11 Jan.	317	929	14 Feb.
190	805	27 Nov.	254	868	1 Jan.	318	930	3 Feb.
191	806	17 Nov.	255	868	20 Dec.	319	931	24 Jan.
192	807	6 Nov.	256	869	9 Dec.	320	932	13 Jan.
193	808	25 Oct.	257	870	29 Nov.	321	933	1 Jan.
194	809	15 Oct.	258	871	18 Nov.	322	933	22 Dec.
195	810	4 Oct.	259	872	7 Nov.	323	934	11 Dec.
196	811	23 Sept.	260	873	27 Oct.	324	935	30 Nov.
197	812	12 Sept.	261	874	16 Oct.	325	936	19 Nov.
198	813	1 Sept.	262	875	6 Oct.	326	937	8 Nov.
199	814	22 Aug.	263	876	24 Sept.	327	938	29 Oct.
200	815	11 Aug.	264	877	13 Sept.	328	939	18 Oct.
201	816	30 July	265	878	3 Sept.	329	940	6 Oct.
202	817	20 July	266	879	23 Aug.	330	941	26 Sept.
203	818	9 July	267	880	12 Aug.	331	942	15 Sept.
204	819	28 June	268	881	1 Aug.	332	943	4 Sept.
205	820	17 June	269	882	21 July	333	944	24 Aug.
206	821	6 June	270	883	11 July	334	945	13 Aug.
207	822	27 May	271	884	29 June	335	946	2 Aug.
208	823	16 May	272	885	18 June	336	947	23 July
209	824	4 May	273	886	8 June	337	948	11 July
210	825	24 April	274	887	28 May	338	949	1 July
211	826	13 April	275	888	16 May	339	950	20 June
212	827	2 April	276	889	6 May	340	951	9 June
213	828	22 March	277	890	25 April	341	952	29 May
214	829	11 March	278	891	15 April	342	953	18 May
215	830	28 Feb.	279	892	3 April	343	954	7 May
216	831	18 Feb.	280	893	23 March	344	955	27 April
217	832	7 Feb.	281	894	13 March	345	956	15 April
218	833	27 Jan.	282	895	2 March	346	957	4 April
219	834	16 Jan.	283	896	19 Feb.	347	958	25 March
220	835	5 Jan.	284	897	8 Feb.	348	959	14 March
221	835	26 Dec.	285	898	28 Jan.	349	960	3 March
222	836	14 Dec.	286	899	17 Jan.	350	961	20 Feb.
223	837	3 Dec.	287	900	7 Jan.	351	962	9 Feb.
224	838	23 Nov.	288	900	26 Dec.	352	963	30 Jan.
225	839	12 Nov.	289	901	16 Dec.	353	964	19 Jan.
226	840	31 Oct.	290	902	5 Dec.	354	965	7 Jan.
227	841	21 Oct.	291	903	24 Nov.	355	965	28 Dec.
228	842	10 Oct.	292	904	13 Nov.	356	966	17 Dec.
229	843	30 Sept.	293	905	2 Nov.	357	967	7 Dec.
230	844	18 Sept.	294	906	22 Oct.	358	968	25 Nov.
231	845	7 Sept.	295	907	12 Oct.	359	969	14 Nov.
232	846	28 Aug.	296	908	30 Sept.	360	970	4 Nov.
233	847	17 Aug.	297	909	20 Sept.	361	971	24 Oct.
234	848	5 Aug.	298	910	9 Sept.	362	972	12 Oct.
235	849	26 July	299	911	29 Aug.	363	973	2 Oct.
236	850	15 July	300	912	18 Aug.	364	974	21 Sept.
237	851	5 July	301	913	7 Aug.	365	975	10 Sept.
238	852	23 June	302	914	27 July	366	976	30 Aug.
239	853	12 June	303	915	17 July	367	977	19 Aug.
240	854	2 June	304	916	5 July	368	978	9 Aug.
241	855	22 May	305	917	24 June	369	979	29 July
242	856	10 May	306	918	14 June	370	980	17 July
243	857	30 April	307	919	3 June	371	981	7 July
244	858	19 April	308	920	23 May	372	982	26 June

A.H.	A.D.		A.H.	A.D.		A.H.	A.D.	
373	983	15 June	437	1045	19 July	501	1107	22 Aug.
374	984	4 June	438	1046	8 July	502	1108	11 Aug.
375	985	24 May	439	1047	28 June	503	1109	31 July
376	986	13 May	440	1048	16 June	504	1110	20 July
377	987	3 May	441	1049	5 June	505	1111	10 July
378	988	21 April	442	1050	26 May	506	1112	28 June
379	989	11 April	443	1051	15 May	507	1113	18 June
380	990	31 March	444	1052	3 May	508	1114	7 June
381	991	20 March	445	1053	23 April	509	1115	27 May
382	992	9 March	446	1054	12 April	510	1116	16 May
383	993	26 Feb.	447	1055	2 April	511	1117	5 May
384	994	15 Feb.	448	1056	21 March	512	1118	24 April
385	995	5 Feb.	449	1057	10 March	513	1119	14 April
386	996	25 Jan.	450	1058	28 Feb.	514	1120	2 April
387	997	14 Jan.	451	1059	17 Feb.	515	1121	22 March
388	998	3 Jan.	452	1060	6 Feb.	516	1122	12 March
389	998	23 Dec.	453	1061	26 Jan.	517	1123	1 March
390	999	13 Dec.	454	1062	15 Jan.	518	1124	19 Feb.
391	1000	1 Dec.	455	1063	4 Jan.	519	1125	7 Feb.
392	1001	20 Nov.	456	1063	25 Dec.	520	1126	27 Jan.
393	1002	10 Nov.	457	1064	13 Dec.	521	1127	17 Jan.
394	1003	30 Oct.	458	1065	3 Dec.	522	1128	6 Jan.
395	1004	18 Oct.	459	1066	22 Nov.	523	1128	25 Dec.
396	1005	8 Oct.	460	1067	11 Nov.	524	1129	15 Dec.
397	1006	27 Sept.	461	1068	31 Oct.	525	1130	4 Dec.
398	1007	17 Sept.	462	1069	20 Oct.	526	1131	23 Nov.
399	1008	5 Sept.	463	1070	9 Oct.	527	1132	12 Nov.
400	1009	25 Aug.	464	1071	29 Sept.	528	1133	1 Nov.
401	1010	15 Aug.	465	1072	17 Sept.	529	1134	22 Oct.
402	1011	4 Aug.	466	1073	6 Sept.	530	1135	11 Oct.
403	1012	23 July	467	1074	27 Aug.	531	1136	29 Sept.
404	1013	13 July	468	1075	16 Aug.	532	1137	19 Sept.
405	1014	2 July	469	1076	5 Aug.	533	1138	8 Sept.
406	1015	21 June	470	1077	25 July	534	1139	28 Aug.
407	1016	10 June	471	1078	14 July	535	1140	17 Aug.
408	1017	30 May	472	1079	4 July	536	1141	6 Aug.
409	1018	20 May	473	1080	22 June	537	1142	27 July
410	1019	9 May	474	1081	11 June	538	1143	16 July
411	1020	27 April	475	1082	1 June	539	1144	4 July
412	1021	17 April	476	1083	21 May	540	1145	24 June
413	1022	6 April	477	1084	10 May	541	1146	13 June
414	1023	26 March	478	1085	29 April	542	1147	2 June
415	1024	15 March	479	1086	18 April	543	1148	22 May
416	1025	4 March	480	1087	8 April	544	1149	11 May
417	1026	22 Feb.	481	1088	27 March	545	1150	30 April
418	1027	11 Feb.	482	1089	16 March	546	1151	20 April
419	1028	31 Jan.	483	1090	6 March	547	1152	8 April
420	1029	20 Jan.	484	1091	23 Feb.	548	1153	29 March
421	1030	9 Jan.	485	1092	12 Feb.	549	1154	18 March
422	1030	29 Dec.	486	1093	1 Feb.	550	1155	7 March
423	1031	19 Dec.	487	1094	21 Jan.	551	1156	25 Feb.
424	1032	7 Dec.	488	1095	11 Jan.	552	1157	13 Feb.
425	1033	26 Nov.	489	1095	31 Dec.	553	1158	2 Feb.
426	1034	16 Nov.	490	1096	19 Dec.	554	1159	23 Jan.
427	1035	5 Nov.	491	1097	9 Dec.	555	1160	12 Jan.
428	1036	25 Oct.	492	1098	28 Nov.	556	1160	31 Dec.
429	1037	14 Oct.	493	1099	17 Nov.	557	1161	21 Dec.
430	1038	3 Oct.	494	1100	6 Nov.	558	1162	10 Dec.
431	1039	23 Sept.	495	1101	26 Oct.	559	1163	30 Nov.
432	1040	11 Sept.	496	1102	15 Oct.	560	1164	18 Nov.
433	1041	31 Aug.	497	1103	5 Oct.	561	1165	7 Nov.
434	1042	21 Aug.	498	1104	23 Sept.	562	1166	28 Oct.
435	1043	10 Aug.	499	1105	13 Sept.	563	1167	17 Oct.
436	1044	29 July	500	1106	2 Sept.	564	1168	5 Oct.

A.H.	A.D.		A.H.	A.D.		A.H.	A.D.	
565	1169	25 Sept.	629	1231	29 Oct.	693	1293	2 Dec.
566	1170	14 Sept.	630	1232	18 Oct.	694	1294	21 Nov.
567	1171	4 Sept.	631	1233	7 Oct.	695	1295	10 Nov.
568	1172	23 Aug.	632	1234	26 Sept.	696	1296	30 Oct.
569	1173	12 Aug.	633	1235	16 Sept.	697	1297	19 Oct.
570	1174	2 Aug.	634	1236	4 Sept.	698	1298	9 Oct.
571	1175	22 July	635	1237	24 Aug.	699	1299	28 Sept.
572	1176	10 July	636	1238	14 Aug.	700	1300	16 Sept.
573	1177	30 June	637	1239	3 Aug.	701	1301	6 Sept.
574	1178	19 June	638	1240	23 July	702	1302	26 Aug.
575	1179	8 June	639	1241	12 July	703	1303	15 Aug.
576	1180	28 May	640	1242	1 July	704	1304	4 Aug.
577	1181	17 May	641	1243	21 June	705	1305	24 July
578	1182	7 May	642	1244	9 June	706	1306	13 July
579	1183	26 April	643	1245	29 May	707	1307	3 July
580	1184	14 April	644	1246	19 May	708	1308	21 June
581	1185	4 April	645	1247	8 May	709	1309	11 June
582	1186	24 March	646	1248	26 April	710	1310	31 May
583	1187	13 March	647	1249	16 April	711	1311	20 May
584	1188	2 March	648	1250	5 April	712	1312	9 May
585	1189	19 Feb.	649	1251	26 March	713	1313	28 April
586	1190	8 Feb.	650	1252	14 March	714	1314	17 April
587	1191	29 Jan.	651	1253	3 March	715	1315	7 April
588	1192	18 Jan.	652	1254	21 Feb.	716	1316	26 March
589	1193	7 Jan.	653	1255	10 Feb.	717	1317	16 March
590	1193	27 Dec.	654	1256	30 Jan.	718	1318	5 March
591	1194	16 Dec.	655	1257	19 Jan.	719	1319	22 Feb.
592	1195	6 Dec.	656	1258	8 Jan.	720	1320	12 Feb.
593	1196	24 Nov.	657	1258	29 Dec.	721	1321	31 Jan.
594	1197	13 Nov.	658	1259	18 Dec.	722	1322	20 Jan.
595	1198	3 Nov.	659	1260	6 Dec.	723	1323	10 Jan.
596	1199	23 Oct.	660	1261	26 Nov.	724	1323	30 Dec.
597	1200	12 Oct.	661	1262	15 Nov.	725	1324	18 Dec.
598	1201	1 Oct.	662	1263	4 Nov.	726	1325	8 Dec.
599	1202	20 Sept.	663	1264	24 Oct.	727	1326	27 Nov.
600	1203	10 Sept.	664	1265	13 Oct.	728	1327	17 Nov.
601	1204	29 Aug.	665	1266	2 Oct.	729	1328	5 Nov.
602	1205	18 Aug.	666	1267	22 Sept.	730	1329	25 Oct.
603	1206	8 Aug.	667	1268	10 Sept.	731	1330	15 Oct.
604	1207	28 July	668	1269	31 Aug.	732	1331	4 Oct.
605	1208	16 July	669	1270	20 Aug.	733	1332	22 Sept.
606	1209	6 July	670	1271	9 Aug.	734	1333	12 Sept.
607	1210	25 June	671	1272	29 July	735	1334	1 Sept.
608	1211	15 June	672	1273	18 July	736	1335	21 Aug.
609	1212	3 June	673	1274	7 July	737	1336	10 Aug.
610	1213	23 May	674	1275	27 June	738	1337	30 July
611	1214	13 May	675	1276	15 June	739	1338	20 July
612	1215	2 May	676	1277	4 June	740	1339	9 July
613	1216	20 April	677	1278	25 May	741	1340	27 June
614	1217	10 April	678	1279	14 May	742	1341	17 June
615	1218	30 March	679	1280	3 May	743	1342	6 June
616	1219	19 March	680	1281	22 April	744	1343	26 May
617	1220	8 March	681	1282	11 April	745	1344	15 May
618	1221	25 Feb.	682	1283	1 April	746	1345	4 May
619	1222	15 Feb.	683	1284	20 March	747	1346	24 April
620	1223	4 Feb.	684	1285	9 March	748	1347	13 April
621	1224	24 Jan.	685	1286	27 Feb.	749	1348	1 April
622	1225	13 Jan.	686	1287	16 Feb.	750	1349	22 March
623	1226	2 Jan.	687	1288	6 Feb.	751	1350	11 March
624	1226	22 Dec.	688	1289	25 Jan.	752	1351	28 Feb.
625	1227	12 Dec.	689	1290	14 Jan.	753	1352	18 Feb.
626	1228	30 Nov.	690	1291	4 Jan.	754	1353	6 Feb.
627	1229	20 Nov.	691	1291	24 Dec.	755	1354	26 Jan.
628	1230	9 Nov.	692	1292	12 Dec.	756	1355	16 Jan.

A.H.	A.D.		A.H.	A.D.		A.H.	A.D.	
757	1356	5 Jan.	821	1418	8 Feb.	885	1480	13 March
758	1356	25 Dec.	822	1419	28 Jan.	886	1481	2 March
759	1357	14 Dec.	823	1420	17 Jan.	887	1482	20 Feb.
760	1358	3 Dec.	824	1421	6 Jan.	888	1483	9 Feb.
761	1359	23 Nov.	825	1421	26 Dec.	889	1484	30 Jan.
762	1360	11 Nov.	826	1422	15 Dec.	890	1485	18 Jan.
763	1361	31 Oct.	827	1423	5 Dec.	891	1486	7 Jan.
764	1362	21 Oct.	828	1424	23 Nov.	892	1486	28 Dec.
765	1363	10 Oct.	829	1425	13 Nov.	893	1487	17 Dec.
766	1364	28 Sept.	830	1426	2 Nov.	894	1488	5 Dec.
767	1365	18 Sept.	831	1427	22 Oct.	895	1489	25 Nov.
768	1366	7 Sept.	832	1428	11 Oct.	896	1490	14 Nov.
769	1367	28 Aug.	833	1429	30 Sept.	897	1491	4 Nov.
770	1368	16 Aug.	834	1430	19 Sept.	898	1492	23 Oct.
771	1369	5 Aug.	835	1431	9 Sept.	899	1493	12 Oct.
772	1370	26 July	836	1432	28 Aug.	900	1494	2 Oct.
773	1371	15 July	837	1433	18 Aug.	901	1495	21 Sept.
774	1372	3 July	838	1434	7 Aug.	902	1496	9 Sept.
775	1373	23 June	839	1435	27 July	903	1497	30 Aug.
776	1374	12 June	840	1436	16 July	904	1498	19 Aug.
777	1375	2 June	841	1437	5 July	905	1499	8 Aug.
778	1376	21 May	842	1438	24 June	906	1500	28 July
779	1377	10 May	843	1439	14 June	907	1501	17 July
780	1378	30 April	844	1440	2 June	908	1502	7 July
781	1379	19 April	845	1441	22 May	909	1503	26 June
782	1380	7 April	846	1442	12 May	910	1504	14 June
783	1381	28 March	847	1443	1 May	911	1505	4 June
784	1382	17 March	848	1444	20 April	912	1506	24 May
785	1383	6 March	849	1445	9 April	913	1507	13 May
786	1384	24 Feb.	850	1446	29 March	914	1508	2 May
787	1385	12 Feb.	851	1447	19 March	915	1509	21 April
788	1386	2 Feb.	852	1448	7 March	916	1510	10 April
789	1387	22 Jan.	853	1449	24 Feb.	917	1511	31 March
790	1388	11 Jan.	854	1450	14 Feb.	918	1512	19 March
791	1388	31 Dec.	855	1451	3 Feb.	919	1513	9 March
792	1389	20 Dec.	856	1452	23 Jan.	920	1514	26 Feb.
793	1390	9 Dec.	857	1453	12 Jan.	921	1515	15 Feb.
794	1391	29 Nov.	858	1454	1 Jan.	922	1516	5 Feb.
795	1392	17 Nov.	859	1454	22 Dec.	923	1517	24 Jan.
796	1393	6 Nov.	860	1455	11 Dec.	924	1518	13 Jan.
797	1394	27 Oct.	861	1456	29 Nov.	925	1519	3 Jan.
798	1395	16 Oct.	862	1457	19 Nov.	926	1519	23 Dec.
799	1396	5 Oct.	863	1458	8 Nov.	927	1520	12 Dec.
800	1397	24 Sept.	864	1459	28 Oct.	928	1521	1 Dec.
801	1398	13 Sept.	865	1460	17 Oct.	929	1522	20 Nov.
802	1399	3 Sept.	866	1461	6 Oct.	930	1523	10 Nov.
803	1400	22 Aug.	867	1462	26 Sept.	931	1524	29 Oct.
804	1401	11 Aug.	868	1463	15 Sept.	932	1525	18 Oct.
805	1402	1 Aug.	869	1464	3 Sept.	933	1526	8 Oct.
806	1403	21 July	870	1465	24 Aug.	934	1527	27 Sept.
807	1404	10 July	871	1466	13 Aug.	935	1528	15 Sept.
808	1405	29 June	872	1467	2 Aug.	936	1529	5 Sept.
809	1406	18 June	873	1468	22 July	937	1530	25 Aug.
810	1407	8 June	874	1469	11 July	938	1531	15 Aug.
811	1408	27 May	875	1470	30 June	939	1532	3 Aug.
812	1409	16 May	876	1471	20 June	940	1533	23 July
813	1410	6 May	877	1372	8 June	941	1534	13 July
814	1411	25 April	878	1473	29 May	942	1535	2 July
815	1412	13 April	879	1474	18 May	943	1536	20 June
816	1413	3 April	880	1475	7 May	944	1537	10 June
817	1414	23 March	881	1476	26 April	945	1538	30 May
818	1415	13 March	882	1477	15 April	946	1539	19 May
819	1416	1 March	883	1478	4 April	947	1540	8 May
820	1417	18 Feb.	884	1479	25 March	948	1541	27 April

A.H.	A.D.		
949	1542	17	April
950	1543	6	April
951	1544	25	March
952	1545	15	March
953	1546	4	March
954	1547	21	Feb.
955	1548	11	Feb.
956	1549	30	Jan.
957	1550	20	Jan.
958	1551	9	Jan.
959	1551	29	Dec.
960	1552	18	Dec.
961	1553	7	Dec.
962	1554	26	Nov.
963	1555	16	Nov.
964	1556	4	Nov.
965	1557	24	Oct.
966	1558	14	Oct.
967	1559	3	Oct.
968	1560	22	Sept.
969	1561	11	Sept.
970	1562	31	Aug.
971	1563	21	Aug.
972	1564	9	Aug.
973	1565	29	July
974	1566	19	July
975	1567	8	July
976	1568	26	June
977	1569	16	June
978	1570	5	June
979	1571	26	May
980	1572	14	May
981	1573	3	May
982	1574	23	April
983	1575	12	April
984	1576	31	March
985	1577	21	March
986	1578	10	March
987	1579	28	Feb.
988	1580	17	Feb.
989	1581	5	Feb.
990	1582	26	Jan.
990	1582	[1]	
991	1583	25	Jan.
992	1584	14	Jan.
993	1585	3	Jan.
994	1585	23	Dec.
995	1586	12	Dec.
996	1587	2	Dec.
997	1588	20	Nov.
998	1589	10	Nov.
999	1590	30	Oct.
1000	1591	19	Oct.
1001	1592	8	Oct.
1002	1593	27	Sept.
1003	1594	16	Sept.
1004	1595	6	Sept.
1005	1596	25	Aug.
1006	1597	14	Aug.
1007	1598	4	Aug.

A.H.	A.D.		
1008	1599	24	July
1009	1600	13	July
1010	1601	2	July
1011	1602	21	June
1012	1603	11	June
1013	1604	30	May
1014	1605	19	May
1015	1606	9	May
1016	1607	28	April
1017	1608	17	April
1018	1609	6	April
1019	1610	26	March
1020	1611	16	March
1021	1612	4	March
1022	1613	21	Feb.
1023	1614	11	Feb.
1024	1615	31	Jan.
1025	1616	20	Jan.
1026	1617	9	Jan.
1027	1617	29	Dec.
1028	1618	19	Dec.
1029	1619	8	Dec.
1030	1620	26	Nov.
1031	1621	16	Nov.
1032	1622	5	Nov.
1033	1623	25	Oct.
1034	1624	14	Oct.
1035	1625	3	Oct.
1036	1626	22	Sept.
1037	1627	12	Sept.
1038	1628	31	Aug.
1039	1629	21	Aug.
1040	1630	10	Aug.
1041	1631	30	July
1042	1632	19	July
1043	1633	8	July
1044	1634	27	June
1045	1635	17	June
1046	1636	5	June
1047	1637	26	May
1048	1638	15	May
1049	1639	4	May
1050	1640	23	April
1051	1641	12	April
1052	1642	1	April
1053	1643	22	March
1054	1644	10	March
1055	1645	27	Feb.
1056	1646	17	Feb.
1057	1647	6	Feb.
1058	1648	27	Jan.
1059	1649	15	Jan.
1060	1650	4	Jan.
1061	1650	25	Dec.
1062	1651	14	Dec.
1063	1652	2	Dec.
1064	1653	22	Nov.
1065	1654	11	Nov.
1066	1655	31	Oct.
1067	1656	20	Oct.
1068	1657	9	Oct.
1069	1658	29	Sept.
1070	1659	18	Sept.
1071	1660	6	Sept.

A.H.	A.D.		
1072	1661	27	Aug.
1073	1662	16	Aug.
1074	1663	5	Aug.
1075	1664	25	July
1076	1665	14	July
1077	1666	4	July
1078	1667	23	June
1079	1668	11	June
1080	1669	1	June
1081	1670	21	May
1082	1671	10	May
1083	1672	29	April
1084	1673	18	April
1085	1674	7	April
1086	1675	28	March
1087	1676	16	March
1088	1677	6	March
1089	1678	23	Feb.
1090	1679	12	Feb.
1091	1680	2	Feb.
1092	1681	21	Jan.
1093	1682	10	Jan.
1094	1682	31	Dec.
1095	1683	20	Dec.
1096	1684	8	Dec.
1097	1685	28	Nov.
1098	1686	17	Nov.
1099	1687	7	Nov.
1100	1688	26	Oct.
1101	1689	15	Oct.
1102	1690	5	Oct.
1103	1691	24	Sept.
1104	1692	12	Sept.
1105	1693	2	Sept.
1106	1694	22	Aug.
1107	1695	12	Aug.
1108	1696	31	July
1109	1697	20	July
1110	1698	10	July
1111	1699	29	June
1112	1700	18	June
1113	1701	8	June
1114	1702	28	May
1115	1703	17	May
1116	1704	6	May
1117	1705	25	April
1118	1706	15	April
1119	1707	4	April
1120	1708	23	March
1121	1709	13	March
1122	1710	2	March
1123	1711	19	Feb.
1124	1712	9	Feb.
1125	1713	28	Jan.
1126	1714	17	Jan.
1127	1715	7	Jan.
1128	1715	27	Dec.
1129	1716	16	Dec.
1130	1717	5	Dec.
1131	1718	24	Nov.
1132	1719	14	Nov.
1133	1720	2	Nov.
1134	1721	22	Oct.
1135	1722	12	Oct.

[1] Transfer from Julian to Gregorian calendar.

A.H.	A.D.			A.H.	A.D.			A.H.	A.D.		
1136	1723	1	Oct.	1200	1785	4	Nov.	1264	1847	9	Dec.
1137	1724	20	Sept.	1201	1786	24	Oct.	1265	1848	27	Nov.
1138	1725	9	Sept.	1202	1787	13	Oct.	1266	1849	17	Nov.
1139	1726	29	Aug.	1203	1788	2	Oct.	1267	1850	6	Nov.
1140	1727	19	Aug.	1204	1789	21	Sept.	1268	1851	27	Oct.
1141	1728	7	Aug.	1205	1790	10	Sept.	1269	1852	15	Oct.
1142	1729	27	July	1206	1791	31	Aug.	1270	1853	4	Oct.
1143	1730	17	July	1207	1792	19	Aug.	1271	1854	24	Sept.
1144	1731	6	July	1208	1793	9	Aug.	1272	1855	13	Sept.
1145	1732	24	June	1209	1794	29	July	1273	1856	1	Sept.
1146	1733	14	June	1210	1795	18	July	1274	1857	22	Aug.
1147	1734	3	June	1211	1796	7	July	1275	1858	11	Aug.
1148	1735	24	May	1212	1797	26	June	1276	1859	31	July
1149	1736	12	May	1213	1798	15	June	1277	1860	20	July
1150	1737	1	May	1214	1799	5	June	1278	1861	9	July
1151	1738	21	April	1215	1800	25	May	1279	1862	29	June
1152	1739	10	April	1216	1801	14	May	1280	1863	18	June
1153	1740	29	March	1217	1802	4	May	1281	1864	6	June
1154	1741	19	March	1218	1803	23	April	1282	1865	27	May
1155	1742	8	March	1219	1804	12	April	1283	1866	16	May
1156	1743	25	Feb.	1220	1805	1	April	1284	1867	5	May
1157	1744	15	Feb.	1221	1806	21	March	1285	1868	24	April
1158	1745	3	Feb.	1222	1807	11	March	1286	1869	13	April
1159	1746	24	Jan.	1223	1808	28	Feb.	1287	1870	3	April
1160	1747	13	Jan.	1224	1809	16	Feb.	1288	1871	23	March
1161	1748	2	Jan.	1225	1810	6	Feb.	1289	1872	11	March
1162	1748	22	Dec.	1226	1811	26	Jan.	1290	1873	1	March
1163	1749	11	Dec.	1227	1812	16	Jan.	1291	1874	18	Feb.
1164	1750	30	Nov.	1228	1813	4	Jan.	1292	1875	7	Feb.
1165	1751	20	Nov.	1229	1813	24	Dec.	1293	1876	28	Jan.
1166	1752	8	Nov.	1230	1814	14	Dec.	1294	1877	16	Jan.
1167	1753	29	Oct.	1231	1815	3	Dec.	1295	1878	5	Jan.
1168	1754	18	Oct.	1232	1816	21	Nov.	1296	1878	26	Dec.
1169	1755	7	Oct.	1233	1817	11	Nov.	1297	1879	15	Dec.
1170	1756	26	Sept.	1234	1818	31	Oct.	1298	1880	4	Dec.
1171	1757	15	Sept.	1235	1819	20	Oct.	1299	1881	23	Nov.
1172	1758	4	Sept.	1236	1820	9	Oct.	1300	1882	12	Nov.
1173	1759	25	Aug.	1237	1821	28	Sept.	1301	1883	2	Nov.
1174	1760	13	Aug.	1238	1822	18	Sept.	1302	1884	21	Oct.
1175	1761	2	Aug.	1239	1823	7	Sept.	1303	1885	10	Oct.
1176	1762	23	July	1240	1824	26	Aug.	1304	1886	30	Sept.
1177	1763	12	July	1241	1825	16	Aug.	1305	1887	19	Sept.
1178	1764	1	July	1242	1826	5	Aug.	1306	1888	7	Sept.
1179	1765	20	June	1243	1827	25	July	1307	1889	28	Aug.
1180	1766	9	June	1244	1828	14	July	1308	1890	17	Aug.
1181	1767	30	May	1245	1829	3	July	1309	1891	7	Aug.
1182	1768	18	May	1246	1830	22	June	1310	1892	26	July
1183	1769	7	May	1247	1831	12	June	1311	1893	15	July
1184	1770	27	April	1248	1832	31	May	1312	1894	5	July
1185	1771	16	April	1249	1833	21	May	1313	1895	24	June
1186	1772	4	April	1250	1834	10	May	1314	1896	12	June
1187	1773	25	March	1251	1835	29	April	1315	1897	2	June
1188	1774	14	March	1252	1836	18	April	1316	1898	22	May
1189	1775	4	March	1253	1837	7	April	1317	1899	12	May
1190	1776	21	Feb.	1254	1838	27	March	1318	1900	1	May
1191	1777	9	Feb.	1255	1839	17	March	1319	1901	20	April
1192	1778	30	Jan.	1256	1840	5	March	1320	1902	10	April
1193	1779	19	Jan.	1257	1841	23	Feb.	1321	1903	30	March
1194	1780	8	Jan.	1258	1842	12	Feb.	1322	1904	18	March
1195	1780	28	Dec.	1259	1843	1	Feb.	1323	1905	8	March
1196	1781	17	Dec.	1260	1844	22	Jan.	1324	1906	25	Feb.
1197	1782	7	Dec.	1261	1845	10	Jan.	1325	1907	14	Feb.
1198	1783	26	Nov.	1262	1845	30	Dec.	1326	1908	4	Feb.
1199	1784	14	Nov.	1263	1846	20	Dec.	1327	1909	23	Jan.

A.H.	A.D.		A.H.	A.D.		A.H.	A.D.	
1328	1910	13 Jan.	1360	1941	29 Jan.	1391	1971	27 Feb.
1329	1911	2 Jan.	1361	1942	19 Jan.	1392	1972	16 Feb.
1330	1911	22 Dec.	1362	1943	8 Jan.	1393	1973	4 Feb.
1331	1912	11 Dec.	1363	1943	28 Dec.	1394	1974	25 Jan.
1332	1913	30 Nov.	1364	1944	17 Dec.	1395	1975	14 Jan.
1333	1914	19 Nov.	1365	1945	6 Dec.	1396	1976	3 Jan.
1334	1915	9 Nov.	1366	1946	25 Nov.	1397	1976	23 Dec.
1335	1916	28 Oct.	1367	1947	15 Nov.	1398	1977	12 Dec.
1336	1917	17 Oct.	1368	1948	3 Nov.	1399	1978	2 Dec.
1337	1918	7 Oct.	1369	1949	24 Oct.	1400	1979	21 Nov.
1338	1919	26 Sept.	1370	1950	13 Oct.	1401	1980	9 Nov.
1339	1920	15 Sept.	1371	1951	2 Oct.	1402	1981	30 Oct.
1340	1921	4 Sept.	1372	1952	21 Sept.	1403	1982	19 Oct.
1341	1922	24 Aug.	1373	1953	10 Sept.	1404	1983	8 Oct.
1342	1923	14 Aug.	1374	1954	30 Aug.	1405	1984	27 Sept.
1343	1924	2 Aug.	1375	1955	20 Aug.	1406	1985	16 Sept.
1344	1925	22 July	1376	1956	8 Aug.	1407	1986	6 Sept.
1345	1926	12 July	1377	1957	29 July	1408	1987	26 Aug.
1346	1927	1 July	1378	1958	18 July	1409	1988	14 Aug.
1347	1928	20 June	1379	1959	7 July	1410	1989	4 Aug.
1348	1929	9 June	1380	1960	26 June	1411	1990	24 July
1349	1930	29 May	1381	1961	15 June	1412	1991	13 July
1350	1931	19 May	1382	1962	4 June	1413	1992	2 July
1351	1932	7 May	1383	1963	25 May	1414	1993	21 June
1352	1933	26 April	1384	1964	13 May	1415	1994	10 June
1353	1934	16 April	1385	1965	2 May	1416	1995	31 May
1354	1935	5 April	1386	1966	22 April	1417	1996	19 May
1355	1936	24 March	1387	1967	11 April	1418	1997	9 May
1356	1937	14 March	1388	1968	31 March	1419	1998	28 April
1357	1938	3 March	1389	1969	20 March	1420	1999	17 April
1358	1939	21 Feb.	1390	1970	9 March	1421	2000	6 April
1359	1940	10 Feb.						

6. DYNASTIES AND RULERS

Detailed genealogical tables will be found in the following books:

S. Lane-Poole. *The Mohammadan Dynasties. Chronological and Genealogical Tables with Historical Introductions.* London, 1894. Reprinted Paris, 1925.

E. de Zambaur. *Manuel de généalogie et de chronologie pour l'histoire de l'Islam.* 2 vols. Hanover, 1927.

Where one date is given, it is that of the ruler's accession.

(i) ORTHODOX CALIPHS
(Medina)

A.H.		A.D.
11–40		632–61
11	Abū-Bakr	632
13	'Umar (ibn al-Khaṭṭāb)	634
23	'Uthmān	644
35–40	'Alī	656–61

(ii) UMAYYAD CALIPHS
(Damascus)

A.H.		A.D.
41–132		661–750
41	Mu'āwiya I	661
60	Yazīd I	680
64	Mu'āwiya II	683
64	Marwān I	683
65	'Abdal-Malik	685
86	al-Walīd I	705
96	Sulaymān	715
99	'Umar II (ibn 'Abd al-'Azīz)	717
101	Yazīd II	720
105	Hishām	724
125	al-Walīd II	743
126	Yazīd III	744
126	Ibrāhīm	744
127–132	Marwān II	744–50

(iii) 'ABBĀSID CALIPHS
(Baghdad)

A.H.		A.D.
132–656		750–1258
132	Abū'l-'Abbās as-Saffāḥ	750
136	Abū Ja'far al-Manṣūr	754
158	al-Mahdī	775
169	al-Hādī	785
170	Hārūn ar-Rashīd	786
193	al-Amīn	809
198	al-Ma'mūn	813
218	al-Mu'taṣim	833
227	al-Wāthiq	842
232	al-Mutawakkil	847
247	al-Muntaṣir	861
248	al-Musta'īn	862
251	al-Mu'tazz	866
255	al-Muhtadī	869
256	al-Mu'tamid	870
279	al-Mu'taḍid	892
289	al-Muktafī	902
295	al-Muqtadir	908
320	al-Qāhir	932
322	ar-Rāḍī	934
329	al-Muttaqī	940
333	al-Mustakfī	944
334	al-Muṭī'	946
363	aṭ-Ṭā'i'	974
381	al-Qādir	991
422	al-Qā'im	1031
467	al-Muqtaḍī	1075
487	al-Mustaẓhir	1094
512	al-Mustarshid	1118
529	ar-Rāshid	1135
530	al-Muqtafī	1136
555	al-Mustanjid	1160
566	al-Mustaḍī	1170
575	an-Nāṣir	1180
622	aẓ-Ẓāhir	1225
623	al-Mustanṣir	1226
640–56	al-Musta'ṣim	1242–58

(iv) UMAYYADS OF CORDOVA

A.H.		A.D.
138–422		756–1031
138	‘Abd ar-Raḥmān I	756
172	Hishām I	788
180	al-Ḥakam I	796
206	‘Abd ar-Raḥmān II	822
238	Muḥammad I	852
273	al-Mundhir	886
275	‘Abdallah	888
300	‘Abd ar-Raḥmān III (Al-Khalīfa An-Nāṣir)	912
350	al-Ḥakam II al-Mustanṣir	961
366	Hishām II al-Mu’ayyad	976
399	Muḥammad II al-Mahdī	1009
400	Sulaimān al-Musta‘īn	1009
400	Muḥammad II (again)	1010
400	Hishām II (again)	1010
403	Sulaimān (again)	1013
407	‘Alī b. Ḥammūd [1]	1016
408	‘Abd ar-Raḥmān IV al-Murtaḍā	1018
408	al-Qāsim b. Ḥammūd [1]	1018
412	Yaḥyā b. ‘Alī [1]	1021
413	al-Qāsim (again) [1]	1022
414	‘Abd ar-Raḥmān V al-Mustaẓhir	1023
414	Muḥammad III al-Mustakfī	1024
416	Yaḥyā (again) [1]	1025
418–22	Hishām III al-Mu‘tadd	1027–31

[1] Of the Ḥammūdid dynasty.

(v) FĀṬIMID CALIPHS
(Mahdīya, later Cairo)

A.H.		A.D.	A.H.		A.D.
297–567		909–1171	297–567		909–1171
297	Al-Mahdī ‘Ubaid Allāh	909	427	al-Mustanṣir	1036
322	al-Qā’im	934	487	al-Musta‘lī	1094
334	al-Manṣūr	945	495	al-Āmir	1101
341	al-Mu‘izz	952	524	al-Ḥāfiẓ	1130
365	al-‘Azīz	975	544	aẓ-Ẓāfir	1149
386	al-Ḥākim	996	549	al-Fā’iz	1154
411	aẓ-Ẓāhir	1021	555–67	al-‘Āḍid	1160–71

(vi) MAMLŪKS

(*a*) BAḤRĪ MAMLŪKS
(Cairo)

A.H.		A.D.
648–792		1250–1390
648	Shajar ad-Durr	1250
648	al-Mu‘izz ‘Izz ad-Dīn Aybak	1250
655	al-Manṣūr Nūr ad-Dīn ‘Alī	1257
657	al-Muẓaffar Saif ad-Dīn Quṭuz	1259
658	aẓ-Ẓāhir Rukn ad-Dīn Baibars al-Bunduqdārī	1260
676	as-Sa‘īd Nāṣir ad-Dīn Baraka Khān	1277
678	al-‘Ādil Badr ad-Dīn Salāmish	1279
678	al-Manṣūr Saif ad-Dīn Qalāūn	1280
689	al-Ashraf Ṣalāḥ ad-Dīn Khalīl	1290
693	an-Nāṣir Nāṣir ad-Dīn Muḥammad	1293
694	al-‘Ādil Zain ad-Dīn Katbughā	1294
696	al-Manṣūr Ḥusām ad-Dīn Lājīn	1296
698	an-Nāṣir Muḥammad (again)	1298
708	al-Muẓaffar Rukn ad-Dīn Baibars Jāshankīr	1308

(*a*) BAHRĪ MAMLŪKS (*continued*)

A.H.		A.D.
648–792		1250–1390
709	an-Nāṣir Muḥammad (third time)	1309
741	al-Manṣūr Saif ad-Dīn Abū Bakr	1340
742	al-Ashraf 'Alā ad-Dīn Kūjūk	1341
742	an-Nāṣir Shihāb ad-Dīn Aḥmad	1342
743	aṣ-Ṣāliḥ 'Imād-ad-Dīn Ismā'īl	1342
746	al-Kāmil Saif ad-Dīn Sha'bān	1345
747	al-Muẓaffar Saif ad-Dīn Ḥājjī	1346
748	an-Nāṣir Nāṣir ad-Dīn Ḥasan	1347
752	aṣ-Ṣāliḥ Ṣalāḥ ad-Dīn Ṣāliḥ	1351
755	an-Nāṣir Ḥasan (again)	1354
762	al-Manṣūr Ṣalāḥ ad-Dīn Muḥammad	1361
764	al-Ashraf Nāṣir ad-Dīn Sha'bān	1363
778	al-Manṣūr 'Alā ad-Dīn 'Alī	1376
783	aṣ-Ṣāliḥ Ṣalāḥ ad-Dīn Ḥājjī	1381
784	Barqūq (see Burjīs)	1382
791–92	Ḥājjī again, with title of al-Muẓaffar	1389–90

(*b*) BURJĪ MAMLŪKS

(Cairo)

A.H.		A.D.
784–922		1382–1517
784	aẓ-Ẓāhir Saif ad-Dīn Barqūq	1382
	(Interrupted by Ḥājjī 791–2)	
801	an-Nāṣir Nāṣir ad-Dīn Faraj	1399
808	al-Manṣūr 'Izz ad-Dīn 'Abd al-'Azīz	1405
809	an-Nāṣir Faraj (again)	1406
815	al-'Ādil al-Musta'īn ('Abbāsid Caliph)	1412
815	al-Mu'ayyad Shaikh	1412
824	al-Muẓaffar Aḥmad	1421
824	aẓ-Ẓāhir Saif ad-Dīn Ṭaṭār	1421
824	aṣ-Ṣāliḥ Nāṣir ad-Dīn Muḥammad	1421
825	al-Ashraf Saif ad-Dīn Bars-bay	1422
842	al-'Azīz Jamāl ad-Dīn Yūsuf	1438
842	aẓ-Ẓāhir Saif ad-Dīn Jaqmaq	1438
857	al-Manṣūr Fakhr ad-Dīn 'Uthmān	1453
857	al-Ashraf Saif ad-Dīn Īnāl	1453
865	al-Mu'ayyad Shihāb ad-Dīn Aḥmad	1460
865	aẓ-Ẓāhir Saif ad-Dīn Khūshqadam	1461
872	aẓ-Ẓāhir Saif ad-Dīn Bilbey	1467
872	aẓ-Ẓāhir Tīmūrbughā	1468
873	al-Ashraf Saif ad-Dīn Qāït-Bey	1468
901	an-Nāṣir Muḥammad	1495
904	aẓ-Ẓāhir Qānsūh	1498
905	al-Ashraf Jānbalāt	1499
906	al-Ashraf Qānṣūh al-Ghūrī	1500
922	al-Ashraf Tūmān-Bey	1516–17

(vii) SELJŪQS

(Persia and Iraq)

A.H.		A.D.
429–552		1037–1157
429	Ṭughril	1037
455	Alp-Arslān	1063
465	Malik Shāh	1072
485	Nāṣir ad-Dīn Maḥmūd	1092
487	Barqiyāruq	1094
498	Malik Shāh II	1104
498	Abu Shujā' Muḥammad	1104
511–52	Sinjar	1117–57

(viii) OTTOMAN SULTĀNS

(Brusa, later Adrianople, later Constantinople)

A.H. 699–1341		A.D. 1299–1923
699	'Uthmān I (Osman)	1299
726	Orkhān	1326
761	Murād (Amurath) I	1360
792	Bāyazīd (Bajazet) I	1389
805	Muḥammad I (Mehmet)	1402
824	Murād II	1421
855	Muḥammad II	1451
886	Bāyazīd II	1481
918	Selīm I	1512
926	Sulaimān I (Solyman)	1520
974	Selīm II	1566
982	Murād III	1574
1003	Muḥammad III	1595
1012	Aḥmad I	1603
1026	Muṣṭafā I	1617
1027	'Uthmān II	1618
1031	Muṣṭafā I (restored)	1622
1032	Murād IV	1623
1049	Ibrāhīm I	1640
1058	Muḥammad IV	1648
1099	Sulaimān II	1687
1102	Aḥmad II	1691
1106	Muṣṭafā II	1695
1115	Aḥmad III	1703
1143	Maḥmūd I	1730
1168	'Uthmān III	1754
1171	Muṣṭafā III	1757
1187	'Abd al-Ḥamīd I	1773
1203	Selīm III	1789
1222	Muṣṭafā IV	1807
1223	Maḥmūd II	1808
1255	'Abd al-Majīd I	1839
1277	'Abd al-'Azīz	1861
1293	Murād V	1876
1293	'Abd al-Ḥamīd II	1876
1327	Muḥammad V Rashād	1909
1336	Muḥammad VI Waḥīd ad-Dīn	1917
1341	'Abd-al-Majīd II	1923

(ix) MONGOLS

MONGOL IL-KHANS OF PERSIA

(Tabriz)

A.H. 654–736		A.D. 1256–1336
654	Hūlāgū (Hülākü)	1256
663	Abāqā	1265
680	Aḥmad	1281
683	Arghūn	1284
690	Gaikhātū	1291
694	Baidū	1295
694	Ghāzān Maḥmūd	1295
703	Ūljaitū	1304
716	Abū Sa'īd	1316
736	Arpā	1335
736	Mūsā	1336

(x) SHĀHS OF PERSIA

(Tabriz, later Ispahan, later Tehran)

ṢAFAVIDS

A.H. 907–1148		A.D. 1502–1736
907	Ismā'īl I	1502
930	Ṭahmāsp I	1524
984	Ismā'īl II	1576
985	Muḥammad Khudābanda	1578
985	'Abbās I	1587
1038	Ṣafī I	1629
1052	'Abbās II	1642
1077	Sulaimān I	1667
1105	Ḥusain I	1694
1135	Ṭahmāsp II	1722
1144–48	'Abbās III	1731–36

AFGHANS

1135	Maḥmūd	1722
1137–42	Ashraf	1725–29

AFSHARIDS

A.H.		A.D.	A.H.		A.D.
1148	Nādir	1736	1161–1210	Shāh Rukh . .	1748–96
1160	ʻĀdil	1747			

ZANDS

A.H.		A.D.	A.H.		A.D.
1163	Karīm Khān . .	1750	1196	ʻAlī Murād (again)	1782
1193	Abū'l-Fatḥ . .	1779	1199	Jaʻfar	1785
1193	ʻAlī Murād . .	1779	1203–9	Luṭf ʻAlī . . .	1789–94
1193	Muḥammad ʻAlī .	1779			
1193	Ṣādiq	1779			

QĀJĀRS

A.H.		A.D.	A.H.		A.D.
1193	Āqā Muḥammad .	1779	1313	Muẓaffar ad-Dīn .	1896
1211	Fatḥ ʻAlī . . .	1797	1324	Muḥammad ʻAlī .	1906
1250	Muḥammad . .	1834	1327	Aḥmad . . .	1909
1264	Nāṣir ad-Dīn . .	1848			

PAHLAVIS

A.H.		A.D.	A.H.		A.D.
1344	Riẓā	1925	1360	Muḥammad . .	1941–

(xi) THE LINE OF MUḤAMMAD ʻALĪ IN EGYPT

	A.D.		A.D.
Muḥammad ʻAli Pasha . .	1805	ʻAbbās Hilmī (Khedive) .	1892
ʻAbbas Pasha	1848	Ḥusain Kāmil (Sultan) . .	1914
Saʻīd Pasha	1854	Fu'ād (Sultan)	1917
Ismaʻil Pasha	1863	(became King) . . .	1922
(became Khedive) . .	1867	Fārūq (King)	1936–
Tawfīq (Khedive) . . .	1880		

(xii) KINGS OF IRAQ

	A.D.		A.D.
Faiṣal I	1921	Faiṣal II	1939–
Ghāzī	1933		

(xiii) PRESIDENTS OF SYRIA

	A.D.		A.D.
Ṣubḥī Bey Barakāt . . .	1922	Hāshim Bey al-Atāsī . .	1936
Aḥmad Nāmī Bey Dāmād .	1926	Shaikh Tāj ad-Dīn al-Ḥasanī	1941
Shaikh Tāj ad-Dīn al-Ḥasanī	1928	ʻAṭā Bey al-Ayyūbī . .	1943
Muḥammad ʻAlī Bey al-ʻĀbid	1932	Shukrī Bey al-Quwwatlī .	1943–1949

(xiv) PRESIDENTS OF THE LEBANON

	A.D.		A.D.
Charles Dabbās	1926	Dr. Ayyūb Thābit . . .	1943
Ḥabīb Pasha as-Saʻd . .	1934	Petro Trād	1943
Émile Eddé	1936	Bishāra al-Khūrī . . .	1943–
Alfred an-Naqqāsh . . .	1941		

(xv) KINGS OF TRANSJORDAN

	A.D.
ʻAbdallah	1946–

(xvi) PRESIDENTS OF TURKEY

	A.D.		A.D.
Mustafa Kemal Atatürk	1923	Ismet Inönü	1938–

(xvii) FRENCH HIGH COMMISSIONERS IN SYRIA-LEBANON

	A.D.		A.D.
Gen. Gouraud	1920	Gen. Dentz	1940
Gen. Weygand	1923	Gen. Catroux (with change of title to Delegate-General	1941
Gen. Sarrail	1924	M. Helleu	1943
M. de Jouvenel	1925	M. Chataigneau	1943
M. Ponsot	1926	Gen. Beynet	1944–
Count de Martel	1933		
M. Puaux	1939		

(xviii) BRITISH HIGH COMMISSIONERS FOR PALESTINE AND TRANSJORDAN (until 1946)

	A.D.		A.D.
Sir Herbert Samuel	1920	Sir Harold MacMichael	1937
Lord Plumer	1925	Lord Gort	1944
Sir John Chancellor	1928	Sir Alan Cunningham	1945–8
Sir Arthur Wauchope	1931		

SECTION II

INDIA AND PĀKISTĀN

1. The romanization of words.
2. Names and titles :
   (i) Family and personal names. (ii) Titles.
3. Place-names and geographical terms.
4. Select glossary.
5. Systems of dating.
6. Dynasties and rulers.
   I. Hindu dynasties.
      (i) The Mauryas. (ii) The Guptas. (iii) The House of Pushyabhūti. (iv) The Imperial Pratīhāras. (v) The Pālas of Bengal. (vi) The Senas of Bengal. (vii) Early Chālukya kings. (viii) The Rāshtrakūta Dynasty. (ix) Chālukya dynasty of Kalyāna. (x) The Pallava kings. (xi) Chola kings. (xii) Yādavas of Vijayanagar. (xiii) Tuluva and Āravīdu kings of Vijayanagar. (xiv) Rānās of Mewār. (xv) Bhonslās (Chhatrapati). (xvi) The Peshwās. (xvii) The Gāikwār Family. (xviii) The Holkar Family. (xix) The Sindhiā Family. (xx) Mahārāja Ranjīt Singh's Family.
   II. Muslim Dynasties.
      (i) The Ghaznavids. (ii) The rulers of Ghūr. (iii) Kings of Delhi. (iv) Kings of Bengal. (v) Kings of Mālwa. (vi) Kings of Gujarāt. (vii) Kings of Khāndesh. (viii) The Sharqī kings of Jaunpūr. (ix) Bahmanī kings of the Deccan. (x) Sultānates of the Deccan. (xi) Nawābs of Oudh. (xii) Nawābs of Arcot. (xiii) Nawābs of Bengal. (xiv) Nizāms of Hyderabad. (xv) Amīrs of Afghānistān.
   III. Governors-General.
      (i) Governors-General of Fort William in Bengal. (ii) Governors-General of India. (iii) Governors-General and Viceroys.

I. THE ROMANIZATION OF WORDS

Indian names are drawn mainly from three linguistic sources, Dravidian, Sanskritic and Islamic (Arabic and Persian), all containing characters and sounds unknown in the languages of those European peoples, including the English, whose contact with India through the ages has been closest. Distortion in transcription into these European languages, therefore, has been considerable. For example, Greek writers, who provide sources for our knowledge of the ancient history of India, could not easily represent the palatals and the *h* of Sanskrit. Later the Portuguese and Dutch found the same difficulty, and, like the Greeks before them, had to represent palatals by sibilants; *j*, for instance, by *z*. The Portuguese used a *b* for *w*; and also provided their own word-terminations in the masculine *-o*. They frequently added extra vowels to overcome difficulty in pronouncing groups of Indian consonants. The Dutch and English practice of using Portuguese interpreters and the more general employment of usually uneducated European troops in India spread distortions of Indian terms widely in Europe from the sixteenth century onwards. These distortions, the identification of which, generally speaking, is a task for specialists, are fully illustrated in Yule and Burnell's *Hobson-Jobson.*

The fifty or sixty letters or signs of the Indian alphabets can be represented precisely in the English alphabet only by adding a complicated system of diacritical marks, at once puzzling and unattractive to the ordinary reader. However, in the late nineteenth century the Government of India, after an exhaustive inquiry as to the best practicable course, prescribed a simplified method of transliteration which has since been adopted in the official publications such as the *Imperial Gazetteer of India* and by most authors who have an accurate acquaintance with India. This system, used for example in the last four volumes of the *Cambridge History of India* and, with slight modifications, in this section of this *Handbook,* is far more widely known than any alternative, and is the only one which need seriously concern the European general reader. It is the Hunterian system and may be outlined as follows:

(1) A large number of Indian proper names such as Calcutta, Madras, Bombay, Delhi, which have obtained an historical or popular fixity of spelling, have been retained, although they represent unscientific transliteration.

(2) Where no English form has established itself, and where, therefore, little or no embarrassment will be given to the European eye, the letters used are meant to correspond as closely to the actual pronunciation as the English alphabet allows. Thus—

(*a*) Consonants are intended to be pronounced as in English. No attempt is made, for instance, to distinguish between the

Persian refinement of pronunciation between *v* and *w*. The chief exceptions are that

j is always palatal as in the English *jet*
g is always guttural as in the English *get*
ch is always palatal as in the English *church*

Aspirated sounds, such as *bh, chh, dh, gh, kh, th,* etc., which are rarely present in English, are important in Sanskritic languages but not in Persian.

It should be noted that in this section of this *Handbook* the Sanskrit palatal and cerebral sibilants, transliterated *ś* and *ṣ* respectively according to the system of the Royal Asiatic Society which is mentioned below, are both transliterated as *sh* pronounced as in the English wi*sh*. This is done for the convenience of the western reader, although he should be aware that the educated, precise speaker properly pronounces the palatal *s* as a palatal, and the cerebral *s* at the back of the mouth, thus approximating rather to *kh*.

(*b*) Five long vowels, *ā, ē, ī, ō, ū,* are employed.

ā has the sound of *a* in *father*
ē has the vowel sound in *grey*
ī has the sound of final *i* in *intrigue*
ō has the sound of *o* in *note*
ū has the sound of *u* in *rural*

The three short vowels *a, i, u* are sounded as in wom*a*n, p*i*n, p*u*t.

Early British attempts by Sir William Jones and Dr. Gilchrist to determine the principles on which the detailed and mutual adjustment of Oriental and Roman alphabets ought to be grounded, and the varying systems of transliteration used down to the middle of the nineteenth century, are well described by H. H. Wilson in the preface to his *Glossary of Indian Terms* (London, 1855). He also includes a comparative table of equivalents in the characters of the English and Oriental languages.

The precise and detailed system of transliteration most generally used by orientalists in England is that recommended by the Royal Asiatic Society in its *Journal* (e.g. January 1935) and described in the section on romanization in the N. and M.E. section of this *Handbook* (pp. 3–6).

2. NAMES AND TITLES

(i) FAMILY AND PERSONAL NAMES

A system of surnames, especially among the middle and upper classes, has evolved in India under western influence, but Hindu surnames had existed earlier and become recognized, being listed, for example, under the later Mughal rulers in 'the chronicles of families'.

I. HINDU NAMES. Hindu surnames, as one would expect, are largely drawn from religious, caste, sect and tribal names, and very frequently carry a functional sense. Personal (or given) names are chiefly drawn from attributes or appellatives of the deities, and of the epic and Puranic heroes. Hindu names may conveniently be analysed under the following headings:

(*a*) *Religious names.* The ancient Indian system of name-giving was not rigid, and although Hindu treatises laid down the most minute refinements, these were not in practice observed. A detailed scheme was formulated for the bestowal of astrological names, the child being called not only with reference to the month of birth, but also the presiding deity, appropriately masculine or feminine according to the sex of the child. Such names clearly were of good omen, giving the children a share in the attributes of the original bearer and providing also the opportunity of pronouncing holy names as frequently as possible. The personal (or given) names of most Hindus, male and female, are taken from the names of chief deities of the Hindu pantheon, like Shiva, Vishnu, Brahma, Indra and others and their consorts. Names invoking the protection of the gods are also common: Devaprasāda, 'Favour of the Gods'; Indrapālita, 'Protected by Indra'; Mitradatta, 'Given by Mitra'; Devadatta, 'God-given'.

(*b*) *Caste and sect names.* Such personal names, especially those connected with the founder or heroes of the caste, are frequently found. Vaishnavites, for example, often use Vishnu as a component of their names, or one of his epithets (e.g. Hari, Keshava, Nārāyana, Mādhava) or the name of one of his incarnations, especially Rāma and Krishna (with the synonyms Gopāla, Govinda, Rādhāvallabha) or of his female counterpart (Lakshmī, Shrī). Likewise, Shaivites assume the names of Shiva (Rudra, Shankara, Sharva) or of his female counterpart (Durgā, Gaurī).

Among the main caste divisions the following name-components are common: for *Brāhmans*, the endings -sharman, -deva; for *Kshatriyas*, the endings -varman, -rāja; for *Vaishyas*, the endings -gupta, -bhūti, -datta. While these endings are recommended in the ancient lawbook, *Manusmriti*, for the caste-groups under which they are mentioned, much confusion has taken place in practice and a modern name ending in one of these terminations is no infallible guide to its owner's class.

Occupation is usually a mark of caste, and many Hindu names carry an occupational sense, e.g. Mehtā (clerk), Kulkarnī (accountant), Patel (headman), Joshī (astrologer), Shroff (money-changer), Chaudharī (headman).

Typical examples of Hindu names built up from divine and functional or family components are:

Surendranath ('Having as lord chief of the gods') Banerjea (perhaps implying a Brāhman teacher):

Keshab Chandra ('Having Keshava [Vishnu] as his moon') Sen (the family name).

Hindus in the north and east of India generally bear a given or personal name and a family or surname on the English model, the name Jawāharlāl ('Darling jewel') Nehru providing a good example of this practice. But in the west and south of India names are rather more complicated. In the western Dravidian area a full name gives first the tribal and village name, secondly the father's name, and thirdly the personal name. In the Kanarese area where Marāthā influence is strong we find the exact reverse. Among the Marāthī-speaking and Gujarātī people we have first the personal name, then the father's name, then a family name taken from a place or function with or without modifications. Thus the following names from west India, Rāmakrishna Gopāl Bhāndārkar and Bāl Gangādhar Tilak, and the Gujarātī name Mohandās Karamchand Gāndhī, are formed as follows:

Rāmakrishna (the personal name) Gopāl (the father's name) Bhāndārkar (a family name meaning 'treasurer');

Bāl (the personal name meaning 'boy') Gangādhar (the father's name meaning 'Holder of the Ganges', i.e. Shiva) Tilak (the family name);

Mohandās (the personal name) Karamchand (the father's name) Gāndhī (the family name meaning 'a perfume merchant').

The name Singh (Sinha), meaning 'a lion', borne by men of the princely or military castes, is now affixed to the personal name by nearly all Sikhs and many Rājpūts and by some men of other castes, too.

(c) *Ancestral and regal names and epithets.* The Hindu concept that a forefather may be reincarnated in his descendants gives rise to the naming of a child after one of his ancestors, especially his grandfather. In the dynasties of ancient Indian kings a number of such instances occur; in the Gupta Empire, for example, Chandragupta I is first followed by Samudragupta and then by his grandson Chandragupta II. In ancient India appellatives were often changed especially to secure success or for distinction, and Hindu kings frequently assumed names for these purposes; thus Chandragupta II was known also as Vikrama or Vikramāditya, and the first three Maurya Emperors, including Ashoka, bore the title Piyadasi ('of amiable appearance').

(d) *Female names.* On marriage a Hindu wife invariably takes the family name of her husband. In addition to what has been said in (a) above, the basis of female personal names is often formed from the simpler and gentler qualities of character and the softer and prettier natural objects, for example, Sarojinī (lotus pool), Padmā (lotus), Mālatī (jasmin), Motī (pearl), Ushā (dawn).

II. MUSLIM NAMES (see also Near and Middle East Section,

pp. 7–9). The Turkish conquerors from central Asia took into India names which were as strange to the Hindus as they are to the British, and central Asian Turkish names soon appeared, such as Alptigīn, Sabuktigīn and Iltutmish. However, the regular Muslim system of personal names soon established itself (see p. 7). Inevitable confusion arises from the Muslim practice of drawing personal names from the strictly limited number of outstanding Hebrew and Islamic heroes and prophets, and, although a second name is often added—for instance, a tribal, place or occupational name as in Alāuddīn Khaljī—the risk of confusion always remains great. The distinction between Muslims and Hindus cannot always be drawn from their names. Through the close contact of Muslims with Hindus over the course of centuries and the conversion of large numbers of Hindus to Islām, some names are held alike by Hindus and Muslims. Patel and Chaudharī are found in both communities. This also applies, for example, to the use as names of titles such as Maḷik and Khān. Many modern Indian Muslim names are not as grammatically correct in their structure as the Islamic nomenclature of the Near East. Like many English names, they consist of groups of words without grammatical relationship, as, for example, Liāquat Alī Khān. Some Indian Muslim surnames such as Jinnah and Chundrigar are not likely to be found outside India, and some forms of Indian Muslim names (for instance, Abdul Rasūl, 'Slave of the Prophet') are probably not quite as acceptable in the older Islamic centres.

III. PĀRSĪ NAMES. As one would expect, many of their personal names are drawn from their ancient heroes in Persia, such as Suhrāb, Rustam, Bahrām, and the risk of confusing individuals is considerable. Pārsī names are usually completed by the addition of the honorific suffix *-jī*, as, for example, in Rustamjī, Bahrāmjī. The Pārsīs, like other Gujarātīs, put first the personal name, second the father's name, and third a functional or local name (or both). In modern times the community has been quick to follow the English practice of using surnames, which have usually been drawn from occupations, such as Modī (steward).

IV. HONORIFICS. Popular usage has created a number of designations, usually drawn from occupations or from social, literary or religious position, which in some cases are being accepted as surnames.

Among Hindus, Shrī (Srī), Shrījut, Shrīmat (fem. Shrīmatī) before a name denote the same as the English 'Mr.' or 'Esq.'. Jī (meaning 'life, soul') at the end of a name (for example, Gāndhījī) denotes affectionate and deep respect. A similar meaning is given to Bābū, at one time a title of respect, which now means no more than 'Mr.'. Among Brāhmans the specialization of functions gave rise to such terms as Āchārya (religious teacher), Pandit (Sanskrit scholar), Chaube (learned in the four Vedas); in Bengal, the name Tagore (from Thākur, meaning 'lord') has become the surname of one of the most famous Brāhman families. Bābā, literally 'father', is a mode of address to ascetics. Mahātmā ('great soul') is especially applied to Gāndhī of recently living men, implying that he had transcended the limitations of the flesh and the world. Lālā

(' writer ') and Munshī (' writer '), both Persian terms, are used by Hindus. To female names in general in south India, -ammā is affixed as a respectful term of address meaning ' Lady ' or ' Mistress ' : for example, Sītamma. To men -appa is sometimes applied.

Among Muslims, honorific designations are just as prevalent. Maulānā (as, for instance, in Maulānā Abul Kalām Āzād) is a title denoting a man of erudition ; others are Mīr or Saiyid (a descendant of Muhammad), Hājjī (one who has made the pilgrimage to Mecca), Munshī (writer), Maulavī (Islamic lawyer), Hāfiz (a Muslim who has memorized the Koran).

(ii) TITLES

I. HINDU. The Hindu titles *Rājā* and *Mahārāja*, which imply sovereignty, were originally held in ancient India by important rulers, and in the period of the Mauryan Empire (4th-3rd centuries B.C.) the emperors themselves—for instance, Ashoka—did not hesitate to use them ; but in later ages, for example, in the Gupta Empire (4th-6th centuries A.D.), such titles were held only by subordinate princes ; the more powerful rulers, like Chandragupta I, meanwhile assuming higher-sounding personal titles such as *Mahārājādhirāja* (' Supreme King of Great Kings '). Moreover, as the emperors began to take on the attributes and character of divine beings—probably through Greek and Chinese influences—their personal titles faithfully reflected this development, and, whereas Ashoka was merely *Devānampiya* (' Beloved of the Gods '), the Kushān emperors of the first two centuries A.D. were named *Devaputra* (' Son of Heaven '), and later rulers *Parameshvara* (' Supreme Lord ').

In the Gupta and post-Gupta periods hereditary feudal titles were common, the following, for example, being applied to feudatories : *Sāmanta*, *Mahāsāmanta*, *Māndalika*, *Mahāmāndalika*.

Under Mughal rule the titles of *Rājā* and of its equivalents, *Rāo*, *Rānā* and *Rāi*, were bestowed on Hindu civil officers of high rank (e.g. *Rāi-rāiān*), whence they later became family designations, e.g. Rām Mohan Roy. Under the British Government these titles of nobility were also widely conferred on Hindu subjects, so that although the title of *Rājā* may still denote a subordinate chief or prince, it is also often held by socially eminent persons, such as important landholders and officials ; and *Rāi* and *Rāo* have been assumed by many men of position.

See also above, p. 53, § IV.

II. MUSLIM. The Muslim conquerors brought into India a regular system of noble titles consisting of three ranks, *Khān*, *Amīr* and *Malik*, which, although not hereditary, may conveniently be compared with the British duke, earl and baron. The title *Khān* as used by the Mongol nomads was strictly confined to the chief of the horde, for example, Chingīz Khān, and the title *Amīr* to his main commanders, but in India this precise application disappeared and their value tended to fall. Under the Turkish kings of Delhi the title *Khān* came to denote their principal nobles, especially those of Persian and Pathān descent, and *Amīr*—and its plural form *Umarā*

—the second rank of courtiers: for the third rank, *Malik*, an Arabic term implying sovereignty, was applied. During the 15th century these titles depreciated and the term *Khān* was widely adopted, but the Emperor Akbar (1556–1605) restricted its use once more to courtiers of merit, and *Amīr* to courtiers in general. As the Mughal Empire declined, titles resumed their natural tendency to degenerate, and new, longer and more sonorous designations were added: *Khān-Khānān* ('Khān of Khāns'); *Khān-bahādur*; *Bahādur ul-Mulk* ('Hero of the Kingdom'). Today the term *Khān* has become a common affix to the names of Muslims of all ranks, especially adopted by those classes of converts from Hinduism, though properly it appears as the surname of Indians claiming a Pathān descent. The British Government has also conferred the titles *Khān Bahādur* and *Khān Sāhib* on subordinate Indian officials.

See also above, p. 53, § IV.

III. British. Besides creating new Orders of Chivalry, 'The Most Exalted Order of the Star of India' (1861), and 'The Most Eminent Order of the Indian Empire' (1877), each including three classes, the British freely adapted Indian titles to be awarded only to Indians, *Dīwān Bahādur, Sardār Bahādur, Khān Bahādur, Rāi Bahādur, Rāo Bahādur, Khān Sāhib, Rāo Sāhib.* In 1919 an Indian, Sir Satyendra Sinha, was raised to the peerage with the title of Lord Sinha of Raipur.

3. PLACE-NAMES AND GEOGRAPHICAL TERMS

A large proportion of Indian place-names are formed, as in English, by the addition of a suffix (or less frequently of a prefix) to a personal name or designation; the latter usually being the name of the founder or being, human or divine, in whose honour the place was founded. The linguistic source, whether Sanskritic, Dravidian or Persian, whence the suffix or prefix is taken usually indicates the age of the name itself, but clearly does not establish the history of the place. The name Allāhābād, for example, made up by the addition of the Persian suffix -ābād ('made populous by'), was given in the time of Akbar (1556–1605) to the long-established Hindu city of Prayāga.

The commonest suffixes drawn from the Sanskritic languages are:

-gad, -gud, -gadi, -gadhi, -gadh, -garh, -gurh (a hill-fort)
-ghāt, corruptly -ghaut or -gaut (river-crossing or mountain-pass)
-grām, -gāum, -gāon and corruptly -gong (a village)
-hāt (market)
-kot, -kota, (written also -cote), -koth, -kotta (fort)
nagar, -nugur, corruptly -nuggur and -nagore (town, city), e.g. Vijayanagar (City of Victory) and Chandernagore (Moon-city)
-pur, -pura, corruptly -poor and -pore (town), e.g. Serāmpur (Shrī-rām-pur, i.e. Rāma's town) and Cawnpore (Kānhpur, i.e. Krishna's town)

Common Sanskritic prefixes are Deo- (a god), Rai- (a king).

The Dravidian languages provide:

-konda (hill)
-pattanam, corruptly -patam (town or village), e.g. Masulipatam (Fish town). Also found in Sanskrit
-palle, -palli, -palliya (hamlet)
-pet (town)
-ūr, -oor, -ūru, -ūra and corruptly -ore, e.g., Vellore, Coimbatore, Tanjore

The Persian language provides:

-ābād ('made populous by'). This suffix is widely found. Originally the meaning was 'populous, cultivated'. A village designated in the revenue return as 'Ābād' was one from which revenue might be levied. Examples of its use as a suffix are Akbar-ābād (City of Akbar), Aurangābād (City of Aurangzīb), Murshidābād (City of Murshid Qulī Khān)
-bāgh (garden)
-bandar (harbour)
-dūn, -doon (valley), e.g. Dehra Dūn
-ganj, gunj, corruptly -gunje (market)
-shahr (city)

Shāh (a king) is a common Persian prefix. Mahal (palace) is an often-used term.

4. SELECT GLOSSARY

Words in this glossary are given in the simplified system of transliteration described in the first part of this section of the *Handbook*. Useful supplementary material can be found in the following works:

J. Dowson, *A Classical Dictionary of Hindu Mythology and Religion, Geography, History and Literature*. London, 1914.
G. Watt, *Dictionary of Economic Products of India*. London, 1890.
G. C. Whitworth, *An Anglo-Indian Dictionary*. London, 1885.
H. H. Wilson, *A Glossary of Judicial and Revenue Terms of British India*. London, 1855.
H. Yule and A. C. Burnell, ed. by W. Crooke, *Hobson-Jobson*. London, 1903.

'ADĀLAT. A court of justice. Under the Muslim governments there were four main courts:

1. *Nizāmat 'Adālat.* The Supreme Court of Criminal Justice, nominally presided over by the Nāzim, or viceroy of the province.

2. *Dīwānī 'Adālat.* The Civil Court of the Dīwān, the chief officer in charge of the revenue of the principality.

3. *Faujdārī 'Adālat.* The Court of the Faujdār or chief of the magistracy and police of a district; the subordinate, or District Criminal Court.

4. *'Adālat al-Qāzī.* The Court of the Qāzī, the chief judge of a town or district in civil causes and questions regarding Islām.

Under the British Government these courts were continued until 1793, when the judicial and revenue departments were separated and Zilā and Provincial Courts established, subordinate to one Supreme 'Adālat in each presidency, distinguished as the *Sadr 'Adālat*, or a Court of Final Decision, subdivided into the

Sadr Dīwānī 'Adālat, High Court of Civil Jurisdiction.
Sadr Nizāmat (or Faujdārī) 'Adālat, High Court of Criminal Justice.
'Adālat Akbar, Court of Appeal.
'Adālat Asghar, an inferior subordinate Court of Justice.

This system ended in 1862 on the introduction of the Penal Code and the institution of the High Courts of Judiciary.

ADIGAR. A south Indian title for a rural headman. In Ceylon used as the title of a chief minister of the Kandyan kings.

AHIMSĀ. The Hindu doctrine of non-violence; particularly linked in political use with Mahātmā Gāndhī. As a religious doctrine also Buddhist and Jain.

ĀĪN-I-AKBARĪ. A compendium of documents of Akbar's time (1556–1605) illustrating the Emperor's activities in each department of the administration.

AKĀLĪ. A class of armed devotees among the Sikhs, worshippers of 'Him who is without time, eternal' (Akāl). To-day the Akālī party is the main political organization of the Sikhs.

Akhbār. News, intelligence, a newspaper; especially the written intelligence of the proceedings of native courts and princes, circulated to other courts and princes by their appointed agents—a regular practice under the native administrations.

Aligol. Irregular foot-soldiers in the Marāthā service without discipline or regular arms.

'Ālim. A wise man; a doctor of the law.

Āltamghā. A royal grant under the seal of some of the former native princes of Hindūstān, and recognized by the British Government.

'Amaldār. A governor of a district, a collector of revenue; the latter especially in central and south India. Also, any officer.

Amātya. One of the principal officers of state in ancient India and among the Marāthās.

'Āmil. In the 13th to the 15th centuries an executive official. Under Akbar a collector of reserved revenue. In the 18th century also a governor, i.e. officer in charge of general administration.

Amīn. A trustworthy person: under the Mughals a title given to Civil Court officials and land survey assistants. See N. and M.E. Glossary, p. 11.

Amīr. A nobleman, a Muslim of high rank. See N. and M.E. Glossary, p. 11.

Arthashāstra. A Hindu text on political administration, especially that traditionally attributed to Kautilya, a famous minister of Emperor Chandragupta Maurya (*fl.* 320 B.C.)

Ārya. The name of the fair-skinned tribes which invaded north India in the second millennium B.C. In Ancient India the word later came to mean free men living according to orthodox Hindu tradition; hence the ancient name of north India, Āryāvarta. Also a title of respect.

Ārya Samāj. A militant Hindu missionary movement founded by Dayānanda Sarasvatī in the last quarter of the 19th century to counter the challenge of Christianity and Islām.

Āshram(-a). Hermitage.

Avatār(-a). The descent or incarnation of a deity; his appearance on earth for some important purpose. Vishnu, for example, appears in ten different forms, a fish, a tortoise, etc., culminating in the deified legendary heroes Rāma and Krishna, the most popular deities of contemporary Hinduism.

Bābū. Properly a title of respect attached to a name as 'Mr.' or 'Esq.' and formerly applied to persons of distinction. Now often used disparagingly; sometimes signifying a native clerk who writes English.

Bādshāh. A king. Pers. pādshah (pādishah).

Bahādur. A hero, a warrior; under the Mughals, a title of honour given to the nobles of the court, usually associated with other titles. At the Delhi court the usual gradation of titles was (ascending): (1) Bahādur, (2) Bahādur Jang, (3) Bahādur ud-Daulah, (4) Bahādur ul-Mulk. Under the British it was given to persons of inferior, though respectable station and to distinguished native officers.

BAKHSHĪ. A paymaster under the Mughals, whose duty it was to keep accounts of payments on military tenures, such as those of Mansabdārs and Jāgīrdārs. The term was also applied to his staff.

BAKHSHĪSH. See N. and M.E. Glossary, p. 13.

BALUTĀ. A collective name of the chief village servants such as the carpenter, blacksmith, who are rewarded by allowances of grain.

BANDE MĀTARAM. 'Hail to thee, Mother', a song composed by Bankim Chandra Chatterjī shortly after the Indian Mutiny. It gained acceptance in the early 20th century as an Indian national anthem and is sung at Congress functions.

BANJĀRĀ. See BRINJARRY.

BANYĀ (BANYĀN). A Hindu trader, especially from Gujarāt. A member of the trading caste.

BĀRGĪR. A trooper of irregular cavalry mounted on a horse which is supplied by the State or the chief he serves. (See SILAHDĀR.)

BATTA. See BHATTĀ.

BAY (THE). In the jargon of the East India Company servants this meant the Bay of Bengal and their factories in the area.

BEGUM. A princess, a Muslim lady of rank. Now in the sense of Mrs.

BETEL. See BĪRĀ.

BHĀGA. In Ancient India the king's share of the produce of the land. Fixed by theorists at one-sixth, it was usually much more in practice.

BHAGAVADGĪTĀ. See MAHĀBHĀRATA.

BHAKTI. Devotion. A term employed by those schools of Hinduism advocating the worship of a personal deity by prayer and praise. While the cult of bhakti is very old, most of the modern forms date from medieval times. These modern sects have become most influential in popular Hinduism.

BHĀNG. The dried leaves and small stalks of hemp used to cause intoxication either by smoking or when eaten mixed into a sweetmeat. Cf. the Arab hashīsh.

BHATĀ (BATTA). Additional pay or allowance to public servants or soldiers employed on special duties. It grew to be a constant allowance of European officers in India, and the question of the right to it on several occasions created great agitation under the East India Company.

BHONSLĀ. The surname of Shivājī, founder of the Marāthā Empire, and of several of the rulers of the Marāthā dynasty of Berar.

BĪGHĀ. A measure of land, varying in extent in different parts of India. In the north-west the standard bīghā is equal (from Akbar's time) to five-eighths of an acre; in Bengal to one-third of an acre. Under the Company the acre superseded the bīghā in official returns.

BĪRĀ. (Anglicized Betel.) Small pieces of areca nut, spice, catechu and quicklime rolled in a leaf of the *piper betel* to be slowly masticated. Much used in all parts of India and Ceylon.

BRĀHMAN(-A). 1. A man of the first rank or priestly caste of Hindus, properly charged with the duty of expounding the

Veda, and conducting the ceremonies essential in Hinduism. Nowadays Brāhmans are engaged in most secular walks of life, especially as cooks.

2. A class of ancient Sanskrit treatises on sacrificial ritual, usually spelt 'brāhmana'.

BRĀHMO SAMĀJ. 'Assembly of Brahmists', Brahma being the Supreme Being according to Hindu philosophic systems. A movement formed in Bengal in 1830 by Rām Mohan Roy to reform Hinduism.

BRINJARRY. A word constantly used in the despatches of Sir Arthur Wellesley; properly 'banjārā'. The Brinjarries of the Deccan were dealers in grain and salt who followed the armies in the Company's wars in south India in the early 19th century, and formed the great resource of the commissariat.

BUDDHISM. A religion originating in India in the 6th century B.C. and founded by Gautama Buddha, who is believed to have lived from *c.* 563 to 483 B.C. Buddha belonged to the Kshatriya, the warrior caste-group of Hindus. Buddhism does not believe in caste, and preaches a creed of practical simplicity. It spread over India, but its influence was later undermined by Hinduism, and Buddhism to-day is stronger outside India.

BURGHER. From Dutch burger, 'citizen', now used in Ceylon to indicate any person who claims to be of partly European descent.

CALIPH. See N. and M.E. Glossary, p. 14.

CANUNGO. See QĀNŪNGO.

CARNATIC. Under the East India Company, the area of the east coast low country north and south of Madras, though earlier used in reference to the Telugu and Kanarese people and their language and the wider area they occupied.

CASTE. Subdivisions of Hindu society said to number over 3,000. According to Indian social view, castes are either high or low. In the Madras Presidency castes are also 'Right-hand' and 'Left-hand', a distinction representing the agricultural groups on the one side and the artisans, etc., on the other.

CĀZĪ. See QĀZĪ.

CHAKLĀ. A large division of a province introduced by Shāh Jahān.

CHAKRAVARTĪ. The title assumed by the most exalted ancient Hindu sovereigns; a universal emperor.

CHAPRĀSĪ. A messenger or orderly wearing a chaprās, or belt of office.

CHAUDHARĪ. Headman of a profession or trade. A holder of landed property classed with the Zamīndār and Tāluqdār.

CHAUKĪDĀR. A watchman, police or customs peon.

CHAUTH. The claim, nominally to one-fourth of the revenue, made by the Marāthās on country which they overran but did not administer.

CHIT. A note, a letter. Under the Marāthā Government, an under-secretary of state who wrote and answered letters. *Chitnīs* means a letter-writer, secretary.

CHOULTRY. A resting-place, a hall: used in the early Company days, a place of business, or court house.

CIRCARS. The territory to the north of the Coromandel coast.

CIVILIAN. A term which came into use in the 1760's as a designation of the covenanted European servants of the East India Company, and was later appropriated to describe the Indian Civil Servants. The members of the Company's Civil Service were classified for the first five years as writers, then as factors, then in the 9th year as junior merchants and thereafter as senior merchants. These names emerged from the early commercial character of the Company's transactions, and were abolished in 1833.

COAST (THE). Used to signify the Madras or Coromandel coast.

COLLECTOR. Chief British administrative officer of an Indian district or zilā, especially charged with the collection of revenue and with magisterial powers. First introduced by Warren Hastings, these posts under the British were mostly held by members of the Indian Civil Service.

COMMISSIONER. A British official controlling a division consisting of several districts or zilās.

CONGRESS, THE INDIAN NATIONAL. Founded in 1885 by a group of Indians and Englishmen. At first an intellectuals' organization, and after 1919 enjoying mass support, it bore the brunt of the struggle for Indian independence.

COOLEE. See KŪLĪ.

COROMANDEL. See COAST (THE).

COSS. See MEASURES under KOS.

COWL (COWLE). See QAUL.

COTWAL. See KOTWĀL.

COVENANTED SERVANTS. See CIVILIAN.

CRORE. See KROR.

CURRENCY. No evidence has been found to suggest that money was current in the early Indus civilization or at the time of the Rigveda. The first traces of a monetary system occur in the literature of the later Vedic period, and a regular coinage based on the *rattī* (Sanskrit *raktikā*, a weight of 1·83 gr.) existed in Mauryan times. Certainly the use of money was well established in northern India before Ashoka's time (274 B.C.).

The most important ancient Indian coins were as follows:

Copper—the *pana* or *kārshāpana* of 80 rattīs
Silver—the *tanka* of 8 rattīs (= 4 copper pana)
kārshāpana, dharana, purāna or *dramma* of 32 rattīs
Gold—the *dīnāra* of 32 rattīs
suvarna or *kārshāpana* of 80 rattīs
nishka, a gold weight of 320 rattīs

The cowrie shell (*varātaka*) was also used as currency, and its value was reckoned at $\frac{1}{80}$ pana.

The kingdoms of the Deccan called the dīnāra by various names, such as *hon, hūn, honnu, varāha* or *Bhāgavata.* The latter name was corrupted by the Portuguese into *pagoda.* The $\frac{1}{2}$ pagoda was known as *kāshu*, which term also denoted a copper coin originally of equal weight—in its latter meaning *kāshu* was anglicized as 'cash'. The *panam* (westernized as fanam) was a small gold coin valued at $\frac{1}{10}$ pagoda. Silver coins of similar weight were also called *panam*, which must not be confused with the larger northern *pana*.

The above weights were by no means strictly adhered to and the terms were very loosely applied. Thus the word *tanka* was used in the medieval period for large coins both in silver and gold. Gold coins—*dinārs*—and silver, including in south India even *pagodas*—and especially the *tanga* or *tanka* consisting of 100 *rattīs* weight—were struck in the 13th and 14th centuries by the Delhi kings, and these were first formally introduced as the *rupee* in 1542 by Sher Shāh. The *rupee* (rūpiya from the Sanskrit rūpya, ' wrought silver ') became the standard coin of the Muslim and the British Indian monetary system. Different rupees were minted by the British—the *Sicca* and the *Arcot* rupee, to mention two varying in weight and purity—until in 1836 the universal *rupee* was established. Until 1899 the *rupee* was free to fluctuate ; but in that year it was fixed at 1*s*. 4*d*. In 1920 it was fixed at 2*s*., and in 1927 at 1*s*. 6*d*. At this rate the equivalents are :

Rupees	*Sterling*
1	1*s*. 6*d*.
100,000 (1 lākh)	£7,500
10,000,000 (1 kror)	£750,000

1 rupee = 16 annas
1 anna = 4 pice
1 pice = 3 pies

CUTCHERRY. See KACHHĒRĪ.

DACOITY. A robbery committed by dacoits ; a gang robbery.

DAFĀDĀR. Commandant of a body of horse, or police.

DAFTAR. A record, register, account. An office in which public records are kept, more correctly daftar-khāna.

DAFTARDĀR. A record-keeper, especially in revenue matters.

DARBĀR (DURBĀR). A court, an audience or levee : or executive government of an Indian State.

DAROGHĀ. The chief officer, sometimes governor, in various departments under the native governments, later applied to humbler persons, especially the head of a police, customs, or excise station. Under the Company's police system the Daroghā was a head constable.

DASTAK. A passport or permit. In the early days of the Company, a document authorizing the free transit of certain goods.

DASTŪR. Custom, permission. Under Akbar, a schedule of assessment-rates stated in money. The orders and rules of government.

DEH. A village in the Indian sense, that is, a small area recognized as an administrative unit, not necessarily inhabited.

DECCAN. India south of the Vindhyas.

DEPRESSED CLASSES. See SCHEDULED CLASSES.

DESHMUKH. Under native government, an hereditary official with police and revenue authority in a district ; under the British, a revenue official.

DHARMA. The Hindu Sacred Law ; virtue, legal or moral duty.

DHARMASHĀSTRA. An ancient authoritative writing on Hindu law and institutions. The Hindu code.

DHARNĀ. Sitting and fasting at the door of a house to compel payment of a debt. As long as the person sits, so long also is the person from whom payment is demanded obliged to fast, because, if the suitor perished, the consequences of the sin would fall on him. The practice was forbidden in 1810 by the East India Company, but in modern times Mahātmā Gāndhī found a new and extended political use for the custom.

DĪN-I-ILĀHĪ. 'The Divine Faith'; the eclectic, vaguely theistic religion founded by Akbar.

DISTRICT. The zilā or administrative unit of British India, at the head of which stood the collector and district magistrate.

DIVYA. An oath, especially an ordeal, various kinds of which were admitted by the Hindu laws.

DĪWĀN. A royal court, a council of state, a tribunal of revenue or justice. A minister, or chief officer of state. In the 13th and 14th centuries it meant a ministry. Under the Mughals it was applied to the chief financial minister of the State and of a province; in the latter being charged with the collection and remittance of revenue and invested with wide judicial powers in all civil and financial causes. Under Marāthā government the Dīwān was the chief minister after the Pradhān.

The title of Dīwān, or office of Dīwānī, carrying the right to receive the revenue-collections of Bengal, Bihar, and Orissa, was conferred upon the East India Company by the nominal emperor, Shāh 'Ālam, in 1765. The word, denoting the head officer of any revenue or financial department, was retained under the British Government. In the 19th century the word meant the Civil Courts. See N. and M.E. Glossary, p. 16.

DOĀB. A tract of land lying between two rivers, especially that between the Ganges and Jumna.

DRĀVIDA. The country in which the Dravidian group of languages is spoken; the country below the Eastern Ghats to Cape Comorin.

DŪBRĀJ. (Corruption of YUVARĀJA, 'young prince'.) The heir of a Rājā.

DURBĀR. See DARBĀR.

DURGĀ. A popular Hindu goddess, especially in Bengal. The wife of Shiva and the destroyer of evil beings.

DVIJA. A twice-born man, first by his actual birth and secondly by his spiritual birth or investiture with the sacrificial cord. The term properly designates a man of any one of the three first caste-groups, the Brāhman, Kshatriya and Vaishya, but is now generally used of the first, since investiture is not now invariably practised by the two latter groups.

EXCLUDED CASTES. See SCHEDULED CLASSES.

FACTOR. See CIVILIAN.

FACTORY. A trading establishment. See China Glossary, p. 181.

FAKHR-UL-TUJJĀR. The provost of the merchants; an honorific title granted by the Mughal Government to any eminent banker or merchant. Literally, 'The pride of the merchants'.

FAQĪR. A poor or indigent person. The most general application is to a Muslim religious mendicant who wanders about the countryside living on alms.

FARMĀN. A mandate, an order, a patent.

FARZ. A divine or positive command that is not to be disobeyed: especially applied to the five indispensable Muslim obligations of purification, prayer, almsgiving, fasting, and pilgrimage.

FASLĪ. Belonging to the harvest or season when cultivated. The harvest year, a mode of computing time throughout India and one of the forms used under Muslim rule in giving a date to all public orders and regulations, started on 10 September 1555.

FATWĀ. A judicial sentence; usually applied to the written opinion of the Muslim law-officer of a court on a question of Islamic law. See N. and M.E. Glossary, p. 16.

FAUJDĀR, FAUJDĀRĪ. In the 14th century a military officer, corresponding roughly to general of division, and directly under the general in chief command. In the 16th–18th centuries an officer in charge of the general administration of a portion of a province. From the 17th century the general, as distinct from the revenue, administration, and under the British concerned with criminal, as distinct from civil, jurisdiction. In modern times a police sub-inspector.

FAUJDĀRĪ 'ADĀLAT. Until 1862 the chief criminal court under the East India Company at Madras and Bombay, usually called Nizāmat 'Adālat in Bengal. (See 'ADĀLAT.)

FISCAL. Dutch Fiscaal, and used in Ceylon for 'sheriff'.

GĀDĪ (GADDĪ). The throne. A cushion, or any padded seat or carpet on which a person sits. The seat of rank or royalty.

GAEKWAR. The title of the Marāthā rulers of Baroda.

GANESH(-A). A Hindu divinity, characterized by an elephant's head, who, in his character of remover of obstacles, is worshipped at the start of an undertaking.

GAUTAMA (GOTAMA). According to Buddhist legend, the surname of the family from which the Buddha sprang.

GAZ. See MEASURES.

GENTOO. (Derived from the Portuguese 'gentio', a gentile or heathen.) A Hindu in contradistinction from the Muslims; a native of India.

GHĀT. A landing-place, steps on the river-bank, a quay. A pass through mountains; the mountains themselves, especially applied to the eastern and western ranges of south India.

GOMĀSTA. See GUMĀSHTĀ.

GOTAMA. See GAUTAMA.

GOVERNOR, GOVERNOR-GENERAL. The title of Governor in the British possessions in India goes back to the first charter of Charles II. In 1780 the custom began of selecting governors for the senior provinces of Bengal, Madras and Bombay from the English political world. In 1773 the Governor of Bengal, Warren Hastings, was made Governor-General and a decade later the Governor-General was given effective powers 'to superintend, direct and control' all British possessions in India.

As the British conquest of India proceeded other governorships were created until, at the time of the passing of the India Act of 1935, there were eleven provinces in British India each with its governor. From 1858, when the government of India passed from the Company to the Crown, the Governor-General assumed also the title of Viceroy.

GUMĀSHTĀ (GOMĀSTA). An agent, steward, confidential representative.

HĀJ (HĀJJĪ). See N. and M.E. Glossary, p. 17.

HĀKIM. Any high executive Muslim officer, whether viceroy of a province or governor of a smaller area.

HARIJANS. See SCHEDULED CLASSES.

HAVĀLADĀR (HAVILDĀR). One holding an office of trust, especially used by Marāthās in ministerial matters. Under the British a sepoy non-commissioned officer corresponding to sergeant.

HAZĀRĪ. Commander of a thousand, either actually or nominally, in which latter event it was an honorary title at the Mughal court.

HIJRA. See N. and M.E. Glossary, p. 18.

HIMĀLAYA. 'The abode of snow.'

HĪNAYĀNA. See S.E. Asia Glossary, p. 116.

HINDUISM. A way of life, rather than a creed, followed by the Hindus. The term covers not merely creed and worship but law, both public and private, and, through its acceptance of the caste-system, practically the whole of social and economic life.

HINDŪSTĀN. 'The country of the Hindus', India. Used to describe the area bounded by the Narbada river and the Sutlej and Indus; and exclusive of Bengal and Bihar. Nowadays sometimes used in contradistinction to Pākistān (*q.v.*).

HOLKAR. The family name of one of the Marāthā leaders who became independent as the Peshwā's power declined, whence it is used as the title of the ruler of the Indore state.

HONG (THE). See China Glossary, p. 183.

HŪNAS. The Huns, who invaded India in the middle of the 5th century A.D. and penetrated deep into the Ganges valley, causing great devastation. Some authorities believe them to be the ancestors of many later Rājpūt families.

HUZŪR (HUZOOR). The presence, the royal presence, the presence of a superior; also the place where he presides.

IJLĀS. A Muslim assembly of jurists for the decision of an intricate or important cause.

ILĀHĪ. Divine; title of the era instituted by the Emperor Akbar, commencing with the first year of his reign, A.H. 963 or A.D. 1556.

IMĀM. See N. and M.E. Glossary, p. 18.

IN'ĀM. A gift or reward. Sometimes applied to land held rent-free and in hereditary and perpetual occupation.

I.C.S. The Indian Civil Service, which in 1858 succeeded the Company's covenanted service. It formed the main administrative service in India and its members (numbering some eleven hundred in 1946) provided most of the collectors, judges and heads of departments in both central and provincial governments; and also political agents and residents (*q.v.*).

INDIGO. A plant extensively cultivated in India, and the dark blue dye made from it.

INTERLOPER. One who traded outside the service of the East India Company, which had a charter of monopoly.

ISLĀM. Literally ‘Resignation to the will of God’. The Muslim religion.

‘IZZAT. Honour, credit, reputation.

JAGANNĀTH(-A). ‘Lord of the world’, a name especially applied to Vishnu in the form in which he is worshipped at the temple of Jagannāth at Purī in Orissa.

JĀGĪR. A tenure common under Mughal rule, in which the collection of the revenues of a given tract of land along with the power of government were made over to a servant of the State. The assignment was either conditional or unconditional. In the former event, some public service such as the levy and maintenance of troops was engaged for. The assignment was usually for life, lapsing on the holder's death to the State, though often renewed to his heir on payment of a nazrānā or fine. Particularly in Marāthā territories these jāgīrs came to be accepted by the British as family properties.

JAINISM. A religion founded in the 6th century B.C. by Vardhamāna Mahāvīra, differing from Hinduism. Jains are met with in considerable numbers, especially among the bankers and merchants in central and northern India.

JAMĀBANDĪ. The settlement of the amount of land-revenue assessed on an estate, village or district.

JAMĀDĀR. In the Indian army the title of the second rank of Indian officer in a company of sepoys, the sūbadār being the first.

JARĪPATKĀ. The pennon of the Peshwā's standard, or his flag in general. A golden sash presented by the Peshwā to general officers in his service.

JĀTAKA. A popular story or folk tale connected with the life of the Buddha in a former birth. A large collection of Pāli jātakas contains valuable information about conditions in ancient India.

JAUHAR. The practice of some classes of Hindus, especially Rājpūts, of putting their wives and children to death when unable to resist an enemy, and then sacrificing themselves.

JIHĀD. A sacred war of Muslims against the infidel.

JIRGA. The council of headmen which governs each Afghan tribe.

JIZYA. The personal tax imposed by Islamic Law on non-Muslim subjects. See N. and M.E. Glossary, p. 19.

JOINT FAMILY. A Hindu institution under which the sons of the family remain even after marriage under the parental roof, the income of all being held in common and the needs of each member met from the common pool.

JUNIOR MERCHANT. See CIVILIAN.

JUGGERNAUT. See JAGANNĀTHA.

KA‘BA. See N. and M.E. Glossary, p. 19.

KACHHERĪ, KACHAHRĪ (CUTCHERRY). A court, hall; an office where any public business is transacted.

KĀFILA. See QĀFILA.

KĀLĪ. A popular goddess, the wife of Shiva, so named from her black complexion. The same as Devī or Durgā.

KĀNŪNGO. See QĀNŪNGO.

KARMA. Act, action, work; any act of piety; fate as the consequence of acts.

KATHĀ. A favourite entertainment among the Marāthās, consisting of the public recitation of a narrative—interspersed with music and singing—of the gods, or of individuals, with allusions to passing events or persons.

KAUL (COWL or COWLE). See QAUL.

KĀYASTH(-A). A caste (or member of it) alleged to have originally sprung from a Kshatriya father and Vaishya mother, the occupation of which is that of the writer or accountant.

KĀZĪ. See QĀZĪ.

KHADDAR (KHĀDĪ). Hand-spun and hand-woven cloth.

KHALĪFA (CALIPH). See N. and M.E. Glossary, p. 14.

KHĀLISA (KHĀLSĀ). 1. The exchequer, the office of government under the Mughals in which the business of the revenue department was transacted. This was for a time maintained by the East India Company. As applied to lands it refers to the property reserved to the State, not made over in Jāgīr or Inām to any other parties.

2. The collective denomination of the Sikh Government, church and people.

KHĀN. A title born by Muslim nobles, especially when of Persian or Pathān descent. Also a common adjunct to Afghan or Pathān names. Its value has degenerated to a vague title like 'Esq.'. See p. 54.

KHĀN-KHĀNĀN. 'Lord of lords', a title borne by nobles of the Delhi court under the Mughals at a time when the value of 'Khān' was sinking.

KHĀNAM. The title of a lady of rank, or of the wife of a Khān.

KHARĀJ (KHIRĀJ). Tax, tribute; originally the tribute levied by Muslims on conquered infidels; and in India meaning the revenue raised from the land as the State's share of the profits.

KHĀS. Select, noble: under Mughal rule applied to the chief officers of the State and nobles of the court.

KHILĀT. Any article of costume presented by a superior authority to an inferior as a mark of distinction.

KHOT. A farmer of land revenue. Now the holder of a special land tenure.

KHUDĀĪ KHIDMATGĀRS. 'Servants of God'. A political organization among Pathāns of the North-West Frontier province allied with the Indian National Congress in the struggle against Britain for independence.

KISĀN. 'Peasant'. The Kisān party is a peasant political movement in northern India formed in the 1930's to ameliorate the lot of the Indian peasantry.

KORAN. See QURĀN.

KOS (COSS). A measure of distance varying in different parts of India from one to two miles, usually the latter. The Kos = 5,000 Gaz. (See MEASURES.)

KOTWĀL. City governor, chief officer of police and a magistrate for a city or town. Commander of a fort.

KRISHNA. Black, hence the name of the popular divinity Krishna, from his dark blue or black complexion.

KROR (CRORE). One hundred lākhs or ten millions.

KSHATRIYA. The name of the second or military and regal group of castes, or a member of it. The warrior, the king.

KŪLĪ (COOLEE). Daily hire or wages : a day-labourer, a cooly.

KUMĀRA (KUNWĀR). A youth, a prince.

KUMĀRĪ. A young girl, princess. A name of the goddess Durgā, as a maiden, to whom a temple dedicated at the extremity of the peninsula has long given to the adjacent cape the name of Kumārī, corrupted to Comorin.

KUSHĀNS. A central Asian people, known to the Chinese as Yueh-chih, who invaded India in the 1st century A.D. The most important Kushān king was Kanishka, who ruled a large empire in north-west India, Afghanistan and central Asia, and was a famous patron of Buddhism.

LĀKH. One hundred thousand. The Indian method of writing and reading numbers expressed in figures is by thousands, lākhs and crores. Thus, 1,02,30,000 reads one crore, two lākhs, thirty thousand.

LAKSHMĪ. Wife of Vishnu and goddess of wealth and prosperity.

LĀTHĪ. A stick or pole usually made from bamboo and sometimes bound with iron rings, making a formidable weapon.

LINGA(-M). A mark, a characteristic sign. The distinguishing mark of gender or sex : the male organ : the phallus, as the type of Shiva, and as worshipped in all parts of India. Usually of stone or marble, it is set up in temples especially appropriated for the worship of Shiva.

MADRASA. A college, an academy.

MAHĀ. Great.

MAHĀBHĀRATA. A great Indian epic gradually built up from a narrative begun perhaps as early as 500 B.C. Later priestly writers have enriched it with masses of didactic matter. One of the world's greatest philosophic poems, the Bhagavadgītā (Song of the Lord), is included in it.

MAHĀL. Under Akbar, a revenue subdivision usually corresponding with parganā (*q.v.*). An estate ; also a department of revenue.

MAHĀRĀJA. A sovereign prince ; applied in courtesy to all rājās.

MAHĀRĀNĪ. Wife of a rājā or a queen in her own right. Applied in courtesy to Hindu ladies of rank.

MAHĀRĀSHTRA. The Marātha country.

MAHĀSABHĀ. 'Great Assembly.' A militant Hindu political organization.

MAHĀYĀNA. See S.-East Asia Glossary, p. 118.

MAJLIS. An assembly, a party, a court.

MAJUMDĀR. A native revenue-accountant who kept the account of the Jamā', or government collections, under the native governments. In Hindūstān he was subordinate to the 'āmil, and he audited the accounts of the qānūngo.

MALIK. In the 13th and 14th centuries a rank of nobility, inferior to Amīr. Later an honorific title used more vaguely. See N. and M.E. Glossary, p. 22.

MĀMLATDĀR. The head revenue native officer of a district. Under Mughal rule he exercised undefined and extensive personal powers. Under the British the title was applied to the officer in charge of a Tāluq (*q.v.*).

MAN, MUN, commonly MAUND. See WEIGHTS.

MANSAB. A military title conferred by the Mughals, regulated by the supposed number of horse the holder could bring into the field, varying from ten to ten thousand.

MANSABDĀR. A noble holding a mansab.

MANTRIN. In ancient India, a minister of state, the confidential adviser.

MANU. In Hindu mythology, the first man. Traditional author of *Manusmriti* or Mānavadharmashāstra, the most important of the dharmashāstras (*q.v.*).

MĀPPILLA (MOPLAH). A name originally applied to Arab traders and their descendants, but now used to include all indigenous west-coast Muslims in Malabar.

MĀRWĀRĪ. A native of Mārwār in Rājpūtānā, often settled in other parts of India and usually following the business of banker, broker and merchant. Mārwārī bankers are mostly of the Jain religion.

MASNAD. The large cushion used by Indian princes in place of a throne.

MAULĀNĀ. The title of a person of learning or respectability; teacher, doctor.

MAULAVĪ. A judge or Doctor of the Law. A term often applied to learned Muslims.

MAUND. See WEIGHTS.

MEASURES. In ancient India the usual units of measure were:

4	hasta (cubits of 18 inches)	= 1 danda
2000	danda	= 1 krosha or kos
4	krosha	= 1 yojana

Long distances were usually measured by yojana.

The short krosha of 1,000 danda was also in use.

Under Akbar the kos was laid down as equal to 5,000 gaz, and the gaz standardized at 33 inches. In Bengal the kos or krosha, the most usual popular measure of distance in India, is reckoned at about 2 miles, in the north-west at much nearer one mile. The Bengal bigha usually equals ·625 of an acre.

MĪR (MEER). A chief, head or leader. Under the Mughals the title of head of a department. Also a title borne by the Sayyids, or those persons who claim descent from the family of Muhammad.

MOHUR. See CURRENCY and MUHAR.

MOPLAH. See MĀPPILLA.

MOSLEM. See MUSLIM.

MUFASSAL (MOFUSSIL). Properly separate, distinct, particular; under pre-British rule a subordinate or separate district. The country as opposed to the Sadr or principal town or station; in Bengal the country, the provinces, as opposed to Calcutta.

MUFASSAL 'ADĀLAT. A provincial court of justice.

MUFTĪ. A Muslim law-officer, whose duty it was to expound the law which the Qāzī was to execute. See N. and M.E. Glossary, p. 23.

MUGHAL, THE GREAT. The name first given by the Portuguese, and later by Europeans generally, to the kings of Delhi of the house of Timur.

MUHAR (MOHUR). See CURRENCY. A seal, a seal-ring, a gold coin of the value, in account, of sixteen rupees.

MUHTASIB. A superintendent of markets and police; an officer appointed to take cognizance of improper behaviour.

MUQADDAM. A chief, a leader, especially the headman of a village or of a caste or corporation. See N. and M.E. Glossary, p. 24.

MUNSHĪ. A writer, a secretary: applied by Europeans usually to teachers or interpreters of languages.

MUNSIF. A judge, applied under the Company to a native civil judge of the lowest rank. Later, a summary civil court of first instance.

MUSLIM, MUSALMĀN. 'Resigning' or 'submitting' (oneself to God), i.e. accepting Islām. The name given by Muhammad to the Faithful. The term Musalmān has been formed from the Persian plural, Muslimān.

MUSLIM LEAGUE, THE ALL-INDIA. Founded in 1906 to protect Indian Muslim political interests. From 1940 it adopted as its goal Pākistān—the partition of India into separate Hindu and Muslim states.

NABOB. A term applied in England, particularly in the 18th century, to Anglo-Indians who returned with fortunes from the East. See NAWĀB.

NĀIB. In the 13th and 14th centuries a deputy, a lieutenant, viceroy. A deputy collector. See N. and M.E. Glossary, p. 25.

NAWĀB (NABOB). A viceroy or governor of a province under the Mughal government, whence it became a mere title of any man of high rank upon whom it was conferred, without office being attached to it.

NAWĀRĀ. A large boat, a barge. Under Mughal rule in Bengal the term was applied to a flotilla stationed at Dacca to protect the branches of the Ganges and Brahmaputra against pirates from Arakan; it also applied to the assessments of revenue set apart for its maintenance by the State.

NIRVĀNA. A technical term in the philosophy of the Buddhists for the condition to which they aspire, namely, the cessation of sentient existence. In Jain usage, the passage of the saint from the world.

NĀZIM. An administrator, governor, viceroy. The superior officer of a province charged with the administration of criminal law.

NIZĀM. An administrator: the viceroy of the Deccan, a title retained by the rulers of Hyderabad. Nizām-ul-mulk, 'administrator of the kingdom'.

NIZĀMAT. The office of the Nizām.

NIZĀMAT 'ADĀLAT. The chief criminal court of the East India Company.

NAZR, NAZAR. A present. A fine paid to the State, or its representative, on succeeding to office or property.

NISHĀN-I-DĪWĀN. The official stamp of the Dīwān.

OMRAH. See UMARĀ.

PĀDISHĀH. A king. See BĀDSHĀH and also N. and M.E. Glossary, p. 25.

PAGODA. The European designation of a Hindu temple in the south of India, derived from Tamil pāgavadam, from Sanskrit bhāgavatam, 'belonging to the Lord'; also the gold coin formerly minted at Madras, from its having the device of a temple on one face. See CURRENCY.

PAIMĀISH. The assessment system. Synonym, Zabt.

PĀKISTĀN. The Muslim state of north-west and north-east India which came into existence in 1947. The name means 'Land of the Pure'.

PĀLI. An ancient Indian Prākritic tongue which became the sacred language of Hīnayāna Buddhism (*q.v.*).

PANCHĀYAT. A native court of arbitration (properly of five persons), chosen by the parties themselves or by the officers of government for the determination of petty disputes.

PANDIT. One learned in Sanskrit lore. An adviser in the Supreme Court on Hindu law. To-day the term is used occasionally as an honorific and bestowed on distinguished Hindus.

PARGANĀ. A subdivision of a district comprising numerous villages.

PARIAHS. See SCHEDULED CLASSES.

PĀRSĪ. A Zoroastrian of Persian origin: a race chiefly settled in western India and distinguished as merchants, shipbuilders and traders. Their ancestors fled from Persia to India upon the conquest of the former by the Muslims in the 8th century.

PARWĀNA. An order, a written precept or command from one in authority to a dependant.

PATEL. The headman of a village, who has general control and management of village affairs.

PATWĀR or PATWĀRĪ. A village accountant, whose duty it was to keep and produce, when required by government officers, all accounts relating to lands.

PĀTĪL. See PATEL.

PATTĀ (POTTA). A deed of lease; a document given by the collector to the Zamīndār, or by some other receiver of revenue, specifying the condition on which the lands are held.

PEON. A term (taken from the Portuguese *peão*) commonly used by Europeans in the sense of 'a foot soldier', an inferior police official: sometimes a courier. In modern use, a messenger.

PERGUNNAHS. 'The Twenty-four.' The official name of the district immediately enclosing Calcutta, ceded to the British in 1757. See PARGANĀ.

PESHKASH (PESHCUSH). Tax, tribute paid to government, especially on first receiving an appointment.

PESHWĀ. Originally the chief minister of the Marāthā power; in the 18th century becoming prince of an independent Marāthā state. The Peshwā's power ceased with the surrender of Bājī Rāo to the British in 1817.

PHADNĪS (PHADNAVĪS, FADNAVĪS, FURNAVEES). At first in the Marāthā districts, he was the head Kārkūn of the District Kachherī, in charge of its accounts. A public officer of the Marāthā Government through whom all orders and grants were issued and to whom all accounts were sent. The title is familiar as the designation of Nānā Fadnavīs, the prime mover of the policy of the Marāthā court at Poona in its later phases.

PINDĀRĪS. Originally bodies of irregular horse allowed to attach themselves to Mughal armies, employed especially in collecting forage and permitted, in lieu of pay, to plunder. Later in the early 19th century, organized associations of mounted marauders in Central India, finally suppressed by the British in 1817.

POLIGAR. A class of semi-feudal petty chieftains in south India (Tamil pālaiyakkāran).

POTTA. See PATTĀ.

PRĀKRIT(-A). An ancient Indian language approximating to the vernacular speech, as opposed to Sanskrit, the formal language. The chief Prākrits are Ardha-māgadhī, Māgadhī, Shaurasenī, Māhārāshtrī and Pāli (*q.v.*).

PRASHASTI. A panegyric on a Hindu king, often in verse. The term is used especially for prashastis engraved on rocks, pillars, monuments, temple walls and copper plates, usually in connection with edicts or grants of land. They are one of our most valuable sources for the history of ancient India.

PRADHĀN (PADHĀN, PURDHĀN). An eminent person, a prime minister. The common title of the eight chief civil and military officers of the Marāthā state, as established by Shivājī in the 17th century.

PRESIDENCY (and PRESIDENT). The chief of a principal East India Company factory was styled 'President' in the 17th century and the area of his jurisdiction the Presidency.

PŪJĀ. Worship, adoration.

PURĀNA. A Hindu sacred book of later composition than the Vedas. Purānas deal mainly with mythology and cosmology, but contain valuable historical information also.

PUROHIT(-A). A Brāhman chaplain to a king or nobleman; sometimes a village priest.

QĀFILA. A body or convoy of travellers.

QĀNŪNGO. The parganā accountant and registrar. The position existed under early Hindu governments. The Qānūngo was an 'interpreter of custom', and the person to whom Muslim administrators looked for information concerning the customs of their Hindu subjects. The office was abolished in Bengal in 1793.

QAUL. A word, promise or contract. In revenue transactions, the document granted by the collector or proprietor.

QĀZĪ. A Muslim judge appointed under Muslim Governments to administer civil and criminal law, chiefly in towns, according to the principles of the Sharīʻa (see p. 28). Under the Mughals, the judicial assistant of the governor. Under the East India Company these judicial capacities ceased, and, excepting for their employment as legal advisers on Muslim law in the courts, their duties were confined to the preparation and attestation of deeds of conveyance and other legal instruments, and the general superintendence and legalization of the ceremonies of marriage, funerals and other Muslim domestic occurrences.

QURĀN. Literally 'the reading'. The name of the sacred book of the Muslims.

RĀI. A title denoting a prince, derived from *rājā*: under the Mughals a title given to Hindu civil officers of high rank.

RAĪYAT (RYOT). A cultivator, a peasant.

RAĪYATWĀRĪ (RYOTWĀRĪ). A system under which the revenue-settlement was made by government officers with each actual cultivator of the soil for a given term, without the intervention of a third party. This mode chiefly prevails in the Madras Presidency.

RĀJ (Sanskrit *rājya*). A kingdom, a rule, sovereignty.

RĀJĀ. A king, prince. A title given by Indian Governments to Hindus of rank. Also assumed by petty chiefs.

RĀMA (RĀM). A name given to three of the ten avatars of Vishnu. The name repeated, *Rām Rām*, is a greeting used by Hindus.

RĀMĀYANA. A great Indian epic which recounts the adventures of Rāma, king of Kosala (Oudh), at an epoch which is quite uncertain.

RĀNĀ. A title held by Hindu princes in central and northern India.

RĀNĪ. A Hindu queen.

RĀO. A Hindu title for a chief or prince, derived from *rājā*. Amongst the Marāthās given to distinguished persons, military and civil.

RĀYA. A king, a prince. Used in Mysore as an honorific affix to the name of a Brāhman; in Bengal a family name (e.g. Rāmamohan Rāya), and often spelt as *Ray* and *Roy*. Also the title (sometimes Rāyalu, Rāyel) of the Hindu sovereigns of Vijayanagar, the last Hindu principality of importance in south India.

RED SHIRTS, THE. See KHUDĀĪ KHIDMATGĀRS.

RESIDENT (THE). 1. Down to Warren Hastings' time the term denoted the chiefs of the Company's establishments in the provinces.

2. Thereafter the title applied to the representatives of the governor-general at the more important native courts.

RIGVEDA. The oldest sacred book of the Hindus, containing over a thousand hymns in archaic Sanskrit. Composed during the second millennium B.C.

RISĀLADĀR (RISSĀLDĀR). A native officer commanding a troop of horse.

RUDRA. One of the names of Shiva.

RUPIYA (RUPEE). See CURRENCY.

RYOT. See RAĪYAT.

SABHĀ. An assembly, or hall of audience. In ancient India also the circle of advisers round the emperor or rājā.

SĀDHU. Pious; particularly applied to an ascetic.

SADR (SADAR, SUDDAR). Supreme; the chief seat of government, the Presidency, as opposed to the provinces or Mufassal (*q.v.*). Usually applied to denote establishments in the judicial and revenue administration of the State.

SADR-'ADĀLAT. The chief court of justice. Until 1862 it formed in Bengal and the North-West Province the chief court of appeal from the district courts, but in the year mentioned it was merged in the High Court of Judiciary. See 'ADĀLAT.

SADR-DĪWĀNĪ-'ADĀLAT. The chief civil court. See 'ADĀLAT

SADR-FAUJDĀRĪ or NIZĀMAT-'ADĀLAT. The chief criminal court. See 'ADĀLAT.

SADR AMĪN. A chief commissioner or arbitrator, the title of a class of native civil judges created under the East India Company.

SADR-KACHHERĪ (SUDDAR CUTCHERRY). The principal revenue office of a district.

SĀHIB. A master: a respectable European's designation, like Mr., Sir.

SAHUKĀR (SOWKAR). A banker and dealer in exchanges, usually belonging to the Hindu Mārwārī community from Rājpūtānā.

SAID (SAYYID and SAIYID). A lord, a chief. A designation assumed by Muslims who claim descent from Husain, the son of Alī and grandson of Muhammad.

SAIDĪ. See SĪDĪ.

SAKA, SHAKA. 1. The Scythians, a people which invaded India in the 1st century B.C. and ruled a considerable area of the north and west. Shaka rule persisted in Gujarāt until the 4th century A.D. The term was later sometimes used to denote any foreigner.

2. An era reckoned, according to popular tradition, from the reign of a Shaka prince of south India, Shālivāhana. But he is mythical, being perhaps a compound of the tribal name *Shaka* and the dynasty of the *Sātavāhanas,* who were genuine Hindus. The era may have started from the coronation of the Shaka satrap, Nahapāna, or possibly, though less probably, from that of Kanishka. It became very common in peninsular India. It may be said to commence in the 79th year of the Christian era and is to be equated with the latter by adding 78¼.

SAMVATSARA (SAMVAT). A year, particularly applied to the years of the era of Vikrama, beginning with the year 58 B.C.

SAN (SUN). A year; like Samvat also applied to the years of an era, of which two varieties have been used, the Bengālī and the Vilāyatī, the former in Bengal, the latter in the Deccan. These eras were first established by the Emperor Akbar. The first month of this luni-solar year is Baisākh (April–May), and to convert the Bengālī to the Christian era, 593 must be added to any period within the first nine months, 594 for the other three: to convert the Vilāyatī, 592 within the first four months, 593 for the other eight. Thus the Bengal San beginning on the first Baisākh 963 + 593 = A.D. 1556. The Vilāyatī San beginning on the first of *Āswin* 963 + 592 = A.D. 1555.

SANAD (SUNNUD). A grant, a charter.

SANNYĀSĪ. A Hindu who has renounced all worldly ties and

possessions in order to devote himself to the spiritual life, living on alms.

SANSKĀRA. An essential ceremony of Hindu initiation, indispensable to constitute the perfect purification of a Hindu.

SANSKRIT. The sacred language of the Hindus and the chief literary language of ancient India.

SARDESMUKH. The head of the Marāthā Desmukh (*q.v.*); officers in an extensive district.

SARKĀR (SIRCĀR, SIRKĀR). A treasury: a revenue district. Also an extensive subdivision of a sūbah (*q.v.*); in this sense usually written Circar—e.g. Northern Circars. Nowadays, denotes the Government, the State.

SĀRĪ. A long robe worn by Hindu women, wrapped round the body and passed over the head.

SARRISHTADĀR. A registrar, a record-keeper, particularly the head native officer of a court of justice or collector's office.

SHĀSTRA. A scripture, a work of authority. It may denote either a single work of the class, or the writings collectively; thus, *a Dharma-shāstra* may imply the code of Manu or any work of authority on the laws and institutes of the Hindus; whilst *the Dharma-shāstra* means the whole science of law and the body of social institutions.

SATĪ (SUTTEE). (Literally, 'good woman'.) The rite of widow-burning practised especially among the Rājpūts: a Hindu wife who consummated a life of duty by burning herself on the funeral pile of her husband. The rite was forbidden by the East India Company in 1829.

SATYĀGRAHA. (Literally, 'insistence on truth'.) Non-violent resistance.

SAYYID. See SAID.

SCHEDULED CLASSES. Castes or communities which, through ancestry, profession, or custom, are looked upon as impure by orthodox Hindus, and with whom no social contact can be made. Also known as 'Untouchables', 'Pariahs', 'Depressed classes', 'Excluded castes', and 'Harijans'. The latter title, ('People of God') coined by Mahātmā Gāndhī, is widely employed in contemporary India.

SENĀPATI. In ancient India, the commander-in-chief.

SENIOR MERCHANT. See CIVILIAN.

SEPOY. See SIPĀHĪ.

SER (SEER). See WEIGHTS.

SHĀH. A king; a title also borne by some Muslim ascetics.

SHĀH-BANDAR. Harbour master, and usually head of the customs. A Muslim port-official.

SHĀH-ZĀDA. A prince, the son of a king.

SHARĪ'A. See N. and M.E. Glossary, p. 28.

SHĪ'A. See N. and M.E. Glossary, p. 28. The lower orders of Muslims in India are of this sect.

SHRENĪ. In ancient India a corporation of persons following the same occupation. The Shrenī corresponds in many respects to the medieval gild.

SHŪDRA. The fourth or servile caste-group of the Hindus.

SIBANDĪ. Irregular soldiery.

SĪDĪ (SAIDĪ, SĪDDHĪ). A name given to the descendants of natives of Africa in the west of India, some of whom were distinguished officers of the Muslim princes of the Deccan, especially of Bijāpur. They provided chief naval officers for the Mughal power on the coast of Gujarāt.

SIKH. 'A disciple': the name of the militant community in the Punjab, followers of Nānak Shāh (born 1469), a dissenter from Brāhmanic Hinduism. The orthodox Sikh wears 'the five K's'; the *Kes*, unshorn hair; the *Kachh*, drawers reaching only to the knee; the *Karā*, iron bangle; the *Kirpan*, sword (or *Khanda*, small dagger); and *Khanga*, or hair-comb.

SIKKA (SICCA). A coining die, a stamp, royal signet; a stamped coin, especially of the kings of Delhi, adopted also by the East India Company. See CURRENCY. Our word 'sequin' comes (through Italian 'zecchino') from the same Arabic root.

SILAHDĀR. A horse-soldier who provides his own horse and arms, especially among the Marāthās.

SIPĀHĪ (SEPOY). A native soldier.

SIPĀH-SĀLĀR. A commander-in-chief.

SHIV(-A), SIVA. The third member of the Hindu triad, the deity presiding over destruction and renovation, frequently worshipped in the form of the *Linga* (*q.v.*). Those Hindus who recognize the supremacy of Shiva are called Shaivites. See VISHNU.

SŪBAH. A province: one of the larger subdivisions of the Mughal Empire, such as Oudh, Bengal, Bihar.

SŪBAHDĀR (SUBEDĀR). Viceroy; governor of a province. A local commandant. Under the British the chief native officer of a company of sepoys.

SŪFĪ. A Muslim mystic.

SULTĀN. A sovereign prince. See N. and M.E. Glossary, p. 29.

SUNNĪ. See N. and M.E. Glossary, p. 29. The Persians and lower classes of Muslims in India are *Shī'ahs*; most of the other Muslim peoples and most of the educated and respectable classes of Indians are *Sunnīs*.

SUNNUD. See SANAD.

SUPREME COURT, THE. An English Court established at Calcutta in 1773 by the Regulating Act, and afterwards at Madras and Bombay. Controversy over the extent of its jurisdiction continued until final definition took place in the Act of Parliament of 1781. The use of the name ceased with the creation of High Courts in 1862.

SUTTEE. See SATĪ.

SWADESHĪ. ('Of one's own country.') Made in India. The name given to the political movement, first beginning in Bengal in 1905, to boycott foreign goods.

SWĀMĪ. A master, a lord; applied especially as a title to the head of a religious order or establishment.

SWARĀJ. The share of the revenue claimed by the Marāthās from any conquered country, the same as CHAUTH (*q.v.*). Literally and nowadays, 'self-rule'.

TĀLUQ (TĀLUK, TALOOK). Dependency. The term came into use at the end of the 17th century. A division of a province; an estate, applied to proprietary land usually smaller than a zamīndārī. A Tāluq was sometimes granted by the Mughal Government at a favourable assessment as a mark of favour or on clearing waste lands. By the East India Company's permanent assessment of Bengal in 1793 Tāluqs were deemed of two kinds: those like the zamīndārīs paying revenue direct to the Government, and secondly those paying through a third party. In the north-west a tāluq forms an estate, the profits of which are divided among different proprietors; in Bombay, the division of a zilā.

TĀLUQDĀR (TĀLUKDĀR). The holder of a Tāluq.

TAHSĪL. Collection, especially of the land-revenue. In the Deccan, a statement prepared by the village accountant of the revenue receivable.

TAHSĪLDĀR. A collector of revenue.

THĀKUR (THAKOOR). An idol, a deity; any individual entitled to reverence or respect, and so applied in different parts of India. In the west commonly used by Rājpūt chiefs; in the Deccan borne by headmen; in Bengal in the form Tagore used as a surname.

THĀNĀ. A military post: police station.

THĀNĀDĀR. Officer in charge of a thānā.

THUG. A cheat, a knave. A class of robbers and assassins suppressed by the East India Company in the 1830's.

TOL. A school kept by a Pandit or Brāhman teacher providing instruction in Sanskrit.

'ULEMĀ. An assembly of 'ālims (*q.v.*).

UMARĀ. Nobles. The higher officials at the Mughal court, a title sometimes applied to an individual.

UNTOUCHABLES. See SCHEDULED CLASSES.

URDŪ. A camp, a royal encampment. The mixed language formed by a copious influx of Arabic, Persian and Turkish words upon a basis of Hindī and Sanskrit which first grew up in the court and camp: 'the camp-language'.

VAISHNAVA. A worshipper of Vishnu; also a group of Hindu bankers and merchants who fall in this category.

VAISHYA. The name of the third caste of Hindus, whose means of subsistence, according to Manu, were agriculture, trade and the keeping of cattle.

VAKĪL. See WAKĪL.

VARNA. (Literally, 'colour'.) A division of the Hindu community. There are four varnas, namely, Brāhmans, Kshatriyas, Vaishyas, and Shūdras (*q.v.*). Each varna includes a number of castes.

VAZĪR. See WAZĪR.

VEDA. The name of the chief scriptural authorities of the Hindus: the sacred books of the Brāhmans.

VEDĀNTA. A system of pantheistic philosophy based upon scattered texts of the Vedas and Upanishads.

VICEROY. See GOVERNOR GENERAL.

VISHNU. The second of the three principal deities of the Hindus, the preserving power personified. Those Hindus who recognize the supremacy of Vishnu are called Vaishnavites. See SHIVA.

WAHHĀBĪ. A follower of the doctrines of an Arabian reformer of Islam, 'Abdul-Wahhāb. See N. and M.E. Glossary, p. 30.

WAKĪL (VAKĪL). In the 13th and 14th centuries the highest ceremonial officer at the Delhi court. Under the Mughals, he was the prime minister, and superior to the Wazīr. By the 19th century, the term meant an authorized public pleader in a court of justice.

WAZĪR (VAZĪR). In the 13th and 14th centuries the prime minister with responsibility for revenue and financial administration. Under the Mughals, if there was a Wakīl, the Wazīr was revenue and finance minister ; otherwise he was in charge of general, as well as revenue, administration. See N. and M.E. Glossary, p. 30.

WEIGHTS. From early times by Indian custom standard weights were based on the weight of seeds. The ancient rattī, the seed of the *Abrus precatorius*, was used as the basis of weights for gold, silver and drugs. 96 rattīs equalled 1 tolā. Five tolās equalled one chhitak.

The maund (mān) with varying values has been current in western Asia as a unit of weight from early times, and certainly in India from at least the 8th century. The maund contained 40 sers, but the weight of the ser differed widely over India and over the course of time.

The principal units to-day are the maund, the ser and the tolā. The standard maund is 82·28 lb. and the ser 2·057 lb.

1 maund = 40 sers
1 ser = 16 chhitaks

WRITER. See CIVILIAN.

YOGA. In Hindu philosophy, union with the Supreme Spirit ; a system of ascetic practices pursued as a method of obtaining this.

YUGA. An age, especially a subdivision of a great age, or aggregate of four Yugas, which are the Krita, or Satya-Yuga, the Tretā-Yuga, the Dvāpara-Yuga and the Kali-Yuga, the duration of which is severally computed at years 1,728,000, 1,296,000, 864,000 and 432,000, making a Mahā-Yuga of 4,320,000 years : the world is now (1947) in the year of the Kali age 5048.

YUVARĀJ(-A) and YUVA-MAHĀRĀJ. In ancient India the young Rājā, properly the eldest son of a Rājā who succeeds to the Rāj by right of primogeniture : also applied to a young prince associated with his father in the government before his death.

ZABT. The assessment system. Synonym, Paimāish.

ZAMĪNDĀR. Literally, ' a landholder ', without necessarily implying a particular claim or title. Under the Mughal power treated as the collector of revenues, removable at will. The East India Company in Bengal, Bihar and Orissa in 1793 by the Permanent Settlement accepted all recognized zamīndārs and independent Ṭāluqdārs as actual proprietors of the land in return for a fixed annual payment. In the north-west there exists a zamīndārī tenure whereby a number of proprietors or tenants hold the land in common and one of them—termed the zamīndār—represents all in accepting responsibility for paying the government revenue.

ZAMORIN. A title borne for many centuries by the ruling Hindu sovereign of Calicut.

ZANĀNA (ZENĀNA). The female apartments: the women of a family.

ZILĀ (ZILLAH). A division, a district. Under the British the area under the jurisdiction of a collector, or of a collector and magistrate combined, or in the Punjab of a deputy commissioner.

ZOROASTRIANISM. The religion of the Pārsīs of India. See PĀRSĪ.

5. SYSTEMS OF DATING

I. HINDU. 'Ages' lasting for thousands of years are frequently referred to in Sanskrit texts. One of the best known, though not one of those found on ancient documents, is the *Kali-yuga*, or Kali age, supposed to be the last and worst of the four ages that make up a great age. Starting in 3102 B.C. from the death of Krishna, it is to last through 432,000 years of progressive deterioration until it ends in the general dissolution of existing forms. This era seems to have been a late invention. Scholars have also identified a considerable number of now-forgotten eras attributable to various conquerors of ancient India and usually dating from their accession to the throne. The idea of suzerainty over all the rulers of a large region is deeply rooted in Indian conceptions of government, and the establishment of this supreme lordship was usually marked by the foundation of an era. The two most significant Hindu eras of the historical period are the Vikrama or Samvat (year) and the Shaka (Saka), both of which are still used.

The *Vikrama Samvat era* began in 58 B.C., and, according to Indian tradition, was established by Vikramāditya, a legendary king of Ujjain, who was said to have defeated the Shakas. Some scholars attribute its foundation to the Shaka king Azes I. Its use became widespread. The year A.D. 1948 may be said to be 2006 of the Vikrama era. Discrepancies occur because the era year is assumed to begin in March-April in eastern India and in October-November in the west.

The *Shaka* (*Saka*) *era*, which has obtained a wide currency in India, especially in the south, is believed by some to have been founded by the Kushān king Kanishka, and dated from his supposed accession in A.D. 78. Possibly, and more probably, it was founded to commemorate the accession of the Satrap Nahapāna. The year A.D. 1948 is 1870 of the Shaka era. See also Saka in the Glossary.

II. BUDDHIST AND JAIN. Two religious eras in common use are those of the Buddhists in Burma and Ceylon, said to date from the death of the Buddha (*c.* 483 B.C.), and of the Jains in north India, said to date from the death of Mahāvīra (*c.* 468 B.C.). The Buddhist era actually begins in 544 B.C. and the era of Mahāvīra in 528 B.C.

III. MUSLIM. (See N. and M.E. Calendars and systems of dating, pp. 32–40). The *Hijra era*, denoted by A.H. (Anno Hegirae), was introduced into India by the Muslim conquerors. The Muslim year, which follows the moon, not the sun, and normally contains only 354 days, created an increasing divergence between the months and the actual seasons of the year, which was administratively inconvenient in a country whose state revenues were largely drawn from the land. In A.H. 963 Akbar therefore established a solar year purely for revenue purposes, which is known as *faslī* (harvest year) and is still familiar in India. Necessarily it has gradually fallen behind the Hijra system of dating. Akbar also introduced the

Ilāhī, or *Divine era*, dating from his accession in A.D. 1556, but his successors, whilst treating each emperor's reign as a new era, accepted the Hijra as the permanent basis of their chronology.

IV. EUROPEAN. For those using Portuguese, Dutch and English sources, it is worth recalling that the system of accepting 25 March as the beginning of the year was abandoned in Portugal in 1556, in Holland in 1583 and in England in 1752. The Julian calendar was replaced by the Gregorian in Portugal in 1582, in Holland in 1583 and in England in 1752.

6. DYNASTIES AND RULERS

Detailed genealogical tables of Hindu and Muslim dynasties in India will be found in the following works:

R. C. Majumdar, H. C. Raychaudhuri, and K. Datta. *An Advanced History of India*. London, 1946.

S. Lane Poole, *The Mohammadan Dynasties*. London, 1894.

Cambridge History of India. Vols. III and IV. Cambridge, 1937.

Detailed lists of the members of the British-Indian Governments in London and in India in the period of British rule over India are to be found in the following work:

Lists of the Heads of Administrations in India and of the India Office in London. Calcutta, 1929.

Lists of the Directors and Chairmen of the East India Company and their periods of service in the century from 1758 to 1858 will be found in the following works:

C. H. Philips. *The East India Company, 1784–1834*. Manchester, 1940.

C. H. and D. Philips. *Alphabetical List of Directors of the East India Company*. (Journal of the Royal Asiatic Society, October 1941.)

Where only one date is given, it is that of the ruler's accession.

I. HINDU DYNASTIES

(i) THE MAURYAS

The power of this dynasty centred on Magadha or south Bihār and became sufficiently great to justify the use of the word 'empire'. The early rulers were:

(1) Chandragupta	*c.* 324 B.C.
(2) Bindusāra	*c.* 302
(3) Asoka (Ashokavardhana) . . .	*c.* 273

Not improbably the empire was divided among the sons of (3) on the latter's death in *c.* 232. Some authorities say that one of these, Kunāla, was succeeded in turn by Bandhupālita (Dasharatha), Samprati, Shālishūka, Devavarman, Shatadhanus, and by the last of the line, Brihadratha, who was overthrown by his own commander-in-chief, Pushyamitra, about 187 B.C.

(ii) THE GUPTAS

This dynasty first emerged in Bihār and ultimately established a great empire over northern India, extending also into the south. The early rulers were:

Chandra Gupta I	320 A.D.
Samudra Gupta	*c.* 330
Chandra Gupta II (Vikramāditya) . .	*c.* 380
Kumāra Gupta I (Mahendrāditya) . .	*c.* 415
Skanda Gupta (Vikramāditya) . .	*c.* 455

After the probable end of Skanda Gupta's reign about A.D. 467 the last period of the empire is obscure, though some sort of unity was maintained until the reign of Budha Gupta (*c.* 477–95); and Gupta rule in northern Bengal continued at least until 544.

(iii) THE HOUSE OF PUSHYABHŪTI

(Capitals: Thānesar and Kanauj)

	A.D.
(1) Prabhākaravardhana, son of Ādityavardhana	
(2) Rājyavardhana II, son of (1)	*c.* 605
(3) Harshavardhana, son of (1)	606

The empire of Harsha dissolved on his death in *c.* 647, and two centuries passed before an imperial power, the Pratīhāras, again established itself in the Ganges valley.

(iv) THE IMPERIAL PRATĪHĀRAS

(Capital: Kanauj)

	A.D.
(1) Nāgabhata I	*c.* 750
(2) Devarāja, nephew of (1)	
(3) Vatsarāja, son of (2)	*c.* 783
(4) Nāgabhata II, son of (3)	*c.* 815
(5) Rāmabhadra, son of (4)	
(6) Bhoja I, son of (5)	*c.* 836
(7) Mahendrapāla I, son of (6)	*c.* 893
(8) Mahīpāla, son of (7)	*c.* 914
(9) Bhoja II, (?) son of (7)	
(10) Vināyakapāla, (?) son of (7)	
(11) Mahendrapāla II, (?) son of (10)	*c.* 946
(12) Devapāla, son of (8)	*c.* 948
(13) Vijayapāla, son of (8)	*c.* 960

The power of the Pratīhāras under (14) Rājyapāla was broken in 1018 by the capture of Kanauj by Mahmūd of Ghaznī. This list from Mahīpāla onwards is quite tentative.

(v) THE PĀLAS OF BENGAL

(Capital: Pātaliputra, i.e. Patna)

	A.D.
(1) Gopāla	
(2) Dharmapāla, son of (1)	*c.* 752–*c.* 794
(3) Devapāla, son of (2)	
(4) Vigrahapāla I, nephew of (3)	
(5) Nārāyanapāla, son of (4)	*c.* 875
(6) Rājyapāla, son of (5)	
(7) Gopāla II, son of (6)	
(8) Vigrahapāla II, son of (7)	
(9) Mahīpāla I, son of (8)	*c.* 1026
(10) Nayapāla, son of (9)	
(11) Vigrahapāla III, son of (10)	*c.* 1074
(12) Mahīpāla II, son of (11)	
(13) Shūrapāla II, son of (11)	
(14) Rāmapāla, son of (11)	
(15) Kumārapāla, son of (14)	*c.* 1142
(16) Gopāla III, son of (15)	
(17) Madanapāla, son of (14)	

(vi) THE SENAS OF BENGAL

(Capital: Vijayapura)

	A.D.
(1) Vijaya Sena	
(2) Ballāla Sena, son of (1)	*c.* 1159
(3) Lakshmana Sena, son of (2)	*c.* 1178
(4) Vishvarūpa Sena, son of (3)	
(5) Keshava Sena, son of (3)	

(vii) EARLY CHĀLUKYA KINGS

(Capital: Vātāpi, i.e. Bādāmi in Bombay)

	A.D.		A.D.
Pulakeshin I		Vinayāditya	680
Kīrttivarman I	566	Vijayāditya	696
Mangalesha	c. 597	Vikramāditya II	733
Pulakeshin II	609	Kīrttivarman II	746–53
Vikramāditya I	655		

About 753 the Chālukyas were overthrown by the Rāshtrakūtas.

(viii) THE RĀSHTRAKŪTA DYNASTY

(Capital: Mānyakheta or Mālkhed in Hyderabad)

	A.D.		A.D.
(1) Dantivarman I		(13) Indra III, grandson of (12)	915
(2) Indra I, son of (1)		(14) Amoghavarsha II, son of (13)	917
(3) Govinda I, son of (2)		(15) Govinda IV, son of (13)	918
(4) Karka I, son of (3)		(16) Amoghavarsha III (Vaddiga), grandson of (12)	c. 934
(5) Indra II, son of (4)		(17) Krishna III, son of (16)	939
(6) Dantivarman II (Dantidurga), son of (5)	754	(18) Khottiga, son of (16) .	968
(7) Krishna I, son of (4) .	768	(19) Karka II (or Amoghavarsha IV) grandson of (16)	972
(8) Govinda II, son of (7) .	783	(20) Indra IV	973–82
(9) Dhruva, son of (7)			
(10) Govinda III, son of (9)	793		
(11) Amoghavarsha I, son of (10)	814		
(12) Krishna II, son of (11)	877		

In 973 this dynasty was overthrown by Taila II, who claimed descent from the early Chālukyas of Vātāpi.

(ix) CHĀLUKYA DYNASTY OF KALYĀNA

	A.D.
(1) Taila II	973
(2) Satyāshraya, son of (1)	997
(3) Vikramāditya V, nephew of (2)	1008
(4) Ayyana II, nephew of (2)	1014
(5) Jayasimha II (Jagadekamalla), nephew of (2) . .	1015
(6) Someshvara I, son of (5)	1042
(7) Someshvara II, son of (6)	1068
(8) Vikramāditya VI, son of (6)	1076
(9) Someshvara III, son of (8)	1127
(10) Jagadekamalla II, son of (9)	1138
(11) Taila III, son of (9)	1151
(12) Someshvara IV, son of (11)	1184–1200

After 1190 the empire of Kalyāna broke into smaller states.

(x) THE PALLAVA KINGS

Centred on Kānchī (Conjeevaram), near Madras, this dynasty emerged as a power in the 4th century A.D. One of its early kings, Vishnugopa, was captured and liberated by Samudra Gupta about the middle of the 4th century. The following list and dates are tentative.

	A.D.		A.D.
Simhavarman IV . . .	c. 436	Parameshvaravarman I .	c. 674
Vishnugopa	c. 450	Narasimhavarman II	
Simhavishnu		Parameshvaravarman II	
Mahendravarman I		Mahendravarman III	
Narasimhavarman I . .	c. 642–68	Nandivarman II . . .	c. 717–82
Mahendravarman II			

The dynasty ended with the overthrow of Aparājita by Āditya Chola late in the 9th century.

(xi) CHOLA KINGS

This south Indian dynasty grew in strength until by the 11th century it ruled over almost the entire peninsula. Its position slowly weakened until it came to an end in the 13th century.

	A.D.		A.D.
Vijayālaya	c. 846	Rājendradeva II . . .	1052
Āditya I	c. 871	Rājamahendra . . .	1060
Parāntaka I	907	Vīrarājendra	1063
Rājāditya I	947	Adhirājendra	1067
Gandarāditya	949	Rājendra III	1070
Arinjaya	956	Vikrama-Chola . . .	1118
Parāntaka II (Sundara Chola)	956	Kulottunga Chola II . .	1133
Āditya II	956	Rājarāja II	1146
Madhurāntaka Uttama .	969	Rājādhirāja II . . .	1163
Rājarāja	985	Kulottunga III . . .	1178
Rājendra I	1012	Rājarāja III	1216
Rājādhirāja I	1044	Rājendra IV	1246–79

(xii) YĀDAVAS OF VIJAYANAGAR

	A.D.
(1) Harihara I, son of Sangama	1339
(2) Bukka I, son of Sangama	1354
(3) Harihara II, son of (2)	1379
(4) Bukka II, son of (3)	1406
(5) Deva Rāya I, son of (3)	1406
(6) Vijaya-Bukka (Vīra Vijaya), son of (5) . .	1422
(7) Deva Rāya II, son of (6)	1422
(8) Mallikārjuna, son of (7)	1446
(9) Virūpāksha II, son of (7)	1465

(xiii) TULUVA AND ĀRAVĪDU KINGS OF VIJAYANAGAR

	A.D.
(1) Narasa Nāyaka, son of Īsvara	1473
(2) Vīra Narasimha, son of (1)	1505
(3) Krishnadeva Rāya, son of (1)	1508
(4) Achyuta Rāya, half-brother of (3) . . .	1530
(5) Venkata I, son of (4)	1542
(6) Sadāshiva, cousin of (5)	1542
(7) Rāma Rāya, son of Ranga I, Āravīdu family	1542
(8) Tirumala, brother of (7)	1565
(9) Ranga II, son of (8)	1570
(10) Venkata II, son of (8)	1586
(11) Ranga III, nephew of (10)	1614

(xiv) RĀNĀS OF MEWĀR

		A.D.
(1)	Hamīr, son of Ari Simha	
(2)	Kshetra Simha, son of (1)	c. 1364
(3)	Laksha, son of (2)	c. 1382
(4)	Mokala, son of (3)	c. 1418
(5)	Kumbha, son of (4)	c. 1430
(6)	Udaya Karan, son of (5)	1469
(7)	Rāyamalla, son of (5)	1474
(8)	Sangrāma (Sangā) I, son of (7)	1509
(9)	Ratna Simha, son of (8)	1527
(10)	Bikramājit, son of (8)	1532
(11)	Ranbīr, nephew of (8)	1535
(12)	Udaya Smha, son of (8)	1537
(13)	Pratāpa Simha I, son of (12)	1572
(14)	Amara Simha I, son of (13)	1597
(15)	Karan, son of (14)	1620
(16)	Jagat Simha, son of (15)	1628
(17)	Rāja Simha I, son of (16)	1652
(18)	Jay Simha, son of (17)	1680
(19)	Amara Simha II, son of (18)	1699
(20)	Sangrāma Simha II, son of (19)	1711
(21)	Jagat Simha II, son of (20)	1734
(22)	Pratāpa Simha II, son of (21)	1752
(23)	Rāja Simha II, son of (22)	1754
(24)	Ari Simha II, son of (21)	1761
(25)	Hamīr II, son of (23)	1773
(26)	Bhīm Simha, son of (23)	1778
(27)	Jawān Simha, son of (25)	1828
(28)	Sardār Simha, adopted son of (26)	1838
(29)	Sarūp Simha, adopted brother	1842
(30)	Shambhu, adopted nephew	1861
(31)	Sujān Simha, first cousin	1874
(32)	Fateh Simha	1884
(33)	Bhopāl Simha, son of (31)	1930

(xv) BHONSLĀS (CHHATRAPATI)

		A.D.			A.D.
(1)	Shivājī I, son of Shāhjī	1674	(5)	Shāhū, son of (2)	1708
(2)	Shambhūjī, son of (1)	1680	(6)	Rām Rāja, grandson of (4)	1749
(3)	Rājarām, brother of (2)	1689	(7)	Shāhū, son of (6)	1777
(4)	Tārā Bāī, widow of (3)	1700	(8)	Pratāp Singh, son of (7)	1810

(xvi) THE PESHWĀS

		A.D.
(1)	Bālājī Viswanāth, son of Viswanāth	1714
(2)	Bājī Rāo I, son of (1)	1720
(3)	Bālājī Bājī Rāo, son of (2)	1740
(4)	Mādhava Rāo Ballāl, son of (3)	1761
(5)	Nārāyan Rāo, son of (3)	1772
(6)	Raghunāth Rāo (Raghobā), son of (2)	1773
(7)	Mādhava Rāo Nārāyan, son of (5)	1774
(8)	Bājī Rāo II, son of (6)	1796-1818

(xvii) THE GĀIKWĀR FAMILY

		A.D.			A.D.
(1)	Pilājī, son of Jhingojī, brother of Dāmājī I.	1721	(4)	Sayājī Rāo I, son of (2)	1771
(2)	Dāmājī II, son of (1)	1732	(5)	Fateh Singh, son of (2)	1771
(3)	Govind Rāo, son of (2)	1768	(6)	Mānājī, son of (2)	1789
			(7)	Govind Rāo, son of (2)	1793

(xvii) THE GĀIKWĀR FAMILY (*continued*)

	A.D.		A.D.
(8) Ānand Rāo, son of (7)	1800	(12) Malhār Rāo, son of (9)	1870
(9) Sayājī Rāo II, son of (7)	1818	(13) Sayājī Rāo III, adopted son	1875
(10) Ganpat Rāo, son of (9)	1847		
(11) Khande Rāo, son of (9)	1856		

(xviii) THE HOLKAR FAMILY

	A.D.
(1) Malhār Rāo Holkar, son of 'Cundajee' (Khandājī)	1728
(2) Ahalyā Bāī, wife of Khande Rāo, son of (1)	1765
(3) Tukojī I	1795
(4) Jaswant Rāo I, son of (3)	1798
(5) Malhār Rāo II, son of (4)	1811
(6) Hari Rāo	1834
(7) Tukojī Rāo II, son of (6)	1843
(8) Shivājī Rāo, son of (7)	1886
(9) Tukojī Rāo III, son of (8)	1903
(10) Jaswant Rāo II, son of (9)	1926–

(xix) THE SINDHIĀ FAMILY

	A.D.		A.D.
(1) Mādhava Rāo (Mahādājī) Sindhiā, son of Ranojī (died 1750)	1761	(3) Jankojī Rāo, son of (2)	1827
(2) Daulat Rāo Sindhiā	1794	(4) Jayājī Rāo, son of (3)	1843
		(5) Mādhava Rāo II, son of (4)	1886
		(6) Jīvājī Rāo, son of (5)	1925

(xx) MAHĀRĀJA RANJĪT SINGH'S FAMILY

	A.D.		A.D.
(1) Nodh Singh, son of Budh Singh	1716	(5) Kharak Singh, son of (4)	1839
(2) Charrat Singh, son of (1)	1752	(6) Nao Nehāl Singh, son of (5)	1840
(3) Mahān Singh, son of (2)	1774	(7) Shēr Singh, son of (4)	1841
(4) Ranjīt Singh, son of (3)	1792	(8) Dalīp Singh, son of (4)	1843–9

II. MUSLIM DYNASTIES

(i) THE GHAZNAVIDS

	A.H.		A.D.
(1)	366	Sabuktigīn, slave of Alptigīn	976
(2)	387	Ismā'īl, son of (1)	997
(3)	388	Mahmūd, son of (1)	998
(4)	421	Muhammad, son of (3)	1030
(5)	421	Mas'ūd I, son of (3)	1030
(6)	432	Maudūd, son of (5)	1040
(7)	440	Mas'ūd II, son of (6)	1048
(8)	440	Bahā-ud-dīn Alī, son of (5)	1048
(9)	444	Abdur Rashīd, son of (3)	1052
(10)	444	Tughril (usurper)	1052
(11)	444	Farrukhzād, son of (5)	1053
(12)	451	Ibrāhīm, son of (5)	1059
(13)	492	Mas'ūd III, son of (12)	1099
(14)	508	Shērzād, son of (13)	1114
(15)	509	Arslān Shāh, son of (13)	1115
(16)	512	Bahrām Shāh, son of (13)	1118
(17)	547	Khusrau Shāh, son of (16)	1152
(18)	555–82	Khusrau Malik, son of (17)	1160–86

(ii) THE RULERS OF GHŪR

A.H.		A.D.
–	Qutb-ud-dīn	–
543	Saif-ud-dīn Sūrī	1148
544	‘Alā-ud-dīn Husain (the Jahānsūz)	1149
556	Saif-ud-dīn Muhammad	1161
558	Ghiyās-ud-dīn Muhammad	1163
569	Mu‘izz-ud-dīn Muhammad Ghūrī	1174

(iii) KINGS OF DELHI

1. ‘*Slave Dynasty*’

	A.H.		A.D.
(1)	602	Qutb-ud-dīn Aibak, slave of Mu‘izz-ud-dīn Muhammad Ghūrī	1206
(2)	607	Ārām (adopted son)	1210
(3)	607	Shams-ud-dīn Iltutmish, slave of (1)	1211
(4)	633	Rukn-ud-dīn Fīrūz Shāh, son of (3)	1236
(5)	634	Raziyyat-ud-dīn, daughter of (3)	1236
(6)	637	Mu‘izz-ud-dīn Bahrām, son of (3)	1240
(7)	639	‘Alā-ud-dīn Mas‘ūd, son of (4)	1242
(8)	644	Nāsir-ud-dīn Mahmūd, son of (3)	1246
(9)	664	Ghiyās-ud-dīn Balban, father-in-law of (8)	1266
(10)	686–9	Mu‘izz-ud-dīn Kaiqubād, grandson of (9)	1287–90

2. *The Khaljī Sultāns*

	A.H.		A.D.
(1)	689	Jalāl-ud-dīn Fīrūzshāh	1290
(2)	695	Rukn-ud-dīn Ibrāhīm, son of (1)	1296
(3)	695	‘Alā-ud-dīn Sikandar Sānī Muhammad Shāh, nephew of (1)	1296
(4)	715	Shihāb-ud-dīn ‘Umar, son of (3)	1316
(5)	716	Qutb-ud-dīn Mubārak, son of (3)	1316
(6)	720	Nāsir-ud-dīn Khusrau, slave of (5)	1320

3. *The House of Tughluq*

	A.H.		A.D.
(1)	720	Ghiyās-ud-dīn Tughluq Shāh I, slave of Balban	1320
(2)	725	Muhammad Ibn Tughluq, son of (1)	1325
(3)	752	Fīrūz Shāh III, nephew of (1)	1351
(4)	790	Ghiyās-ud-dīn Tughluq II, grandson of (3)	1388
(5)	791	Abū Bakr, grandson of (3)	1389
(6)	792	Nāsir-ud-dīn Muhammad Shāh, son of (3)	1390
(7)	795	‘Alā-ud-dīn Sikandar (Humāyūn Khān), son of (6)	1394
(8)	795	Nusrat Shāh, disputed succession 1395, died 1398 or 1399, grandson of (3)	1394
(9)	795–816	Mahmūd Shāh, son of (6)	1394–1413

4. *The Sayyids*

	A.H.		A.D.
(1)	817	Khizr Khān	1414
(2)	824	Mu‘izz-ud-dīn Mubārak, son of (1)	1421
(3)	838	Muhammad Shāh, grandson of (1)	1434
(4)	849	‘Alā-ud-dīn ‘Ālam Shāh, son of (3)	1445

5. *The Lodīs*

	A.H.		A.D.
(1)	855	Bahlūl Lodī	1451
(2)	894	Nizām Khān Sikandar Lodī, son of (1)	1489
(3)	923	Ibrāhīm Lodī, son of (2)	1517
(4)	932	Invasion of Bābur	1526

6. *The Sūrs*

	A.H.		A.D.
(1)	945	Shēr Shāh	1538–9
(2)	952	Islām (Salīm) Shāh, son of (1)	1545
(3)	961	Mubāriz Khān Muhammad 'Ādil Shāh, nephew of (1)	1554
(4)	962	Ibrāhīm Shāh, cousin of (1)	1555
(5)	962	Ahmad Khān Sikandar Shāh, cousin of (1)	1555
	962	Mughal conquest	1555

7. *The Mughal Emperors*

	A.H.		A.D.
(1)	932	Zāhir-ud-dīn Bābur	1526
(2)	937	Muhammad Humāyūn, son of (1)	1530
(3)	963	Jalāl-ud-dīn Akbar, son of (2)	1556
(4)	1014	Nūr-ud-dīn Muhammad Jahāngīr, son of (3)	1605
(5)	1037	Dāvar Bakhsh, grandson of (4)	1627
(6)	1037	Khurram Shihāb-ud-dīn Muhammad, Shāh Jahān, son of (4)	1628
(7)	1068	Murād Bakhsh, son of (6)	1657
(8)	1068	Shāh Shujā, son of (6)	1657
(9)	1068	Muhyi-ud-dīn Muhammad Aurangzīb 'Ālamgīr, son of (6)	1658
(10)	1118	'Azam Shāh, son of (9)	1707
(11)	1119	Kām Bakhsh, son of (9)	1707
(12)	1119	Mu'azzam Shāh 'Ālam I, Bahādur Shāh I, son of (9)	1707
(13)	1124	'Azīm-ush-Shān, son of (12)	1712
(14)	1124	Mu'izz-ud-dīn Jahāndar Shāh, son of (12)	1712
(15)	1124	Muhammad Farrukhsiyar, grandson of (12)	1713
(16)	1131	Rafī-'ud-darajāt, grandson of (12)	1719
(17)	1131	Rafī-'ud-daulah, Shāh Jahān II, grandson of (12)	1719
(18)	1131	Muhammad Shāh, grandson of (12)	1719
(19)	1132	[Muhammad Ibrāhīm, grandson of (12)]	1720
(20)	1161	Ahmad Shāh, son of (18)	1748
(21)	1167	'Azīz-ud-dīn 'Ālamgīr II, son of (14)	1754
(22)	1173	Shāh Jahān III, great grandson of (9)	1759
(23)	1173	Mīrzā 'Abdullah 'Alī Gohar, Shāh 'Ālam II, son of (21)	1759
(24)	1202	[Bīdār Bakht, son of (20)]	1788
(25)	1221	Akbar Shāh II, son of (23)	1806
(26)	1253–76	Bahādur Shāh II, son of (25)	1837–58

(iv) KINGS OF BENGAL

1. *Eastern Bengal*

A.H.		A.D.
737	Fakhr-ud-dīn Mubārak Shāh	1336
747–53	Ikhtiyār-ud-dīn Ghāzī Shāh	1346–52

2. *Western Bengal and all Bengal*

A.H.		A.D.
740	'Alā-ud-dīn 'Alī Shāh	1339
746	Hājī Shams-ud-dīn Ilyās Shāh, Bhangārā	1345
759	Sikandar Shāh	1357
796	Ghiyās-ud-dīn 'Azam Shāh	1393
813	Saif-ud-dīn Hamza Shāh	1410
815	Shihāb-ud-dīn Bāyazīd	1412
817	Ganesh of Bhātūriā	1414
817	Jadu, alias Jalāl-ud-dīn Muhammad Shāh	1414
820	Danuja-mardana	1417
821	Mahendra	1418
835	Shams-ud-dīn Ahmad Shāh	1431
846	Nāsir-ud-dīn Mahmūd Shāh	1442
865	Rukn-ud-dīn Bārbak Shāh	1460
879	Shams-ud-dīn Yūsuf Shāh	1474
886	Sikandar Shāh II	1481
886	Jalāl-ud-dīn Fath Shāh	1481
892	Bārbak the Eunuch, Sultān Shāhzāda	1486
892	Malik Indīl, Fīrūz Shāh	1486
895	Nāsir-ud-dīn Mahmūd Shāh II	1489
896	Sīdī Badr, Shams-ud-dīn Muzaffar Shāh	1490
899	Sayyid 'Alā-ud-dīn Husain Shāh	1493
925	Nasīr-ud-dīn Nusrat Shāh	1518
940	'Alā-ud-dīn Fīrūz Shāh	1533
940	Ghiyās-ud-dīn Mahmūd Shāh	1533
946	Humāyūn, Emperor of Delhi	1538
946	Shēr Shāh Sūr	1539
947	Khizr Khān	1540
952	Muhammad Khān Sūr	1545
962	Khizr Khān, Bahādur Shāh	1555
968	Ghiyās-ud-dīn Jalāl Shāh	1561
971	Tāj Khān Kararānī	1564
980	Sulaimān Kararānī	1572
980	Bāyazīd Khān Kararānī	1572
980–4	Dāūd Khān Kararānī	1572–6
984	Annexed by Akbar	1576

(V) KINGS OF MĀLWA

1. *Ghūrīs*

	A.H.		A.D.
(1)	794	Dilāwar Khān Ghūrī	1392
(2)	808	Hūshang Shāh, son of (1)	1405
(3)	838	Muhammad, son of (2)	1435
(4)	839	Ma'ūd	1436

2. *Khaljīs*

	A.H.		A.D.
(1)	839	Mahmūd I Khaljī	1436
(2)	873	Ghiyās, son of (1)	1469
(3)	905	Nāsir, son of (2)	1500
(4)	916	Mahmūd II, son of (3)	1510
	937	Annexed by Gujarāt	1531

(vi) KINGS OF GUJARĀT

	A.H.		A.D.
(1)	798	Zafar Khān, Muzaffar I	1396
(2)	814	Ahmad I, grandson of (1)	1411
(3)	846	Muhammad Karīm, son of (2)	1442
(4)	855	Qutb-ud-dīn Ahmad, son of (3)	1451
(5)	862	Dāūd, son of (2)	1458
(6)	862	Mahmūd I, Begath, son of (3)	1458
(7)	917	Muzaffar II, son of (6)	1511
(8)	932	Sikandar, son of (7)	1526
(9)	932	Nāsir Khān Mahmūd II, son of (7)	1526
(10)	932	Bahādur, son of (7)	1526
(11)	943	Mīrān Muhammad, grandson of (7)	1537
(12)	943	Mahmūd III, grandson of (7)	1537
(13)	961	Ahmad II	1554
(14)	967	Muzaffar III, son of (12)	1562
	980	Annexed by Akbar	1572

(vii) KINGS OF KHĀNDESH

A.H.		A.D.	A.H.		A.D.
784	Malik Rāja	1382	926	Mīrān Muhammad	1520
801	Malik Nāsir	1399	943	Ahmad Shāh	1537
840	'Ādil Khān I	1437	943	Mīrān Mubārak II	1537
844	Mubārak Khān	1441	974	Mīrān Muhammad II	1566
861	'Ādil Khān II	1457	984	Hasan Shāh	1576
907	Dāūd	1501	985	'Alī Khān	1577–8
914	Ghaznī Khān	1508	1006	Bahādur Shāh	1597
914	Hasan Khān	1508	1009	Annexed by Akbar	1601
914	'Ādil Khān III	1509			

(viii) THE SHARQĪ KINGS OF JAUNPŪR

	A.H.		A.D.		A.H.		A.D.
(1)	796	Khwāja-i-Jahān	1394	(5)	862	Muhammad, son of (4)	1458
(2)	802	Mubārak, adopted son of (1)	1399	(6)	862	Husain, son of (4)	1458
(3)	804	Ibrāhīm, son of (2)	1402		881	Annexed by Delhi	1477
(4)	840	Mahmūd, son of (3)	1436				

(ix) BAHMANĪ KINGS OF THE DECCAN

	A.H.		A.D.
(1)	748	'Alā-ud-dīn Hasan Bahman Shāh	1347
(2)	759	Muhammad I, son of (1)	1358
(3)	776	Mujāhid, son of (2)	1375
(4)	779	Dāūd, son of (1)	1378
(5)	780	Muhammad II, son of (1)	1378
(6)	799	Ghiyās-ud-dīn, son of (5)	1397
(7)	799	Shams-ud-dīn, son of (5)	1397
(8)	800	Fīrūz, son of (4)	1397
(9)	825	Ahmad I, son of (4)	1422
(10)	839	'Alā-ud-dīn Ahmad II, son of (9)	1436
(11)	862	Humāyūn, son of (10)	1458
(12)	865	Nizām, son of (11)	1461
(13)	867	Muhammad III, son of (11)	1463
(14)	887	Mahmūd, son of (13)	1482
(15)	924	Ahmad III, son of (14)	1518
(16)	927	'Alā-ud-dīn, son of (14)	1521
(17)	928	Walī-ullāh, son of (14)	1522
(18)	931–4	Kalīm-ullāh, son of (15)	1525–7

(x) SULTĀNATES OF THE DECCAN

1. *The 'Imād Shāhīs of Berār*

A.H.		A.D.	A.H.		A.D.
895	Fath Allāh . . .	1490	970	Burhān.	1562
910	'Alā-ud-dīn . . .	1504	976–82	Tufāl (usurper) . .	1568–7
937	Daryā.	1529			

2. *The Nizām Shāhī Dynasty of Ahmadnagar*

	A.H.		A.D.		A.H.		A.D.
(1)	895	Malik Ahmad, son of Nizām-ul-mulk Bahrī	1490	(6)	997	Ismā'īl . . .	1589
(2)	915	Burhān, son of (1).	1509	(7)	999	Burhān II . .	1591
(3)	960	Husain, son of (2) .	1553	(8)	1002	Ibrāhīm . . .	1595
(4)	973	Murtazā Shāh I, son of (3) . . .	1565	(9)	1004	Bahādur . . .	1596
(5)	995	Mīrān Husain . .	1586	(10)	1004	(Ahmad II) . .	1596
				(11)	1012	Murtazā Shāh II	1603
				(12)	1040–43	Husain Shāh II .	1630–33

3. *The Barīd Shāhī Dynasty of Bīdar*

A.H.		A.D.	A.H.		A.D.
894	Qāsim I	1487	994	Qāsim II	1586
910	Amīr I	1504	999	Amīr Barīd Shāh . .	1589
949	'Alī	1542	1010	Mīrzā 'Alī	1601
987	Ibrāhīm	1579	1018	'Alī Barīd Shāh . .	1609

4. *The 'Ādil Shāhī Dynasty of Bijāpur*

	A.H.		A.D.		A.H.		A.D.
(1)	895	Yūsuf 'Ādil Khān .	1490	(7)	1037	Muhammad . .	1627
(2)	916	Ismā'īl, son of (1) .	1510	(8)	1068	'Alī II . . .	1657
(3)	941	Mallū, son of (2) .	1534	(9)	1083	Sikandar . . .	1672
(4)	941	Ibrāhīm, son of (2).	1534	(10)	1097	Annexed by Aurangzīb . .	1686
(5)	965	'Alī, son of (4) . .	1558				
(6)	988	Ibrāhīm II, nephew of (5)	1580				

5. *The Qutb Shāhī Dynasty of Golkundā*

	A.H.		A.D.		A.H.		A.D.
(1)	918	Qulī Shāh . . .	1512	(6)	1020	Muhammad Qutb Shāh . . .	1612
(2)	950	Jamshīd, son of (1)	1543	(7)	1035	'Abdullah . . .	1626
(3)	957	Subhān Qulī . .	1550	(8)	1083–98	Abul Hasan Qutb Shāh .	1672–87
(4)	957	Ibrāhīm, brother of (2).	1550				
(5)	988	Muhammad Qulī Qutb Shāh . .	1580				

(xi) NAWĀBS OF OUDH

	A.H.		A.D.
(1)	1137	Sa'ādat Khān, son of Mīr Muhammad Nāsir . .	1724
(2)	1152	Safdar Jang, nephew of (1)	1739
(3)	1168	Shujā-ud-daula, son of (2)	1754
(4)	1189	Āsaf-ud-daula, son of (3)	1775
(5)	1212	Wazīr 'Alī, son of (4)	1797
(6)	1213	Sa'ādat 'Alī	1798
(7)	1230	Ghāzī-ud-dīn Haidar, son of (6)	1814
(8)	1243	Nāsir-ud-dīn Haidar, son of (7)	1827
(9)	1253	'Alī Shāh, son of (6)	1837
(10)	1258	Amjad 'Alī Shāh, son of (9)	1842
(11)	1264	Wājid 'Alī Shāh, son of (10)	1847
	1273	Oudh annexed by the East India Company . .	1856

(xii) NAWĀBS OF ARCOT

	A.H.		A.D.
(1)	1102	Zulfiqār Alī Khān	1690
(2)	1115	Dāūd Khān	1703
(3)	1122	Muhammad Sayyid Sa'ādat-ullāh Khān I	1710
(4)	1145	Dost 'Alī Khān, nephew of (3)	1732
(5)	1153	Safdar 'Alī Khān, son of (4)	1740
(6)	1155	Sa'ādat-ullāh Khān II, son of (5)	1742
(7)	1157	Anwār-ud-dīn Muhammad	1744
(8)	1163	Walā Jāh, Muhammad 'Alī, son of (7)	1749
(9)	1210	'Umdat-ul-Umarā, son of (8)	1795
(10)	1216	'Azīm-ud-daula, nephew of (9)	1801
(11)	1235	'Azam Jāh, son of (10)	1819
(12)	1284–91	'Azīm Jāh Bahādur, son of (10)	1867–74

(xiii) NAWĀBS OF BENGAL

	A.H.		A.D.
(1)	1115	Murshid Qulī Ja'far Khān	1703
(2)	1140	Shujā-ud-dīn, son-in-law of (1)	1727
(3)	1152	Sarfarāz Khān, son of (2)	1739
(4)	1153	Ilah-vardī Khān	1740
(5)	1170	Sirāj-ud-daula, grandson of (4)	1756
(6)	1171	Mīr Ja'far	1757
(7)	1174	Mīr Qāsim, son-in-law of (6)	1760
(8)	1177	Mīr Ja'far	1763
(9)	1179	Najm-ud-daula, son of (6)	1765
(10)	1180–1184	Saif-ud-daula, son of (6)	1766–70

(xiv) NIZĀMS OF HYDERABAD

	A.H.		A.D.
(1)	1137	Mīr Qamar-ud-dīn, Nizām-ul-mulk Āsaf Jāh	1724
(2)	1161	Mīr Muhammad Nāsir Jang, son of (1)	1748
(3)	1164	Muzaffar Jang	1750
(4)	1164	Mīr Āsaf-ud-daula Salābat Jang, son of (1)	1751
(5)	1175	Nizām 'Alī, son of (1)	1762
(6)	1217	Mīr Akbar 'Alī Khān Sikandar Jāh, son of (5)	1802
(7)	1245	Nāsir-ud-daula, son of (6)	1829
(8)	1274	Afzal-ud-daula, son of (7)	1857
(9)	1286	Mīr Mahbūb 'Alī Khān, son of (8)	1869
(10)	1330–	Mīr 'Usmān 'Alī Khān Bahādur Fath Jang, son of (9)	1911–

(xv) AMĪRS OF AFGHĀNISTĀN

1. *The Durrānī Shāhs*

	A.H.		A.D.
(1)	1160	Ahmad Shāh, Durrānī	1747
(2)	1187	Timūr Shāh, son of (1)	1773
(3)	1207	Zamān Shāh, son of (2)	1793
(4)	1215	Mahmūd, son of (2)	1800
(5)	1218	Shujā, son of (2)	1803
(6)	1224	Mahmūd, son of (2)	1809
(7)	1234	Ayyūb, son of (2)	1818

2. *Barakzāi Wazīrs and Amīrs*

	A.H.		A.D.
(1)	1160	Jamāl Khān, Barakzāi	1747
(2)	1187	Pāyinda Khān, son of (1)	1773
(3)	1215	Fath Khān, son of (2)	1800
(4)	1242	Dost Muhammad Khān, Amīr of Kabul, son of (2)	1826
(5)	1280	Shēr 'Alī, son of (4)	1863
(6)	1296	Yaqūb Khān, son of (5)	1879
(7)	1297	'Abd-ar-Rahmān, grandson of (4)	1880
(8)	1319	Habīb-ullah, son of (7)	1901
	1338	Amān-ullah, son of (8)	1919
	1352–	Muhammad Zahīr Shāh	1933–

III. GOVERNORS-GENERAL

(i) GOVERNORS-GENERAL OF FORT WILLIAM IN BENGAL

(Regulating Act of 1773)

The names of those temporary and officiating are in italics

1774 (20 October)	Warren Hastings
1785 (8 February)	*Sir John Macpherson*
1786 (12 September)	Earl (Marquess) Cornwallis
1793 (28 October)	Sir John Shore (Lord Teignmouth)
1798 (17 March)	*Sir A. Clarke*
1798 (18 May)	Earl of Mornington (Marquess Wellesley)
1805 (30 July)	Marquess Cornwallis (for the second time)
1805 (10 October)	*Sir George Barlow*
1807 (30 July)	Baron (Earl of) Minto I
1813 (4 October)	Earl of Moira (Marquess of Hastings)
1823 (13 January)	*John Adam*
1823 (1 August)	Baron (Earl) Amherst
1828 (13 March)	*William Butterworth Bayley*
1828 (4 July)	Lord William Cavendish-Bentinck

(ii) GOVERNORS-GENERAL OF INDIA

(Charter Act of 1833)

The names of those temporary and officiating are in italics

1834 (16 June)	Lord William Cavendish-Bentinck
1835 (20 March)	*Sir Charles (Lord) Metcalfe*
1836 (4 March)	Baron (Earl of) Auckland
1842 (28 February)	Baron (Earl of) Ellenborough
1844 (15 June)	*William Wilberforce Bird*
1844 (23 July)	Sir Henry (Viscount) Hardinge
1848 (12 January)	Earl (Marquess) of Dalhousie
1856 (29 February)	Viscount (Earl) Canning

(iii) GOVERNORS-GENERAL AND VICEROYS

(Government of India Act, 1858)

The names of those temporary and officiating are in italics

1858 (1 November)	Viscount (Earl) Canning
1862 (12 March)	Earl of Elgin and Kincardine I
1863 (21 November)	*Sir Robert Napier (Baron Napier of Magdala)*
1863 (2 December)	*Sir William T. Denison*
1864 (12 January)	Sir John (Lord) Lawrence
1869 (12 January)	Earl of Mayo
1872 (9 February)	*Sir John Strachey*
1872 (23 February)	*Lord Napier of Merchistoun*

(iii) GOVERNORS-GENERAL AND VICEROYS (*continued*)

1872 (3 May)	Baron (Earl of) Northbrook
1876 (12 April)	Baron (Earl of) Lytton I
1880 (8 June)	Marquess of Ripon
1884 (13 December)	Earl of Dufferin (Marquess of Dufferin and Ava)
1888 (10 December)	Marquess of Lansdowne
1894 (20 January)	Earl of Elgin and Kincardine II
1899 (6 January)	Baron (Earl) Curzon of Kedleston
1904 (30 April)	*Lord Ampthill*
1904 (13 December)	Baron (Marquess) Curzon of Kedleston (re-appointed)
1905 (18 November)	Earl of Minto II
1910 (23 November)	Baron Hardinge of Penshurst
1916 (4 April)	Baron Chelmsford
1921 (2 April)	Earl of Reading
1925 (10 April)	*Lord Lytton II*
1925 (6 August)	Earl of Reading
1926 (3 April)	Lord Irwin
1929 (29 June)	*Lord Goschen*
1931 (18 April)	Earl of Willingdon
1934 (16 May-August)	*Sir George Stanley*
1936 (18 April)	Marquess of Linlithgow
1943 (20 October)	Earl Wavell
1947 (24 March to 15 August)	Viscount Mountbatten

SECTION III

SOUTH-EAST ASIA AND THE ARCHIPELAGO

1. (i) The romanization of Burmese, Siamese and Malayan words.
   (ii) The French system of romanization.
2. Personal names and titles.
3. Place-names :
   (i) Burma. (ii) Siam. (iii) Malaya and Indonesia.
4. Select glossary.
5. Calendars and systems of dating.
6. Dynasties and rulers.
   (i) Kings of Burma. (ii) Kings of Arakan. (iii) Kings of Siam. (iv) Rulers of Java (*a.* Hindu Period; *b.* Muslim Period). (v) Mohammedan Sultans of Atjeh (Achin) in Sumatra. (vi) Sultans of Palembang in Sumatra. (vii) Governors-General of the Netherlands East Indies. (viii) The Khmer Kingdom of Cambodia. (ix) Kingdom of Lang-Xang or Luang Prabang. (x) Kings of Champa. (xi) Kings of Annam and Tongking. (xii) Governors and Governors-General of French Indo-China.

(i) THE ROMANIZATION OF BURMESE, SIAMESE AND MALAYAN WORDS

There is no exact and scientific system, especially in the case of Burmese and Siamese. The one in general use in English works to-day is called the Hunterian; it has roughly Italian values for vowels and English ones for consonants. It aims at indicating an approximation to the actual pronunciation of the words, not necessarily the spelling in the original language. From the philological point of view this may be somewhat unsatisfactory, since in the case of Siamese in particular the many words of Sanskrit or Pali origin have considerably changed their pronunciation in modern times.

The system of phonetic romanization has for many years been a hotly debated matter in Siam, and the last word has not yet been said. The most recent contribution to the subject is to be found in the introduction to the late G. B. McFarland's *Thai-English Dictionary* (London, 1944); though, as he was an American, the value of his representations of certain vowel sounds is questioned by English scholars. For further discussion of this thorny problem reference may be made to the *Journals of the Siam Society*, vols. iii (part 2), iv (part 1), ix (parts 3 and 4), x (part 4), xxvi, xxviii and xxxiii (part 1). In vol. xxvi (1933) are set forth the findings of a Royal Commission appointed to investigate the subject. A useful guide is Glossary No. 6, *Thai (Siamese)*, published by the Royal Geographical Society for the Permanent Committee on Geographical Names for British Official Use, and prepared by the Rev. H. S. O'Neill.

The Hunterian System was prescribed by the Government of Burma in *Tables for the Transliteration of Burmese into English* (Rangoon, 1908). A more easily obtainable vade-mecum is the *Short Glossary of Burmese*, published by the War Office in January 1945. Long before 1908, in fact, conventions approximating to the present system had been growing up. They may be traced by comparing Appendix M. (pp. 381–91) of Yule's *Narrative of the Mission to the Court of Ava in 1855* (London, 1858) with the first edition of Taw Sein Ko's *Elementary Handbook of the Burmese Language* (Rangoon, 1898), where the system was in all essentials fully fledged. For the method used by most writers at the beginning of the 19th century—e.g. in Adoniram Judson's Dictionary—there is a useful glossary in Symes's *Account of an Embassy to the Kingdom of Ava in 1795* (London, 1800), pp. 501–3. Another work of the same period, Father Sangermano's *Description of the Burmese Empire*, the English translation of which by William Tandy was published in Rome in 1833, employs an orthography invented by the writer and based upon Italian values.

The languages of Indo-China were all in their original forms monosyllabic; hence intonation is part of the meaning of words. Save in linguistic works, however, tonal signs are not used in transliteration. In words of more than one syllable, with the exception of imported words, each syllable represents a word, and the correct pronunciation of the combination may present formidable difficulties to readers unfamiliar with the language, since they cannot always tell where one syllable ends and the next begins. The spread of Hindu and Buddhist civilization throughout much of Indo-China at an early date has given its languages a vast number of Pali and many Sanskrit words. And not only has the pronunciation of these changed through the process of assimilation, but in the case of Siamese their spelling has been considerably simplified during the past half-century or so. No assistance can be given here in dealing with such problems as these: it would involve going into technical details beyond the needs (and the patience) of the ordinary reader.

While Burmese and Siamese borrowed alphabets of Indian origin, the Malay peoples, on being converted to Islam, adopted Arabic characters, with certain conventions, to represent the sounds of their language. The old Dutch method of romanization reproduced the Arabic letters in Roman equivalents. The modern phonetic system aims at reproducing the actual pronunciation.

As already mentioned, modern romanized Burmese, Malay and Siamese gave Italian values to the five vowels. Those in closed syllables are short; in open ones in Malay they may be either long or short. The Burmese carefully distinguish between the *e* acute and the *e* grave as in French. In modern transliteration the grave accent is usually employed, but rarely the acute. Older writers tend to render both vowels indiscriminately by *ay*, *ey* and *eh*.

Neither Burmese nor Siamese has any distinctive sign for the neutral vowel. In Malay it is represented by *ĕ*. Some old writers used *a* for the purpose. Crawfurd, in his *History of the Indian Archipelago* (1820) and *Descriptive Dictionary of the Indian Islands and Adjacent Countries* (1856), used *â*. Marsden, *Grammar of the Malayan Language* (1812), and older Dutch writers used simply *e*. The missionary press in Singapore sometimes omitted any vowel, or inserted ʼ or ʹ. Thus there are the following spellings of the same word: bassar, bâsar, besar, bsar, bʼsar, bʹsar and bĕsar.

All three languages have the two diphthongs *ai*, pronounced *i* as in *light*, and *au*, pronounced *ow* as in *cow*. The latter is sometimes spelt *ou* in Burmese. In addition, Burmese has *ei*, pronounced *ay* as in *away*, and Shan has *oi*, pronounced as in *boil*.

In the pronunciation of consonants the following special points should be noted:

(1) In all three languages *ng* at the beginning of a syllable is pronounced like the final *ng* in *sing*.

(2) The Burmese final *n* represents a nasalization of the preceding vowel sound; hence older writers usually transliterate it by *ng*; e.g. *Aeng* in Yule's map, for the An Pass between Burma and Arakan.

(3) Modern Burmese has no *r* sound. Old Burmese used it freely

and it still survives in Arakanese. During the 18th century the Burmese began to change it to *y*; e.g. *Mranma* (Burma) became *Myanma*. But even by the end of the century the change was incomplete, and the old spelling is still found in some European works. Thus both Symes and Sangermano spell *Sayedawgyi* (royal secretary), *yahan* (monk), *yon* (court-house) and *ywa* (village), *Seredohgry, rahan, rhoom* and *rua*.

(4) Both Burmese and Siamese in common with others of the Indo-Chinese group have two main classes of guttural, palatal, labial and dental consonants, the unaspirated and the aspirated. In transliterating Burmese the modern practice is to indicate the aspirated consonant by placing *h* before it. In Siamese it is often represented by the addition of *h* after the consonant; e.g. *phya, thien*. But, as this misleads people into pronouncing such combinations as in English, writers now prefer to indicate the aspirate by an apostrophe; e.g. *p'ya, t'ien*.

(5) Since both Burmese and Siamese have considerably more consonants than the Roman alphabet—Burmese has thirty-two, Siamese forty-four—it is impossible to represent in Roman characters those that are in effect slightly different intonations of some basic consonant, e.g. *kh* with six different variations in Siamese and *t* with no less than eight.

(6) In romanized Siamese *ch* usually stands for two classes of sounds, one soft like *j*, the other hard like *tch* in *pitch*. Some writers distinguish between them by using *j* to represent the soft sound, except in the names of well-known places such as Chiengmai and Chiengsen, the spellings of which have become established by long usage. French writers use *x* to represent the sound. In the case of Burmese *ch* is approximately the *ch* of English *chew*. *Ky* in present-day pronunciation of Burmese is the same sound made with the tip of the tongue held against the lower teeth, *gy* is the *j* of English *jam*. Symes renders *ky* by *ki* or *ke*; e.g. *kyaung* (monastery) he spells *kioum* or *keoum*.

(7) The Burmese letter rendered by *s* to-day may present difficulties to readers of older historical works. Symes transliterates it by *ch*. Thus for *sitke* (police officer), *Sagaing* (place-name) and *Sawbwa* (Shan chief) he has *chekey, Chagaing* and *Chobwa*. He also uses *s* or *ss* for the letter now transliterated by *th*; e.g. Kathe (Cassay), Pathein (Persaim), Thayetmyo (Sirriapmew).

(8) In Malay a glottal stop at the end of a word after a vowel is represented by either *k* or an apostrophe. In Burmese, final *k* and *t* are both glottal stops. Hence in the past *t* has sometimes been transliterated by *k* or *ck*; e.g. Nabeck for Nabet, a village in the Sagaing district.

(9) In all three languages:

g is pronounced as in *good*, never as in *germ*,
s is pronounced as in *sister*, never as in *his*,
l is pronounced as the first *l* in *little*, not as the second,
y is a semi-vowel as in English, e.g. *yet*,
w is a semi-vowel as in English, e.g. *want*,
h is always sounded distinctly.

COMPARATIVE TABLE TO ILLUSTRATE METHODS OF ROMANIZING

BURMESE

Hunterian	*Yule*	*Sangermano*	*Symes*	*Meaning*
Alaungpaya	Alompra	Alompra	Alompra	Founder of last dynasty.
Atwinwun	Atwénwoon	Attovun	Attawoon	Wun of the Interior, i.e. palace.
Ein-she-thakin Ein-she-min	Ein-shé-men	—	EngyTeekien	Heir apparent.
Hlutdaw	Hlwot-dau	—	Lotoo	Supreme Council of State.
Hsinbyushin	Senphyoo-yen	Zempiuscien	Shembuan	Lord of the White Elephant.
Kala	Kala	—	Colar	Native of India.
Kyaung	Kyoung	—	Kioum	Monastery.
Mingyi	Mengyi	—	Mungai	'Great Ruler', title of Wungyi.
Myothugyi	Myothoogyi	Miodighi	Miouthoogee	District chieftain.
Myowun	Myowoon	—	Maywoon	Provincial governor.
Moksobomyo	Moutsho-bomyo	Mozzobomio	Monchaboo	Old name for Shwe-bo.
Paya	Phya	—	Praw	'Lord'; term applied to a pagoda.
Sayedawgyi	Tsaré-dau-gyi	—	Seree Dogee	Royal secretary.
Sawbwa	Tsaubwa	Zaboa	Chobwa	Shan chief of highest rank.
Sitké	Sitké	Zicchè	Chekey	Provincial police officer.
Talaing	Talaing	—	Talien	Burmese name for Mon people.
Thandawzin	Thandau-zen	—	Sandozien	'Royal voice announcer.'
Wundauk	Woondouk	—	Woondock	'Supporter of the burden'; Minister of second class.
Wungyi	Woongyi	Vunghi	Woongee	Minister of highest grade; 'great burden'.
Yazawin	Yazawen	Razaven	—	Court chronicle.
Yewun	Yéwoon	Ieun	Raywoon	Lieut. to Myowun, lit. 'Wun of the Water'.
Yon	Yoom	Ion	Rhoom	Court-house.
Ywa	Yuá	Ioa	Rua	Village.

Where a Malay sound lies between *o* and *u* or between *e* and *i*, modern spelling differs from older forms as shown in the following table :

Modern : *Older*	*Modern* : *Older*	*Modern* : *Older*	*Modern* : *Older*
ong : ung	ul : ol	eh : ih	ip : ep
oh : uh	up : op	ek : ik	is : es
ok : uk	us : os	ing : eng	ir : er
um : om	or : ur	im : em	it : et
un : on	ut : ot	in : en	i : e
	u : o	il : el	

The main differences between the modern phonetic and the old Dutch spelling of Malay are as follows:

Modern	*Old Dutch*
ĕ	e
u	oe
y	j
j	dj
ch	tj
kh	ch

(ii) THE FRENCH SYSTEM OF ROMANIZATION

The Latin alphabet was first applied to the Annamite language by French missionaries in the 17th century. Three or four centuries earlier the language had been reduced to writing by the adoption of Chinese characters. This form of writing is known as *chũ-nôm* (' southern characters '). In the course of time the French system, revised and simplified by missionaries early in the 19th century, became the *quõc-ngũ* (' national language '), officially recognized by the French when they annexed Tongking, Annam and Cochin China. All the other systems of writing in French Indo-China derive, like those of Burma and Siam, from Indian scripts. In applying Roman characters to them the French linguists found themselves up against the same problem as in the case of Siamese, namely the impossibility of spelling words in such a way as to satisfy at the same time the needs of philology and of pronunciation. Cambodian in particular constantly writes letters which are not pronounced. The French aim has always been to write words in such a way that they can be pronounced correctly, and the linguistic experts of the École Français de l'Extrême Orient, since its foundation at Hanoi in the year 1900, have achieved standards of phonetic perfection which make formidable demands upon the ordinary English reader called upon to tackle the bewildering variety of diacritical signs employed in modern French transliteration. The subject may best be studied in the pages of the *Bulletin de l'École Français de l'Extrême Orient à Hanoi*, notably vol. ii, for Cambodian, vol. xvii, for Lao, vol. xxxi, for Siamese, and vol. xxxviii, for Cham. The following table is offered as a useful guide to pronunciation:

VOWELS

a	open, long, as in *rare*.
ă	open, short, as in *mal*.
â	extremely closed, like *eu* in *heure*.
â̆	closed, short, like *eu* in *neuf*.
o	open, long, as in *encore*.
ŏ	open, short, as in *code*.
ô	closed, long, as in *rose*.
ô̆	closed, short, as in *sot*.
u	long, like *ou* in *cour*.
ŭ	same sound short, as in *bouc*.
u'	long, intermediate between *u* and *eu*.
ŭ'	same sound short.
o'	open, long, like *e* in *je*.
ŏ'	same sound short.
e	open, long, as in *très*.
ĕ	open, short, as in *pelle*.
ê	closed, long, as in *dé*.
ê̆	closed, short, as in *état*.
i	long, as in *rire*.
ĭ	short, as in *ville*.

DIPHTHONGS

Normally the first vowel is long and the second short.

CONSONANTS

k	as *c* in *café*.
g	hard, as in *gare*.
kh	aspirated *k*.
gh	aspirated *g*.
n	as in French.
nh	aspirated *n*.
n, ng	as in *longue*.
ngh	aspirated *ng*.
ñ	between the *gn* of *pagne* and the *ni* of *niais*.
m	as in French.
č	rather like the liquid *t* in *pitié*.
ch	aspirated *c*.
ç	between *s* (French) and *th* (English).
s	hard, as in *sot*.
š	as French *ch* or English *sh*.
z	as in French.
x	soft *ch*, almost *j*.
d	as in French.
dh, d'	aspirated *d*.
đ	like English *d*, pronounced with the tip of the tongue touching the sockets of the teeth.
t	as in French.
th, t'	aspirated *t*.
j	somewhere between the English *John* and the *di* of *diable*.
j́	like the *di* of *dieu*.
p	as in French.
ph	aspirated *p*, tending towards *f*.
f	as in French.
b	as in French.
bh	aspirated *b*.
b̆	between *p* and *b*.
r	as in French, but more vibrant.
l	as in French.
v	like English *w* or French *ou* in some cases, like *v* in others.
y	like *y* in *yole*.
h	strongly aspirated.

2. PERSONAL NAMES AND TITLES

Neither the Burmese nor the Malays use patronymics: thus girls retain their maiden names unaltered after marriage. In Burma Ma Pyaw (Miss Soft), after marriage to Maung Shwe (Mr. Gold), remains Ma Pyaw. If necessary, she will be referred to as 'Ma Pyaw wife of Maung Shwe'. Ordinary names are all Burmese, but Buddhist monks drop their Burmese names for Pali ones. The personal names of Malays are either Malay or Arabic, both classes being combined with the Arabic *bin* (son of) or *binti* (daughter of).

The Siamese adopted a system of patronymics for the first time in the reign of Rama VI (1911–25). Previously each individual was referred to by his title, of which the number has always been legion, or by his or her personal name. Rama VI permitted each family to register a clan name, based on Sanskrit. The determining factor in selecting these was usually some family tradition, so that they often refer to an exploit of some ancestor or a district with which a family has been closely connected. Except in the higher grades of society surnames are used only for official purposes. The pronunciation of these names is frequently quite different from the accepted romanized version of the original Sanskrit; hence visiting-cards printed in English may be very confusing to anyone unfamiliar with the pronunciation.

In both Burma and Siam it used to be the common practice for a child's name to be selected in accordance with its horoscope. The practice is called in Burma *Gyothin Nanthin Hmē*, 'to name according to the planet and day of the week', and consists of choosing a name beginning with one of the letters proper to the day of the week on which the child was born. The consonants are divided into groups which are assigned to the weekdays. Sunday (*Taningan-wene*) has all the vowels. The name given at birth is not necessarily retained throughout life: it may be changed before puberty as often as is desired, so long as due notice is given to all relatives and friends. Modern conditions of life, however, have introduced powerful deterrents in the shape of registers of property and, not least important, of school attendance. Hence it is, as a rule, only criminals who have more than one name.

The title corresponding to Mr. for a young man in Burma is Maung ('younger brother') placed before his name, even though Maung may be one of his names. Actually Maung Maung is quite a common name. Young men will often refer to each other by the title Ko ('elder brother'). In later life Maung gives way to U ('uncle'). The title for a girl or young woman is Ma, corresponding to Miss. This in later life is changed to Daw. There is no title corresponding to Mrs.

In Siam the ordinary term of address for a man of any age is Na-i, corresponding to the Burmese Maung. Miss in polite language is Nang-sao; familiarly it is Meh. A married woman is addressed as Nang. Old men may be familiarly addressed as P'o ('grandpa').

Malay forms of polite address, not indicating any actual relationship, are dato', to' (grandfather), nenek (grandmother), ayah, bapa (father), ĕmak (mother), abang (elder brother), kakak (elder sister), pĕnghulu (to a minor headman), che' guru (to a pundit), tuan kadli (to a priest or Mahommedan magistrate).

In Burma kings and statesmen have rarely been referred to by their personal names; in most cases these have been completely forgotten. On ascending the throne a king took a long Pali title, which was too long for convenience, and by which he was rarely referred to. In history, or in conversation, he might be referred to by the name of the appanage from which as a prince he had drawn his revenues (e.g. Thibaw Min), by some term indicating personal relationship to his successors (e.g. Bodawpaya), or by some phrase expressing some of his claims to distinction (e.g. Hsinbyushin, 'Lord of the White Elephant') or even some of his failures (e.g. Tayokpyemin, 'the king who ran away from the Chinese'). A Wungyi of the Hlutdaw might be known by name, by the name of his office or by the territorial designation or title conferred on him by the king (e.g. Kyaukmaw Mingyi). There were no hereditary titles of nobility. Burma in the days of the kings was full of titles, which varied in dignity according to the number of syllables. The social system, however, had surprisingly few grades compared with that of Siam.

In Siam, as in Burma, kings were always referred to by titles; it was not customary to use a king's personal name, and in most cases it has been completely forgotten. On succeeding to the throne each king had his title inscribed on a gold plate. Unfortunately, when Ayut'ia was destroyed by the Burmese in 1767, these were all lost, so that even the titles by which the chronicles refer to the kings of the earlier period cannot be relied upon.

It was once the common custom to give children numbers for names. The names used were Ai (one), Yi (two), Sam (three), Sai (four), Ngoa (five), Lok (six), Chet (seven), Pet (eight), Chao (nine) and Chong (ten). The Shans still use these names, but they are rarely found among the Siamese. The second king of the Ayut'ia dynasty, Boromoraja I, was named P'angoa, an archaic form of the name 'five'.

Princes of the royal family were referred to by the term Chao Nai ('Chief'), but more often by titles showing their actual rank. Thus the son of a king by a queen would be distinguished by the title Somdet Chao Fa, while the son of a king by a lady below the rank of queen would receive the title P'ra Ong Chao. Princes of these ranks on attaining manhood would be accorded one of the following titles according to rank, Krom P'aya, Krom P'ya, Krom Luang, Krom K'un or Krom Mun. Owing to the practice of polygamy the numbers of the royal family were legion, and the titles indicating the exact rank of each individual far too numerous for detailed treatment here.

There were five main grades of higher officials in order of rank, Somdet Chao P'ya, Chao P'aya, P'aya, P'ra and Luang. Below them were the members of the corps of royal pages (Mahatlek) arranged in the three grades of Chao Mun, Cha Mun and Cha. In older works the title P'aya is rendered by the now obsolete form

Ocya. The hereditary governor of a province (muang) bore the title Chao Muang. Subordinate provincial officers were ranked in the four grades, K'un, Mun, Kamnan and Pantanai.

In Malaya and Indonesia official titles are mainly Arabian or Indian, e.g. Sultan, Raja, Mufti, Haji, Sayid, Sharif, Sharifa, Wakil, etc.

Persons are addressed by a great variety of titles in order to indicate rank. The following list may be useful:

Patek, used when addressing a Raja or higher officer of state, not a European.

Tuan (master), polite address to a European, tuanku to a reigning Sultan, tuan puteri is 'princess' in literary style.

Tĕngku, ĕngku, tunku, are used in addressing a Raja. E.g. Tĕngku Besar is the title of the Crown Prince of Pahang; he is addressed as Tĕngku.

Shah Alam (sovereign of the world) and yang di-pĕrtuan (his highness) are literary forms of address to princes, as also is baginda.

Bandahara (Jav. bendara), 'lord', is a title applied to higher officers of state.

Laksamana was in former days the equivalent of Admiral.

Orangkaya, a general title for Chiefs in the Malay Peninsula.

Sĕri, the Malay form of the Indian honorific Sri.

Bĕsar (great), honorific title of a high official.

Khoja (Pers. Khwāja), a title of respect given in former times to Indian or Arab merchants.

Hamba (slave), a form of first person used by any class in addressing a superior.

In the countries forming French Indo-China kings are usually referred to in European historical works or other records by the particular European word for king, or, in the case of Annam, emperor, according to the language employed. In the countries in which Indian civilization prevailed at an early date a large number of titles derived from Sanskrit or Pali were used to designate the royal person; some of them appear from time to time in official correspondence. Thus in Cambodia we find Rās (King), Brah Pād (Sacred Feet), Kambujadhipati (Sovereign of Kambuja), Peramapubitr (Supreme Purification), Narottama (Elevated among Men), and so on. The usual designation at Luang Prabang is the Siamese Somdet P'ra-Chao (Great Master of Life).

Higher civil and military officials were always referred to by Europeans as 'mandarins'. In old Annam there were two orders, each with nine degrees. The three highest degrees conferred the title ông lớn (Excellency); next came four to which was attached the title ông quan (Mandarin); below were two inferior degrees for subordinate employees not properly within the mandarinate. In Cambodia the higher dignitaries were classified in four categories called samrăp and distinguished by the numbers ek, tou, trey and chetva, derived from Sanskrit. In each of these in turn were ten grades called săk. Luang Prabang divided its higher mandarinate into Right, Left and Centre. The P'aya Muong-Sen was the first Mandarin of the Right, the P'aya Muong Tiane the first Mandarin of the Left and the P'aya Muong-Khang the first Mandarin of the Centre. As the Siamese and Laotian languages are local dialects of the Tai language, Lao titles are practically the same as Siamese. Moreover, settling as they did in lands previously held by the Khmers, and in which Indian culture predominated, they, like the Cambodians, adopted their higher titles from Sanskrit or Pali. Thus the three grand dignitaries next in rank to the King were the Oupahat (Uparāja) or Second King, the Ratsavong (Rājavamça) or First Prince and the Ratsabout (Rājaputra) or Second Prince.

In Laos and Cambodia patronymics have never been used. As in Burma, both sexes have only the personal names given at birth in accordance with the horoscope, or assumed later. Anyone with any office would be addressed by the title conferred by his office. As the Chinese clan system prevailed in Annam and Tongking, the first member of the name is the 'family' name; but as there are only about a dozen of these, and some of them have been adopted in comparatively recent times from the names of popular kings (e.g. Trân, Lê, Nguyên, etc.), this part of the name does not indicate common descent. And though, as the hereditary part of the name, it corresponds to our surname, it is never, in Annam, used as such. The parts of the name which follow—usually two, rarely three—are given by the father according to taste or as advised by astrologers. The first may mean 'happy' (phúc), 'strong' (manh), 'beautiful' (văn), etc. The second is fairly often borrowed from the name of a king or distinguished person. There is no indication of sex in the case of a man's name; but the middle member of a woman's name, next after the family name, is always Thê. The most common family names are Trân, Lê, Nguyên, Pham, Ly, Du'o'ng, Vũ, Mac and Đô.

3. PLACE-NAMES

(i) BURMA

Most towns and villages are named after physical features or natural objects. Common components are:

Haung, old.	Nge, small.
In, small lake.	Pin, tree.
Kan, tank.	Se, dam, weir.
Kon, high ground.	Seik, landing-place.
Chaung, stream.	Taung, hill.
Kyi, big.	Taw, jungle.
Kyun, island.	Thit, new.
Le, rice land.	Wa, mouth.
Myo, town.	Ywa, village.

Thus we have the towns Magwè, 'the bend of the river', Myitkyina, 'near the great river', Tantabin, 'one toddy palm', Toungoo (really Taungngu), 'the spur of the hill', and Ava (a corruption of Inwa), 'the entrance to the lake'. Mandalay, the last royal capital, founded by Mindon Min in 1857, takes its name from the hill at the base of which it lies, probably a corruption of Mandara, the sacred mountain of Hindu mythology.

Rangoon is a corruption of Yangon, 'the end of the strife', a name given by Alaungpaya to the village of Dagon when he conquered it in 1755. The village seems to have taken its name from the Shwe Dagon pagoda. Dagon is thought to be derived from the Pali Tikumbha, a 'three-hilled city'.

Many names are associated with local traditions or aetiological tales, in which the substratum of truth is hard to find. From Prome southwards Mon influence is marked and the Burmese name is often a corruption of an earlier Mon one. Thus Martaban, the once-famous port on the Sittang estuary, comes from the Mon Muhtamaw, 'rocky promontory'. Cosmin, the name given by European travellers of the 16th and 17th centuries to the port on the Irrawaddy delta now called Bassein (Bur. Pathein), has puzzled many scholars. It was probably a corruption of the old Pali name, Kusima, once borne by the city.

(ii) SIAM

Place-names in Siam contain far more derivations from Pali or Sanskrit than those of Burma. These two classical languages are being digested into Siamese at very much the same stage of assimilation as Greek and Latin into English about 500 years ago. The official name for Bangkok consists of the Siamese words Krungt'ep ('city of the divine messenger') plus a whole string of Pali titles, together making a compound word longer than the longest Welsh name. The first title in the string, mahanakorn, is a corruption of the Pali *Maha Nagara*, 'great city'. Ayut'ia, the former capital, referred to by Europeans of the 16th and 17th centuries variously as

Judea, Odia, Hudia, was so called after *Ayodhya*, the Hindu city of Rama, a Sanskrit word meaning 'not to be warred against'. Suk'ot'ai, the oldest known settlement of the Mon-Khmer people, and capital of an independent Tai kingdom from 1238 to 1378, comes from the Pali *Sukhodaya*, 'the abode of happiness'. Rajaburi is the Pali word for 'king's town'.

Most of the names in their Siamese forms are composite and normally consist of monosyllabic couples, e.g. Krung Kao, 'the old city', i.e. Ayut'ia. Bangkok appears to be a combination of *ban*, 'village', and *kok*, 'wild olive tree'. Lan-chan, an earlier name for Luang Prabang, means 'a million elephants'. The Siamese tendency was to give ostentatious names to their cities. Thus the ancient city of Kampengpet signified 'walls of diamond' and according to La Loubère the native name for Ayut'ia was Sijon Thijan, 'terrestrial paradise'. *Chieng*, as in Chieng-mai, is the Siamese word for 'town'. Its Chinese versions are *Keng, Cheng* and *Chung*. Other commonly used terms are *nakon*, 'country', *hoa muang*, 'head of a province', and *wieng*, 'fortified place'. *Krung* is used only of a capital city. *The Royal Geographical Society's Glossary, No. 6, Thai* (*Siamese*), is a useful guide to place-names.

(iii) MALAYA AND INDONESIA

Here Malay names predominate, though there are a few, such as Singapore (Skt. Sinhapura = 'lion city'), which derive from Sanskrit. The following are common components:

Ayer, water.
Batu (Jav. watu), stone or rock.
Bukit, hill or mountain.
Chi (abbrev. form of chai), water, with significance of river.
Desa, country as distinct from town, village in Java.
Gunong, mountain.
Kali, river (Java).
Laut, sea.
Naga, snake, dragon.
Nusa, island (Java).
Pasar, bazaar.
Pulao, island.
Sungai, river.
Tanah, land, region.
Tanjong, headland, cape.
Ujong, point, promontory.

Penang is so named from the Malay *pinang*, 'areca-nut', because the island was thought to resemble one in shape. Junk-Ceylon is a corruption of the Malay *Ujong Salang*, 'the promontory of the heavily-tossing vessel'. Malacca is the Malay *malaka*, 'myrobalan tree', a corruption of the Sanskrit *amlaka*, 'acid'. Sumatra probably comes from the Sanskrit *samudra*, 'sea'. Java, a name of great antiquity, was in its original form (Mal. and Jav.) *Jawa*, and as such appears in a Sanskrit inscription of A.D. 762 in the Batavia Museum. The word implies wealth in cereals and probably derives from the Sanskrit *jawa*, 'millet', 'barley'. Boro-budur, the great Buddhist monument at Kadu in Java, seems to mean 'myriad Buddhas'. Ujongtanah, the Malay name for the extreme end of the Peninsula, means 'land's end'. Achin, the state and town at the north-west angle of Sumatra, comes from the Malay *acheh*, 'wood leech'. Celebes, according to Skeat, is a variant of *Si-Lebih*, 'of Lebih', a man's name, since many Malay place-names are derived from those of people. Kedah (Quedda) may be derived from the Arabic *kedah*, ' goblet ', though some authorities think it comes from the Indian word *kheda*, the stockade trap into which elephants are driven. This, however, in Malay is *kubu*. The origin of the name for the Spice Islands, the Moluccas, is unknown. The Portuguese called them the Maluko islands. The suggested derivation is the Arabic *Jazirat-al-Muluk*, ' isles of the kings ', because each had its own king. But if, as Skeat suggests, they are the *Mi-li-ku* referred to in the 7th-century Chinese history of the Tang dynasty, the name is too old to be Arabic. A valuable guide to the study of the place-names of the whole region is John Crawfurd's *Descriptive Dictionary of the Indian Islands and Adjacent Countries* (London, 1856).

(iv) FRENCH INDO-CHINA

The following are common components of place-names:

Annamese

Yên-lac, peace, tranquillity.
Hā-nôi, on the river (the Red River).
Viñh-yên, peace, prosperity.
Hai'-phòng, port, harbour (lit. ' water ' and ' to guard ' or ' protect ').
Phú-tho, prosperity (lit. ' wealth ' and ' long life ').
Cho'-bò', river market (lit. ' market ' and ' river bank ').
Cho'-lón, big market.
Ninh-giang, peaceful river.
Cao-băng, high land.
Hu'ng hóa, prosperous trade.
Cho' mói, new market.
So'n tây, eastern mountain.
Sông cái, main river.
Băc ninh, peaceful north.
Luc-an-châu, sixth peaceful territory.
Hā đông, populous river.
Tam đ'ao, three mountains.
Lôc Biǹh, decorative vase.
Phô mo'í, new street.
Môc châu, woodland.
Hu'o'ng so'n, fragrant mountain.
Yên trung, peaceful centre.
C'u'a viêt, gate of the Viet.
Tan kỳ, three regions.
Cùng so'n, last mountain.

Cambodian

Arak, spirit.
Bânteai, fortified enclosure.
Barai, artificial lake.
Beng, pool.
Dâng, land.
Khet, district.
Kompǒng, wharf, or river-bank market.
Kŭk, cell, sanctuary.
Phnǒm, hill.
Phsar, market.
Phum, village.
Prah, sacred.
Prâsat, tower, temple.
Prei, forest.
Spean, bridge.
Stu'ng, river.
Sre, rice field.
Srok, country.
Thnot, sugar-palm.
Tǒnle, large lake.
Trâpeang, pool.
Tu'k, water.
Vat, temple.
Veal, plain.

N.B. Villages are often named after local trees, e.g. Phum sendaek (bean tree), Phum lâvea (fig tree).

4. SELECT GLOSSARY

A = Annam, B = Burma, C = Cambodia, Ch = Champa, L = Laos, M = Malaya or Indonesia, S = Siam

ABBYOURAC (C). A king who has abdicated in order to ensure a successor of his own choice.

ABHISEKANAMA (Ch). The royal name taken by a king upon accession.

ADALAT (B). See India Glossary, p. 57.

ADAT (M). Local custom. See N. and M.E. Glossary, p. 11.

AFDEELING (M). Subdivision of a residency in Dutch Indonesia; under an assistant resident in the European Civil Service. It normally coincided with a Regency, the head of which belonged to the highest rank of the Native Civil Service.

AGILA. Eagle-wood of commerce, Mal. *Kalambah.* An aromatic wood from Cambodia. The word traces back to a corrupt form of the Sanskrit name for the wood, which caused the Portuguese to call it *d'aguila,* whence the French *bois d'aigle* and the English eagle-wood. Used as incense in Europe.

AHMUDAN (B). Classes of the population liable to regular service, military or non-military, in the old social organization of Burma.

AKAUKWUN (B). Collector of customs.

AKUNWUN (B). Provincial revenue officer under Burmese rule; in British times became officer in charge of the revenue office of a deputy commissioner.

AMPO (S). District, part of a Muang (*q.v.*).

AN-SAT (A). Provincial judge in a major province, governor of a minor province.

ARECA (CATECHU). Betel-nut, with many names in Malay lands, e.g. Mal. *pinang,* Jav. *jambi,* Bal. *banda.*

ARRACK. Ardent spirit, Arabic *Araq.* See N. and M.E. Glossary, p. 12.

ASU (B). A regiment or organization of all persons liable through heredity for some form of service, e.g. as soldiers or, in some cases, as dancers, menials, etc. They were members of the *ahmudan* (*q.v.*) class.

ATHI (B). People not of the *ahmudan* class, who were liable for military service only in an emergency or for the twelve state duties, i.e. village or civil duties.

AYADAW MYE (B). State land as opposed to *bobabaing* (*q.v.*) or private land.

BAJAU (M). Wandering maritime Malays with gipsy habits.

BAKO (C). The special caste from whose ranks the Khmers chose a new king, when the royal family failed of heirs. Thought to be the descendants of Brahmans (see India Glossary, p. 59), and as such played an important part in all royal ceremonies.

BALACHONG (M). Pounded and pickled prawns and sardines in universal use as a condiment. Mal. *belachan.*

BALAI (M). Hall of audience, court of an official.

BALAT (C). Assistant to a provincial governor.

BAN (L). Village.

BATIG SLOT (M). The surplus revenue of Netherlands India under the Cultuurstelsel, which formed a 'contribution' to the revenues of Holland.

BO (B). Military officer; term also applied to a dacoit leader. *Bogyi* (great captain) commonly referred to Burman officers in Burmese units, but was sometimes used by the Burmese in addressing Britishers.

BOBABAING (B). Private land as opposed to *ayadaw mye* (*q.v.*). Owners had rights of alienation without restriction.

BO-CHANH (A). Director of bureaux in a major province, governor of a minor province.

BOEDI-OETOMO (M). Javanese nationalist association founded in 1908. Appealed to the intelligentsia.

BONZE. A Japanese word applied by Europeans to Buddhist monks throughout Indo-China. The native term in Cambodia is *Bikkhu*, corresponding to *Pongyi* in Burma, *P'ra Song* in Siam and *Ti-khu'u* in Annam. The old Khmer term was *Chao Ku*, which is still sometimes used in Siam. European visitors to Siam in the 17th century noted that the Siamese term for Bonze was *Chao Ku*. See Japan Glossary, p. 225.

BUDDHIST SECTS (C). In 1864 the Thommayut was founded by Samdac Prah-sokon, a monk, who introduced changes in the style of draping the yellow robe, in the manner of carrying the begging-bowl and in the days on which confession should be made. Those who clung to the traditional methods were thenceforward known as the Mohanikay.

BUDDHIST TERMS (C). *Mohasankhrac*, Chief of the Order; *Sankhanayok*, Principal Abbot; *Bikkhu*, Monk; *Samanera*, Probationer; *Vat*, Monastery; *Sangha*, The Brotherhood of Monks; *Treybeidak*, Three Baskets of the Law; *Prah-piney*, Instructions for the Brotherhood; *Prah-saut*, Narrative Portion of the Scriptures; *Prah-apphithom*, The Doctrine. For Burma and Siam, see Comparative Table of Religious Terms, p. 127.

BUGIS (M). Malay name for the dominant people of Celebes.

BYEDAIK (B). Privy Council of the Court of Ava, lit. 'bachelors' quarters'. *Bye* is a corruption of a Mon word *blai*.

CAI (A). Manager of an estate or overseer of a gang of labourers.

CAMPHOR TREE (M). *Kapur*, the Malay name, is a corruption of Skt. *karpura*.

CATECHU (M). Cutch of European trade, Mal. *kachu*.

CHAMYE (B). Old rendering of *sa mye* (eating land), land bestowed by the king as an appanage. Land allotted to soldiers was *ne mye lok mye*.

CHANG (S). Elephant, cf. Bur. *hsin*.

CHAO CHIWIT (S). Usual title for the king, lit. 'Lord of Life'.

CHAO-MAHA-OUPAHAT (L). Second King or Heir Presumptive. See *Maha Uparat* (S), *Uparaza* (B) and *Obbarac* (C).

CHAU MU'O'N (L). Chief of a principality, corresponding to a province elsewhere in French Indo-China. Also spelt *Chao Muang*.

CHINDIT (B). Corruption of Bur. *chinthè*, leogriph guarding a sacred building.

CHUA (A). A Buddhist pagoda. See *Paya* (B), *Bote, Prachedi* (S).

COMAR (C). Name applied to the country of Cambodia by the early Arab geographers; a corruption of Khmer, the name of the people. The Chinese name for the country was *Chin-la*.

CRACHIN (A). A wet season which affects the regions bordering on the China Sea to the north of Tourane during the second half of cold weather, January to February.

CUNAU (A). A brown dye made from the wild tea plant and used extensively by villagers in Annam and Tongking for dyeing clothes.

CULTUURSTELSEL (M). The 'culture system' of the period 1830–50, whereby dues were paid in kind instead of in cash. Established by Van den Bosch in Java only.

CURRENCY (A). Before the French occupation there was a hotch-potch of coins, metals and standards: no monetary system of units and multiples existed. Bazaar currency consisted of the copper or zinc *sa-pek*, called the *dong*, with a square hole in the middle for filing, in imitation of the Chinese cash. A string of 60 was called a *mas*, ten strings a *kwan*. The coins had no fixed value: they were really counters; their value varied with the supply.

In trade above the bazaar level silver ingots and foreign coins were bartered according to kind and weight. The chief coin in use at the ports was the Mexican dollar, called piastre. There were also British, Dutch and Spanish silver pieces. With the French occupation the piastre came into use in the inland regions. The depreciation in the value of silver in the latter part of the 19th century caused the *sa-pek*'s exchange rate to fluctuate in relation to the piastre. The value of the latter fell from 8 strings in 1883 to 6 in 1898. In 1904 five-*sa-pek* zinc pieces worth $\frac{1}{600}$ of a piastre were issued, but were withdrawn in 1914 owing to further changes in the value of silver. As a result the *sa-pek* was driven out of domestic trade by the piastre and the cent. In 1864 the French attempted to circulate a five-franc écu legally valued at $\frac{90}{100}$ of a piastre; this failed because the coin's intrinsic value was $\frac{93}{100}$ of a piastre. Hence in 1885 they coined a trade piastre with the same exchange rate as the Mexican.

In the old Kingdom of Champa silver money was not unknown, but was not current. Merchandise was bartered for rice, wine and other foodstuffs. (See China Glossary, *s.v.* Dollar.)

CURRENCY (B.) Save for the tin currency in use in Tenasserim at the time of the British annexation in 1826, Burma had no coinage of her own until Mindon Min (1853–78) introduced the peacock coinage on the British India model. In the 16th and 17th centuries the main currency was ganza (Skt. *kansa*, bell-metal), which was weighed out by the viss. One viss was said to be worth 1*s*. 4*d*. in the early 17th century. Gradually its copper content decreased until it was pure lead. Its value correspondingly declined. Foreign merchants used imported silver dollars or Indian gold pagodas and fanums. In the 18th century under the Alaungpaya dynasty silver became the standard currency for commerce, being weighed by the tical and tested by an assayer. Purest current silver (*Baw*) contained 3%–4% alloy. *Ngwe-ni* (flowered silver) contained 85% *Baw* and 15% copper. The tical was roughly equal to a rupee. Ganza, when pure lead, was reckoned at $\frac{1}{500}$ the value of silver. The tin coinage of Tenasserim consisted of a large pice, *hkèbya*, of which eleven weighed one lb. avoirdupois. Fifty went to a sicca rupee. There was also a smaller coin, the coss, valued at $\frac{1}{12}$ of a *hkèbya*. *Coss*, like Chinese *cash*, Tamil *kasu* and Portuguese *caixa*, seems to have been a derivation from the Sanskrit *karsha*, a copper coin. Arakan in the 17th century used the Mughal *tanga* and, for small purchases, cowrie shells imported from the Maldives. These latter were never in use in Burma.

CURRENCY (S). The coin in commonest use in the early days of European trade was the *baht*, referred to by them as 'tical'. Originally a rounded lump of silver, it was equal to a rupee, and was stamped on one side with a Siamese crown or a *chakr* (sacred wheel). In 1862 it was issued as a flat minted coin. Large sums were reckoned in *chang* (80 *baht*). Smaller silver coins were *song saleung* ($\frac{1}{2}$ *baht*), *saleung* ($\frac{1}{4}$ *baht*) and *fuang* ($\frac{1}{8}$ *baht*). Below these in value were cowrie shells (*bia*), several hundred of which went to the *baht*. Similar coins in gold representing five, ten and twenty *baht* were once in use, but the attempt in 1862 to issue a flat gold coinage failed. From about the same time a copper coinage was substituted for cowrie shells. Early in the present century a new coinage, based on the decimal system, came into circulation, consisting of the *satang* ($\frac{1}{100}$ *baht*), a copper coin, and nickel coins of five and ten *satang* value.

DAI-LY-THI (A). Tribunal of appeal to the emperor.

DAMAR (M). Resin, used as tar or pitch in Europe.

DANDAVASO BHATAH (C). Captain of the Royal Guards.

DAMAUGYA (B). Lit. 'first dah drop'; land originally waste or unoccupied, to which a title was acquired by occupation and cultivation with the permission of the local land officers. In Lower Burma in British times it became land to which a title had been acquired by squatting for twelve years.

DAMMATHAT (B). Code of Civil Law.

DE-DOC (A). Provincial general, subordinate to a Tong-doc. See China Glossary, *s.v.* Tyidu.

DESA (M). A village tract, district, from Skt. *desa*, country as distinct from town. *Desa-diensten*, compulsory services rendered to the village.

DINH (A). Communal centre used for meetings of the Council of Notables of the *Xa* or *Thon*; a temple for the worship of the spirits protecting the village.

DURIAN (M). A fruit with esculent seeds; has the same name all over the far east. A pure Malayan word.

DYAK or DAYAK (M). Lit. 'up-country', whence *orang Dayak*, the people of the interior. People inhabiting Borneo.

EGGA MAHA THINAPADI (B). Adaptation of Pali *Agga maha senapadi*, title used in addressing a Wungyi, possibly on occasions when it would signify commanding general.

FERINGI (B). Pers. *Farangi, Firingi* ; Arabic *Al-Faranj, Ifranji, Firanji* ; a Frank, old term in use all over Asia for a European ; applied in S.E. Asia specifically to an Indian-born Portuguese, and in the 17th century in particular to those in the service of Arakan, who made Dianga, close to Chittagong, their headquarters for slave raids into Bengal. See N. and M.E. Glossary, *s.v.* Frank.

FESTIVALS (B). All public festivals are called *Pwè*. The New Year's Festival, *Thingyan*, falling in March or April, is called by Europeans the 'Water Festival'. Next in importance comes the full moon of *Thadingyut*, or 'End of Lent', with the *Tawadeingtha* festival, referred to by Europeans as the 'Festival of Lights'. Besides these there are many local festivals connected with famous pagodas.

FESTIVALS (S). The chief ones are *Khao Wasah* (beginning of the rains), *Ok Wasah* (end of the rains), the *Khan Wisakha*, which commemorates the birth, death and attainment of Buddhahood of Gautama, on the full moon of the sixth lunar month (April or May), the *Thot Krathin* (presentation of robes to monks) in October, the *P'rabat* or *P'ra P'utta Bat* (adoration of the sacred footprint) in January or February, the *P'u Khao T'ong* Fair at the 'Golden Hill' shrine outside Bangkok at the end of December or beginning of January and the *Kaw P'ra Sai*, held during the dry season. All are Buddhist. The *Songkran* marks the beginning of the New Year according to the Maha Sakarat or Çaka era. There are festivals in connection with every stage in the process of rice cultivation. The first of these is the *Loh ching cha* ('Pulling the Swing'), which falls in late December or early January and is Brahman in origin. Equally ancient is the *Kahn Raak Na* ('Ceremony of the First Ploughing'), which takes place at the beginning of the rains during the first half of May. It was originally performed by the king in person, and links up with similar ceremonies in China and Burma. So far as Siam and Burma are concerned it was a Brahman custom introduced in early times from India.

GAMBOGE (M). A gum deriving its name from Kamboja, the Malay name for the country of Cambodia, the chief source of supply.

GANH (A). The balancing-pole for carrying merchandise.

GAUNG (B). Village official, subordinate to a headman.

GUN (B). Properly dressed cotton.

HEERENDIENSTEN (M). Compulsory services rendered to the Dutch Government.

HINAYANA. The 'Lesser Vehicle', the purer form of Buddhism prevailing in Burma, Ceylon, Siam, Cambodia and Laos ; often referred to as 'Southern Buddhism'. Its sacred language is Pali.

HLE (B). A boat. (Hlè, however, means 'cart'.)

HMANNANDAWGYI (B). Lit. 'Glass Palace', one of the principal rooms of the palace. Gives its name to the most famous of the court chronicles, the *Hmannan Yazawin*, 'Glass Palace Chronicle'.

HTI (B). Umbrella, also the architectural feature at the top of a pagoda. See *Payong* (M.)

HUYEN (A). Division of a *phu* (*q.v.*), described by the French as the equivalent of the arrondissement.

INDIGO. The dark-blue dye of the *Indigofera tinctoria*. Mal. *tarum* = the plant, *nila* = the dye.

JAK (Ch). A measure of rice of unknown volume. The sole measurement of land was according to its taxable value in terms of *jak*.

JAKSA (Jav.). Judge-advocate, or Court Prosecuting Officer in Dutch Indonesia.

JUNK (M). The Portuguese *junca* is a corruption of the Mal. *jong* and Jav. *ajong*, meaning 'a large vessel'. See China Glossary, p. 184.

KADAW PWE (B). Royal reception of presents from feudatories. Lit. 'Beg-pardon festival'. British envoys objected to the obligation to attend it on account of the implication that their government 'placed its head under the Golden Feet'.

KALA (B). Burmese, Mon and Shan name for Indians of all sorts. Seems to be derived from Skt. or Pali *kula*, 'family', 'caste', hence the Burmese word indicates 'caste people'. It appears in inscriptions of the Pagan period. Europeans were sometimes referred to as *kalapyu*, 'white kalas'.

KAMPONG (M). A group of houses, hamlet.

KAMVUJA (C). The name by which the Khmers of Cambodia called their country. Early European travellers render it Camboia or Camboja. The names Khmer and Kamvuja both appear as early as the 9th century A.D. in Cambodian and Cham inscriptions.

KAWI (M). The ancient and recondite language of literature, law and religion in Java and Bali.

KAZIN (B). Small artificial ridges forming partitions between fields.

KHAO PLEUAK (S). Paddy as distinct from *khao san*, husked rice.

KHAND (C). A canton, the equivalent to a *Tong*, in Annam.

KHET (C). Province; see *muang* (S), *myo* (B), *phu* (A).

KHUM (A). A subdivision of a canton, rendered 'commune' by the French. The smallest administrative unit.

KLING (M). Name given by Malays and Javanese to the Kalinga nation of south India, and now to all Indians.

KLONG (S). A canal.

KOMAKHOUNE (L). Title of the third and fourth princes of the royal family in Luang Prabang.

KRAMA (M). Javanese name for their ceremonial dialect. Apparently derived from *Kerama* (*Kerma*), a Malay word meaning a 'curse', 'evil spell'.

KRAMAKAR (C). A subordinate provincial official.

KRATON (Jav.). Palace of a native ruler.

KRIS (M). Abbrev. of *keris*, 'dagger'.

KROMAKAN (L, S). A type of functionary who administered justice and possessed certain executive powers in a principality.

These officers were divided into two categories, the *Phann* and the *Phya*. In Siam the *Kromakan* was a sort of Justice of the Peace.

KRUNG (S). Capital or royal city. *Krung Kao*, 'old capital', signifies Ayut'ia, *Krung Tep*, 'heavenly capital', is a name for Bangkok.

KWAI (S). Buffalo; cf. Bur. *chwè*.

KWIN (B). Piece of land used as survey unit by the Land Records Department; about one square mile.

KYAT (B). Popular expression for rupee; used also for tical weight.

LAC, LACCA. Resinous incrustation produced on certain trees; once in great demand for the manufacture of sealing-wax, varnishes, dyestuff and for stiffening men's hats.

LAKE (S). Departments of the public service into which the whole population was divided. *Lake Sui* signified those exempted from personal service but obliged to contribute produce in kind.

LAMAING MYE (B). Land cultivated by the king's labourers, possibly *adscripti glebae*.

LEDAW (B). Royal lands. In Kyauksè, however, the phrase used was *pè daw*, 'royal acres', which denoted approximately what is called above *ayadaw*, and all land (including service land and *lamaing mye*) not held in private ownership.

LONGYI (B). Modern Burmese skirt worn in slightly different forms by both men and women; akin to the Malay *sarong* and the Siamese *panaung*. The *paso*—the primitive kilt—and the *tamein*—open at one side—are older forms of dress, now largely ceremonial. Usually of silk woven in variegated colours.

LUANG PENG (S). Interpreter of law in the courts.

LUGYI (B). Village elder.

LUK KUN (S.). Supreme Court of Law, Court of Appeal until 1862 when the *San Dika* was established.

MAHAYANA. 'The Great Vehicle', the Tibetan and Chinese form of Buddhism prevailing in Annam and Tongking, and formerly in Burma and Cambodia. Often called 'Northern Buddhism'. Its sacred language is Sanskrit.

MAHASENAPATI (Ch). Title indicating the commander-in-chief of an army; see India Glossary, *s.v.* Senapati.

MAHA UPARAT (S). Heir Apparent or Royal Deputy, first mentioned in the reign of King Trailok near the end of the 15th century. Often referred to as *Wang Na*, a title rendered in English in the 19th century by 'Second King', the king himself being styled 'First King'. *Uparat* is a corruption of a Pali word with the same meaning. The Burma edition of the word is *Uparaza*, a title by which the *Ein-she-min* was often known.

MALIM (MAALIM) (M). Mate of a native ship, Arabic *mu'allim*. See N. and M.E. Glossary, p. 23.

MANDARIN. The name applied to all high officers of state in Indo-China by Europeans, although in Annam and Tongking only was there a mandarinate of the Chinese type. In Annam there were two orders, civil and military, each of nine degrees. The civil was known as the *quan văn*, the military as the *quan vô*. Each degree had two classes. Thus on the civil side 1a was a grand functionary without title, 1b comprised the members of the *noi cac* or Aulic Council, 2a included the heads of the six ministries and the Tông-đôc of each major province, 2b included the *tuan phu* of each minor province, 3a comprised the *bo chanh* and *quan-bo* (assessors to ministers) and the heads of the administrative services in provinces, 4a included the *quan-ân* or provincial judges, and so on. The three superior degrees on both sides conferred the title of *ông lo'n* and the next four degrees that of *ông quan*. There was a system of examinations which alone gave access to the mandarinate. It was established under Li-thanh-tôn in the 11th century A.D., and conferred three ‘ degrees ’, called tu-tai, cu'-nho'n and tiên-si, which the French render baccalauréat, licencié and doctorat. Candidates were examined in the teachings of Confucius. Training for these was given in the three official schools, Quôc-tu-giam, Thai-hoc and lan-kha-tu-viên.

In Cambodia mandarins were in four categories called *samrăp*, distinguished by the Sanskrit numerals *ek, tou, trey* and *chetva*. In each *samrăp* there were ten grades, called *săk*. Champa had a higher mandarinate of three classes, the *Louen to sing*, the *Ko Louen tche ti* and the *Yi ti kia lan*. Below them was a provincial hierarchy of more than 200 categories. The Laos imitated Siam. See China Glossary, p. 186.

MANTRIS. Officer in Dutch Indonesia subordinate to Wedono (*q.v.*). The Malay word *mantĕri* (*mĕntĕri, mantri*) means ‘ a minister of state ’, and in some states is applied to the Chief Minister. See India Glossary, *s.v.* Mantrin.

MEASURES (B). The main unit of linear measure is the *taung* (cubit of 18 inches). Four *taung* = one *lan* (fathom), seven *taung* = one *ta* (bamboo), 7,000 *taung* = one *taing* (Burmese mile = 2 miles 193 yards 2 feet 8 inches). Grain is measured by the standard village basket (*tin*) containing 48 lb. of paddy or 75 lb. of clean rice.

MEASURES (M). Linear measure was by finger length, span, foot, pace and fathom, the last of which, the *depa*, represents the span of the outstretched arms. The lowest measure of capacity was the *chupak* (coconut shell). Four made a *gantang* and 800 *gantangs* a *koyan*. The largest Javanese measure of land was a *jong* (lit. ‘ ship ’), half of which was a *kikil* (lit. ‘ leg ’), half of which in turn was a *bau* (Dutch *bouw*), which the Dutch standardized at 1·75 acres.

MEASURES (S). Based on measurements of the human body, *niu* (finger-width), *keuap* (hand-span), *sauk* (cubit), and *wa* (span of the outstretched arms). 20 *wa* = 1 *sen*, 400 *sen* = 1 *yot*. The *wa* is the unit for square measure: 100 sq. *wa* = 1 *ngan*, 4 *ngan* = 1 *rai* ($\frac{2}{5}$ acre).

The *tanan* (coconut-shell) is the unit for cubic measure. 20–25 *tanan* = 1 *sat* (basket), 80 *sat* = 1 *kwien* (cart-load). These are cultivators' measures for paddy. The rice-miller uses the *tang* (bucket) equal to about half a bushel. 80 *tang* = 1 rice-miller's *kwien* = 1 ton.

In the teak trade the unit in use is the *yok*, which is 64 *sauk* in length, 1 *sauk* in width and 1 *niu* in depth, or about 11½ English cubic feet.

MEKHŬM (C). Headman of a hamlet.

MESRŎK (C). Headman of a village.

MILITARY TERMS (B). In the pre-British army regiments were classified as *myin* (cavalry), *thenat* (musketeers), *amyouk* (artillery), *hlan-kaing* (spearmen), *daing* (engineers), and *hle-thin* (boat corps or navy). Every five or so men formed a group (*o za*), which may be termed a mess; two such units formed a *kyat*, led by an *akyat*; five *kyats* formed a *thwethauksu* under the command of a *thwethaukgyi*, who held a position somewhat like that of a sergeant in the British army. Two *thwethauksus* formed what approximated to a company commanded by a *tathmu* (captain). The *asu* (regiment) was commanded by a *bo* (colonel), assisted by two staff officers, named according to the weapon used, e.g. *thenat saye, amyouksaye, myinsaye,* etc. Above the regimental commanders was a general in command of each branch of the army, and named accordingly. Thus there is the *Thenat Wun,* the *Amyouk Wun,* the *Myin Wun,* while the commander of the war boats is the *Hlethin Atwinwun.* All these last-named would invariably be leading statesmen. After enrolment a recruit was tattooed with the badge of his regiment: he then became a full-blown private, or *hse-daw-hto ahmudan.* In time of war he might be required to drink the oath-water (*thitsa-ye*). The palace guard consisted of two brigades, each of six regiments, the *Atwin chauk su* or Inner Brigade and the *Apyin chauk su* or Outer Brigade. The commanding officer of each brigade was a *thenat saye gyi,* and held the rank of *Thandawsin* at the court of Ava.

MINISTERS OF STATE (B). There were two classes of ministers, those of the Royal Household, whose authority was restricted to the palace, and those who were responsible for the more important administrative offices of the State. In later days this distinction tended to break down in practice, though the two categories remained, so far as nomenclature was concerned. The first class comprised the officials of the *Byedaik,* the Secret Department of the Court, who bore the title of *Atwinwun,* eight in number in the 19th century. Below them were the *Thandawzin* ('heralds'), *Simitunhau* (lamp-lighters) and *Ataukdaw* (spies). The second class formed the Hlutdaw, or Council of State, and were entitled *Mingyi* ('great ruler'), or *Wungyi* ('bearer of the great burden'). Below them in rank were two high officials, the *Myinzugyiwun* ('governor of the chief cavalry regiment') and the *Athiwun* ('governor of those not in royal service'). Each *Wungyi* was served by a *Wundauk* ('sharer of the burden'), who had charge of one or more departments of official business. The title of *Wundauk* might also be conferred upon important local governors. The chief officials in the departmental secretariats of the Hlutdaw were designated *Nakandaw* ('receivers of royal orders'). Below them in order of rank were the *Sayedawgyi* ('great chief clerk'), *Ameindawye* ('writer of the great orders'), *Athonsaye* ('writer of use'), *Ahmadawye* ('recorder of orders') and *Aweyauk* ('distant arrivals', i.e. receiver of letters coming from a distance). There were also two *Thandawgans* who opened letters of apology received from great feudatories unable to attend a *Kadaw Pwè* ('beg-pardon festival'), a kind of royal levee held three times a year at the palace.

MINISTERS OF STATE (S). The king was assisted by six chief ministers, the *Chakkri* (Minister of the Interior), the *Wang* or *Thorama* (Minister of the Royal Household), the *Baladep* or *Bholadeb* (Minister of Lands), the *P'ra Klang* (Minister of Finance), the *Kalahom* (Minister of War), and the *Yomarat* (Lord Prefect of the City). In addition there was the *Wang Lang* and a *Prasadet* (Minister for Public Worship). Ministers might belong to the *P'aya* (*Ocya*), the *Chao P'aya* or the *Somdet Chao P'aya* classes. Earlier (in the 17th century) a four-minister régime is found, the *Chatu Sadom* (*Chatta sadampa*, 'Four Stakes') 'supporting the realm'. They were the *Khun Muang* (Interior), *Khun Wang* (Royal Household), *Khun Klang* (Finance) and *Khun Na* (Agriculture).

MOKOT (L). The pointed tiara seen on images of the Buddha.

MONSOON (M). Possibly a corruption of the Arabic *mawsim*, 'season'.

MONTON (S). Administrative circle composed of provinces.

MUANG (S). Older name for province, now *changwad*. See *mu'o'n* (L).

MU'O'N (L). Principality in northern Laos equivalent to a province elsewhere. A Siamese term.

MYANMA (B). Burmese name for their land and its people. Rendered *Buraghma* by 18th-century Europeans, hence the modern name. The Chinese name, *Mien*, appears first in the 13th century, and is apparently derived from the first syllable of the Burmese word.

MYO (B). Fortified town, district or province. Under the Burmese kings a *myothugyi* governed a *myo*, which was an *athi* area including perhaps ten village tracts; a *myowun* governed a province of which the *myo* was the chief town. The *myothugyi* was the backbone of the administration of Upper Burma. Under the British he was given authority over *ahmudans* as well as *athis*.

MYOOK (B). Township officer in British administration.

MYOSA (B). (1) Official to whom the revenues of a district or province were assigned, (2) a Shan chief, lower than Sawbwa, in some of the minor states. Lit. 'Eater of a *myo*'.

NAKHODA (M). Master of a native vessel, from Pers. *nā-khudā*.

NAGA (M). Skt. for fabulous snake or dragon, frequently used in place-names.

NANMADAWPAYA (B). Title of the principal queen at the court of Ava.

NANGSEU DAM (S). Coarse local paper used for literary works before the introduction of printing. Similar to *parabaik* in Burma.

NAT (B). A spirit. Features largely in Burmese animistic beliefs. Similar to Siamese *P'i*.

NGAY DIEN (A). Fields reserved for religious foundations for the support of widows, orphans and the aged.

NGEUN (S). Silver. Bur. *ngwe*.

NHA QUE (A). A peasant.

NHA THO' (A). A worship house dedicated to the spirits of the dead.

NITI (S). A form of literature consisting of old sayings, traditions and maxims.

NOI CAC (A). The Advisory Council of the emperor, referred to by the French as the Aulic Council.

NU'O'C-MAM (A). A condiment in universal use, made of pickled fish, like Burmese *ngapi* and *Balachong* (*q.v.*).

NUSA, NUSWA (M). Jav. 'island', similar to Malay *pulau*. Prefixed to names of small islands. Nusa-Kambangan, 'duck island', is the only large island to which the term is applied.

OBBARAC (C). Vice-king, heir presumptive. See *Maha Uparat* (S), *Uparaza* (B). Sometimes called *Uparaj* in Cambodia.

ONG LON, ONG QUAN (A). See MANDARIN.

OPIUM (M). Malay *apium* from Arabic *afyan*. Barbosa renders it *amfiam*. See China Glossary, p. 187.

PADANG (M). Plain or open field.

PEIKTHA (B). The Indian viss, see WEIGHTS.

PANGERAN (M). A Javanese title of very high rank, equivalent to the Malay *tengku*.

PATAMABYAN (B). One who has passed the Patama examination in the Buddhist scriptures. The reason for the name is obscure. Perhaps it comes from the fact that ability to recite parts of the scriptures (*pyan*) was the preliminary test.

PATIH (M). Chief minister at a native court.

PAYA (B). 'Lord', the word applied to a pagoda, which is usually, but not always, a solid, conical erection placed over sacred relics. The term is also applied to temples such as those of Pagan (11th to 13th centuries A.D.), e.g. the Ananda, with south Indian architectural affinities, being massive structures with narrow corridors leading to small chapels or to colossal figures of a Buddha. The Shwe Dagon at Rangoon is a solid cone.

PAYONG (M). Umbrella.

PÈ (B). Unit of land measurement, 1·75 acres.

PENANG (M). Malay *Pinang*, 'areca palm' island.

PHI (L). Spirits worshipped by animists; identical with p'i-worship in Siam and nat-worship in Burma.

PHO-BAN (L). Headman of a village, lit. 'father of the village'.

PHU' (A). Rendered 'departement' by the French; a division of a *tinh*. See China Glossary, *s.v.* FUU.

PISANG (PULO) (M). Lit. 'banana island', the name given to six different islets in the Malay archipelago.

PO (B). Silk.

PONGSAWARDAN (S). Modern reconstructions of the official annals of the court of Ayut'ia, destroyed by the Burmese at the capture of the city in 1767.

PONSAVADAN (L), PONSAVODAR (C). Official chronicles. *Ponsawardan mu'an Lao* = Annals of the Lao Country; *Ponsavadan*

Kasat Vien-chan = Annals of the Rulers of Vien-chan (Vientiane); *Raca Ponsavodar* = Royal Chronicles of Cambodia. The equivalent Burmese term is *Yazawin*.

PRAH BAT (C). Footprint of the Buddha.

PRAH THOMMASATH (C). The oldest Cambodian legal document, a Khmer gloss of a Sanskrit text. The title is a corruption of *Prah Dharmasastra*.

PRAMANA (Ch). A province, subdivision of a grand circle. A purely administrative term. When a province was held as a feudal appanage the term *vijaya* was applied.

PRAU, PERAHU (M). Mal. or Jav. word for any sailing or rowing vessel; referred to by Europeans as 'prauwe', 'prow' or 'parao'.

PU PRAP (S). Deliverer of judgment in a court of law.

PUROHITAS (Ch). Official in charge of the royal sacrificial ceremonies. See India Glossary, p. 72.

PYATTHAT (B). The many-tiered pavilion of multiple receding roofs which is a distinctive feature of royal or monastic architecture.

QAFILAH (M). Arabic term for a consignment of goods sent overland; lit. 'caravan'. Appears in 17th-century works as *caffula*.

RAI (A). Temporary fields prepared for crops by burning off natural forest growth.

RATAN (M). Mal. *rotan*, possibly a corruption of *rautan*, a paring.

RAWA (M). A morass or lake.

REGERINGSREGLEMENT (M). A Constitutional Regulation in Netherlands India, especially those of 1806, 1815, 1818, 1827, 1830, 1836, 1854, etc.

RESIDENCY (M). Administrative unit in Netherlands India corresponding to a District in British India; officer in charge was called a Resident.

RONGGENG (M). A dancing-girl.

RUA (S). A boat.

SAGU (M). Mal. or Jav. name for the mealy pith of the sago palm, which is exported for refining into European sago.

SAMPAN (M). Word used all over the Far East for a kind of harbour-boat or dinghy. Probably a purely Chinese word. Annamese *tamban*.

SAMRAP (C). See MANDARIN.

SAPANG, SEPANG (M). Wood of the *Caesalpina Sappan*, a dye-wood once in great demand, the brazil-wood of medieval commerce.

SARIKAT ISLAM (M). A nationalist association formed in 1911. Popular and Mohammedan in appeal.

SARONG (M). The Malay skirt.

SHABUNDER (B, M). From the Pers. *Shahbandar*, 'King of the Haven'. The title of an officer who was the harbour-master at a port, with whom foreign traders and shipmasters had to deal. In Burma was usually an Armenian or Indian-born Portuguese. See India Glossary, p. 75.

SHWEMYODAW (B). The capital city, lit. 'royal golden city', often referred to as *Yadanabon*, 'filled with gems', from Pali *Ratanapunna*. The royal palace contained general features widespread over much of Asia, e.g. the palace of Kublai Khan at Peking. All the capitals of Burma were built to the same general plan. A description of Pagan extant in Pali verse from the last quarter of the 12th century might have been written of Mandalay, built in 1857. Yule was of opinion that the palaces of Asoka and Vikramaditya were of the same character.

SHWEDAIK (B). The Treasury, lit. 'gold building', at the capital. The officer in charge was the *Shwedaik Wun*. *Shwedaik Sayin* was the term applied to the book in which Bodawpaya's Revenue Inquest of 1784 was entered up.

SINGKEK (M). Chinese contract coolies imported into Malaya; a Chinese word, lit. 'new-comer'.

SOMDET-PHRA-CHAO (L). Usual title of the king, lit. 'Great Master of Life'; see CHAO CHIWIT (S).

SONG SO-LEN (A). Festival of the Sacrifice to the Imperial Tombs.

SULUT (B). Name applied to villages or areas in which the *athi* class predominated.

SUNGAI (M). Mal. 'river' = Jav. *kali* or *sunda chai*; a word of frequent occurrence in place names.

SURAU (S). A Malay chapel in Siam.

SUSUHUNAN (M). Title of the Sultan of Mataram in Java.

TA DIEN (A). Tenant farmer.

TAI (S). Plough.

T'AI (S). Siamese name for their nation, lit. 'freeman'.

TALAING (B). Burmese name for the Mon people of Lower Burma. The word is unknown in this connection before Alaungpaya's conquest of the Mon kingdom of Pegu in the middle ofthe 18th century. Forchhammer connects it with a Mon word meaning 'slave'.

TALAPOIN (B). Portuguese name for a Buddhist monk; probably a Mon word.

TANAH (M). Land, earth, ground, from Skt. *thana*.

TANJONG (M). Headland, cape; of very frequent occurrence in place-names.

TARAKARN (S). Recorder in a court of law.

TCHEOU (Ch). The highest administrative division of the kingdom; the province was a subdivision of it.

TET-CA (A). The New Year Festival, a form of ancestor worship.

THAT (L). A stupa built of brick or stone over sacred relics, a pagoda. See CHUA (A), PAYA (B).

THATHAMEDA (B). House-tax levied by King Mindon and retained by the British.

THON (A). The smallest administrative unit, also called *Xa*.

THUGYI (B). Headman.

TI-KHU'U (A). A Buddhist monk.

TIMAH (M). Mal. or Jav. word for tin or lead. *Timah putih* = tinned iron, *timah sari* = zinc or spelter, *timah itam* = lead.

TINH (A). A province, under a *Tong-đoc*.

TONG (A). A subdivision of a province, usually rendered 'canton' by the French. Similar to *Khand* (C). Under a *Cai-tong* assisted by a *Pho-tong*.

TONG-ĐOC (A). Provincial governor of the first class. See China Glossary, *s.v.* Tzoongdu.

TRACHANG (S). A balance similar in design to a Fairburn weighing machine ; from Malay *daching*.

TRANH (A). *Imperata cylindrica*, a grass covering wide stretches of uncultivated land where forest does not predominate.

TRI-PHU (A). Officer in charge of a *phu* ('departement ').

TRI-HUYEN (A). Officer in charge of a *huyen* ('arrondissement ').

TUAN-PHU (A). A governor of the second class, in charge of a minor province.

UJONG, HUJONG (M). Mal. or Jav. word for point, headland, promontory ; e.g. Ujung-tanah, the name for the end of the Malay Peninsula.

UPARAZA (B). Pali title for the Heir Apparent or *Ein-she-min*. The usual contraction was *Uparit, Upayit*. The 18th-century English rendering is 'Upper Raja'. See MAHA UPARAT (S).

VAT (C). Buddhist monastery ; Siamese *wat*, Burmese *kyaung*.

VIHARA (C). A temple as distinct from a pagoda.

VIJAYA (Ch). A province held as a feudal appanage by a royal prince or high officer of state. See *pramana* (Ch).

V.O.C. (M). Verenigde Oostindische Compagnie ; the Dutch United East India Company, founded in 1602, came to an end on 31 December 1799.

WEDONO (M). Jav. title for the assistant to a *patih*.

WEIGHTS (B). Burma used the Indian viss (3 lb. 5 oz. 5 dr.) and its subdivisions, giving them Burmese names : viss = *peiktha*, tical (100 to the viss) = *kyat*. The *kyat* was subdivided into 4 *mat*, the *mat* into 2 *mu*, and the *mu* into 2 *pè*. Rice was sold by the *tin*, which was reckoned at 16 *pyi* or measures. See MEASURES (B).

WEIGHTS (Ch). The smallest unit was the *dram* (= 3·09 grammes). 12 *dram* = a *thil* or *thei*. These were used only for gold or precious wares. Heavier weights were the *karsa* or *kar* (280 grains) and its multiples :

4 *karsas* = a *pala*,
100 *palas* = a *tulā*,
20 *tulās* = a *bhāra*.

Others of unknown value were the *penda* (a multiple of the *thil*), the *kattika* and the *pana*.

So far as the remainder of French Indo-China is concerned, the only weights likely to be encountered by historical readers are those of Indian or Chinese origin used by European traders. Reference should therefore be made to the treatment of this subject in the cases of Burma, Siam and Malaya.

WEIGHTS (M). 'The original measures of the Malays and Javanese were evidently by capacity and not by weight' (Crawfurd). Hence foreigners brought with them their own systems. The Chinese used the *tael*, the *catty* (16 *taels*), and the *pikul* (100 *catties* or 133⅓ lb.). *Pikul* is a Malay word meaning 'to carry a heavy load necessitating the use of the shoulder' or 'a man's load'. The commercial form of the word is *picul*.

The Arabs introduced the *bahar*, known in Malaya as a *bahara*, equal to 3 *pikuls*. To-day the *pikol* of Netherlands Indonesia weighs 136·161 lb. or 61·76 kg., and 16 *pikols* = 1 ton. (1 ton [English] = 16·47 *pikols*.) The Singapore *picul* of 60·45 kg. weighs slightly less than the Dutch *pikol*. The *Bahar* sometimes differed for different articles of merchandise. A *bahar* of *agar-agar*, the succulent sea-weed used by the Chinese in making bird's-nest soup, was equal to no less than 12 *pikuls*, one of cinnamon to 6 *pikuls* and one of *tripang*, the sea-slug known as *bêche-de-mer*, to 3 *pikuls*. The additional percentage was termed a *picota*.

For weighing gold, Indian gold weights, based on the weight of seeds, were used; thus the *masha* weighed 10 abrus seeds. But it was found that the Spanish dollar gave greater fixity of weight than any seed or bean, and Malay weights are now based on the Spanish dollar:

12 *saga* = 1 *mayam*,
16 *mayam* = 1 *bungkal* = 832 grains, the weight of 2 Spanish dollars.

The weights of Achin were: 4 *copangs* = 8 *mace*, 5 *mace* = 1 *mayam*, 16 *mayam* = 1 *tael*, 5 *taels* = 1 *buncal*, 20 *buncals* = 1 *catty*, 200 *catties* = 1 *bahar*. The Achin catty weighed 2 lb. 1 oz. 13 dr. The Chinese called the *catty kin* or *chin*; the word *catty* is Malayo-Javanese.

WEIGHTS (S). The *baht* (= 15 grammes) was the unit of weight, like the tical or *kyat* in Burma, see CURRENCY (S).

40 *baht* = 1 Chinese *catty*,
100 *catties* = 1 picul, known in Siamese as *hap* ('man-load').

WUTTAGAN (B). Pagoda land, i.e. the revenues were devoted to the upkeep of a religious shrine or monastery. Burmese records usually refer to such land as *Kaung phaya wut mye*.

XA (A). A commune under a *Xa-tru'o'ng* or *Ly-tru'o'ng* ('mayor') assisted by a *pho-ly* ('adjutant'). See THON (A).

XIEN (CHIENG) (L). Principality in southern Laos, equivalent of a province elsewhere. See MU'O'N (L).

YAZAWIN (B). Vernacular chronicles, of which Burma has a rich collection. The main record for the period up to 1752 is the *Hmannan Yazawin* and thereafter the *Konbaungset*, which are court chronicles. Local records are called *Thamaing*, and were often maintained at pagodas.

YOKRABAT (S). Prosecutor in a court of law.

YON (B). A court-house, dignified by the title *Yondaw* at the capital or in a provincial capital. Referred to by Europeans of the 16th–18th centuries as the Rounday or Runday.

YUVARĀJA (Ch). The Heir Apparent. It was the Sanskrit term meaning 'young king', borrowed from ancient India by the monarchies of Indo-China. See MAHA UPARAT (S), UPARAZA (B).

COMPARATIVE TABLE OF RELIGIOUS TERMS IN USE IN BURMA AND SIAM

Burma	*Siam*	*Meaning*
Thathanabaing	Sangk'arach	Chief of the Order of Monks.
Sayadaw Gaing Ok	Chao Kana Yai	Principal Abbot (of the largest division).
Pongyi, Rahan	Pra Song	Monk.
Upazin	Nane	Probationer.
Koyin	Sisya	Acolyte.
Kyaung	Wat	Monastery.
Thinga (Sanga)	Kana Chammayatika	The brotherhood (of monks).
Paya	Bote, Prachedi	Temple, pagoda.
Bidagat	Trai Pitok	Three Baskets of the Scriptures.
Wini	P'a Winai	Instructions for the Brotherhood.
Thut	P'ra Sai	Narrative portion of the Scriptures.
Abidamma	P'ra Baramat	The doctrine pure and simple.
Zayat	Sala	Rest-house (adjoining a shrine).
Tarapat	Talapat	Monk's fan
Shinpyu	Kahu ta'chuk	Initiation ceremony for boys on attaining puberty.
Wa	Wasah	Buddhist Lent.
Waso	K'ao Wasah	Festival of beginning of Lent.
Thadingyut	Ok Wasah	Festival of end of Lent.
Thingyan	Songkran	New Year Water Festival.

5. CALENDARS AND SYSTEMS OF DATING

The oldest era, once in use throughout Further India, begins in 691 B.C. It is Brahman in origin, but Buddhists attribute it to Anjana, grandfather of Gautama. In Siam it is called the Maha Sakarat. Crawfurd refers to it as the Grand Epoch. Another early era, still in use in Siam under the name P'ra Putta Sakarat, begins in 543 B.C., the traditional date of Gautama's attainment of Nirvana. It is not unknown in Burma. Crawfurd calls it the Sacred Era. The Shaka (Saka) Era, perhaps introduced into southern India by Kanishka in A.D. 78, and probably carried by his missionaries to the Indo-Chinese peninsula, was used in Siam until the middle of the 16th century A.D. In Burma it was known as the Prome Era, being attributed to a legendary King Sumundri of that city. It was also the era used by the compilers of the chronicles of the kingdoms of Cambodia, Luang Prabang and Champa. See also India, Systems of Dating, p. 80.

The era used by the Burmese court chronicles, such as the Mahayazawin and the Hmannanyazawin, is the Khaccapañcha, which begins in March, A.D. 638. It is known officially to-day as the Burmese Era and dates in it are distinguished by the letters B.E. Its establishment is traditionally ascribed to Popa Sawrahan, who, according to the chronicles, reigned at Pagan A.D. 613–40. It was imposed upon Siam in 1569 by Bayinnaung of Burma, when he conquered Ayut'ia, and was officially in use until 1889. The Siamese call it the Chula Sakarat to distinguish it from the Maha Sakarat. Although the British on annexing Burma substituted the Christian Era and Gregorian Calendar for official use, the Burmese system is still in use, particularly for the dating of the great national festivals. Crawfurd, *Journal of an Embassy to the Court of Ava in the year 1827*, Appendix VIII, prints a translation of a Burmese chronological table ranging from 691 B.C. to A.D. 1822, showing dates according to all the various eras that have been in use.

In 1889 King Rama V of Siam introduced a new civil era dating from the accession of the first king of the Bangkok dynasty in 1789. After twenty years it was abandoned in favour of the P'ra Putta Sakarat early in the reign of Rama VI. The P'ra Putta Sakarat has been brought into correspondence with the Gregorian Calendar in regard to length of months and number of days, but the year begins on 1 April.

A very old Siamese practice is that of grouping years into cycles of sixty. This is done by combining a sub-cycle of twelve, to each year of which is given the name of an animal, with another of ten, consisting of the Pali numerals from one to ten. The two sub-cycles run concurrently so that at the end of every sixty years each year in the animal sub-cycle returns to the same position in the ten-year sub-cycle. Each of these periods of sixty years is called a Great Cycle.

The animal sub-cycle runs:

(1) Pee Chuet,	year of the	Rat		(7) Pee Mamia	year of the	Horse
(2) ,, Chalu	,, ,,	Bull		(8) ,, Mamè	,, ,,	Goat
(3) ,, K'an	,, ,,	Tiger		(9) ,, Wawk	,, ,,	Monkey
(4) ,, T'aw	,, ,,	Hare		(10) ,, Raka	,, ,,	Cock
(5) ,, Marong	,, ,,	Dragon		(11) ,, Chaw	,, ,,	Dog
(6) ,, Maseng	,, ,,	Snake		(12) ,, Kun	,, ,,	Pig

The ten-year sub-cycle runs:

Eka Sok . . .	First year	Sapta Sok . .	Seventh year
T'o Sok . . .	Second ,,	Att'a Sok. . .	Eighth ,,
Tri Sok . . .	Third ,,	Nop'a Sok . .	Ninth ,,
Chatawa Sok. .	Fourth ,,	Samrid Sok . .	Year completing the decade
Bencha Sok . .	Fifth ,,		
Chaw Sok . .	Sixth ,,		

Siamese chronicles usually indicate a date by giving not only the year of the Sakarat but also the name of the animal and the year of the decade. So elaborate a method is normally of little value save for the purpose of checking a possible error in the Sakarat year. The animal sub-cycle is the method in most general use among the people. Thus a man, when asked for the year of his birth, will usually give the name of the animal corresponding to the Sakarat year, but not the year itself. In A.D. 1638 King Prasad T'ong, fearing lest the Chula Sakarat year 1000, which was the year of the tiger 10, would be ill-omened, changed its animal to the pig, thereby passing over nine animals. He tried unsuccessfully to persuade King Thalun of Burma to adopt his scheme. The Court of Ava did not use the animal cycle, although it was generally observed elsewhere throughout Indo-China. Even in Siam this drastic alteration failed to secure general recognition.

The year in Burma (and formerly in Siam) is a lunar one of 354 days. It is divided into twelve months of alternately 29 and 30 days. To bring it into line with solar time a thirteenth month is added in approximately every third year. The months are known simply by numbers in Siam. In Burma they have the following names: (1) Tagu, (2) Kason, (3) Nayon, (4) Wazo, (5) Wagaung, (6) Tawthalin, (7) Thadingyut, (8) Tazaungmon, (9) Nattaw, (10) Pyatho, (11) Tabodwe, (12) Tabaung. Days of the month are numbered by the waxing (Bur. *lazan*, Siam. *kheun*) and waning (Bur. *labyigyaw*, Siam. *raam*) of the moon, the first day being the first of the waxing and the sixteenth the first of the waning. New Year's Day might be any day in Tagu or Kason in Burma, and fell in either March or April. Now it is regularly 13 April.

Both Burma and Siam have a seven-day week in which each day bears the name of a heavenly body, thus:

Burma	*Siam*	*Heavenly Body*	*Great Britain*
Taninganwe-ne	Van-a-thed	Sun	Sunday
Taninla-ne	Van-chan	Moon	Monday
Inga-ne	Van-ang-k'an	Mars	Tuesday
Boddahu-ne	Van-p'ood'	Mercury	Wednesday
Kyathapade-ne	Van-pra-had'	Jupiter	Thursday
Thaukkya-ne	Van-sook'	Venus	Friday
Sane-ne	Van-sao	Saturn	Saturday

The Malayan calendar is the Muhammadam. European dominance imposed the Christian Era and Gregorian Calendar for official purposes. The Malays had no era before they adopted the Hijra: they had a solar year and reckoned in it by reigns of kings.

The only people in Indonesia to use an era before the spread of Islam or the advent of the Portuguese were the Javanese and the Balinese, who adopted the Shaka Era. Up to the year A.D. 1633 it was used in Java with solar reckoning. In that year, however, lunar reckoning was adopted, and, as no intercalation was practised, the Javanese Era and the Shaka Era diverged. Thus the year A.D. 1820, which is the Shaka year 1742, is 1747 in the Javanese Era.

The calendar in use throughout the dominions of the old empire of Annam was the Chinese. Annamese days and months were ordinarily numbered; there were no days of the week, only of the half-month as in Burma. The months are (1) Thang Giêng, (2) Thang Hai, (3) Thang Ba, (4) Thang Tu', (5) Thang Năm, (6) Thang Sau, (7) Thang Bay, (8) Thang Tam, (9) Thang Chin, (10) Thang Mu'oi, (11) Mot I' and Chap (the last, 12th or 13th, as the case may be, as they are lunar).

6. DYNASTIES AND RULERS

(i) KINGS OF BURMA

The Burmese Chronicles give three lists of early kings who are purely legendary. First come 33 kings of Tagaung; these are followed by 17 kings of Mauroya and Tagaung and these in turn are followed by 27 kings of Tharakhettara (Śrī Kṣetra or Old Prome) dating from Thambawa, who is said to have come to the throne in 483 B.C., and ending with the death of Thupinya in A.D. 95. Then come the kings of Pagan, beginning in A.D. 108, the first 40 of whom must be considered legendary. The 41st is Anawrahta, a historical character of importance. The Pyu inscriptions of Śrī Kṣetra, deciphered by Blagden, have yielded a list of kings of a Vikrama Dynasty, founded there in the 7th century A.D. or earlier and lasting to 832 (*Journal of the Burma Research Society*, vii. 37), referred to by G. H. Luce (*Journal of the Burma Research Society*, xxvii. 239).

The Pagan Dynasty

(1)	Anawrahta, founder of the empire	1044
(2)	Sawlu, son of (1)	1077
(3)	Kyanzittha, son of (1)	1084
(4)	Alaungsithu, grandson of (3)	1112
(5)	Narathu, son of (4)	1167
(6)	Naratheinhka, son of (5)	1170
(7)	Narapatisithu, brother of (6)	1173
(8)	Htilominlo or Nantaungmya, son of (7)	1210
(9)	Kyaswa, son of (8)	1234
(10)	Uzana, son of (9)	1250
(11)	Narathihapate or Tarokpyemin, son of (10)	1254
(12)	Kyawswa, son of (11)	1287
(13)	Sawhnit (myosa in rank), son of (12)	1298
(14)	Uzana (myosa in rank), son of (13), last male ruler of the dynasty	1325

Rulers of Pinya, Sagaing and Ava

Thihathu (a Shan), at Pinya	1312
A son of Thihathu	1324
Ngasishin, son of Thihathu	1343–50
Sawyun (a son of Thihathu), established at Sagaing	1315

(1)	Thadominbya (founder of Ava), descendant of Sawyun	1364
(2)	Minkyiswasawke, descendant of Narathihapate of Pagan	1368
(3)	Minhkaung, son of (2)	1401
(4)	Thihathu, son of (3)	1422
(5)	Kalekyetaungnyo, cousin of (4)	1426
(6)	Mohnyinthado, unrelated to royal house	1427
(7)	Minrekyawswa, son of (6)	1440
(8)	Narapati, brother of (7)	1443
(9)	Thihathura, son of (8)	1469
(10)	Minhkaung, son of (9)	1481
(11)	Shwenankyawshin, son of (10)	1502
(12)	Thohanbwa, usurper	1527
(13)	Hkonmaing, Sawbwa of Hsipaw	1543
(14)	Mobye Narapati, son of (13)	1546
(15)	Sithukyawhtin, Shan Sawbwa unrelated to predecessor	1552–5

The Mon Kingdom of Pegu

Capital at Martaban 1287–1369 and at Pegu 1369–1539

Wareru, a Mon adventurer who established himself as Chief of Martaban in 1281 and was recognized as overlord of Lower Burma from 1287	1287
INTERREGNUM	1296–1353

Wareru's murder in 1296 was followed by a 'time of troubles' during which, according to the chronicles, the following members of his family wielded some kind of authority:

Khun Law, brother	1306
Zaw An or Thin Hmaing, nephew	1310
Zaw Zip or Binnya Randa, nephew	1323
Binnya Elaw, cousin of above	1330

Binnya U, cousin of above	1353
Razadarit (Binnya Nwe), son of above	1385
Binnya Dammayaza, son of above	1423
Binnya Ran, brother of above	1426
Binnya Waru, nephew of above	1446
Binnya Kyan, cousin of above	1450
Shin Sawbu (Queen), sister of Binnya Ran	1453
Dammazedi, son-in-law of above	1472
Binnya Ran, son of above	1492
Takayutpi, son of above	1526

The independent kingdom was conquered by Tabinshwehti in 1539.

The Burmese Dynasty of Toungoo

Capital transferred to Pegu in 1539 and from Pegu to Ava in 1635

Thinhkaba, first chief to style himself king	1347–58
Pyanchi, son of above	1358–77
Sawluthinhkaya	1421–36
Sithukyawhtin	1471–82
Minkyinyo, first of a continuous line	1486–1531
Tabinshwehti, son of above	1531–50
Bayin Naung, brother-in-law of above	1551–81
Nanda Bayin, son of above	1581–99
INTERREGNUM	1599–1605
Anaukpetlun, nephew of above	1605–28
Minredeippa, son of above	1628–29
Thalun, brother of Anaukpetlun	1629–48
Pindale, son of above	1648–61
Pye, brother of above	1661–72
Narawara, son of above	1672–73
Minrekyawdin, cousin of above	1673–98
Sane, son of above	1698–1714
Taninganwe, son of above	1714–33
Mahadammayaza-Dipati, son of above	1733–52

The Alaungpaya Dynasty

Capitals at Shwebo (1752–65), Ava (1765–60), Amarapura (1760–1823), Ava (1823–37), Amarapura (1837–60) and Mandalay (1860–85)

(1) Alaungpaya of Shwebo	1752
(2) Naungdawgyi, son of (1)	1760
(3) Hsinbyushin, brother of (2)	1763
(4) Singu Min, son of (3)	1776
(5) Maung Maung, son of (4), reigned only seven days	1781
(6) Bodawpaya, son of (1)	1781

(7)	Bagyidaw, grandson of (6)	1819
(8)	Tharrawaddy, brother of (7)	1838
(9)	Pagan Min, son of (8)	1846
(10)	Mindon Min, brother of (9)	1853
(11)	Thibaw, son of (10)	1878

The last king, Thibaw, was deposed in 1885 and his kingdom annexed to British India on 1 January 1886. From the kingdom of Burma, as it was at the beginning of Bagyidaw's reign, Great Britain annexed Arakan and Tenasserim in 1826 and Pegu in 1852.

(ii) KINGS OF ARAKAN

The chronicles begin with the first dynasty of Dinnyawadi (2666 B.C.–825 B.C.), containing 54 kings. The second dynasty, comprising 53 kings, is said to have reigned from 825 B.C. to 746 B.C. Neither names nor dates can be relied upon even where actual historical characters are mentioned, but the great majority of the names are entirely mythical. Inscriptions show that there was a Candra dynasty in Arakan which reigned from the middle of the 4th century A.D. for 230 years and numbered 13 kings. Candrodaya of the inscriptions may possibly be equated with Sandasurya of the chronicles, whose date of accession is given as A.D. 146. (See Johnson, E. H., *Some Sanscrit Inscriptions of Arakan* in the *Bulletin of the School of Oriental and African Studies*, xi. 2, pp. 357–85.) The capital of the Candra dynasty is given the Indian name of Vaisali by the inscriptions. The chronicles contain a We-tha-li dynasty of 12 kings reigning for 230 years, from 788 to 1018, as follows:

Maha-taing-chandra	788
Suriya-taing-chandra, son of above	810
Mawla-taing-chandra, son of above	830
Pawla-taing-chandra, son of above	849
Kala-taing-chandra, son of above	875
Tula-taing-chandra, son of above	844
Sri-taing-chandra, son of above	903
Thinhka-taing-chandra, son of above	935
Chula-taing-chandra, son of above	951
Amyahtu, chief of the Myu tribe	957
Yehpyu, nephew of above	964
Nga-pin-nga-ton, son of Chula-taing-chandra	994

This dynasty, according to the chronicles, was followed by six more, each taking its name from its capital city. All the capitals come within the Akyab district in northern Arakan. The following lists are based upon Harvey's revision of Phayre's (Harvey, *History of Burma*, pp. 370–2).

First Pyinsa Dynasty

Hkittathin, grand nephew of Chula-taing-chandra	1018
Chandrathin, brother of above	1028
Minyinpyu, son of above	1039
Nagathuriya, son of above	1040
Thuriyaza, son of above	1052
Ponnaka, son of above	1054
Minpyugyi, son of above	1058
Sithabin, usurper	1060
Minnangyi, son of Minpyugyi	1061
Minlade, son of above	1066
Minkala, son of above	1072
Minbilu, son of above	1075
Thinhkaya, usurper	1078
Minthan, son of above	1092
Minpati, son of above	1100

The Parin Dynasty

Letya-min-nan, grandson of Minbilu	1103	Thagiwinnge, son of above	1115
Thihaba, son of above	1109	Kawliya, son of above	1133
Yazagyi, son of above	1110	Datha Raja, son of above	1153
Thagiwingyi, son of above	1112	Ananthiri, son of above	1165

The Hkrit Dynasty

Min Onsa, brother of Ananthiri	1167	Keinnayok, son of above	1176
Pyinsakawa, son of above	1174	Salinkabo, usurper	1179

The Second Pyinsa Dynasty

Misuthin, son of Pyinsakawa	1180	Minhkaunguge, son of above	1207
Nga Yanman, son of above	1191	Kabalaunggyi, son of above	1208
Nga Pogan, son of above	1193	Kabalaungnge, son of above	1209
Nga Yahkaing, son of above	1195	Letyagyi, son of above	1210
Nga Kyon, son of above	1198	Letyange, son of above	1218
Nga Su, son of above	1201	Thanabin, son of above	1229
Nga Swethin, son of above	1205	Nga Nathin, son of above	1232
Minhkaunggyi, son of above	1206	Nga Nalon, son of above	1234

The Launggyet Dynasty

Alawmahpyu, son of Nga Nalon	1237	Min Hti, son of Min Bilu	1279
Yazathugyi, son of above	1243	Ossanange, of the blood	1385
Sawlu, son of above	1246	Thiwarit, brother of above	1387
Ossanagyi, son of above	1251	Thinhse, brother of above	1390
Sawmungyi, son of above	1260	Razathu, son of above	1394
Nankyagyi, son of above	1268	Sithabin, usurper	1395
Min Bilu, son of above	1272	Myinhsainggyi, usurper	1397
Sithabin, usurper	1276	Razathu, restored	1397
		Theinhkathu, brother of above	1401

The Mrohaung (Mrauk-u) Dynasty

Narameikhla (Min Sawmun), son of Razathu	1404
Alī Khān, brother of above	1434
Basawpyu (Kalima Shah), son of above	1459
Dawlya, son of above	1482
Basawnyo, uncle of above	1492
Yanaung, son of Dawlya	1494
Salingathu, uncle of above on mother's side	1494
Minyaza, son of above	1501
Kasabadi, son of above	1523
Min Saw-o, brother of Salingathu	1525
Thatasa, son of Dawlya	1525
Minbin, son of Minyaza	1531
Dikha, son of above	1553
Sawhla, son of above	1555
Minsetya, brother of above	1564
Minpalaung, son of Minbin	1571
Minyazagyi (Salim Shah), son of above	1593
Minhkamaung (Husein Shah), son of above	1612
Thirithudamma, son of above	1622
Minsani, son of above, reigned 28 days	1638
Narapatigyi, great grandson of Thatasa	1638
Thado, nephew of above	1645
Sandathudamma, son of above	1652
Thirithuriya, son of above	1684
Waradhammaraza, brother of above	1685
Munithudhammaraza, brother of above	1692
Sandathuriyadhamma, brother of above	1694
Nawrahtazaw, son of above, reigned 15 days	1696

Mayokpiya, usurper	1696
Kalamandat, usurper	1697
Naradipati, son of Sandathuriyadhamma	1698
Sandawimala, grandson of Thado	1700
Sandathuriya, grandson of Sandathudamma	1706
Sandawizaya, usurper	1710
Sandathuriya, son-in-law of above	1731
Naradipati, son of above	1734
Narapawara, usurper	1735
Sandawizaya, cousin of above	1737
Katya, usurping foreigner, held palace for 3 days	1737
Madarit, brother of Sandawizaya	1737
Nara-apaya, uncle of above	1742
Thirithu, son of above	1761
Sandapayama, brother of above	1761
Apaya, brother-in-law of above	1764
Sandathumana, brother-in-law of above	1773
Sandawimala, usurper	1777
Sandathaditha, lord of Ramree	1777
Thamada, chief, deposed by Burmese 1785	1782

Kingdom annexed by the Burmese in 1785 and in 1826 by the English.

(iii) KINGS OF SIAM

The Ayut'ia Monarchy

The transliteration used is that of W. A. R. Wood, *A History of Siam* (1926); Pallegoix's transliteration of 1854 is given in parentheses. The dates are those of accession.

(1)	Rama T'ibodi (Rama-Thibodi), founder of the kingdom	1350
(2)	Ramesuen (Rame-Súen), first reign, son of (1)	1369
(3)	Boromoraja I (Borom-Raxa), sometimes called P'angoa, uncle of (2)	1370
(4)	T'ong Lan (Phra-Cháo-Tong-Lan), son of (3)	1388
(2)	Ramesuen (Rame-Súen), second reign	1388
(5)	Ram Raja (Phaja-Ram), son of (2)	1395
(6)	Int'araja (Intharaxa), nephew of (3)	1408
(7)	Boromoraja II (Borom-Raxa-Thiràt), son of (6)	1424
(8)	Boroma Trailokanat (Boroma-Trai-Lôkhanàt), son of (7)	1448
(9)	Boromoraja III (Phra-Borom-Raxa), son of (8)	1488
(10)	Rama T'ibodi II (Phra-Rama-Thibodi), brother of (9)	1491
(11)	Boromoraja IV (Phra-Borom-Raxa), son of (10)	1529
(12)	Ratsada (Raxa-Kuman), son of (11)	1534
(13)	P'rajai (Xaja-Raxa-Thiràt), half-brother of (11)	1534
(14)	Keo Fa (Phra-Jot-Fa), son of (13)	1546
(15)	K'un Worawongsa (no name given), usurper	1548
(16)	Maha Chakrap'at (Maha-Chakraphat-Raxa-Thirāt), brother of (13)	1549
(17)	Mahin (Mahinthara-Thirat), son of (16)	1569
(18)	Maha T'ammaraja or P'ra Sri Sarap'et (Thamma-Raxa-Thiràt), Chief of Suk'ot'ai	1569
(19)	Naresuen (Phra Naret), called the Black Prince, son of (18)	1590
(20)	Ekat'otsarot (Eka-Thotsarot), son of (19)	1605
(21)	Songt'am (Phra-Chào-Song-Tham) or Int'araja II, son of (20)	1610
(22)	Jett'a (not mentioned), son of (21)	1628
(23)	Prasat Tong (Phra-Chào-Prasat-Thong), usurper	1630
(24)	Chao Fa Jai (Chào-Fa-Xai), son of (23)	1656
(25)	Sri Sut'ammaraja (Sutham-Raxa), brother of (23)	1656
(26)	Narai (Phra-Chào-Xamphu'ok or Phra Narai), brother of (24)	1657
(27)	P'ra P'etraja (Phra-Phet-Raxa) or Ramesuen, usurper	1688
(28)	P'rachao Sua (Chào-Dua), son of (27)	1703

The Ayut'ia Monarchy (continued)

(29) Pu'mint'araja or T'ai Sra (no name given), son of (28) . 1709
(30) Boromokot or Maha T'ammaraja II (no name given), brother of (29) 1773
(31) Ut'ump'on or Dok Madüa (Chào-Dok-Ma-Dua), son of (30) 1758
(32) Boromoraja V or Ekat'at (no name given) 1758–67

The Bangkok Monarchy

(1) P'ya Taksin (Phaja-Tak), a Chinese leader in Siamese service 1767
(2) Rama I or P'ra P'utt'a Yot Fa Chulalok (Phra-Phuti-Chao-Luáng), founder of last dynasty 1782
(3) Rama II (Phëndin-Klang), son of (2) 1809
(4) Rama III or P'ra Nang Klao (Chào-Fa-Mongkut), son of (3) 1824
(5) Rama IV or P'ra Chom Klao (Somdet-Phra-Paramander-Maha-Mongkut), half-brother of above 1851
(6) Rama V or Chulalongkorn, son of (5) 1868
(7) Rama VI or Maha Vajiravudh, son of (6) 1910
(8) Prajadhipok, brother of (7) 1925
(9) Ananda Mahidol, son of (8) 1935–46

(iv) RULERS OF JAVA

A. HINDU PERIOD

Kings of Java before 1222

I. West Java

	A.D.		A.D.
Devavarman (?) . .	132	Dvaravarman (?) . .	435
Pūrnavarman . . .	c. 400	. . . .	.
P'o-to-kia	424	Jayabhūpati . . .	1030

II. Middle Java

	A.D.		A.D.
Simo (?)	674	rake Garung . . .	829 or 839
rake Matarām, Sañjaya	732	rake Pikatan . . .	864 ?
rake Panangkaran . .	778	rake Kayuvangi . .	879–82
rake Panunggalan . .	—	rake Vatuhumalang .	886
Varak	—		

III. East Java

	A.D.		A.D.
Devasimha	—	A. . . . nana (?) . .	760
Gajayāna	—		

IV. East and Middle Java

	A.D.		A.D.
rake Vatukura, Balitung	898–910	rake Layang, Tulodong	919–21
rake Hino, Daksa . .	915	rake Pangkaya, Vava .	924–8

V. East Java

	A.D.		A.D.
rake Hino, Siṇḍok . .	929–47	Kāmeçvara I . . .	1115–30
Lokapāla	950	Jayabhaya	1135–57
Makutavangçavarddhana	—	Sarvveçvara I . . .	1160
Dharmavangça Anantavikrama	991–1007	Aryyeçvara	1171
rake Halu, Airlangga .	1019–42	Kroñearyyadipa, Gandra	1181
rake Halu, Juru (? Janggala)	1060	Kāmeçvara II . . .	1185
Jayavarsa (Kaḍiri) . .	1104	Sarvveçvara II, Çṛngga	1194–1200
		Kertajaya	1216–22

Kings of Singhasāri and Madjapahit

	A.D.		A.D.
Rājasa	1222–7	Jayanagara	1309–28
Anūṣapati	1227–48	Tribhuvanā	1329–50
Tohjaya	1248	Rajasanagara (Hayam Wuruk)	1350–89
Viṣṇuvarddhana	1248–68	Vikramavarddhana	1389–1429
Kertanagara	1268–92	Suhita	1429–47
Jayakatwang	1292–3	Bhre Tumapĕl	1447–51
Kertarājasa Jayavarddhana	1293–1309		

East Java Kings after 1451

	A.D.
Rajasavarddhana (Bhre Pamotan)	1451–3
INTERREGNUM	1453–6
Hyang Pūrvaviçeṣa (Bhre Vengker)	1456–66
Singhavikramavarddhanā (Bhre Pandan Salar)	1466–78 (?)
Raṇavijaya	1486
Pateudra	1516

West Java Kings after 1222

	A.D.		A.D.
Niskalavastu	—	Ratu Dewata	1333–57
Deva Niskala	—	Sanghyang	1522

B. MUSLIM PERIOD

Sultans of Demak

	A.D.
Patih Yunus	1511–21
Pangeram Trangganan	1521–50

Sultans of Bantam

	A.D.
Faletahan (Sunan Gunung Djati)	1526–52
Hasanuddin	1552–70
Maulana Jusup	1570–80
Maulana Mohammed	1580–96
. . . .	
Abu'l-Ma'ali Ahmad, Rahmat-Allah	1631
. . .	1634
. . . .	
Abu'n-Nasr Muhammad 'Arif, Zain al-'Ashiqin	1752

(Sultanate abolished by Sir Stamford Raffles)

Sultans of Mataram

	A.D.
Sutavijaya Senopati, overlord of East Java, founder of Empire of Mataram (now Surakarta)	1582–1601
Mas Djolang	1601–13
Tjakrakusuma Ngabdurrahman (Sultan Agung), after 1625 with title of Susuhunan	1613–45
Prabu Amangkurat I (Sunan Tegalwangi)	1645–77
Amangkurat II	1677–1703
Amangkurat III (Sunan Mas)	1703–5
Pakubuwana I (Sunan Puger)	1705–19
Amangkurat IV	1719–25
Pakubuwana II	1725–49
Pakubuwana III	1749–88

The third Javanese War (1749–55) ends with the division of Mataram into the states of Surakarta and Djocjakarta.

Surakarta

	A.D.		A.D.
Pakubuwana IV	1788–1820	Pakubuwana VIII	1858–61
Pakubuwana V	1820–3	Pakubuwana IX	1861–93
Pakubuwana VI	1823–30	Pakubuwana X	1893–
Pakubuwana VII	1830–58		

Djocjakarta

	A.D.
Abdurrahman Amangkubuwana I (Mangkubumi)	1755–92
Abdurrahman Amangkubuwana II (Sultan Sepuh)	1792–1810
Abdurrahman Amangkubuwana III	1810–14
Abdurrahman Amangkubuwana IV	1814–22
Abdurrahman Amangkubuwana V	1822–55
Abdurrahman Amangkubuwana VI	1855–77
Abdurrahman Amangkubuwana VII	1877–1921
Abdurrahman Amangkubuwana VIII	1921–

(v) THE MUHAMMADAN SULTANS OF ATJEH (ACHIN) IN SUMATRA

	A.D.
Alī Mughāyat Shāh	1496
Ṣalāḥ ad-Dīn ibn ʻAlī	1528
Alā ad-Dīn al-Qahhār ibn ʻAlī	1537
Ḥusain	1568
Sulṭān Muda (a few days)	1575
Sulṭān Srī ʻAlam	1575
Zain al-ʻĀbidīn	1576
ʻAlā ad-Dīn of Perak = Manṣūr Shāh	1577
Sulṭān Boyong	? 1589
ʻAlā ad-Dīn Riʻāyat Shāh	1586
ʻAlī Riʻāyat Shāh	1604
Iskandar Muda = Meukuta ʻAlam	1607
Iskandar Thānī	1636
Ṣāfiyat ad-Dīn Tāj al-ʻĀlam bint Iskandar Muda (widow of Iskandar Thānī)	1641
Naqīyat ad-Dīn Nūr al-ʻĀlam	1675
Zaqīyat ad-Dīn ʻInāyat Shāh	1678
Kamālat Shāh Zīnat ad-Dīn	1688
Badr al-ʻĀlam Sharīf Hāshim Jamāl ad-Dīn	1699
Perkara ʻAlam Sharīf Lamtūī	1702
Jamāl al-ʻĀlam Badr al-Munīr	1703
Jauhar al-ʻĀlam Amīn ad-Dīn (a few days)	1726
Shams al-ʻĀlam (a few days)	1726
ʻAlā ad-Dīn Aḥmad Shāh	1727
ʻAlā ad-Dīn Shāh Jahān	1735
Maḥmūd Shāh (until 1781)	1760
Badr ad-Dīn (until 1765)	1764
Sulaimān Shāh	1775
ʻAlā ad-Dīn Muḥammad	1781
ʻAlā ad-Dīn Jauhar al-ʻĀlam I (until 1802 under Regent)	1795
Sharīf Saif al-ʻĀlam	1815
Jauhar al-ʻĀlam II	1818
Muḥammad Shāh ibn Jauhar al-ʻĀlam I	1824
Manṣūr Shāh	1838
Dutch occupation	1874

(vi) SULTANS OF PALEMBANG IN SUMATRA

Abd ar-Rahīm	1648
Muhammad Manṣūr	1694–1706
. . .	.
Badr ad-Dīn Maḥmūd I	1715–50
. . .	.
Bahā ad-Dīn Muhammad	1775
Badr ad-Dīn Maḥmūd II	1803–22

(vii) GOVERNORS-GENERAL OF THE NETHERLANDS EAST INDIES

Pieter Both	1609
Gerard Reynst	1614
Laurens Reaal	1616
Jan Pieterzoon Coen	1618
Pieter de Carpentier	1623
Jan Pieterzoon Coen	1627
Jacques Specx (acting)	1629
Hendrik Brouwer	1632
Anthony van Diemen	1636
Cornelis van de Lijn	1645
Carel Reyniersz	1650
Johan Maetsuycker	1653
Rijklof van Goens	1678
Cornelis Speelman	1681
Johannes Camphuijs	1684
Willem van Outhoorn	1691
Johan van Hoorn	1704
Abraham van Riebeeck	1709
Christoffel van Swoll	1713
Henricus Zwaardecroon	1718
Matheus de Haan	1725
Dirk Durven	1729
Dirk van Cloon	1732
Abraham Patras	1735
Adriaan Valckenier	1737
Johannes Thedens	1741
Gustaaf W. van Imhoff	1743
Jacob Mossel	1750
P. A. van der Parra	1761
Jeremias van Riemsdijk	1775
Reinier de Klerk	1777
William A. Alting	1780
Pieter van Overstraten	1796
Johannes Siberg	1801
Albert H. Wiese	1805
Herman W. Daendals	1808
Jan Willem Hanssens	1811
Thomas Stamford Raffles (Lt.-Gov. of the English East India Company)	1811
John Fendall (Lt.-Gov. of the English East India Company)	1816
Commissiaries-General of William I of the Netherlands	1816
G. A. Baron van der Capellen	1818
L. P. J. Viscount du Bus de Ghisignies (Commissary-General)	1826
J. Count van den Bosch	1830
J. C. Baud	1833
D. J. de Eerens	1836
P. Merkus	1840
J. C. Reynst	1844
J. J. Rochussen	1845
A. J. Duymaer van Twist	1851
C. F. Pahud	1856
L. A. J. W. Baron Sloet van den Beele	1861
P. Mijer	1866
J. Loudon	1872
J. W. van Lansberge	1875
F.'s Jacob	1881
C. Pijnacker Hordijk	1888
C. H. J. van der Wijk	1893
W. Rooseboom	1899
J. B. van Heutsz	1904
A. F. van Idenburg	1909
J. P. Count of Limburg-Stirum	1916
D. Fock	1921
A. C. D. de Graeff	1926
B. C. de Jonge	1931
A. W. L. Tjarda van Starkenborgh Stachouwer	1936

(viii) THE KHMER KINGDOM OF CAMBODIA

(A) ANCIENT CAMBODIA TO THE END OF THE PERIOD COVERED BY EPIGRAPHY

	A.D.
Çroutavarman (founder of the dynasty)	reigning *c.* 400
Çrestavarman	?–?
Kaundinya Jayavarman	?–514
Rudravarman	514–*c.* 550
Bhavavarman I (capital at Bhavapura)	?–? (reigning in 598)
Mahendravarman	*c.* 600–?
Içanavarman (capital at Içanapura)	?–? (reigning 616, 626)
Bhavavarman II	?–? (reigning 639)
Jayavarman I	?–? (reigning 657, 681)
Jayadevi (widow of Jayavarman I)	?–? (reigning 713)

In 716 the kingdom split into two sections, which were reunited in 802 by Jayavarman II. During this period two kings are mentioned in inscriptions.

Pushkara (or Pushkaraksha) of Çambhupura	?–? (reigning 716)
Baladitya of Aninditapura	?–?

Aymonier, *Le Cambodge* (1900–4), and most French writers use the numbering of the Jayavarmans given here. In his later *Histoire de l'ancien Cambodge*, however, Aymonier counts Kaundinya Jayavarman as Jayavarman I and renumbers the later ones accordingly. Cœdès, *Les États Hindouisés D'Indochine et D'Indonésie*, uses the original numbering, which is therefore retained here.

Jayavarman II (capital at Hariharalaya)	802–50
Jayavarman III	850–77
Indravarman I	877–89
Yaçovarman I (capital at Angkor)	889–900
Harshavarman I	900–*c.* 922
Içanavarman II	?–? (reigning 925)
Jayavarman IV	928–42
Harshavarman II	942–4
Rajendravarman	944–68
Jayavarman V	968–1001
Udayadityavarman I	1001
Suryavarman I	1002–50
Udayadityavarman II	1050–66
Harshavarman III	1066–80
Jayavarman VI	1080–1107
Dharanindravarman I	1107–13
Suryavarman II	1113–*c.* 1145
Dharanindravarman II	*c.* 1160–81(?)
Jayavarman VII	1181–*c.* 1220
Indravarman II	?–1243
Jayavarman VIII	1243–95
Çrindravarman	1295–1307
Çrindrajayavarman	1307–27
Jayavarmadiparameçvara	1327–?

(B) THE PERIOD OF THE CHRONICLES

At present there is a hiatus between the last kings of epigraphy and the first of the Cambodian chronicles. There is as yet no authoritative list of the latter; the following must be considered as only a provisional one:

Nippean Bāt (Nirvânapâda)	1340–6
Sitheant-rāchā	1346–7
Srey Lompongsa-rāchā	1347–53
Obbarac Srey Sauryotey	1353
INTERREGNUM: three Siamese kings	1353–7
Srey Sauryovonge	1357–66
Prah-Barom Rama	1366–73
Thommasoka	1373–94
INTERREGNUM	1394–1401
Srey Sauryovonge	1401–17
Barommasoka	1417–31
Rama Thupdey	1432–59
Srey Rāchā	1459–73
Thommo-rāchā (Poñā Yāt)	1673–1504
Srey Sokonthor-bat	1504–8
Nāy Kan (usurper)	1508–26

Ang Chan	1516–28 (at Parsat)
	1528–66 (at Lovek)
Barom Rãchã	1566–76
Sotha I	1576–?
Chettha I	?–1594
Prah Rama (usurper)	1594–6
Poñã Tan	1596–8
Poñã Ang	1598–9
Chaopoñã Youm (regent)	1599–1600
Srey Sauryopor	1600–18
Chettha II	1618–22
INTERREGNUM	
Poñã To	*c.* 1625–30
Poñã Non	1630–40
Ang Non	1640–2
Rama Thupdey Chan	1642–59
Batom Rãchã	1660–72
Chettha III	1672–3
Obbarac Ang Non	1673–5
Chettha IV	1675–1702
Thommo-rãchã	1702–4
Chettha IV (2nd reign)	1704–6
Thommo-rãchã (2nd reign)	1706–10
Ang Em	1710–?22
Sottha II (Ang Chey)	?1722–38
Thommo-rãchã (3rd reign)	1738–47
Ang Tong	1747–9
Chettha V	1749–55
Ang Tong (2nd reign)	1755–8
Prah Outey	1758–75
Ang Mon	1775–9
INTERREGNUM	
Ang Eng	1779–96
INTERREGNUM	
Ang Chan	1806–34
Ang Mey	1834–41
Ang Duong	1841–59
Norodom	1860–1904
Sisovath	1904–

(ix) KINGDOM OF LANG-XANG OR LUANG PRABANG

Local chronicles preserve a list of thirty-five indigenous rulers of Muong-Swa up to the year A.D. 1316, the date of the birth of Fa-Ngoun, the founder of the kingdom of Lang-Xang. No dates are given. On the precise historical value of the list no verdict is possible as yet. The following is the list as given by Le Boulanger, *Histoire du Laos Français*:

(1) Phaya-Nan-Tha (of Ceylon ?)
(2) Phaya-Inthapatha (of Cambodia), who married his predecessor's widow.
(3) Thao-Phou-Tha-Saine, son of (2).
(4) Phaya-Ngou-Lueum, son of (3).
(5) Thao-Phe-Si, son of (4).
(6) Ay-Saleukheuk, son of (5).
(7) Ay-Tiet-Hai, son of (6).
(8) Thao-Tiantha-Phanit, a betel-nut merchant who came from Vientiane.
(9) Khoun-Swa, a Kha chief.
(10) Khoun-Ngiba, son of (9).
(11) Khoun-Viligna, son of (10).
(12) Khoun-Kan-Hang, son of (11).
(13) Khoun-Lo, eldest son of a Tai prince.
(14) Khoun-Swa-Lao, son of (13).
(15) Khoun-Soung.
(16) Khoun-Khet.
(17) Khoun-Khoum.
(18) Khoun-Khip.
(19) Khoun-Khap.

(20) Khoun-Khoa.
(21) Khoun-Khane.
(22) Khoun-Phèng.
(23) Khoun-Phéng.
(24) Khoun-Pheung.
(25) Khoun-Phi.
(26) Khoun-Kham.
(27) Khoun-Houng.
(28) Thao-Thene, son of (27).
(29) Thao-Nhoung.
(30) Thao-Nheuk.
(31) Thao-Phin.
(32) Thao-Phat.
(33) Thao-Vang.
(34) Phaya-Lang-Thirat.
(35) Phaya-Souvanna-Kham-Phong, son of (34), father of Thao-Phi-Fa and grandfather of Fa-Ngoun.

The Lan-Xang Dynasty

	Date of Accession A.D.
(1) Fa-Ngoun, founder of the state	1353
(2) Sam-Sène-Thaï (Oun-Hueun), son of (1)	1373
(3) Lan-Kham-Dèng, son of (2)	1416
(4) Phommathat, son of (3)	1428
(5) Pak-Houeï-Luong, son of (2)	1429
(6) Thao-Sai, brother of (5)	1430
(7) Phaya-Khai, son of (3)	1430
(8) Xieng-Sai, son of (2)	1433
(9) Son of (3), name unknown	1434
(10) Kam-Kheut, son of a palace slave	1435
(11) Sai-Tiakaphat, son of (2)	1438
(12) Thène-Kham (Souwanna-Ban-Lang), son of (11)	1479
(13) La-Sène-Thaï, brother of (12)	1486
(14) Som-Phou, son of (13)	1496
(15) Visoun, son of (11)	1501
(16) Phothisarath, son of (15)	1520
(17) Setthathirath, son of (16)	1548
(18) Sène-Soulintha (Regent)	1571
(19) Maha-Oupahat, uncertain, possibly a brother of (17)	1575
(18) Sène-Soulintha (King)	1580
(20) Nakhone-Noi, son of (18)	1582
INTERREGNUM	1583–91
(21) Nokèo-Koumane, son of (17)	1591
(22) Thammikarath, cousin by marriage of (21)	1596
(23) Oupagnouvarath, son of (22)	1622
(24) Phothisarath II, son of (18)	1623
(25) Mone-Kèo, brother of (24)	1627
(26) Oupagnaovarath, son of (25) (27) Tone-Kham, son of (26) (28) Visai, brother of (27)	dates unknown
(29) Souligna-Vongsa, son of (27)	1637
(30) Tian-Thala, son-in-law of (29)	1694
(31) Nan-Tharat, usurper	1700
(32) Saï-Ong-Hué, grandson of (29)	1700

In 1707 the kingdom was split up into two independent states with capitals at Luang Prabang and Vientiane.

Kings of Vientiane

	Date of Accession
(1) Saï-Ong-Hué, No. 32 above	1707
(2) Ong-Long, son of (1)	1735
(3) Ong-Boun, son of (2)	1760
INTERREGNUM	1778–82
(4) Chao-Nan, son of (3)	1782
(5) Chao-In, brother of (4)	1792
(6) Chao-Anou, brother of (5)	1805–28

Kings of Luang Prabang

	Date of Accession
(1) King-Kitsarath, son of (29) above	1707
(2) Khamone-Noi, cousin and son-in-law of (1)	1726
(3) Intha-Som, brother of (1)	1727
(4) Sotika-Koumane, son of (3)	1776
(5) Tiao-Vong, brother of (4)	1781
INTERREGNUM	1787–91
(6) Anourout, son of (3)	1791
(7) Mantha-Thourath, son of (6)	1817
(8) Souka-Seum, son of (7)	1836
(9) Tiantha-Koumane, brother of (8)	1851
(10) Oun-Kham, brother of (9)	1872
INTERREGNUM	1887-94
(11) Zakarine, son of (10)	1894
(12) Sisavang-Vong, son of (11)	1904

(x) KINGS OF CHAMPA

(From Georges Maspero, *Le Royaume de Champa* (1928))

Cham Name in Sanskrit Form	*Chinese Name*	*Annamese Name*	A.D. *Dates of*		*Extremes where Dates Unknown*
			Accession	*End of Reign*	
		FIRST DYNASTY, 192–336 A.D.			
(*Elder Branch*)					
Çrī Māra	K'iu Lien (?)	Khu Liên	192		
X, son of Çrī Māra					
Son and grandson of X (*Younger Branch*)					220–30
	Fan Hiong	Pham Hung			270(?)
	Fan Yi	Pham Đât		336	
		SECOND DYNASTY, 336–420(?)			
	Fan Wen	Pham Văn	336	349	
	Fan Fo	Pham Phât	349		
Bhadravarman I	Fan Hou-ta (or Siu-ta)	Pham Hođat Pham Tu-Đât			377 399–413
Gangārāja	Ti Tchen	Đich Cho'n			
	Manorathavarman				
	Wen Ti				
		THIRD DYNASTY, 420(?)–530(?) Capital: K'iu-son			
	Fan Yang-mai I	Pham Du'o'ng-mai I			421
	Fan Yang-mai II	Pham Du'o'ng-mai II			431–46
	Fan Chen-tch'eng	Pham Thân-thanh			455–72
	Fan Tang-ken-tch'ouen	Pham Đang-căn-thăng			484–91
	Fan Tchou-nong	Pham Chu'-nông		498	492
	Fan Wen-k'ouan Fan Wen-tsan	Pham Văn-to'n			502(?)
Devavarman	Fan T'ien-k'ai	Pham Thiên-kno'i			510–14
Vijayavarman	P'i-Ts'ouei-pa-mo	Bat-tôi-bât-ma			

Rudravarman I	(Kao-che) Lu-t'o-lo-pa-mo	(Cao-thu'c) Luat-đa-la-bât-ma	529(?)		572(?)
Çambuvarman	Fan Fan-tche	Pham Phan-chi			
Kandharpadharma	Fan T'eou-li	Pham Đâu-lê		629(?)	605
Bhāsadharma	Fan Tchen-long		629(?)		
Bhadreçvaravarman				645	640
X, daughter of Kandharpadharma			645		
Prakāçadharma-Vikrāntavarman I	Tchou Ko-ti / Po-chia-cho-pa-mo		653		679
Vikrāntavarman II	Kien-to-ta-mo				686(?)–731
Rudravarman II	Lu-to-lo / Lu-to				749
Fifth Dynasty, 758(?)–859(?)					
Prithivīndravarman					
Satyavarman					774–84
Indravarman I					787–801
Harivarman I					803(?)–817(?)
Vikrāntavarman III					854
Sixth Dynasty, 875(?)–991(?)					
Indravarman II					875–89
Jaya Sinhavarman I					898–903
Jaya Caktivarman					
Bhadravarman II					910
Indravarman III	(Che-li) Yin-to-man			959	918
Jaya Indravarman I	(Che-li) To-pan / Yin-t'o-pan				960–5
Parameçvaravarman I	P'i-mei-chouei / (Che-li) T'o pan Yin-t'ou / P'i-mei-chouei Ho Yin-t'ou / P'i-mei-chouei (Yang Pou) Yin	Ba-mī-thuê / Ba-mī-thuê (Du'o'ng Bô) In (Sa) Lo'i		982	972
Indravarman IV	(Che-li) T'o-pan Wou-je-houan	(Xa Lo'i) Đa-ban Ngô-nhiet-hoan / Ngô-nhiet-hoan	982	986(?)	
	Lieou Ki-tsong	Lieu Ky-tô'ng	986(?)	988(?)	

(X) KINGS OF CHAMPA (*continued*).

Cham Name in Sanskrit Form	*Chinese Name*	*Annamese Name*	A.D. *Dates of* — *Accession*	A.D. *Dates of* — *End of Reign*	*Extremes where Dates Unknown*
		Seventh Dynasty, 991(?)–1044(?) **Capital at Vijaya, modern Binh-đinh**			
Harivarman II	(Yang)-T'o-pai	Băng Vu'o'ng-la (Cu Thi Lo'i) Ha-thanh Bai-ma-la (Du'o'ng) Đa-bai	991(?)		997
Yan Pu Ku Vijaya (Çri)	(Yang P'ou Kiu) P'i-t'ou-yi (Tche-li) (Yang P'ou Kiu) P'i-t'ou (Tche-li)	(Du'o'ng Phô Cu) Bi-tra (Xa Lo'i)			999–1007
Harivarman III	(Che-li) Hia-li-pi-ma (ti)				1010
Parameçvaravarman II	(Che) Mei-p'ai-mo (tie)				1018
Vikrantavarman IV	(Yang P'ou Kou Che-li) P'i-lan-to-kia-pa-mo-(tie)			1030	
Jayasinhavarman II	(Hing Pou Che-li) Tcho-sing-hia-fou	Sa-đâu	1044	1044	
		Eighth Dynasty, 1074(?)–1139(?)			
Jaya Parameçvaravarman I		Ung-ni	1044		1060
Bhadravarman III					1061
Rudravarman III	(Che-li) Lu-t'ou-pan-ma (Tch'ang Yang Pou) (Yang-Pou Che-li) Lu-t'o-p'an-ma (Tip'o)	Chê Cu Đê Cu	1061		1074
		Ninth Dynasty, 1074(?)–1139(?)			
Harivarman IV			1074(?)	1081	
Jaya Indravarman II (1st reign)			1080	1081	
Paramabhodisatva			1081	1086(?)	
Jaya Indravarman II [partly cut off]			1086		1110

Jaya Indravarman III			1139(?)		1145(?)
ELEVENTH DYNASTY, 1145(?)–1318					
Rudravarman IV					1145(?)
Jaya Harivarman I	Tcheou Che-lan-pa Tcheou Che-pa-lan	(Chê) Bi-ri-but	1047		1160
Jaya Harivarman II					
Jaya Indravarman IV			1167(?)	1190	
Division into Two Kingdoms: (A) Kingdom of Vijaya					
Suryajayavarman			1190	1191	
Jaya Indravarman V			1191	1192	
(B) Kingdom of Panran					
Suryavarman			1190	1192	
Re-establishment of United Kingdom of Champa					
Suryavarman (of Panran)			1192	1203	
Champa a Khmer Province (1203–20)					
Jaya Parameçvaravarman II			1220		
Jaya Indravarman VI					1254
Indravarman V	(Che-li) Tcha-ya Sin-ho Pa-la (Ngo-tie wa)		1265(?)		1285
Jaya Sinhavarman III	(Pou-ti)	(Chê) Man		1307	1288(?)
Jaya Sinhavarman IV		(Chê) Chi (Tac) Chi	1307	1312	
		(Chê) Đa-a-ba-niêm (Chê) Năng	1312	1318	
TWELFTH DYNASTY, 1318–1390					
		(Chê) A-nan	1318	1342	
		Tra Hoa (Bô Đê)	1342		
	Ngo-ta Ngo-tcho	(Chê) Bông Nga		1390	1369

(X) KINGS OF CHAMPA (*continued*)

Cham Name in Sanskrit Form	*Chinese Name*	*Annamese Name*	A.D. *Dates of*		*Extremes where Dates Unknown*
			Accession	*End of Reign*	
		THIRTEENTH DYNASTY, 1390–1458			
Jaya Sinhavarman V	Ko Cheng	La Khai	1390	1400	
	Pa Ti-Lai / Tchau-pa Ti-lai	Ba Đich-lai	1400	1441	
Maha Vijaya	Mo-ho Pi-kai	Maha Bi-cai / Maha Bi-lai	1441	1446	
	Mo-ho Kouei-lai	Ma-ha Qui-lai	1446	1449	
	Mo-ho Kouei-yeou	Ma-ha Qui-do	1449	1458	
		FOURTEENTH DYNASTY, 1458–71			
	Mo-ho P'an-lo-yue	Ban-la-tra-nguyêt	1458	1460	
	P'an-lo T'ou-ts'iuan	Ban-la-tra-toan	1460	1471	

(xi) KINGS OF ANNAM AND TONGKING

I. The Legendary Dynasty of the Hông-Bang, 2879 B.C.–258 B.C.

Kingdom named Văn-lang.
Capital at Phong-châu.

II. The Thuc Dynasty

Thuc An-Du'o'ng Vu'o'ng, 257 B.C.–208 B.C.

Kingdom named Au-lac.
Capital at Loa-thanh.

III. The Triêu Dynasty (2nd century B.C.)

Kingdom of Nam-viêt.
Capital at Phien-ngu (Fan-yu).

Triêu Vo-Vu'o'ng *or* Triêu Vo-Đê	207–137
Triêu Van-Vu'o'ng	136–125
Triêu Minh-Vu'o'ng	124–113
Triêu Ai-Vu'o'ng	112
Triêu Vu'o'ng Kiên-Đu'c	111

Kingdom of Nam-viêt loses its independence and is incorporated in China.

IV. The Earlier Li Dynasty (6th century A.D.)

Capital at Song-biên.

Li Nam-Viêt Đê Bôn (Li Bi)	544–8
Triêu Viêt-Vu'o'ng Quang-Phuc (usurper)	549–71
Li Dao-Lang Vu'o'ng Thiên-Bao	549–55
Li Hâu-Đê Phât-Tu'	571–602

602 A.D. Annam again under Chinese domination. Capital removed to Tông-bônh on the site of modern Hanôi.

V. The Ngô Dynasty

Capital at {Hoa-lu'. / Co-loa.}
Kingdom called Đai-co-viêt.

Ngô Vu'o'ng Quyên	939–44
Du'o'ng-Binh Vu'o'ng Tam-Kha (usurper)	945–50
Ngô Nam-Tân Vu'o'ng Xu'o'ng-Van	951–65
and Ngô Thiên-Sach Vu'o'ng Xu'o'ng-Ngâp	951–4

Period of anarchy.

VI. The Đinh Dynasty

Capital at Hoa-lu'.
Kingdom called Đai-cô-viêt.

Đinh Tiên-Hoang Đê	968–79
Đinh Dê-Toan	979–80

VII. The Earlier Lê Dynasty

Capital at Hoa-lu'.

Lê Dai-Hanh Hoang-Đê	980–1005
Lê Trung-Tôn Hoang-Đê	1005–9

VIII. The Later Li Dynasty

Li Thai-Tô (Li Công-Uân)	1009–28
Li Thai-Tôn (Phât Ma)	1028–54
Li Thanh-Tôn	1054–72
Li Nho'n-Tôn	1072–1127
Li Thân-Tôn	1127–38
Li Anh-Tôn	1138–75
Li Cao-Tôn	1175–1210
Li Huê-Tôn	1210–24
Li Chiêu-Hoang	1224–5

IX. The Trân Dynasty

Trân Thai-Tôn . . .	1225–58
Trân Thanh-Tôn . .	1258–78
Trân Nho'n-Tôn. . .	1278–93
Trân Anh-Tôn . . .	1293–1314
Trân Minh-Tôn . . .	1314–29
Trân Hien-Tôn . . .	1329–41
Trân Du-Tôn . . .	1341–69
Du'o'ng Nhu't-Lê (usurper ?). . . .	1369–70
Trân Nghe-Tôn . . .	1370–72
Trân Duê-Tôn . . .	1372–7
Trân Dê-Hiên *or* Trân Phê-Đê.	1377–88
Trân Thuân-Tôn . .	1388–98
Trân Thiêu-Đê . . .	1398–1400

X. The Hô Dynasty

Hô Qui-Li	1400
Hô Han-Thu'o'ng . .	1400–7

XI. The restored Trân Dynasty

Trân Đê-Qui *or* Trân Gian-Đinh Dê . .	1407–9
Trân Đê Qui-Khoang	1409–13

XII. The later Lê Dynasty

Lê Lo'i *or* Binh-Đinh Vu'o'ng . . .	1418
Lê Nga (usurper)	1420
Trân Cao (usurper)	1426
Lê Thai-Tô *or* Cao Hoang-Đê . . .	1428–33
Lê Thai-Tôn *or* Văn Hoang-Đê . . .	1433–42
Lê Nho'n-Tôn *or* Tuyên Hoang-Đê . .	1442–59
Lê Nghi-Dân (usurper)	1459–60
Lê Thanh-Tôn *or* Thuân Hoang-Đê . .	1460–97
Lê Hiên-Tôn *or* Duê Hoang-Đê . . .	1497–1504
Lê Tuc-Tôn *or* Khâm Hoang-Đê. . .	1504
Lê Ui-Muc Dê	1504–9
Lê Tu'o'ng-Du'c Dê	1509–16
Trân Cao (usurpers)	1516
Trân Thang (usurpers)	1516
Lê Bang (usurpers)	1518
Lê Du (usurpers)	1518
Lê Chiêu-Tôn *or* Thân Hoang-Đê . .	1516–26
Lê Hoang-Đê-Xuan (*or* Thung) *or* Cung Hoang Đê	1522–7
INTERREGNUM of the Mac:	
Mac Đăng-Dung	1527–9
Mac Đăng-Doanh	1530–3
Lê Trang-Tôn *or* Du Hoang-Đê . . .	1533–48
Lê Trung-Tôn *or* Vô Hoang-Đê . . .	1548–56
Lê Anh-Tôn *or* Tuân Hoang-Đê . . .	1556–73
Lê Thê-Tôn *or* Nghi Hoang-Đê . . .	1573–99
Nguyên Du'o'ng-Minh (usurpers). . . .	1597
Nguyên Minh-Tri (usurpers)	1597
Lê Kinh-Tôn *or* Huê Hoang Đê . . .	1599–1619
Lê Thân-Tôn *or* Uyên Hoang Đê . .	1619–43
Lê Chân-Tôn *or* Thuân Hoang Đê . .	1643–9
Lê Than-Tôn *or* Uyên Hoang Đê . .	1649–62
Lê Huyên-Tôn *or* Muc Hoang Đê . .	1662–71
Lê Gia-Tôn *or* Mi Hoang Đê . . .	1671–5
Lê Hi-Tôn *or* Chu'o'ng Hoang Đê . .	1675–1705
Lê Du-Tôn *or* Hoa Hoang Đê . . .	1705–29
Lê Đê Duy-Phu'o'ng	1729–32
Lê Thuân-Tôn *or* Gian Hoang Đê . .	1732–5
Lê I-Tôn *or* Huy Hoang Đê . . .	1735–40
Lê Hiên-Tôn *or* Vinh Hoang Đê. . .	1740–86
Lê Mân Hoang-Đê	1786–1804

XIII. *The Mac Dynasty*

Mac Dăng-Dung	1527–9	Mac Toân	1592
Mac Dăng-Doanh	1530–40	Mac Kinh-Chi	1592–3
Mac Phuc-Hăi	1540–6	Mac Kinh-Cung	1593–1625
Mac Phuc-Nguyên	1546–61	Mac Kinh Khoan	1625–38
Mac Mâu-Ho'p	1562–92	Mac Kinh Hoan	1638–77

XIV. *The Trinh Family (of Tongking)*

Trinh Kiêm	1539–69	Trinh Giang	1729–40
Trinh Côi	1569–70	Trinh Dinh	1740–67
Trinh Tong	1570–1623	Trinh Sam	1767–82
Trinh Trang	1623–57	Trinh Can	1782
Trinh Tac	1657–82	Trinh Khai	1782–6
Trinh Côn	1682–1709	Trinh Phung	1786–7
Trinh Cu'o'ng	1709–29		

XV. *The Tây-So'n Dynasty*

(N.B.—Văn-Nhac was the eldest of three brothers Tây-So'n, who, as the rival of the Nguyên of Hue from 1771, became the master of Middle and Lower Annam and proclaimed himself Emperor.)

Nguyên Văn-Nhac,	1778–93
Nguyên Văn-Huê, brother of above	1778–92
Nguyên Quang-Toan, son of above	1792–1802

XVI. *The Nguyên Dynasty of Hue*

Nguyên Du'c-Trung	?	Nguyên Phuc-Khoat	1738–65
Nguyên Văn-Lang, son of above	died 1513	Nguyên Phuc-Thuân	1765–75
Nguyên Hoang-Du	died 1518	Nguyên (Phuc)-Anh	1778–80
Nguyên Kim	died 1545	Gia-Long	1802–19
Nguyên Hoang, Governor of Thuăn-hoa	1558–1613	Minh-Mang	1820–40
Nguyên Phuc-Nguyên	1613–35	Thiêu-Tri	1841–47
Nguyên Phuc-Lan	1635–48	Tu'-Du'c	1848–83
Nguyên Phuc-Tân	1648–87	Nguyên Duc Du'c	1883
Nguyên Phuc-Trăn	1687–91	Nguyên Hiêp-Hoa	1883
Nguyên Phuc-Chu	1691–1725	Kiên-Phuc	1884
Nguyên Phuc-Chu	1725–38	Ham-Nghi	1885
		Dông-Khanh	1886–8
		Thanh-Thai	1889–

(xii) GOVERNORS AND GOVERNORS-GENERAL OF FRENCH INDO-CHINA

Civil Governors

Le Myre de Vilers	July 1879–November 1882
Thomson	January 1883–July 1885
General Begin	July 1885–June 1886
Filippini	June 1886–October 1887
Noël Pardon, Lt.-Gov. intérimaire	23 October 1887–2 November 1887
Piquet, Lt.-Gov. intérimaire	3 November–15 November 1887

Governors-General

Constans	November 1887–April 1888
Richaud	April 1888–May 1889
Piquet	May 1889–April 1891
Bideau (intérimaire)	
De Lanessan	April 1891–October 1894
Rodier (intérimaire)	
Rousseau	December 1894–March 1895
Foures (intérimaire)	
Paul Doumer	February 1897–March 1902

Governors-General (continued)

Paul Beau	October 1902–February 1907
Bonhoure (intérimaire)	
Klobukowsky	September 1908–January 1910
Picquie (intérimaire)	
Luce	February–November 1911
Albert Sarraut (1st term)	November 1911–January 1914
Van Vollenhoven (intérimaire)	
Roume	March 1915–May 1916
Charles (intérimaire)	
Albert Sarraut (2nd term)	January 1917–May 1919
Montguillot (intérimaire)	
Maurice Long	February 1920–April 1922
Baudoin (intérimaire)	
Merlin	August 1922–April 1925
Montguillot (intérimaire, second term)	
Alexandre Varenne	November 1925–April 1928
Pierre Pasquier.	1928

SECTION IV

CHINA

1. The romanization of Chinese words.

   (i) Systems. (ii) A comparative table of initials and finals. (iii) Guide to pronunciation. (iv) Comparative table of Wade and Gwoyeu Romatzyh systems. (v) Bibliographical references.

2. Names and titles.

   (i) Chinese personal names. (ii) Chinese imperial titles.

3. Place-names and geographical terms.

   (i) General. (ii) The names of the eighteen provinces. (iii) A list of common words occurring in place-names. (iv) Bibliographical references.

4. Select glossary.

5. Calendars and systems of dating.

   (i) Dating by 'year-periods'. (ii) Dating by the Sexagenary Cycle. (iii) Dating by the Animal Cycle. (iv) Dating since the Republic. (v) Chinese calendars. (vi) Bibliographical references.

6. Dynasties and rulers.

   (i) Short table of dynasties. (ii) Tables of rulers.

L

1. THE ROMANIZATION OF CHINESE WORDS

(i) SYSTEMS

Before the middle of the 19th century there was little that could be described as systematic about western methods of transcription: since then a number of systems have appeared in different countries and, as a rule following the publication of a dictionary using the method in question, some of them have won fairly wide acceptance within their respective language areas.

Of these, the most important are: Wade-Giles (English); Hirth and Lessing-Wilhelm (German); Vissière and Couvreur (French); Latinxua-Dragunov (Russian); Gardner-Dubs (American); and Gwoyeu Romatzyh (Chinese).

Wade-Giles. This made its first appearance in Sir Thomas Wade's *Peking Syllabary* (Hongkong, 1859), a supplement to the author's *Hsin Ching Lu or Book of Experiments: being the First of a Series of Contributions to the Study of Chinese.* A revised edition (London, 1867) was published as part of the *Yü-yen tzŭ-êrh chi: a Progressive Course Designed to Assist the Student of Colloquial Chinese* (3rd edn., 1903). Although Herbert A. Giles, in the preface to the *Dictionary* (1892), describes it as 'anything but scientifically exact. In some respects it is cumbersome; in others inconsistent', it represented a great advance on the chaos that had gone before, and by using it Giles gave a quasi-official authority to the method. It became standard for the whole of the English-speaking world of sinology, and maintained its pre-eminence almost unchallenged for nearly half a century. By far the larger part of recent historical writing makes use of the Wade-Giles orthography, though the reader must be warned that a proportion of authors using this method regrettably omit aspirates and diacritical marks—for example, T'ai-p'ing will be written Tai-ping, etc.—with resulting confusion as to the correct pronunciation.

Hirth. Based on the work of E. Bretschneider this system was first published in the *Proceedings of the 13th Congress of Orientalists, Hamburg 1902* (Leiden, 1904). A slightly modified English-language version appeared in *Publication 54 of the Carnegie Institute of Research in China*, vol. I, part 2 (Washington, 1907). At the present time the Lessing is rather more widely used than the Hirth in Germany. The most important difference between the two is that Hirth follows Wade in using k' and k, p' and p, t' and t, etc., where Lessing approximates to the Gwoyeu Romatzyh in writing k and g, p and b, t and d, etc., in the initials.

Lessing-Wilhelm. Published in *Lehrgang der nordchinesischen Umgangssprache* (Tsingtao, 1912), and used by W. Rüdenberg in his *Chinesisch-deutsche Wörterbuch* (Hamburg, 1924; 2nd edn., 1936).

Vissière. Published in the author's *Méthode de transcription française des sons chinois* (Paris, 1902). This system, an outstanding example of linguistic nationalism, is used in the two most important French sinological journals (B.E.F.E.O. and *Journal asiatique*) and has been adopted officially by the French Foreign Office.

Gwoyeu Romatzyh. The New Official Chinese Latin Script. The Chinese scholar principally responsible for the working out of this system was Dr. Jaw Yuanrenn (Chao Yüan-jên). It was promulgated by the Chinese Ministry of Education in 1928, and has been used in recent Chinese dictionaries for indicating the pronunciation of characters. An important feature is the incorporation of the four Mandarin tones into the actual spelling of the word in G.R. (for example, the Wade *t'ang*$^{1-4}$ is written *tang, tarng, taang, tanq*). *The beginners' Chinese-English dictionary*, compiled by Dr. W. Simon (London, 1947), is the first European lexicographical work to use G.R.

Western writers on Chinese subjects who use the G.R. method of romanizing are still few in number ; but it is likely that this system will be increasingly adopted in the future, not only by English-speaking scholars but also by those belonging to other non-Chinese language-groups. This, and the fact that, as it is now the official Chinese system, its use by Chinese writers is already growing, make G.R. important for the western student. It is not, perhaps, too much to hope that the present confusion due to the use of different transcription systems in different countries will one day disappear through a general adherence to the New Official Chinese Latin Script.

(ii) A COMPARATIVE TABLE OF INITIALS AND FINALS

This table (modified from Heepe, *Lautzeichen*, pp. 88–9) gives the romanization of Chinese initials and finals in accordance with the Wade-Giles, Hirth, Lessing-Wilhelm, Vissière and Gwoyeu Romatzyh systems, and should be of help in identifying Chinese names in modern English, French and German works. The meaning of the words ' initial ' and ' final ', as here used, is explained in the following quotation : ' For the survey of Chinese sounds . . . an old Chinese " spelling method " has been used. It splits the (monosyllabic) Chinese words up into *initials* and *finals*. In accordance with this system, the term " final " is made to denote all that remains of a Chinese word after taking away its initial consonant, and the term is even extended to those cases where there is no initial consonant, i.e. where the " final " itself represents a Chinese word ' (Simon, *Gwoyeu Romatzyh*, p. 13).

INITIALS

G.R.	*Wade-Giles*	*Hirth*	*Lessing*	*Vissière*
b	p	p	b	p
ch	ch'	tsch'	tsch, tj	tch', k', ts'
d	t	t	d	t
g	k	k	g	k
i	y	y	y	y
j	ch	tsch	dsch, dj	tch, k, ts
k	k'	k'	k	k'
p	p'	p'	p	p'
r	j	j	j	j
s	s, ss, sz	s, ss	s	s, ss
sh	hs	h, s	hs	h, s
sh	sh	sch	sch	ch
t	t'	t'	t	t'
ts	ts', tz'	ts', tz'	ts	ts'
tz	ts, tz	ts, tz	ds	ts

FINALS

G.R.	*Wade-Giles*	*Hirth*	*Lessing*	*Vissière*
au	ao	au	au	ao
e	ê, o	ö, o	ö, o	ö, o
ei	ei	eï	e	ei
el	êrh	ïr	örl	eul
en	ên	ön	ën	en
eng	êng	öng	ëng	eng, ong
ia	ia	ia	ia	ia, ea
ian	ien	ién	iän	ien
iang	iang	iang	iang	iang, eang
iau	iao	iau	iau	iao, eao
ie	ieh	ié	iä	ie, iai
iong	iung	iung	iung	iong
iou	iu	iu	iu	ieou
iu	ü	ü	ü	iu
iuan	üan	üan	üan	iuan
iue	üeh, io	üé, io	üä	iue, io
iun	ün	ün	ün	iun
o, uo	o	o	o	o
ong	ung	ung	ung	ong
ou	ou	óu	ou	eou
u	u	u	u	ou
ua	ua	ua	ua	oua
uai	uai	uai	uai	ouai
uan	uan	uan	uan	ouan
uang	uang	uang	uang	ouang
uei	ui, uei	ui	ui, ue	ouei
uen	un	un	un	ouen
uen	wên	wön	wën	wen
ueng	wêng	wöng	wëng	wong
uo	uo	uo	uo	ouo
y	ŭ, ih	ï	ï	e, eu

Notes : (i) The initials f, h, l, m, and n are used in the same way in all five systems (though note that *hien* in the Vissière can correspond to the Wade *hsien*). (ii) The finals a, ai, an, ang, i, in and ing are used in the same way in all five systems. (iii) When finals beginning with i and u as the first element of a diphthong or triphthong are used as independent words, the i and u are changed to y and w in all the above systems (except the G.R., which retains i and u in the basic—first tone—form, though writing y and w in the other tones).

(iii) GUIDE TO PRONUNCIATION

(*a*) THE TONES

Chinese is a tonal language, and the meaning of a word to the hearer depends as much on the musical accent in which it is said as on its actual sound. For example, *i* in the first tone can mean one, clothes or doctor; in the second tone suspicion, soap or to bequeath; in the third tone a chair, already, to use; and in the fourth tone an idea, easy or an epidemic. There are, in the Mandarin dialect, only some 420 different monosyllables with which to express a large vocabulary, and the difficulties raised by the consequent number of homophones are to some extent eased by the existence of the four tones, which considerably increases the total of distinguishable sounds.

Each tone possesses its characteristic musical quality. The *first* (high level) tone is high in pitch, and is maintained on a level note (cf. in English, an unemotional statement of fact—'*I* did it'). The *second* (high rising) tone begins at a slightly lower pitch than the first and rises to a little above it (a gentle inquiry—' Do you mean *me* ? '). The *third* (low rising) tone begins at a lower pitch than the second, and there is a fractional drop before the rise (an indignantly protesting inquiry—' Do you mean it's *your* book ? '). The *fourth* (high falling) tone has a pitch which falls sharply from a higher to a lower level (indignant denial—' Certainly *not* ! '). In the second and third tones the lower notes tend to be somewhat slurred over and the higher emphasized, and the opposite in the fourth tone.

The four tones of Mandarin (National Language) are indicated in the Wade-Giles system by superior numbers ; in G.R. by systematic modifications in the spelling of the word. The G.R. basic form is reserved for the first tone (except for words beginning with l, m, n and r, where it is used for the second tone).

(*b*) THE INITIALS

G.R.	*Wade-Giles*	*Approximate pronunciation*
ch	ch'	as *ch* in *check,* but palatalized before i (pronounce *chi* as if spelt tchee).
j	ch	as *j* in *jump,* but palatalized before i (pronounce *jia* as if spelt djya).
r	j	somewhere between the sibilant *s* of *pleasure* and the *r* of *rain.*
sh	sh, hs	as *sh* in *shop,* but palatalized before i (pronounce *shi* as if spelt hsyee).
ts	ts', tz'	as *ts* in *bats.*
tz	ts, tz	as *dz* in *adze.*

The other initials have approximately the same sound in both languages.

(*c*) THE FINALS

G.R.	*Wade-Giles*	*Approximate pronunciation*
a	a	as *a* in *father* (Fr. or Ger. *a*).
ai	ai	like *eye.*
an	an	as *arn* in *barn* (or Fr. *âne*).
ang	ang	same as the last, with *ng* instead of *n* (or Ger. *angst*).
au	ao	as *ow* in *owl* (or Ger. *bau*).
e	ê, o	as *or* in *work* (or Fr. *neuf*).
ei	ei	as *ay* in *way.*
el	êrh	Chinese *e* followed by retroflex *l,* something like the *r* in the Amer. pronunciation of *sure.*
en	ên	as *en* in *darken.*
eng	êng	same as the last, with *ng* instead of *n.*
i	i	as *ea* in *eager.*
ia	ia	as *ya* in *yard.*
ian	ien	the first vowel of *anything,* with a *y* before it (or Fr. *Vienne*).*
iang	iang	between the sound of *young* and of Ger. *ang*st with a *y* before it.*
iau	iao	Ger. *au* with a *y* before it.*
ie	ieh	as *ye* in *yet.*
in	in	*in* with a *y* before it.*
ing	ing	the final of *sing* with a *y* before it.*
iong	iung	like Ger. *jung.*
iou	iu	like *you.*

* Note that the *y* is added to these sounds only when they appear as independent words, without any prefixed initial.

G.R.	*Wade-Giles*	*Approximate pronunciation*
iu	ü	Fr. *u* with a *y* before it.*
iuan	üan	same as the last, followed by *an*.
iue	üeh, io	Fr. *u* followed by the first *e* of *ever*.
iun	ün	Fr. *une* with a *y* before it.*
o	o	see under *uo*.
ong	ung	the final of Ger. *jung*.
ou	ou	as *o* in *old*.
u	u	as *oo* in *food*.
ua	ua	as *wa* in *awa'*.
uai	uai	like *Wye*.
uan	uan	Chinese *an* with *w* before it.
uang	uang	Ger. *ang*st with *w* before it.
uei	ui, uei	used without an initial: as in *Weymouth*. With an initial: like *wee* (for 1st and 2nd tones), as in *Weymouth* (3rd tone), as in *Coué* (4th tone).
uen	wên, un	used without an initial: as in *Owen*. With an initial: as in *boon*.
ueng	wêng	Chinese *eng* with *w* before it.
uo, o	uo	as *wa* in *ward*, or *or* in *order*.
y	ŭ, ih	as *u* in *surprise*.

* Note that the *y* is added to these sounds only when they appear as independent words, without any prefixed initial.

(iv) COMPARATIVE TABLE OF WADE AND GWOYEU ROMATZYH SYSTEMS

This table is adapted from W. Simon, *The beginners' Chinese-English dictionary* Table IX, Concordances I and II (pp. lx-lxx). Asterisks are substituted for tonal forms which do not occur in Chinese either as separate words or as elements of compounds.

Wade	*G.R.* (1st)	*G.R.* (2nd)	*G.R.* (3rd)	*G.R.* (4th)
a	a	ar	aa	ah
ai	ai	air	ae	ay
an	an	*	aan	ann
ang	ang	arng	*	anq
ao	au	aur	ao	aw
cha	ja	jar	jaa	jah
ch'a	cha	char	*	chah
chai	jai	jair	jae	jay
ch'ai	chai	chair	chae	chay
chan	jan	*	jaan	jann
ch'an	chan	charn	chaan	chann
chang	jang	*	jaang	janq
ch'ang	chang	charng	chaang	chanq
chao	jau	jaur	jao	jaw
ch'ao	chau	chaur	chao	*
chê	je	jer	jee	jeh
ch'ê	che	*	chee	cheh
chên	jen	*	jeen	jenn
ch'ên	chen	chern	cheen	chenn
chêng	jeng	*	jeeng	jenq
ch'êng	cheng	cherng	cheeng	chenq
chi	ji	jyi	jii	jih
ch'i	chi	chyi	chii	chih
chia	jia	jya	jea	jiah
ch'ia	chia	chya	chea	chiah
chiang	jiang	jyang	jeang	jianq
ch'iang	chiang	chyang	cheang	chianq
chiao	jiau	jyau	jeau	jiaw
ch'iao	chiau	chyau	cheau	chiaw

Wade	*G.R.* (1st)	*G.R.* (2nd)	*G.R.* (3rd)	*G.R.* (4th)
chieh	jie	jye	jiee	jieh
ch'ieh	chie	chye	chiee	chieh
chien	jian	*	jean	jiann
ch'ien	chian	chyan	chean	chiann
chih	jy	jyr	jyy	jyh
ch'ih	chy	chyr	chyy	chyh
chin	jin	*	jiin	jinn
ch'in	chin	chyn	chiin	chinn
ching	jing	*	jiing	jinq
ch'ing	ching	chyng	chiing	chinq
chiu	jiou	*	jeou	jiow
ch'iu	chiou	chyou	cheou	*
chiung	jiong	*	jeong	*
ch'iung	chiong	chyong	*	*
cho	juo	jwo	*	*
ch'o	chuo	*	*	chuoh
chou	jou	jour	joou	jow
ch'ou	chou	chour	choou	chow
chu	ju	jwu	juu	juh
ch'u	chu	chwu	chuu	chuh
chua	jua	*	joa	*
ch'ua	chua	*	*	*
chuai	juai	*	joai	juay
ch'uai	chuai	chwai	choai	chuay
chuan	juan	*	joan	juann
ch'uan	chuan	chwan	choan	chuann
chuang	juang	*	joang	juanq
ch'uang	chuang	chwang	choang	chuanq
chui	juei	*	*	juey
ch'ui	chuei	chwei	*	chuey
chun	juen	*	joen	*
ch'un	chuen	chwen	choen	*
chung	jong	*	joong	jonq
ch'ung	chong	chorng	choong	chonq
chü	jiu	jyu	jeu	jiuh
ch'ü	chiu	chyu	cheu	chiuh
chüan	jiuan	*	jeuan	jiuann
ch'üan	chiuan	chyuan	cheuan	chiuann
chüeh	jiue	jyue	jeue	*
ch'üeh	chiue	chyue	*	chiueh
chün	jiun	*	jeun	jiunn
ch'ün	chiun	chyun	*	*
ê (o)	e	er	ee	eh
ên	en	*	*	enn
êng	eng	*	*	*
êrh	*	erl	eel	ell
fa	fa	far	faa	fah
fan	fan	farn	faan	fann
fang	fang	farng	faang	fanq
fei	fei	feir	feei	fey
fên	fen	fern	feen	fenn
fêng	feng	ferng	feeng	fenq
fo	*	for	*	foh
fou	*	four	foou	fow
fu	fu	fwu	fuu	fuh
ha	ha	har	haa	*
hai	hai	hair	hae	hay
han	han	harn	haan	hann
hang	hang	harng	*	*
hao	hau	haur	hao	haw
hê (ho)	he	her	*	heh
hei	hei	*	heei	*
hên	*	hern	heen	henn
hêng	heng	herng	*	henq

Wade	*G.R.* (1st)	*G.R.* (2nd)	*G.R.* (3rd)	*G.R.* (4th)
hou	hou	hour	hoou	how
hsi	shi	shyi	shii	shih
hsia	shia	shya	*	shiah
hsiang	shiang	shyang	sheang	shianq
hsiao	shiau	shyau	sheau	shiaw
hsieh	shie	shye	shiee	shieh
hsien	shian	shyan	shean	shiann
hsin	shin	shyn	shiin	shinn
hsing	shing	shyng	shiing	shinq
hsiu	shiou	*	sheou	shiow
hsiung	shiong	shyong	*	shionq
hsü	shiu	shyu	sheu	shiuh
hsüan	shiuan	shyuan	sheuan	shiuann
hsüeh	shiue	shyue	sheue	shiueh
hsün	shiun	shyun	*	shiunn
hu	hu	hwu	huu	huh
hua	hua	hwa	*	huah
huai	*	hwai	*	huay
huan	huan	hwan	hoan	huann
huang	huang	hwang	hoang	huanq
hui	huei	hwei	hoei	huey
hun	huen	hwen	hoen	huenn
hung	hong	horng	hoong	honq
huo	huo	hwo	huoo	huoh
i (yi)	i	yi	yii	yih
jan	*	ran	raan	*
jang	*	rang	raang	ranq
jao	*	rau	rao	raw
jê (jo)	*	*	ree	reh
jên	*	ren	reen	renn
jêng	rheng	reng	reeng	*
jih	*	*	*	ryh
jo	*	ruo	*	ruoh
jou	*	rou	roou	row
ju	*	ru	ruu	ruh
juan	*	ruan	roan	*
jui	*	ruei	roei	ruey
jun	*	ruen	*	ruenn
jung	*	rong	roong	*
ka	ga	gar	gaa	gah
k'a	ka	*	kaa	kah
kai	gai	*	gae	gay
k'ai	kai	*	kae	kay
kan	gan	*	gaan	gann
k'an	kan	*	kaan	kann
kang	gang	*	gaang	ganq
k'ang	kang	karng	kaang	kanq
kao	gau	*	gao	gaw
k'ao	kau	*	kao	kaw
kê (ko)	ge	ger	gee	geh
k'ê (k'o)	ke	ker	kee	keh
kei	*	*	geei	*
kên	gen	gern	*	genn
k'ên	*	*	keen	kenn
kêng	geng	*	geeng	genq
k'êng	keng	*	keeng	*
kou	gou	*	goou	gow
k'ou	kou	*	koou	kow
ku	gu	gwu	guu	guh
k'u	ku	*	kuu	kuh
kua	gua	*	goa	guah
k'ua	kua	*	koa	kuah
kuai	guai	*	goai	guay
k'uai	kuai	*	koai	kuay

Wade	*G.R.* (1st)	*G.R.* (2nd)	*G.R.* (3rd)	*G.R.* (4th)
kuan	guan	*	goan	guann
k'uan	kuan	*	koan	*
kuang	guang	*	goang	guanq
k'uang	kuang	kwang	*	kuanq
kuei	guei	*	goei	guey
k'uei	kuei	kwei	koei	kuey
kun	*	*	goen	guenn
k'un	kuen	*	koen	kuenn
kung	gong	*	goong	gonq
k'ung	kong	*	koong	konq
kuo	guo	gwo	guoo	guoh
k'uo	*	*	*	kuoh
la	lha	la	laa	lah
lai	*	lai	*	lay
lan	*	lan	laan	lann
lang	*	lang	laang	lanq
lao	lhau	lau	lao	law
lê	lhe	le	*	leh
lei	lhei	lei	leei	ley
lêng	*	leng	leeng	lenq
li	lhi	li	lii	lih
lia	*	*	lea	*
liang	*	liang	leang	lianq
liao	lhiau	liau	leau	liaw
lieh	lhie	lie	liee	lieh
lien	*	lian	lean	liann
lin	*	lin	liin	linn
ling	lhing	ling	liing	linq
liu	lhiou	liou	leou	liow
lo	lhuo	luo	luoo	luoh
lou	lhou	lou	loou	low
lu	lhu	lu	luu	luh
luan	*	luan	loan	luann
lun	lhuen	luen	*	luenn
lung	*	long	loong	lonq
lü	*	liu	leu	liuh
lüan	*	liuan	leuan	*
lüeh	*	*	*	liueh
lün	*	liun	*	*
ma	mha	ma	maa	mah
mai	*	mai	mae	may
man	mhan	man	maan	mann
mang	*	mang	maang	*
mao	mhau	mau	mao	maw
mei	*	mei	meei	mey
mên	mhen	men	*	menn
mêng	mheng	meng	meeng	menq
mi	mhi	mi	mii	mih
miao	mhiau	miau	meau	miaw
mieh	mhie	*	*	mieh
mien	*	mian	mean	miann
min	*	min	miin	*
ming	*	ming	miing	minq
miu	*	*	*	miow
mo	mho	mo	moo	moh
mou	*	mou	moou	mow
mu	*	mu	muu	muh
na	nha	na	naa	nah
nai	*	*	nae	nay
nan	nhan	nan	naan	nann
nang	nhang	nang	naang	nanq
nao	*	nau	nao	naw
nei	*	*	neei	ney
nên	*	*	*	nenn

Wade	*G.R.* (1st)	*G.R.* (2nd)	*G.R.* (3rd)	*G.R.* (4th)
nêng	*	neng	*	nenq
ni	*	ni	nii	nih
niang	*	niang	*	nianq
niao	*	*	neau	niaw
nieh	nhie	nie	*	nieh
nien	nhian	nian	nean	niann
nin	*	nin	*	*
ning	*	ning	niing	ninq
niu	nhiou	niou	neou	niow
no	*	nuo	*	nuoh
nou	*	*	*	now
nu	*	nu	nuu	nuh
nuan	*	*	noan	*
nun	*	*	*	nuenn
nung	*	nong	*	nonq
nü	*	*	neu	niuh
nüeh	*	*	*	niueh
ou	ou	*	oou	ow
pa	ba	bar	baa	bah
p'a	pa	par	*	pah
pai	bai	bair	bae	bay
p'ai	pai	pair	pae	pay
pan	ban	*	baan	bann
p'an	pan	parn	*	pann
pang	bang	*	baang	banq
p'ang	pang	parng	paang	panq
pao	bau	baur	bao	baw
p'ao	pau	paur	pao	paw
pei	bei	*	beei	bey
p'ei	pei	peir	*	pey
pên	ben	*	been	benn
p'ên	pen	pern	*	penn
pêng	beng	berng	beeng	benq
p'êng	peng	perng	peeng	penq
pi	bi	byi	bii	bih
p'i	pi	pyi	pii	pih
piao	biau	*	beau	biaw
p'iao	piau	pyau	peau	piaw
pieh	bie	bye	biee	bieh
p'ieh	pie	*	piee	*
pien	bian	*	bean	biann
p'ien	pian	pyan	pean	piann
pin	bin	*	biin	binn
p'in	pin	pyn	piin	pinn
ping	bing	*	biing	binq
p'ing	ping	pyng	*	pinq
po	bo	bor	boo	boh
p'o	po	por	poo	poh
p'ou	pou	pour	poou	*
pu	bu	bwu	buu	buh
p'u	pu	pwu	puu	puh
sa	sa	*	saa	sah
sai	sai	*	*	say
san	san	*	saan	sann
sang	sang	*	saang	sanq
sao	sau	*	sao	saw
sê	*	*	*	seh
sên	sen	*	*	*
sêng	seng	*	*	*
sha	sha	shar	shaa	shah
shai	shai	*	shae	shay
shan	shan	*	shaan	shann
shang	shang	*	shaang	shanq
shao	shau	shaur	shao	shaw

Wade	*G.R.* (1st)	*G.R.* (2nd)	*G.R.* (3rd)	*G.R.* (4th)
shê	she	sher	shee	sheh
shei	*	sheir	*	*
shên	shen	shern	sheen	shenn
shêng	sheng	sherng	sheeng	shenq
shih	shy	shyr	shyy	shyh
shou	shou	shour	shoou	show
shu	shu	shwu	shuu	shuh
shua	shua	*	shoa	*
shuai	shuai	*	shoai	shuay
shuan	shuan	*	*	shuann
shuang	shuang	*	shoang	*
shui	*	shwei	shoei	shuey
shun	*	*	shoen	shuenn
shuo	shuo	*	*	shuoh
so	suo	swo	suoo	*
sou	sou	*	soou	sow
ssŭ (szŭ)	sy	*	syy	syh
su	su	swu	*	suh
suan	suan	*	*	suann
sui	suei	swei	soei	suey
sun	suen	*	soen	suenn
sung	song	sorng	soong	sonq
ta	da	dar	daa	dah
t'a	ta	*	taa	tah
tai	dai	dair	dae	day
t'ai	tai	tair	*	tay
tan	dan	*	daan	dann
t'an	tan	tarn	taan	tann
tang	dang	*	daang	danq
t'ang	tang	tarng	taang	tanq
tao	dau	*	dao	daw
t'ao	tau	taur	tao	taw
tê	*	der	*	*
t'ê	te	*	*	teh
tei	*	*	deei	*
têng	deng	*	deeng	denq
t'êng	teng	terng	*	*
ti	di	dyi	dii	dih
t'i	ti	tyi	tii	tih
tiao	diau	*	deau	diaw
t'iao	tiau	tyau	teau	tiaw
tieh	die	dye	*	*
t'ieh	tie	*	tiee	tieh
tien	dian	*	dean	diann
t'ien	tian	tyan	tean	tiann
ting	ding	*	diing	dinq
t'ing	ting	tyng	tiing	tinq
tiu	diou	*	*	*
to	duo	dwo	duoo	duoh
t'o	tuo	two	tuoo	tuoh
tou	dou	*	doou	dow
t'ou	tou	tour	toou	tow
tsa	tza	tzar	*	*
ts'a	tsa	*	tsaa	*
tsai	tzai	*	tzae	tzay
ts'ai	tsai	tsair	tsae	tsay
tsan	tzan	tzarn	tzaan	tzann
ts'an	tsan	tsarn	tsaan	tsann
tsang	tzang	*	tzaang	tzanq
ts'ang	tsang	tsarng	tsaang	*
tsao	tzau	tzaur	tzao	tzaw
ts'ao	tsau	tsaur	tsao	tsaw
tsê	*	tzer	tzee	tzeh
ts'ê	*	*	*	tseh

Wade	*G.R.* (1st)	*G.R.* (2nd)	*G.R.* (3rd)	*G.R.* (4th)
tsei	*	tzeir	*	*
tsên	tzen	*	tzeen	tzenn
ts'ên	tsen	tsern	*	*
tsêng	tzeng	*	*	tzenq
ts'êng	tseng	tserng	*	tsenq
tso	tzuo	tzwo	tzuoo	tzuoh
ts'o	tsuo	tswo	tsuoo	tsuoh
tsou	tzou	*	tzoou	tzow
ts'ou	*	*	*	tsow
tsu	tzu	tzwu	tzuu	tzuh
ts'u	tsu	tswu	*	tsuh
tsuan	tzuan	*	tzoan	tzuann
ts'uan	tsuan	tswan	*	tsuann
tsui	tzuei	*	tzoei	tzuey
ts'ui	tsuei	*	tsoei	tsuey
tsun	tzuen	*	tzoen	tzuenn
ts'un	tsuen	tswen	tsoen	tsuenn
tsung	tzong	*	tzoong	tzonq
ts'ung	tsong	tsorng	*	*
tu	du	dwu	duu	duh
t'u	tu	twu	tuu	tuh
tuan	duan	*	doan	duann
t'uan	tuan	twan	toan	tuann
tui	duei	*	*	duey
t'ui	tuei	twei	toei	tuey
tun	duen	*	doen	duenn
t'un	tuen	twen	toen	tuenn
tung	dong	*	doong	donq
t'ung	tong	torng	toong	tonq
tzŭ	tzy	*	tzyy	tzyh
tz'ŭ	tsy	tsyr	tsyy	tsyh
wa	ua	wa	woa	wah
wai	uai	*	woai	way
wan	uan	wan	woan	wann
wang	uang	wang	woang	wanq
wei	uei	wei	woei	wey
wên	uen	wen	woen	wenn
wêng	ueng	*	woeng	wenq
wo	uo	*	woo	woh
wu	u	wu	wuu	wuh
ya	ia	ya	yea	yah
yai	*	yai	*	*
yang	iang	yang	yeang	yanq
yao	iau	yau	yeau	yaw
yeh	ie	ye	yee	yeh
yen	ian	yan	yean	yann
yin	in	yn	yiin	yinn
ying	ing	yng	yiing	yinq
yu	iou	you	yeou	yow
yung	iong	yong	yeong	yonq
yü	iu	yu	yeu	yuh
yüan	iuan	yuan	yeuan	yuann
yüeh	iue	*	*	yueh
yün	iun	yun	yeun	yunn

(v) BIBLIOGRAPHICAL REFERENCES

Chao, Y. R. 'Languages and dialects in China', *Geographical Journal*, cii (1943), 63–6.
De Francis, J. 'The alphabetization of Chinese', *Journal of the American Oriental Society*, lxiii (1943), 225–40.

Gardner, C. S. 'The western transcription of Chinese', *Journal of the North China Branch of the Royal Asiatic Society*, lxii (1931), 136–47.

Heepe, M. (ed.). *Lautzeichen und ihre Anwendung in verschiedenen Sprachgebieten*. Berlin, 1928.

Karlgren, B. *The romanization of Chinese*. (China Society.) London, 1928.

Karlgren, B. *Sound and symbol in Chinese*. London, 1923.

Simon, W. *Gwoyeu romatzyh. Tables, rules, illustrative examples*. London, 1942.

Simon, W., and Lu, C. H. *Chinese sentence series*. London, 1942. [Part I (pp. 9–62) and bibliographical appendix (pp. 226–30).]

2. NAMES AND TITLES

(i) CHINESE PERSONAL NAMES

I

The 'basic name' of a Chinese consists of two parts: a family name or surname, called the *shinq* (*hsing*^{4}); and a personal or given name, the *ming* (*ming*^{2}). In Chinese usage the *shinq* is always written first, and the *ming* second.

Two-character names were usual up to the time of the *Hann* (*Han*^{4}) dynasty: since then it has become more common for the whole name (*shinq* and *ming*) to be written with three characters (though two- and four-character names are still not infrequently met with). In most names the *shinq* is written with a single character and the *ming* with two, e.g. *Suen Yihshian* (*Sun Yat-sen*); but there are several compound surnames, e.g. *Symaa, Ouyang* (*Ssŭ*^{1}*-ma*^{3}, *Ou*^{1}*-yang*^{2}), and then the given name will commonly be written with a single character.

In selecting *ming* for the children of a numerous family, it is customary to give the sons names in which one of the characters is retained and repeated for all the brothers, the other being changed for each son (and similarly for daughters, though the 'retained' character will normally be a different one). For example, the Northern *Songq* (*Sung*^{4}) statesman *Wang Anshyr* (*Wang*^{2} *An*^{1}*-shih*^{2}) was the third of seven brothers, the personal names of the others being *Anren, Andaw, Angwo, Anshyh, Anlii* and *Anshanq* (*An*^{1}*-jên*^{2}, *An*^{1}*-tao*^{4}, *An*^{1}*kuo*^{2}, *An*^{1}*-shih*^{4}, *An*^{1}*-li*^{3} and *An*^{1}*-shang*^{4}). Even if the *ming* consists of a single character only, the radical part of the character can be retained in combination with different non-radical elements for each name (e.g. the brothers *Su Shyh* (*Su*^{1} *Shih*^{4}) and *Su Cheh* (*Su*^{1} *Chê*^{4}), politicians and writers of the *Songq* (*Sung*^{4}) period: the characters *shyh* and *cheh* are both written with the same radical, 159).

The constant or repeated character is, moreover, often used to 'place' the individual in his generation. It is frequently a word from a family motto, each word in which is used to distinguish a particular generation. For example, if the phrase *Der nae ren jy bao* (*Tê*^{2} *nai*^{3} *jên*^{2} *chih*^{1} *pao*^{3}, Virtue is man's treasure) has been chosen, '*Der*' would appear as part of the *ming* in the great-grandfather's generation, '*Nae*' in the grandfather's, '*Ren*' in the father's, and so on till the reappearance of '*Der*' in the generation of the great-grandchildren.

Although the *ming* is a person's legal name, which he will sign on formal occasions, it is not the first one he receives, and there are many other names by which he will be known or by which he may refer to himself.

The first, chronologically, is his 'childhood name', colloquially called *sheauming* (*hsiao*^{3}*-ming*^{2}, little name), and in literary Chinese known as *ruuming* (*ju*^{3}*-ming*^{2}, milk name). This is given by the head of the family (in the absence of grandparents, then by the parents) and usually makes reference, directly or by implication, to the hoped-for continuity and prosperity of the family. Alternatively, if the parents do not 'know the rules' about selecting an auspicious name for the child, a *sheauming* may be chosen at random (for instance by one of the parents walking out of the house and naming the child after whatever he or she first sees).

At the age of ten, or a little before, the child receives his personal name (the *ming* already referred to). As has been mentioned, this may be chosen with a classical quotation or allusion in mind, or with some reference to a family motto, and will serve to mark the generation to which he, together with his brothers and cousins, belongs.

On the child's going to school a *shuming* (*shu*^{1}-*ming*^{2}) or *shyueming* (*hsüeh*^{2}-*ming*^{2}) (book name or study name) may also be given him by his teacher. This will be used both by his schoolmasters and schoolfellows, and may be retained later in life in anything having to do with literary pursuits.

We come now to the very important *tzyh* (*tzŭ*^{4}, courtesy names) and *haw* (*hao*^{4}, literary names) which most educated people adopt, and which are frequently used alone, i.e. without the *shinq*, in speaking or writing about an individual. These are well illustrated in the note that follows on the different names of *Ju Shi* (*Chu*^{1} *Hsi*^{1}).

At the time of their marriage it is customary for both groom and bride to take a *tzyh* as a marriage name.

Most scholars, in former times, adopted one or more 'studio names' or *byeming* (*pieh*^{2}-*ming*^{2}): and if they held a post in the governing bureaucracy, they often made use of an 'official name' (*guanming*, *kuan*^{1}-*ming*^{2}) as well.

After the death of an illustrious man, a posthumous name was sometimes conferred by imperial decree.

II

To illustrate all this, some of the names and titles of the great Southern *Sonq* (*Sung*^{4}) philosopher and historian *Ju Shi* (*Chu*^{1} *Hsi*^{1}) may be briefly told.

He was born in A.D. 1130 at *Youchi*, *Yanpyngfuu* (*Yu*^{2}-*ch'i*^{1} *Yen*^{2}-*p'ing*^{2}-*fu*^{3}), in present *Fwujiann* (*Fukien*) province. His childhood names were (1) *Chernlaang* (*Ch'ên*^{2}-*lang*^{3}, 'the youngster from *Chern*'—which was the ancient name for *Youchi*) and (2) *Jihyan* (*Chi*^{4}-*yen*^{2}, 'the younger *Yanpyng*'—the elder being his teacher, who was known as *Lii Yanpyng*, *Li*^{3} *Yen*^{2}-*p'ing*^{2}).

The name (3) *Yuanhuey* (*Yüan*^{2}-*hui*^{4}, 'the great one who hides himself') was given him by another of his teachers, *Liou Yannjong* (*Liu*^{2} *Yen*^{4}-*chung*^{1}), and can be taken either as a *tzyh* or a *shyueming*.

The *tzyh* which *Ju Shi* himself most often used was (4) *Jonqhuey* (*Chung*^{4}-*hui*^{4}, 'the second one who hides himself'), a more modest name than the other.

The most commonly used of his *haw* or literary names was (5) *Hueyan* (*Hui*^{4}-*an*^{1}, 'the little hidden-away cottage'), a reference to his very unpretentious style of living. His workroom there was called the *Tzyy-yang* hall, and from this *Ju Shi* was often referred to as *Tzyy-yang* (*Tzŭ*^{3}-*yang*^{2}) (6).

Others of his *haw* were (7) *Hueyueng* (*Hui*^{4}*-wêng*^{1}, 'the old man who hides away'); (8) *Tsangjou duennueng* (*Ts'ang*^{1}*-chou*^{1} *tun*^{4}*-wêng*^{1}, 'the old man from the Isle of the Blessed who hides away'); (9) *Tsangjou binqsoou* (*Ts'ang*^{1}*-chou*^{1} *ping*^{4}*-sou*^{3}, 'the sick old man from the Isle of the Blessed'); (10) *Yunguu laoren* (*Yün*^{2}*-ku*^{3} *lao*^{3}*-jên*^{2}, 'the old gentlemen from the cloudy valley'); (11) *Jonqlaang* (*Chung*^{4}*-lang*^{3}, 'the clear-minded second son').

Among *Ju Shi's* posthumously-awarded names were (12) *Jong Dahfu* (*Chung*^{1} *Ta*^{4}*-fu*^{1}, 'the even-tempered minister of state'); (13) *Tayshy* (*T'ai*^{4}*-shih*^{1}, 'the great teacher'); (14) *Shinngwo gong* (*Hsin*^{4}*-kuo*^{2} *kung*^{1}, 'the duke of *Shinn-an*', which title was later changed to (15) *Hueigwo gong, Hui*^{1}*-kuo*^{1} *kung*^{1}, 'the duke of *Hueijou, Hui*^{1}*-chou*^{1}'); and (16) *Wen gong* (*Wên*^{2} *kung*^{1}, 'the duke of letters').

(ii) CHINESE IMPERIAL TITLES

The period of imperial rule in China began in 221 B.C. with the unification of the major part of what is to-day called 'China Proper' by *Chyn Shyy Hwangdih* (*Ch'in*^{2} *Shih*^{3} *Huang*^{2}*-ti*^{4}), first emperor of the Chyn dynasty; and ended with the formal abdication of the last Manchu emperor in A.D. 1912.

Before 221 B.C. the rulers of the *Jou* (*Chou*^{1}) dynasty had been known as *Wang*, or kings, and the same title had been adopted, towards the end of the *Janngwo* (*Chan*^{4}*-kuo*^{2}) or Warring States period, by the rulers of the larger (nominally vassal) states.

With the *Chyn*, the new title *Hwangdih* (*Huang*^{2}*-ti*^{4}), Emperor, was used for the first time, and it remained for more than two thousand years the expression normally employed. Consonant with the genius of literary Chinese for brevity, we often find this contracted to the ellipsis *Dih* (*Ti*^{4}). (Used in this sense *Dih* must not be confused with earlier and different meanings of the same character.) The form 'Emperor *Wuudih*' ('*Wu*^{3}*-ti*^{4}') sometimes met with in occidental writings is therefore tautologous, and the following forms are to be preferred: either *Wuudih*, or 'Emperor *Wuu*', or (translating the whole) 'the Martial Emperor'.

Like anyone else, a Chinese emperor had a surname and given name. The surname (*shinq, hsing*^{4}) of the first *Ming* emperor was Ju (Chu^{1}), and his given name *Yuanjang* (*Yüan*^{2}*-chang*^{1}). This given name, out of respect, was taboo, and even the inadvertent use of its characters could be severely punished. It was therefore known as *huey* (*hui*^{4}), a word meaning 'taboo' or 'to avoid'.

The three ways of referring to an emperor which are most commonly used are (i) by his *shyh* (*shih*^{4}) or posthumous name; (ii) by his *miawhaw* (*miao*^{4}*-hao*^{4}) or Temple Name, also posthumously bestowed; and (iii) by his *nianhaw* (*nien*^{2}*-hao*^{4}) or year-period, when a single one was retained by the ruler for the whole of his reign.

The *shyh* or posthumous name consisted of one or more adjectives depicting the praiseworthy qualities (real or assumed) of the ruler. Successive dynasties increased and elaborated the *shyh*, and the posthumous names attributed to some of the Manchu emperors include as many as twenty-four adjectives. In practice the longer of these *shyh* were abbreviated; for example, the *shyh* of the *Tarng* (*T'ang*^{2}) emperors were shortened to their first, or first two, words, while for the Ming and Manchu emperors the last word of the *shyh* was customarily used for the whole. The *shyh* is written by the Chinese together with the imperial title: as *Gauhwangdih* (*Kao*^{1}-*huang*^{2}-*ti*^{4}), 'the Eminent Emperor'. (*Gau* was the *shyh* of *Ju Yuanjang*, the founder of the *Ming*.) It can also be written *Gaudih* (*Dih* used for *Hwangdih*), with the same translation.

Miawhaw: most emperors, though not all, were given a Temple Name. This consisted always of two characters only: the first an adjective, and the second either *Tzuu* (*Tsu*^{3}) or *Tzong* (*Tsung*^{1}). *Tzuu*, or Founder, was used for the first emperor of a dynasty, and has sometimes been attributed retrospectively to his more important (though often not imperial) forbears. *Tzong*, for which Prof. Duyvendak has suggested the translation 'Exemplar', was regularly used for the later emperors of a dynastic line. The range of characters used adjectivally in *miawhaw* was restricted by convention. The same combinations of characters tend therefore to recur from dynasty to dynasty—for example, the founder was almost invariably given the Temple Name *Gautzuu* or *Taytzuu*. In referring to an emperor by his *miawhaw* it is therefore necessary to precede it by the name of his dynasty. *Taytzuu*, the Great Founder, was the Temple Name conferred on *Ju Yuanjang*, and to distinguish him from the *Taytzuu* of other dynasties, he is properly referred to as *Ming Taytzuu*.

The *nianhaw* or year-period is a two-character phrase, chosen for its auspicious associations, used to refer to a part or the whole of a ruler's reign. From 1368, the beginning of the *Ming*, the practice was adopted of retaining a single *nianhaw* for the whole of a reign, and the English translation 'reign-title' was probably chosen with this in mind. 'Reign-title' is, however, an inaccurate rendering for Chinese history before the *Ming*, as it was the earlier custom for emperors to change their *nianhaw* at frequent intervals, sometimes even yearly. *Hann Wuudih* (*Han*^{4} *Wu*^{3}-*ti*^{4}), the *Hann* Martial Emperor, was the first to introduce the system of *nianhaw*, and changed them eleven times in the course of his reign (140–87 B.C.). The *nianhaw* in earlier usage, then, applied only to a certain period of years, which hardly ever coincided with an entire reign: for this reason 'year-period' should be accepted as the better translation.

An emperor should only be referred to by his *nianhaw* if its use was retained during the whole of a reign, and consequently only the *Ming* and *Ching* emperors can be so designated.

As with the *shyh*, the *nianhaw* is used by the Chinese together with the imperial title. The *nianhaw* adopted by the founder of the Ming dynasty was *Horngwuu* (*Hung*^{2}-*wu*^{3}). *Horngwuu Hwangdih* is thus yet another way of referring to *Ju Yuanjang*. As *Horngwuu* is simply the name of a year-period, the above expression should not be translated as 'the Emperor *Horngwuu*' but as 'the Emperor of the *Horngwuu* period', or, more briefly, as 'the *Horngwuu* Emperor'. Nor is it correct to use the year-period *Horngwuu* by itself to designate the emperor of that reign, as is so often done for

Ming and Manchu rulers, since it is neither a name nor a title attributed to the emperor himself.

Example: the first emperor of the *Ming* dynasty.

Ju was his family name (*shinq*).
Yuanjang were his (tabooed) given names (*huey*).
Gau (Eminent) was his posthumous name (*shyh*). This is used together with the imperial title, as *Gauhwangdih*, or *Gaudih* ('the Eminent Emperor').
Taytzuu (Great Founder) was his Temple Name (*miawhaw*).
Horngwuu was the year-period he adopted, and was retained by him for the duration of his reign. He may therefore be referred to by it. It is used with the imperial title, as *Horngwuu Hwangdih* (The *Horngwuu* Emperor).

For further information on official names and titles, see the following works:

Dubs, Homer H. 'Chinese imperial designations', *Journal of the American Oriental Society*, lxv (1945), 26–32.
Mayers, W. F. *The Chinese Government: a manual of Chinese titles, categorically arranged and explained.* Shanghai, 1878.

3. PLACE-NAMES AND GEOGRAPHICAL TERMS

(i) GENERAL

Chinese geographical names present problems of variation, transcription and interpretation.

In the first place, for many areas and natural features there exist archaic as well as modern names, and the former are as frequently used and as well understood (by the educated Chinese) as the latter ; e.g. *Syhchuan* (*Szechwan*), archaic name *Shuu* (*Shu*^{3}). Moreover the names of provinces, towns and even villages have often been changed by successive dynasties ; e.g. the town at present known as *Beeipyng* (*Pei*^{3}*-p'ing*^{2}) and before as *Beeijing* (*Peking*), was called under the *Yuan* dynasty *Dahdu* (*Ta*^{4}*-tu*^{1}) or *Jongdu* (*Chung*^{1}*-tu*^{1}), under the *Liau* (*Liao*^{2}) dynasty *Ianjing* (*Yen*^{1}*-ching*^{1}) and earlier *Nanjing* (*Nan*^{2}*-ching*^{1}), while during the *Tarng* (*T'ang*^{2}) period its name was *Ioujou* (*Yu*^{1}*-chou*^{1}).

Transcription raises its own difficulties. Chinese place-names appear in English historical writing usually in either the Post Office or Wade transcriptions. The former was originally a compromise between a number of earlier transcription systems and local dialect pronunciations. It preserves certain dialect (and pre-Wade) forms, such as ki- and occasionally ts- for initial ch- and j-, but in general disdains such (other) niceties as aspirates, diacriticals and tones. On the other hand, it introduces quite arbitrary changes of spelling to meet the practical difficulty of differentiating between place-names that are identically romanized by Wade (assuming that superior tone-numbers are omitted). Example : the provinces *Shansi* and *Shensi*—in Wade *Shan*^{1}*-hsi*^{1} and *Shan*^{3}*-hsi*^{1} (G.R. differentiates them as *Shanshi* and *Shaanshi*). The bibliographical references for this system are : the List of Post Offices (14th Issue, 1936), and the China Postal Atlas, of the same year, both published by the Directorate-General of Posts, Shanghai. The Wade system of transcription is discussed in the section on Romanization, above.

As soon as works in German and French are added to a list of literary sources, other systems of romanization enter and bring with them new complications, thus the capital of *Hwunan* (*Hunan*) province appears as *Tsch'ang-scha* (Hirth), Tch'ang-cha (Vissière), *Ch'ang-sha* (Wade) and *Changsha* (Post Office). Other examples can easily be found in which the choice between competing ‘ sinological nationalisms ’ and unscientific and often misleading simplifications is even more confusing. This multiplicity of national transcription systems and the fact that the Wade hegemony seems to be breaking up (this at least can be deduced from the radical modifications of and departures from the Wade that are being increasingly adopted, as private systems, by English-speaking sinologists) constitute a great part of the case for the use of G.R. romanizations of place-names. It is a further advantage that G.R., since it incorporates the tonal value of a word in the spelling, enables the reader to differentiate between words that—tonal quality apart

—are homophones (e.g. *Shanshi* and *Shaanshi*). G.R. romanization is also noticed in the section on Romanization, above.

Thirdly, there is the question of the interpretation of meanings. The names of places and natural features often reflect historical, social and topographical facts. It is, unfortunately, a peculiar difficulty with Chinese geographical names that, owing to the large number of homophones, it is usually difficult to recognize meanings unless characters are given as well as a romanized transcription. A list of the commoner components of Chinese geographical names is, however, included as part (iii) of this Note, while in part (ii) a brief interpretation is offered of the names of the provinces of China Proper.

(ii) THE NAMES OF THE EIGHTEEN PROVINCES

1 and 2. *Herbeei* (*Hopeh*) and *Hernan* (*Honan*). Respectively North and South of the River. The word Her (*Hê*^{2} or *Ho*^{2}), used without further qualification, almost always refers, as here, to the *Hwangher* (*Huang*^{2}*-hê*^{2}) or Yellow River. Ancient names: *Jih* (*Chi*^{4}), and *Yuh* (*Yü*^{4}).

3 and 4. *Shandong* (*Shantung*) and *Shanshi* (*Shansi*). Respectively East and West of the Mountains. The mountains referred to are the *Tayharngshan* (*T'ai*^{4}*-hang*^{2}*-shan*^{1}), running approximately along the line of the *Shanshi-Herbeei* border. Ancient names: *Luu* (*Lu*^{3}), and *Jinn* (*Chin*^{4}).

5. *Gansuh* (*Kansu*). 'In giving a name to a new and larger political area a new name has frequently been formed by taking one syllable each from two old units within the area. Thus many old names are repeated in new combination' (Spencer, p. 83). *Gansuh*, which may be translated 'Sweet Solitude', is an example of this practice. Ancient name: *Loong* (*Lung*^{3}).

6. *Shaanshi* (*Shensi*). West of Shaan (i.e. Shaanshiann in Hernan). Ancient name: Chyn (Ch'in^2).

7. *Jiangsu* (*Kiangsu*). Name compounded from two places, Jiangning (Chiang'-ning^2) and Sujou (Su'-chou').

8. *Anhuei* (*Anhwei*). Another example of the practice referred to under 5 above. The name can be translated 'Peaceful and Beautiful'. Ancient name: *Woan* (*Wan*^{3}).

9. *Jehjiang* (*Chekiang*). The *Jeh* River province.

10. *Jiangshi* (*Kiangsi*). The River Province—West. The word *Jiang* (*Chiang*^{1}), used without further qualification, usually denotes, as here, the *Yangtzyy* (*Yangtse*) River. Ancient name: *Gann* (*Kan*^{4}).

11. *Fwujiann* (*Fukien*). Name compounded from two places, Fwujo^2 (Foochow) and Jiannjou (Chien^4-chou). Ancient name: *Min* (*Min*^{2}).

12 and 13. *Hwubeei* (*Hupeh*) and *Hwunan* (*Hunan*). Respectively North and South of the Lake. The lake referred to is *Donqtyng* (*Tung*^{4}*-t'ing*^{2}). Ancient names: *Eh* (*E*^{4}), and *Shiang* (*Hsiang*^{1}).

14. *Syhchuan* (*Szechwan*). The Four River province. Ancient name: *Shuu* (*Shu*^{3}).

15. *Gueyjou* (*Kweichow*). May be translated 'Precious District'. Ancient name: *Chyan* (*Ch'ien*^{2}).
16. *Yunnan* (*Yünnan*). South of the Clouds. Ancient name: *Dian* (*Tien*^{1}).
17 and 18. *Goangdong* (*Kwangtung*) and *Goangshi* (*Kwangsi*). Respectively East and West of Goangjou (Canton). Ancient names: *Yueh* (*Yüeh*^{4}), and *Guey* (*Kuei*^{4}).

(iii) A LIST OF COMMON WORDS OCCURRING IN PLACE-NAMES

an (an^1)	peace	jong (chung^1)	middle
ba (pa^1)	eight	jou (chou^1)	district
beei (pei^3)	north	ju (chu^1)	pearl
bo (po^1)	slope	juang (chuang)	cottage, village
charng (ch'ang^2)	long	koou (k'ou^3)	mouth, opening, port
cherng (ch'êng^2)	walled city		
chi (ch'i^1)	seven	liow (liu^4)	six
chuan (ch'uan^1)	river, stream	long (lung^2)	dragon
chyau (ch'iao^2)	bridge	nan (nan^2)	south
dah (ta^4)	large, great	pyng (p'ing^2)	plain
dao (tao^3)	island	pyng (p'ing^2)	peace
dong (tung^1)	east	san (san^1)	three
du (tu^1)	capital (city)	shan (shan^1)	mountain
ell (êrh^4)	two	sheau (hsiao^3)	small
feng (fêng^1)	peak	shi (hsi^1)	west
fuu (fu^3)	prefecture, prefectural city	shiann (hsien^4)	district
		shin (hsin^1)	new
goang (kuang^3)	extensive	shoei (shui^3)	water
hae (hai^3)	sea	shyh (shih^4)	market
her (hê^2)	river	shyr (shih^2)	stone, rock
hwang (huang^2)	yellow	shyr (shih^2)	ten
hwu (hu^2)	lake	syh (ssu^4)	four
jenn (chên^4)	market town	wuu (wu^3)	five
jeou (chiu^3)	nine	yih (i^4)	one
jiang (chiang^1)	river	yih (i^4)	city
jia (chia^1)	family, clan	yuan (yüan^2)	plain
jing (ching^1)	capital (city)	yuh (yü^4)	jade

(iv) BIBLIOGRAPHICAL REFERENCES

Herrmann, Albert. *Historical and commercial atlas of China*. (Harvard-Yenching Inst. Monograph Series, Vol. I.) Cambridge, Mass., 1935.

Playfair, G. M. H. *The cities and towns of China: a geographical dictionary*. Hongkong, 1879.

Simon, W. *The beginners' Chinese-English dictionary*. London, 1947. [Table xv, Geographical Names; pp. xcix–cxxxi.]

Spencer, J. E. 'Chinese place-names and the appreciation of geographic realities', *Geographical Review*, xxxi (1941), 79–94.

4. SELECT GLOSSARY

For all Chinese words the main entry is under the *Gwoyeu Romatzyh* (G.R.) transcription. If the G.R. and Wade-Giles transcriptions begin with the same initial letter, this is the only entry; but if the Wade-Giles initial is different from the G.R., the word also appears in its appropriate place in the Wade-Giles transcription with a cross-reference to the G.R. form. G.R. romanization is always followed (in brackets) by either the Wade-Giles (with superior tone-numbers) or Post Office transcriptions.

ALLOWANCE. See PRIVATE TRADE.

ARROW WAR. The second Anglo-Chinese war (1856–60): so-called from the incident of 8 October 1856, the arrest by Chinese soldiers of the Chinese crew of a Hongkong-registered lorcha, the *Arrow*, flying the British flag.

BAMBOO ANNALS. See JWUSHU JIHNIAN.

BAO (PAO^3). A small administrative area in the present local government system; officially translated as 'borough'. In rural areas it is a subdivision of the shiang (hsiang^1), in urban areas of the jenn (chên^4). See also SHIANN (HSIEN^4).

BAOJEA (PAO^3-CHIA^3) SYSTEM. An old form of local government organization recently re-introduced in China. Ten huh (hu^4) or households make up a jea (chia^3) and ten jea are grouped together in each bao (pao^3). The term baojea is an old one, and governments at various periods of Chinese history have attempted to establish local government systems of this type (notably the Sonq (Sung^4) statesman Wang Anshyr (Wang^2 An^1-shih^2) in the 11th century, and the Manchus in the 17th). The Republican Government decreed the introduction of the baojea system, first in 1932 as a military measure applicable to certain civil-war provinces only, and then in 1935 as the standard of local administration for the whole country. The mathematical tidiness of the scheme has militated against its effective application to the Chinese countryside, and most of the self-governing functions entrusted to the baojea system by the new laws are still carried out by various traditional *de facto* groupings.

BANNER. (1) The basic grouping of the Manchu military organization. The Banner system was devised by Nurhaci, the real founder of the Ching dynasty, who in 1605 succeeded in creating a professional army by transforming the traditional Manchu *niru* ('arrows'—semi-feudal levies in which service was partly hereditary, partly dependent on land-holding) into four Banners which had no specific territorial ties. The number of Banners was increased to eight in 1615. Both Chinese and Mongols who had passed over to the Manchu side were later brigaded with the Manchu Banners, and eventually each of the eight Banners comprised Chinese and Mongol as well as Manchu 'nations', thus bringing up the number of military formations to twenty-four. The Eight Banners (Ba Chyi, Pa^1 Ch'i^2) were distinguished by colours: in order of descending status they were: (i) Bordered Yellow; (ii) Plain Yellow; (iii) Plain White; (iv) Bordered White; (v) Plain Red; (vi) Bordered Red; (vii) Plain Blue; (viii) Bordered Blue.

(2) The tribal-territorial unit of the Mongols. It normally comprised some fifty adult males capable of bearing arms, and was led by its chieftain or dzassak (*q.v.*).

BATTLE OF THE CONCESSIONS. The name applied to the scramble for leased territories and concessions in China by Germany, Russia, France and Britain, which opened in 1898.

BEG. A title used in Turkestan and elsewhere by the Chinese Mohammedans meaning 'chief'. (Lokotsch, nos. 260, 282.) See also N. and M.E. Glossary, under BEY (p. 13).

BEILEH. The Manchu title conferred on the sons of the Ching dynasty imperial princes. Its meaning is 'commander' or 'leader'. Chinese transliteration: Beyleh, Pei^{4}-lê^{4}.

BINGBUH (PING^{1}-PU^{4}). See LIOWBUH.

BOHEA. See TEA

BONZE. As used by Europeans in China, the term generally denotes a Buddhist priest. The name was brought to China from Japan, and is a corruption of the Japanese reading of Chinese characters meaning a religious person or Teacher of the Law. See also S.E. Asia and Japan Glossaries, pp. 113, 225.

BOR (PO^{2}). Earl. The third of the traditional Chinese ranks of nobility. See also TITLES OF NOBILITY.

BOXERS. The Boxer movement had its origin (*c.* 1895) in several secret societies of a mystical, superstitious and generally anti-foreign character. Spreading from Shandong (Shantung) to other parts of northern and north-western China, often with a measure of support from local officials, the secret society known as the Yihher Twan (I^{4}-ho^{2} T'uan^{2}), or Righteous Harmony Militia, gave an increasingly violent expression to the anti-foreign sentiment generated by the Sino-Japanese war (1894) and the Battle of the Concessions (1898). Opponents of the movement changed the last character (Twan) of the name to Chyuan (Ch'üan^{2}), 'fist'. Hence the European name 'Boxer', which also described aptly enough the gymnastic exercises performed by the adepts of the society. Supported by reactionary elements at court, the Boxer Rising of 1900 was followed by the siege and relief of the Legations at Beeijing (Peking). The episode was ended with the signing of the Boxer Protocol, an international instrument which opened a new phase in the relations of China and the Western Powers.

BUH (PU^{4}). A measure of area, about 5 feet square. The moou (mow) consists of 240 buh. Literally, a 'pace'. See also MOOU.

BUND. In China the term bund is applied especially to the banked-up quay along the shore of the former Settlements in the Treaty Ports. In Hongkong alone the word bund is not used, and there the quay is known as the praya (from the Port. *praia*, 'shore'). Bund is from the Hindustani *band*, an artificial embankment, causeway or dyke.

CANDARIN. The trade term for the hundredth part of a tael (*q.v.*).

Sometimes found as Candareen. The Chinese equivalent is fen (fên^1).

CANGUE. A portable pillory, in the form of a square wooden board, worn clamped round the neck and resting on the shoulders. The weight was limited by law to 30 lbs., but while wearing it the victim could neither feed himself nor easily lie down. The wearing of the cangue, as a punishment for minor offences, is said to have been introduced into China by the Tuohbar Wey (To^4-pa^2 Wei^4) (see List of dynasties and rulers). Chinese etymologies have been suggested, but the word is probably from the Portuguese *canga*, 'ox-yoke'. Other forms: conga, congoe.

CASH. The trade name of the only coin formerly made in China: Chinese chyan (ch'ien^2). Ten cash make one candarin; ten candarins one mace; ten mace one tael. From *caixa*, the name given by the Portuguese to the tin coins of Malacca, and brought by them to China. (Lokotsch, no. 1102.)

CATHAY. An old name for China, originally for north China only. It came into European usage via central Asia, and is from the name of the Chihdan (Ch'i^4-tan^1) of Manchuria who established the Liau (Liao^2) dynasty in north-eastern China (see List of dynasties and rulers). In the form *Kitai* it is still the Russian name for China. Other forms: Catai, Cataja, Catay, Cataya, Cathaia, Catheie. See also MANZI.

CATTY. A measure of weight, usually translated as 'pound'. 16 taels or ounces (leang, liang^3) make one catty or pound (jin, chin^1), and 100 catties make one picul (shyr, shih^2 or dann, tan^4). As with most Chinese measures, there are innumerable local and occupational variations. The standard catty-weight used in the levying of Customs duties was stipulated by the Trade Regulations annexed to the Sino-British Treaty of 1858 at $21\frac{1}{3}$ ounces avoirdupois, and by the Sino-French Treaty at 604·53 grammes. The word is from the Malay *kātī*. Other forms: cate, catte, cattie.

CHAM. A medieval corruption of Khan.

CHAN^4 KUO^2. See JANNGWO.

CHÊN^4. See JENN.

CHIA^3. See JEA.

CHIANG^1-CHÜN^1. See JIANGJIUN.

CHIH^1-FU^3. See JYFUU.

CHIH^4-T'AI^2. See TZOONGDU.

CHINA PROPER. China Proper or the Eighteen Provinces (see under SHEENG) is often distinguished from the Outer Territories of Tibet, Chinese Turkestan, Inner Mongolia and Manchuria. The latter were traditionally subject to special territorial or semi-colonial forms of government, and their full assimilation to the provincial system characteristic of the rest of China did not take place until after the inauguration of the Republic.

CHINCHAI (CH'IN^1-CH'AI^1). An imperial envoy. The expression is found in the Jesuit Letters as *kin-thai*.

CHIN^4-SHIH^4. See EXAMINATIONS.

CHIU (CH'Ü^1). See SHIANN.

Chop. Properly speaking a seal-impression, stamp, brand, mark, number or name. Probably from the Hindustani *chhāp* (the verb *chāpnā* means to stamp or print), though it has also been suggested that it derives from the Cantonese pronunciation of *jar* (*cha*^{2}), to prick or puncture. The corresponding Chinese expression is haw (hao^{4}) or tzyhhaw (tzŭ^{4}-hao^{4}). Chop in the sense of brand or mark is used in, for example, a 'chop of tea', i.e. tea bearing the mark of a particular dealer; and 'first-chop', i.e. best quality. Again, a 'chop-dollar' is a dollar stamped by a (Chinese) firm with a private mark as a guarantee of the genuineness of the coin. The practice of chopping dollars seems to have been confined to south China. In Pidgin (*q.v.*) chop acquired the further meaning of a permit or licence, probably from the official seal imprinted on the document. The Grand Chop was the trade term for the port clearance granted by the Hoppo (*q.v.*) to a ship after all Customs charges and dues had been paid. The customs offices on the Canton river were also, in the early days of the trade, known as Chop-houses.

Chou^{1}. See Jou.

Chuenchiou (Ch'un^{1}-ch'iu^{1}). One of the Confucian classics, the Annals of the feudal state of Luu (Lu^{3}), traditionally ascribed to Confucius. The words mean 'Spring and Autumn'. The name is also applied to the period of Chinese history between 722 and 481 B.C., to which the Annals relate.

Chü^{3}-jên^{2}. See Examinations.

Chumpein. See Tzoongbing.

Chung^{1}-kuo^{2}. See Jonggwo.

Chunkoon. See Jiangjiun.

Chuntuck (Chumtuck). See Tzoongdu.

Chu^{2}-shu^{1} Chi^{4}-nien^{2}. See Jwushu Jihnian.

Chyng (Ch'ing^{2}). A square measure equal to a little more than $13\frac{1}{3}$ acres or 5·4 ha. 100 moou make one chyng.

Chyy (Ch'ih^{3}). A linear measure: the Chinese 'foot'. 10 fen (fên^{1}) make one tsuenn (ts'un^{4}), 10 tsuenn make one chyy, 1800 chyy make one lii (li^{3}). There have at different times been several hundred chyy in use in China, varying in length from locality to locality, and from trade to trade. The range is estimated to extend from 8·6 to 27·8 inches. The chyy used in the China trade for measuring ships and cloth was that of the Canton carpenters, and fixed at 14·1 English inches (0·358 metres). It was adopted as the 'foot' of the Chinese Customs tariff in 1843. The common trade name was cubit or covid (*q.v.*).

Co-hong. See Hong.

Comay. The chop (*q.v.*) granted formally by the responsible Chinese official allowing 'free trade'. Used in the earlier days of the China trade, it meant that western merchants could both sell to and buy from any Chinese merchants at the port, as against being restricted in their dealings to specified dealers. From the Chinese *kee mae* (*k'e*^{3} *mai*^{3}), 'able to buy'.

Comprador. The word has had two meanings on the China coast;

(i) Ship-chandler or purveyor of supplies. This is the meaning commonly intended in 18th and early 19th century references. (ii) The chief (Chinese) cashier and broker of a foreign firm, responsible for the Chinese staff (warehouse keepers, shroffs, etc.), attending to money and credit matters in the firm's dealings with Chinese, and generally acting as 'link' between the western businessman and the Chinese merchant. This usage gradually ousted the former one during the last century.

CONCESSION. (1) A grant under the authority of the Chinese Government of the privilege or right to do something—e.g. build a railway or operate a mine or public utility undertaking. Such concessions usually had their origin in some international instrument such as a treaty or special agreement, and normally gave the Concessionary Power a right of control over the railway, mine or other enterprise that infringed Chinese sovereignty. See also BATTLE OF THE CONCESSIONS.

(2) An area conceded by the Chinese Government under treaty at one of the former Treaty Ports and set aside for the residence of foreigners. Municipal and police administration was under the control of the foreign lessee power, though sovereignty over the area remained with the Chinese Government, which also levied a fixed land-tax. See also SETTLEMENT.

CONGFOU (CONGOU). See TEA.

CONSOO FUND. Instituted in 1779–80, this was a guarantee fund administered by the Hong merchants (*q.v.*) to meet liabilities for mercantile debts and official fines, impositions, etc. The money was provided by a direct contribution from the foreign trade in the form of an *ad valorem* tax of 3 per cent. and sometimes 6 per cent. paid by foreign merchants on almost all goods. Consoo is not, as has been suggested, a corruption of 'council', but is from gongsuoo (kung^{1}-so^{3}), the hall or meeting-place of a gongsy (kung^{1}-ssŭ^{1}) or guild. The council hall adjoining the foreign factories at Canton, where the Hong merchants held their own meetings and also their conferences with the foreign traders, was known as the Consoo House.

COUNTRY TRADE. The adjective 'country' was used colloquially by Europeans in the Far East from the 17th century to differentiate Indian from European products. A 'country ship' was thus one that was owned in an Indian port, and, from the point of view of the China merchants, the 'country trade' was the India-China commerce as distinct from that between China and Europe.

COVID. The common trade name for the chyy (ch'ih^{3}), the Chinese 'foot'. A probable Indo-Portuguese corruption of the Port. *côvado,* the Flemish ell. Other forms: covad, cobde, cobdee, covit. See also CHYY.

CUMSHAW. Pidgin (*q.v.*) for a present of any kind. From the Cantonese or Amoy pronunciations of gaanshieh (kan^{3}-hsieh^{4}), 'heartfelt thanks'.

DAW (TAO^{4}). In medieval China the term was applied to a region of considerable size, comparable to the modern province. In the later imperial and early republican periods the daw or circuit was a subdivision of the province. It is now abolished, leaving no administrative area intermediate between the sheeng (shêng^3, province) and shiann (hsien^4, district).

DAWTAIR (TAO^4-T'AI^2). An imperial official administering a daw, tao^4 (*q.v.*). Although a civilian, he had control over the military forces stationed within the fuu of his area. His title is often translated as 'Intendant' or 'Sub-Inspector'. References to the 'Taotai' in trading records are usually to this official in his special capacity as Customs Controller (see GUANDAW).

DIANNSHYH (TIEN^4-SHIH^4). See EXAMINATIONS.

DIAW (TIAO^4). A string of cash. In theory a string is made up of 10 rolls of 100 cash each, and a full diaw therefore passes for 1,000 cash. In practice, money-changers made a charge for 'stringing' by deducting a few cash from each roll. Diaw therefore tended to vary locally, the range normally running from 970 to 990 cash. See also CASH.

DIHBAO (TI^4-PAO^3). The village headman, usually nominated by the shiann (hsien^4) administration from among the elders of the village.

DOTCHIN. A set of scales used by Chinese merchants for weighing silver, etc. From the Chinese *duhcheng* (*tu*^{4}-*ch'êng*^{4}), to weigh.

DUJIUN (TU^1-CHÜN^1). Military governor or (often a more accurate translation) warlord. The period after the fall of the Manchu empire and before the establishment of the authority of the Gwomindaang (Kuo^2-min^2-tang^3) over most of China in the late 'twenties is often referred to as the period of dujiun rule.

DZASSAK. A noble or chieftain commanding one of the Mongol banners (*q.v.*). The position was sometimes hereditary, sometimes conferred by imperial appointment. (Mayers, no. 537.)

EXAMINATIONS. The former competitive Civil Service examinations were: (i) A first examination normally held twice in every three years in shiann (hsien^4) and fuu (fu^3) cities. Successful candidates were known as Shiowtsair (Hsiu^4-ts'ai^2)—the title is often translated 'B.A.', though it is properly to be regarded rather as a qualification than as a degree. (ii) An examination of higher standard held in the provincial capitals, roughly at three-year intervals. Candidates that passed obtained the title Jeuren (Chü^3-jên^2), translated (again somewhat misleadingly) as 'Master's degree'. Jeuren were sometimes appointed to office, but more often proceeded to the next examination. (iii) This was held triennially at the Imperial Capital, and only Jeuren who had not yet taken office could present themselves for it. Successful candidates (in Manchu times some 200 to 350 out of about ten times that number of aspirants) were rewarded with the title of Jinnshyh (Chin^4-shih^4), sometimes translated as 'Doctor'. Jinnshyh were further tested in the Palace Examination (Diannshyh, Tien^4-shih^4) held, in theory at least, in the presence of the emperor, and on a theme set by him. Jinnshyh passing this with high distinction became members of the Hannlin Yuann (*q.v.*).

Extraterritoriality. An arrangement provided for in treaties between China and a number of foreign states whereby citizens of those states while in China were withdrawn from the application of Chinese law and the jurisdiction of Chinese courts in cases in which they appeared as defendants and were instead placed under the jurisdiction and law of special Consular courts established by the Treaty Powers each for its own nationals. The first treaty to embody this kind of arrangement was the Sino-American Treaty of Wanghia, 3 July 1844, which served as model for subsequent treaties. The Chinese rightly regarded extraterritoriality as derogating from their national sovereignty, and conducted a long campaign, especially after the establishment of the Republic, to bring the system to an end. Extraterritorial rights were relinquished by the United Kingdom and the U.S.A. in 1943. See Japan Glossary, p. 226.

Factory. (1) In general, a trading establishment at a foreign port. The factories were not places where goods were made, but the places of residence and business of the factors or commercial agents of the various East India Companies established by the trading countries of Europe. The words were perhaps adopted from the Portuguese *feitor* and *feitoria*.

(2) In particular, the buildings occupied by the foreign merchants at Canton when all the China trade was confined by law to that town.

Fan Kwae. 'Barbarian devils', a formerly common term for foreigners. From the Chinese *fangoei* (*fan*^{1}-*kuei*^{3}). Sometimes found as Fan Qui.

Fantair (Fan^{1}-t'ai^{2}). The colloquial term for a provincial treasurer under the empire. The Fantair was the nominal head of the provincial Civil Service. Official designation, *Fansy* (*Fan*^{1}-*ssŭ*^{1}). (Mayers, no. 275.)

Fan Qui. See Fan Kwae.

Fengshoei (Feng^{1}-shui^{3}). Literally, 'wind and water': the name given to the art of harmonizing the siting of homes, ancestral temples and graves with the local currents of chih (ch'i^{4}, 'the universal breath') as determined by the topographical features (hills, streams, buildings, roads and bridges) of the neighbourhood. Early railway construction in China was often hampered by local opposition, as people believed that the tracks would disturb the fengshoei of the district.

For (Fo^{2}). Buddha or Buddhism. In earlier European accounts it is usually found as Fo or Foh.

Fuu (Fu^{3}). An administrative area in the imperial local government system, often translated 'prefecture' (see under Jyfuu). It normally comprised from 2 to 6 shiann, jou or ting (*qq.v.*). Towards the end of the Manchu period there were 183 fuu in China. The area was abolished in 1912, though the word is still occasionally to be met with in books as a part of place-names (e.g. Shi-an-fuu, Sianfu).

Fuutair (Fu^{3}-t'ai^{2}). See Fuuyuann.

Fuuyuann (Fu^{3}-yüan^{4}). Provincial governor. During the greater part of the Manchu period all the Eighteen Provinces of China

Proper (*q.v.*) with the exception of Jyrlih (Chihli), Gansuh (Kansu) and Syhchuan (Szechwan) (see under TZOONGDU) were under a Fuuyuann. The three provinces Shanshi (Shansi) Hernan (Honan) and Shandong (Shantung) were under the exclusive jurisdiction of their provincial governors. In the remaining twelve provinces the Fuuyuann's authority was shared with a Tzoongdu (Tsung^{3}-tu^{1}) or governor-general. Transcriptions commonly met with in 18th and 19th century records are: Fooyen, Fuion, Fuioon, Fuyuen and Phuen. Colloquial designation: Fuutair (Fu^{3}-t'ai^{2}). See also TZOONGDU.

GAULIANG (KAO^{1}-LIANG^{2}). *Sorghum vulgare,* the staple grain in Manchuria and in much of north China.

GAUTZUU (KAO^{1}-TSU^{3}). See section (ii) of Names and Titles, p. 169.

GINSENG. *Panax repens*, a medicinal plant found in Manchuria, Korea, North America and elsewhere, whose root is supposed to resemble in shape the body of a man (hence the Chinese name renshen (jên^{2}-shên^{1}), of which ginseng is a corruption).

GODOWN. A warehouse in which goods and stores are kept. The word is used in India as well as all over east Asia. It is from the Malay *gadong*. Other forms: gaddone, gadonge, gedonge, godon, godung, goedown, gotton, gudam, zodoun.

GONG (KUNG^{1}). Duke. The first of the traditional Chinese ranks of nobility. See also TITLES OF NOBILITY.

GONGBUH (KUNG^{1}-PU^{4}). See LIOWBUH.

GRAND CHOP. See CHOP.

GUANDAW (KUAN^{1}-TAO^{4}). An added title enjoyed by the Dawtair (*q.v.*) in his capacity as Superintendent of the Customs Houses in his daw. By way of exception there was at Tianjin (Tientsin) a special Guandaw official in addition to the territorial Dawtair. (Mayers, no. 324.) See also HOPPO.

GUNPOWDER. See TEA.

GWOMINDAANG (KUO^{2}-MIN^{2}-TANG^{3}). The National People's Party, founded by Dr. Sun Yat-sen towards the beginning of the present century. In spite of its success in bringing about the revolution of 1911, its authority in the early years of the Republic was limited to a small area in south China. After its reorganization (on the model of the Communist Party of the Soviet Union) in 1923–4 it successfully carried through under the leadership of Chiang Kai-shek the Northern Expedition of 1926–7, thus accomplishing the political unification of the country. The claim of the Gwomindaang to be the sole legal political party in China has since then been effectively challenged only by the Chinese Communist Party.

HAEGUAN (HAI^{3}-KUAN^{1}) TAEL. The unit of account in which duties were levied by the Imperial Maritime Customs. It has never existed as an actual currency, and in practice Customs obligations were always settled in the local currency at an agreed rate of conversion. See also TAEL.

HAKKA. An immigrant community, with its own dialect and customs, now located mainly in Goangdong (Kwangtung), Goangshi (Kwangsi), Jiangshi (Kiangsi) and Fwujiann (Fukien).

HANNLIN YUANN (HAN⁴-LIN² YUAN⁴). The Academy of Literati, first established during the Tarng (T'ang²) dynasty in the 8th century. Under the Manchus its membership was about five hundred. Admission to it was the highest literary distinction open to scholars, and only Jinnshyh graduates were eligible to sit for its examinations. The functions of the Hannlin Yuann included the compilation of the Dynastic Histories, the drafting of edicts, etc. Literal meaning, 'the forest of pencils' (Mayers, no. 201). See also EXAMINATIONS.

HONG. (1) A business firm. From the Chinese harng (hang²), original meaning—a row or series. The extended meaning arose because the Chinese warehouse or factory usually consisted of a series of buildings reaching back in a line from the street front (see under FACTORY). The word hong was applied at Canton especially to the factories of the European merchants.

(2) The guild of Chinese merchants exclusively licensed to trade with the foreigners at Canton. The Hong, or Co-Hong, was first established (*c.* 1720) by the great merchants of Canton, with the support of the local officials. It was essentially a combination to maintain the prices of Chinese exports and restrict competitive bidding for imports, while at the same time it effectively limited the circle of those enjoying the resultant profits of the trade. In 1757 Canton became the only port at which foreign trade was permitted, and three years later the Co-Hong was formally chartered. It was dissolved in 1771, but reconstituted as the Twelve (later the Thirteen) Merchants in 1782. The Hong merchants were given full control of the trade, were to be the sole channel of communication between the Imperial Government and the foreign traders, and were made responsible for the good behaviour of the latter. They were also entrusted with the administration of the Consoo Fund (*q.v.*). The Hong was finally dissolved under the terms of the Treaty of Nanking (1842). Co-Hong is a corruption of the Cantonese pronunciation of *gongharng* (*kung¹-hang²*), though Yule suggests 'an exogamous union between the Latin *co-* and the Chinese hong'. It is also found as Cong-Hong.

HOPPO. The title commonly used by western traders in the 18th and 19th centuries for the Administrator of the Canton Customs (the Guandaw or Customs Dawtair (*qq.v.*) of the Goangdong (Kwangtung) ports). The Hoppo was always a Manchu, and in the official hierarchy took rank after the Tzoongdu (Tsung³-tu¹) or governor-general. The derivation of the name is obscure. Other forms: Hapoa, Happa (Eng.) and Opeou (Fr.).

HOUR (HOU²). Marquis. The second of the traditional Chinese ranks of nobility. See also TITLES OF NOBILITY.

HSIANG¹. See SHIANG.

HSIEN⁴. See SHIANN.

HSING²-PU⁴. See LIOWBUH.

HSIU⁴-TS'AI². See EXAMINATIONS.

HUHBUH (HU⁴-PU⁴). See LIOWBUH.

HUNDRED DAYS' REFORM. The energetic attempt to reform China by edict undertaken by the Guangshiuh (Kuang¹-shü⁴) Emperor and his chief adviser Kang Yeouwei (K'ang^{1} Yu^{3}-wei^{2}) in 1898. The hundred-day period extended from 11 June to 21 September. The reform movement was brought to an end by the reactionary coup d'état of the Empress Dowager.

HWEIHWEI (HUI^{2}-HUI^{2}). The common term in China for Moslems. It appears first in the Liau (Liao^{2}) dynasty records. Its etymology is uncertain.

HYSON and HYSON SKIN. See TEA.

INVESTMENT. See STOCK.

JANNGWO (CHAN^{4}-KUO^{2}). The Warring States. The name is applied to the period of Chinese history between 481 and 221 B.C., during which the westerly state of Chyn (Ch'in^{2}) was establishing its hegemony over its feudal rivals. The period ended with the first imperial unification of China under Chyn Shyyhwangdih (Shih^{3}-huang^{2}-ti^{4}).

JEA (CHIA^{3}). The smallest administrative area in the present local government system: officially translated as 'ward'. It is a subdivision of the bao (pao^{3}). See also BAO, BAOJEA and SHIANN.

JENN (CHÊN^{4}). A subdivision of the shiann (hsien^{4}) or county (*q.v.*) in urban areas. Its counterpart in rural areas is the shiang (hsiang^{1}). It is officially translated as 'urban district'.

JEUREN (CHÜ^{3}-JÊN^{2}). See EXAMINATIONS.

JIANGJIUN (CHIANG^{1}-CHÜN^{1}). Tartar General. During the Manchu period Jiangjiun exercising territorial jurisdiction in the three eastern provinces (Manchuria) were in fact military governors: after 1876 they held the rank and powers of a Tzoongdu (*q.v.*). In China Proper the Jiangjiun, though they outranked even governors-general, normally exercised no authority except over the small Manchu banner forces they commanded. Chunkoon is a commonly found 18th-century transcription. (Mayers, nos. 367, 426.)

JINNSHYH (CHIN^{4}-SHIH^{4}). See EXAMINATIONS.

JONGGWO (CHUNG^{1}-KUO^{2}). China. Literally, 'the Middle Kingdom'.

JOSS. An idol. A Pidgin (*q.v.*) corruption of the Port. *Deos*, borrowed back by Europeans as a 'Chinese' word. Cf. Joss-house, a Chinese temple; and Joss-stick, a stick of incense used in temple ceremonies. Other forms: joos, joost, josie, josin.

JOU (CHOU^{1}). In classical times the jou was a territorial grouping of 2,500 families. Under the empire it was an administrative area similar, though superior in status, to the shiann (hsien^{4}). There were two kinds of jou: the first subject to, and the second administratively independent of, a fuu (fu^{3}) or prefecture. The second class were themselves subdivided into shiann. An early romanization, still met with in place-names in conventionalized spelling, is 'chow'.

JU^{2}. See RU.

JUNK. A large Chinese sailing vessel. The word is probably from the Javanese and Malay *jong* and *ajong*, a large boat, though Chinese etymologies have been suggested. Other forms:

iuncks, iunkes, iunks, juncos, jungos, zonchi, zunci. See S.E. Asia Glossary, p. 117.

Jwushu Jihnian (Chu^{2}-shu^{1} Chi^{4}-nien^{2}). An official chronicle of the feudal state of Liang (Liang^{2}) or Wey (Wei^{4}) ending with the year 299 B.C. and completed by a chronicle of the state of Jinn (Chin^{4}) and of the whole empire from the earliest times.

Jyfuu (Chih^{1}-fu^{3}). Literally the 'knower' of a fuu (*q.v.*): the name by which the official in charge of a prefecture was known. Commonly translated as 'prefect'. (Both 'prefect' and 'prefecture' are, as translations, open to many objections: in general the use of the Chinese term, with explanation, is to be preferred.) (Mayers, no. 281.)

Jyhtair (Chih^{4}-t'ai^{2}). See Tzoongdu.

Jyshiann (Chih^{1}-hsien^{4}). Literally the 'knower' of the shiann (hsien^{4}): the name by which the official in charge of a shiann or county was formerly known. The present title is Shiann-jaang (Hsien^{4}-chang^{3}). The Jyshiann (county or district magistrate) had and has judicial, police and fiscal as well as administrative duties. The Jyfuu and Jyshiann, but especially the latter, were of all the provincial officials those with whom the ordinary people had most contact. They were commonly referred to as the Fuhmuu Guan (Fu^{4}-mu^{3} Kuan^{1}), the 'Father and Mother Officials'. (Mayers, no. 289.)

Kao^{1}-liang^{2}. See Gauliang.

Kotow or Kowtow. A ceremonial prostration and knocking of the head: a form of reverent salutation used toward the emperor or anyone representing him, or even before objects symbolizing the emperor's majesty. The refusal of foreign envoys to perform the required 'three kneelings and nine knockings' was a frequent cause of diplomatic disputes. From the Chinese *ketour* (*kê^{1}-t'ou^{2}*), to knock the head. (Lokotsch, no. 1214.)

Kuan^{1}-tao^{4}. See Guandaw.

Kuhpyng (K'u^{4}-p'ing^{2}) Tael. The unit of account in which all obligations due to the Imperial Government were assessed (with the exception of Customs duties and taxes levied in kind). The standard kuhpyng tael at the Imperial Treasury was equal to 575·8 grains of 'pure' silver (this was the 'receiving rate': the 'paying-out rate' was reckoned 0·2 per cent. lighter). See also Tael, Haeguan Tael and Sycee.

Kung^{1}. See Gong.

Kung^{1}-pu^{4}. See Liowbuh.

Kuomintang. See Gwomindaang.

Leang (Liang^{3}). The Chinese ounce or tael (*q.v.*). It is both a unit of weight and, as a weight of silver of a prescribed fineness, a unit of account. Sixteen leang make a Chinese pound (weight) or catty.

Leased Territory. See Battle of the Concessions.

Lihbuh (Li^{4}-pu^{4}). See Liowbuh.

Lii (Li^{3}). Linear measure, often spoken of as the Chinese 'mile'. The lii is roughly one-third of an English mile, though it varies in length according to local usage. The early Jesuit geographers reckoned 200 lii to a mean degree of the meridian, thus making 1 lii equal 1,826 feet. To-day it is conventionally taken as 1,890 feet.

LIIBUH (LI^{3}-PU^{4}). See LIOWBUH.

LIIFANYUANN (LI^{3}-FAN^{1}-YUAN^{4}). Literally, the Bureau for the Management of the Barbarians: the former imperial 'Colonial Office'. The Liifanyuann had general charge of Mongolian and Tibetan affairs and, until the creation in 1861 of the Tzoonglii Yamen (*q.v.*), was also the body responsible for dealing with the western nations.

LIKIN. An internal tax on goods in transit, introduced in Shandong (Shantung) in 1853 and extended to the whole of China in the middle 1860's. The official rate was one-tenth of one per cent. *ad valorem*, but in practice local collectors enjoyed considerable latitude in fixing rates. It is estimated that at the beginning of the present century goods passing through a single province paid up to 5 per cent. and passing through several provinces up to 20 per cent. The tax was abolished by the Republic. From the Chinese lijin (li^{2}-chin^{1}), literally 'thousandth money'.

LINGUIST. Interpreters were so called in the early days of the China trade. Although their linguistic attainments were usually worse than mediocre (they were, as a class, the creators of Pidgin, *q.v.*), their role was an important one, as the Chinese at that time were forbidden to teach their own language to foreign barbarians.

LIOWBUH (LIU^{4}-PU^{4}). The Six (Administrative) Boards or Ministries of the former Imperial Central Government. In order of importance, they were: (i) the *Lihbuh* (*Li*^{4}-*pu*^{4}) or Board of Civil Office, dealing with Civil Service appointments, promotions, retirements and honours; (ii) the *Huhbuh* (*Hu*^{4}-*pu*^{4}) or Board of Revenue, receiving duties and taxes and having a general regard to fiscal matters; (iii) the *Liibuh* (*Li*^{3}-*pu*^{4}) or Board of Rites, in charge of the correct ordering of ceremonial observances; (iv) the *Bingbuh* (*Ping*^{1}-*pu*^{4}) or Board of War; (v) the *Shyngbuh* (*Hsing*^{2}-*pu*^{4}) or Board of Punishments, responsible for the administration of justice; and (vi) the *Gongbuh* (*Kung*^{1}-*pu*^{4}) or Board of Public Works.

LORCHA. A small sailing vessel with western-built hull and Chinese-style masts and sails. Etymology is uncertain.

MACE. The trade term for the tenth part of a tael (*q.v.*). The word is originally from the Sanskrit *masha*, a bean, and was brought to China by way of Java and Malaya. It corresponds to the Chinese chyan (ch'ien^{2}).

MANDARIN. (1) The Chinese National Language (Gwoyeu, Kuo^{2}-yü^{3}) or Standard Chinese: the general type of speech of the people all over China Proper except in the extreme southern and south-eastern provinces. More narrowly, the dialect of Beeipyng (Peking). Mandarin was so called because the standard was originally set by the speech of the official class.

(2) An official. Mandarins, both civil and military, were ordered under the Manchu dynasty into nine ranks, each of which was itself subdivided into a superior and subordinate grade, distinguished as jenq (chêng^{4}) and tsorng (ts'ung^{2}).

The word is from the Hind. *mantri*, a counsellor or minister of state, and not, as is sometimes suggested, from the Port. *mandar*, to command or govern. See S.E. Asia Glossary, p. 118.

MANZI. A name formerly used for south China, as Cathay (*q.v.*) was for north China. From *Mantzyy* (*Man*²-*tzŭ*³), the Chinese expression for the (southern) barbarians. It also appears in Marco Polo's *Description* as Mangy and Manzy.

MEASURAGE. In the early period of the China trade the port charges payable by commercial vessels were comprehended under the name of measurage duty. 'A ship is not properly imported until she is measured, which measurement is taken from the centre of the mizzen-mast to the centre of the fore-mast for the length, and close abaft the mainmast from side to side for the breadth; the length is multiplied by the breadth, and the product, divided by ten, gives the ship's measurage' (Milburn). Measurement was in covids (*q.v.*). All ships were classified according to size, and the rate at which the duty was levied, in taels per unit of measurage, was lowest for the smaller, and greater for the larger, vessels.

MIAWHAW (MIAO⁴-HAO⁴). See section on Names and Titles, p. 169.

MIDDLE KINGDOM. See JONGGWO.

MOOU (MOU³). A square measure equal to 240 buh (*q.v.*). Though there are considerable local variations, the moou may be taken as roughly equivalent to one-sixth of an acre. Often found as *mow*.

NAN (NAN²). Baron. The fifth of the traditional Chinese ranks of nobility. See also TITLES OF NOBILITY.

NANBEEICHAUR (NAN²-PEI³ CH'AO²). Literally, Southern and Northern Dynasties: the name given by Chinese historians to the period A.D. 420–589.

NIANHAW (NIEN²-HAO⁴). See section on Names and Titles, p. 169.

OPIUM. The dried juice of the unripe capsules of the poppy (*Papaver somniferum*). The poppy, according to Edkins, was unknown in China before the Tarng (T'ang²) period: the habit of opium smoking (as distinct from the Indian practice of eating opium) seems to have developed in China after the introduction of tobacco (17th century). The first edict against the importation of the drug was issued in 1729, when the trade was exclusively in the hands of the Portuguese of Goa. From 1773, the year in which Warren Hastings as governor-general of India took over the monopoly of the sale of opium, it became a staple of the Country Trade (*q.v.*). Further edicts prohibiting its importation were issued in 1796 and 1800, and the determined attempt of the imperial commissioner Lin Tzershyu (Lin²-Tsê²-hsü²) to enforce these edicts was one of the immediate causes precipitating the first Anglo-Chinese war. A great smuggling traffic had grown up early in the century, and this continued and increased after the war. Although opium was not mentioned in the Treaty of Nanking (1842), the revised Customs tariff prescribed by Article 26 of the Anglo-Chinese Treaty of 1858 included opium as a duty of Tls. 30 per picul: this quasi-legalisation ended the smuggling traffic. The volume of imports slackened after the 1860's, due chiefly to increased domestic production. India in 1926 prohibited the export of opium, and the Chinese Government has also made great efforts (so far not outstandingly successful) to restrict home production and eradicate the opium habit.

OPIUM WAR. The name often, though with doubtful historical justification, applied to the first Anglo-Chinese war (1839–42).

PAGODA. Properly, a temple or group of buildings used for religious purposes. The word is either of Persian or of Sanskrit origin, and is used in many eastern countries. It is applied in China especially to a kind of tower, usually but not always octagonal, divided (at least to the external view) into an uneven number of stories, seven, nine, eleven or thirteen (which is the maximum). The Buddhists are credited with the introduction of this architectural form. Pagodas were first built in China in the 3rd century A.D.

PAO[3]. See BAO.

PICUL. A measure of weight. It is the trade term for the Chinese shyr (shih[2]) or dann (tan[4]). Like all Chinese weights and measures, it exhibits considerable local variation. For the purposes of external commerce the Trade Regulations annexed to the Sino-British Treaty of 1858 declared that the 'picul of one hundred catties is held to be equal to one hundred and thirty-three and one-third pounds, avoirdupois'. The Sino-French Treaty of the same year fixed the picul at 60 kilos 453 grammes. From the Malay *pikul* (Lokotsch, no. 1655). See also CATTY, and S.E. Asia Glossary under WEIGHTS (MALAYA).

PIDGIN. The former *lingua franca* of the China coast, used by Chinese merchants, compradors, shopkeepers and servants and by Europeans of all nationalities unfamiliar with the Chinese language. Pidgin originated with the Linguists (*q.v.*) and gained general currency about the beginning of the 18th century. It employs a strictly limited vocabulary, and in its syntax, and its rejection of variant forms to express differences of case, number and tense, and of inflections generally, it bears strong marks of the native speech of its creators. With greater knowledge on the part of European and Chinese of each other's language, Pidgin is rapidly passing out of use. The word itself is said to be a corruption of 'business'. Sometimes (incorrectly) found as 'Pigeon'.

PING[1]-PU[4]. See LIOWBUH.

PO[2]. See BOR.

PRAYA. See BUND.

PRIVATE TRADE. During the period of the East India Company's monopoly the term 'private trade' was applied to the personal commercial ventures which the Company permitted (with limitations as to quantity and kind) to its supercargoes and to the officers of its ships. Supercargoes were rewarded, apart from their salaries, in some or all of the following ways: (i) by receiving the profits on a part of the ship's stock, 'allowed' to them—known as Allowance; (ii) by a permit to take out up to a specified amount in silver, and bring back in gold what they could obtain in exchange for it—known as Permission; (iii) the privilege of conducting a small private venture in goods, outward and inward—known as Privilege. Private trade by captains and other ship's officers, though the Company had vainly attempted to keep it within bounds in the early part of the 18th century, grew steadily in importance during the whole period of the Company's monopoly.

PRIVILEGE. See PRIVATE TRADE.

PU⁴. See BUH.

PUNT. The trade term for the tsuenn (ts'un⁴) or Chinese inch (*q.v.*).

PUNTI. From the local pronunciation of the Chinese beendih (pên³-ti⁴), literally, 'rooted in the land'. It is applied to the 'original' Chinese population of Goangdong (Kwangtung) province to distinguish them from the Hakkas (*q.v.*).

RU (JU²). A Confucian scholar. The term used for the Confucian school is Rujia (Ju²-chia¹), and for the doctrine Rujiaw (Ju²-chiao⁴).

SAMPAN. The name is applied in China to any kind of small boat (Lokotsch, no. 1834). See also JUNK.

SANGWO (SAN¹ KUO²). Literally, Three Kingdoms. They were the three succession states of the Later Hann (Han⁴) dynasty: Shuu (Shu³), Wey (Wei⁴) and Wu (Wu²). Sangwo is the name given by Chinese historians to the period A.D. 221–65, during which these kingdoms flourished. See also List of dynasties and rulers.

SANMINJUUYIH (SAN¹-MIN²-CHU³-I⁴). The Three People's Principles: the title of a book compiled from lectures delivered at Goangjou (Canton) by Suen Yihshian (Sun Yat-sen) in 1924. The three principles are: (i) Mintzwu (Min²-tsu²) or Nationalism; (ii) Minchyuan (Min²-ch'üan²) or Democracy; and (iii) Minsheng (Min²-shêng¹) or People's Livelihood. The book has become the major political and social text of modern China.

SEASON. The word 'season' as used in the literature of the China trade is open to ambiguity, since the time occupied by a single trading voyage, outward and inward, might extend to 24 months or more and fall within three calendar years. Where a date is given (e.g. 'the season of 1780') the year mentioned is usually that in which the ships reached Canton. In the days of sail the period of actual trading on the China coast extended roughly from August of one year to March of the next. Ships outward-bound from England normally received their sailing orders sometime during the first three months of the year, if they were going directly to China, and would sail from the Downs as soon as a favourable wind allowed. Ships routed Bombay and China, Coast (Madras) and China, or Bay (Calcutta) and China, would have already sailed the previous August or September. First arrivals sometimes appeared at Canton as early as July. More ships would arrive all through the late summer, autumn and early winter. The earliest arrivals, soonest filled, would be the first to leave, sailing from Canton about November. More would sail in December, and most would have gone by the end of January, although belated departures might continue into March and even the first week of April. The earliest of the season's ships would complete their return voyage to England by the following autumn, though the majority would not reach home till three months or more later.

SECURITY MERCHANT. In the early period of the China trade, for each foreign ship entering Canton, one or more Chinese merchants were designated by the authorities to stand security for payment of the usual duties, and for the good behaviour of the Europeans during such time as their ship remained in Chinese waters.

SETTLEMENT. A reserved area for foreign residence, often possessing municipal organization, but in which the title-deeds to real property were issued directly by the Chinese Government and not mediately through a foreign consul. See also CONCESSION (2).

SHANNYU (SHAN^{4}-YÜ^{2}). The title borne by the chief of the Shiongnu (Hsiung^{1}-nu^{2}) (Huns ?) during the Hann (Han^{4}) period.

SHEENG (SHÊNG^{3}). Province. The modern provincial system in China goes back to the Mongol period (Yuan dynasty) when, in the 14th century, 'ambulatory departments' (*shyngsheeng, hsing^{2}-shêng^{3}*) were established, 13 in number. The Ming continued this system, with slight modifications, increasing the number of provinces to 15. The Ming provinces were: Shandong (Shantung), Shanshi (Shansi), Hernan (Honan), Shaanshi (Shensi), Fwujiann (Fukien), Jehjiang (Chekiang), Jiangshi (Kiangsi), Hwugoang (Hukwang), Syhchuan (Szechwan), Goangdong (Kwangtung), Goangshi (Kwangsi), Yunnan (Yunnan), Gueyjou (Kweichow), and the two metropolitan provinces Jyrlih (Chihli) and Jiangnan (Kiangnan). This number was increased to 18 under the Manchus: (*a*) by the separation of Anhuei (Anhui) from Jiangnan, the remaining portion of which was then called Jiangsu (Kiangsu); (*b*) by the formation of Gansuh (Kansu) out of a part of Shaanshi; and (*c*) by the partition of Hwugoang into Hwubeei (Hupeh) and Hwunan (Hunan). These eighteen provinces together comprise what is often called 'China Proper'.

Of the outlying territories, Shinjiang (Sinkiang) or Chinese Turkestan was organized as a province in 1884; while the Inner Mongolian and Tibetan regions have also, since the Republic, been recast administratively as provinces, thus bringing the number, with the Dongsansheeng (Tung^{1}-san^{1}-shêng^{3}, Three Eastern Provinces—Manchuria) up to a total of 28. The recent (1946) division of Manchuria into nine provinces raises the present total to 34.

Provincial particularism is strong in China, and provincial governments have normally enjoyed considerable freedom from central control.

SHIANG (HSIANG^{1}). A subdivision of the shiann (hsien^{4}) (*q.v.*) in rural areas. Sometimes translated as 'Rural District'. See also JENN.

SHIANN (HSIEN^{4}). Often translated as 'district', though the present official translation is ‘ county ’, the shiann is the most important civic, political, judicial and fiscal unit in the Chinese polity. It consists usually of a walled township with its surrounding countryside. To-day it is the sole area of local self-government, all others between it and the province having been abolished. *Shiann* are distributed into six grades: size, population density, and the presence or absence of transport facilities are the principal factors determining the classification. The largest are divided into chiu (ch’ü^{1}) or county districts. All shiann are composed of shiang (hsiang^{1}) (in rural areas) and jenn (chên^{4}) (in urban areas), and the latter may be further subdivided into bao (pao^{3}) and jea (chia^{3}), respectively boroughs and wards.

SHIANNJAANG (HSIEN^{4}-CHANG^{3}). See JYSHIANN.

SHIOWTSAIR (HSIU^{4}-TS’AI^{2}). See EXAMINATIONS.

SHROFF. A silver expert employed by banks and commercial firms to check the quality of dollars paid in, and eliminate bad coins. Later the term was extended to cover any employees who collect accounts for a firm. A corruption of the Arabic *ṣarrāf*, a banker.

SHYNGBUH (HSING^{2}-PU^{4}). See LIOWBUH.

SOUCHONG. See TEA.

STOCK. The outward-bound cargo of merchandise and bullion taken to China by the ships of the East India Company and other trading concerns was called the ‘ stock ’. Its sale in China enabled the trader to procure in exchange Chinese goods to take back for sale in Europe or India—these made up what was known as the ship’s investment.

SWANPAN. The Chinese abacus, still widely used for all kinds of calculating work. The word is from the Chinese *suannparn* (*suan*^{4}-*p’an*^{2}), a reckoning tray.

SYCEE or SISEE. Silver in shoe-shaped ingots, used as a means of payment. The shoes could be of any weight, from one to 50 or even 100 ounces. Sycee is from the Cantonese pronunciation of *shih sy* (*hsi*^{4} *ssŭ*^{1}), fine silk, for this lump silver, if pure, can be drawn out when heated into threads resembling silk. Payments due to the emperor had to be in sycee, which was always taken to be silver 1,000 pure: hence if we find in trade accounts the phrase ‘ add 7 per cent. to make it sycee ’, it implies that the actual payment has been made in silver of 93 touch (*q.v.*).

TAEL. The name given by foreign traders to the Chinese leang (liang^{3}) or ‘ ounce ’ (*q.v.*). There are still innumerable standards in use, and tael-weight not only varies from place to place and use to use, but different degrees of fineness in the silver are customarily used in the taels of a single locality.

As a unit of account the tael is a leang weight of silver. In the China trade accounts were kept in taels, mace, candarins and cash: 10 cash made 1 candarin; 10 candarins 1 mace; and 10 mace 1 tael. The Canton tael was actually 579·85 grains, and was normally invoiced by the East India Company at 6*s*. 8*d*.

The word tael is from the Hindustani *tola* by way of the

Malay *tahil*. Other forms: taey, taies, taye, tayel, theyl. See also HAEGUAN and KUHPYNG TAELS.

TAIPAN. Literally, 'great manager'. From the Chinese *dahban* (*ta⁴-pan¹*). The title was normally given to the head of a foreign business firm. It was formerly used as well for foreign consuls.

TAO⁴. See DAW.

TAO⁴-T'AI². See DAWTAIR.

TAYHOW (T'AI⁴-HOU⁴). The former title of an empress dowager (Mayers, no. 3).

TAYPYNG (T'AI⁴-P'ING²). Literally, 'great peace', the dynastic title adopted by the leader of the agrarian revolution in 1850–64, Horng Shiowchyuan (Hung² Hsiu⁴-ch'üan²), and usually applied to the rebellion itself.

TAYTZONG (T'AI⁴-TSUNG¹). 'Great Exemplar'—a Temple Name. See section on Names and Titles, p. 170.

TAYTZUU (T'AI⁴-TSU³). 'Great Ancestor'—a Temple Name. See section on Names and Titles, p. 170.

TAYTZYY (T'AI⁴-TZŬ³). The former title of an imperial heir apparent (Mayers, no. 10).

TEA. The principal sorts of tea imported from China by the East India Company were (i) of the black teas: (*a*) Bohea or Voo-yee, the cheapest variety—this was not imported by individuals, but made up one-sixth of the Company's imports in the last decade of the 18th century; (*b*) Congou or Congfoo, a superior kind of Bohea—it accounted for about half the Company's tea imports; (*c*) Souchong or Se-ow-chong—what entered the trade under this name was really first quality Congou; (ii) of the green teas: (*d*) Singlo, the meanest sort; (*e*) Twankay or Tunkey, a superior kind of Singlo, only imported by the Company; (*f*) Hyson Skin or Bloom tea, the inferior variety of the next; (*g*) Hyson or He-tchune; and (*h*) Gunpowder, a superior kind of Hyson.

TEMPLE NAME. See section on Names and Titles, p. 167.

TIANSHIAH (T'IEN¹-HSIA⁴). The literal meaning is 'under heaven'—a common way of referring to China.

TIANTZYY (T'IEN¹-TZŬ³). Literally, the 'Son of Heaven': a religious title of the rulers of China. It is of great antiquity, occurring in the Shujing (Shu¹-ching¹) or Book of History, and was borne both by the kings (wang) of the Jou (Chou¹) period and by the emperors (hwangdih, huang²-ti⁴) who ruled China after 221 B.C.

TIAO⁴. See DIAW.

T'IEN⁴-SHIH⁴. See EXAMINATIONS.

TING (T'ING¹). An administrative area under the empire, similar, though superior in grade, to the shiann (hsien⁴). Abolished in 1912. See also FUU.

TI⁴-PAO³. See DIHBAO.

TITLES OF NOBILITY. The traditional ranks of nobility were five: *Gong* (*Kung¹*), duke; *Hour* (*Hou²*), marquis; *Bor* (*Po²*), earl; *Tzyy* (*Tzŭ³*), viscount; and *Nan* (*Nan²*), baron. The translations are conventional only. These titles were bestowed on the greater vassals of the Jou (Chou[1]) kings, generally in accordance with the standing of the family (in particular its blood-relationship with the royal family) and the size of the fief. In later times they were awarded for outstanding services to the State, especially military services. Their possessors did not constitute an hereditary class.

TITTUCK. See TYIDU.

TOUCH. The degree of fineness of silver used as a means of payment. See also SYCEE.

TREATY PORT. The ports, coastal and up-river, where under the terms of treaties signed between China and the Powers, foreign countries were permitted to establish consulates, where customs offices were set up, and where foreign merchants were allowed to settle and trade. The first Treaty Ports were opened in accordance with the terms of Art. 2 of the Treaty of Nanking, 1842, and subsequent treaties extended the list. The term later covered not only these but certain other ports opened voluntarily by the Chinese Government. As a result of the ending of the Unequal Treaties, the expression is now an anachronism. See Japan Glossary, p. 232.

TSUENN (TS'UN[4]). Inch. The trade term was ' punt '. See also CHYY.

TU[1]-CHÜN[1]. See DUJIUN.

TWANKAY. See TEA.

TWENTY-ONE DEMANDS. A far-reaching series of demands served on the Chinese Government by Japan in 1915. Full acceptance of the 21 Demands would have turned China into a Japanese semi-colony.

TYIDU (T'I[2]-TU[1]). The official title of the general commanding the troops of a province. The Tyidu's colloquial designation was Tyitair (T'i[2]-t'ai[2]) (Mayers, no. 440). Romanizations frequently found in 18th-century English records are Tittuck and Tytuck, following the Cantonese pronunciation of the Chinese characters.

TYTUCK. See TYIDU.

TZOONGBING (TSUNG[3]-PING[1]). A general of brigade in the Chinese (Green Flag) army under the Manchus. Found in 18th-century English records as Chumpein.

TZOONGDU (TSUNG[3]-TU[1]). Governor-General : often mistranslated ' Viceroy '. The colloquial designation was Jyhtair (Chih[4]-t'ai[2]). The office of Tzoongdu dates from the 18th century. During the greater part of the Manchu period there were eight governors-general ; some with sole responsibility for a single province, others administering (concurrently with provincial governors or Fuuyuann, *q.v.*) a group of two or more adjacent provinces. Their distribution is shown in the following list.

Jyrlih (Chihli)	Under the Jyrlih governor-general. No governor.
Jiangsu (Kiangsu) Anhuei (Anhui) Jiangshi (Kiangsi)	Under the Jiangnan governor-general. In addition each province had its own provincial governor.
Shandong (Shantung)	No governor-general. Under its own governor.

Shanshi (Shansi)	No governor-general. Under its own governor.
Hernan (Honan)	No governor-general. Under its own governor.
Shaanshi (Shensi)	Under the Shaangan governor-general. In addition it had its own governor.
Gansuh (Kansu)	Under the Shaangan governor-general. No provincial governor of its own.
Fwujiann (Fukien) Jehjiang (Chekiang)	Under the Minjeh governor-general. In addition each province had its own provincial governor.
Hwubeei (Hupeh) Hwunan (Hunan)	Under the Hwugoang or Leanghwu governor-general. In addition each province had its own provincial governor.
Syhchuan (Szechwan)	Under the Syhchuan governor-general. No provincial governor of its own.
Goangdong (Kwangtung) Goangshi (Kwangsi)	Under the Leangoang governor-general. In addition each province had its own provincial governor.
Gueyjou (Kweichow) Yunnan (Yunnan)	Under the Yunguey governor-general. In addition each province had its own provincial governor.

Where the Tzoongdu and Fuuyuann exercised concurrent jurisdiction, they worked together in practice rather as colleagues than as superior and subordinate. The Tzoongdu was at the same time the highest ranking official in the province, with control over all military forces (other than the Manchu garrison troops) in his territory. In the official hierarchy he was outranked only by the Jiangjiun or Tartar general (*q.v.*). The name is often found in 18th-century English records as Chumtuck or Chuntuck, following the Cantonese pronunciation of the Chinese characters. (Mayers, no. 273.)

TZOONGLII YAMEN (TSUNG^3-LI^3 YA^2-MÊN^2). The 'Foreign Office' set up in 1861 in fulfilment of the treaty requirements of 1860. By 1878 gradual changes made in its personnel had transformed it into something more like a European cabinet. By the terms of the Boxer Protocol (1901) the Tzoonglii Yamen was reorganized into a Ministry of Foreign Affairs, the Waywuhbuh (Wai^4-wu^4-pu^4). (Mayers, no. 152.)

TZYY (TZU^3). Viscount. The fourth of the traditional Chinese ranks of nobility. See also TITLES OF NOBILITY, p. 192.

UNEQUAL TREATIES. The treaties (from the Treaty of Nanking, 1842, onward) dictated to China by the Western Powers were so called primarily because China, under these treaties, did not enjoy Customs autonomy either in the making of her tariff or in its administration, and because of the articles embodying the system of extraterritoriality (*q.v.*).

VOO-YEE. See TEA.

WANG (WANG^2). King or prince. The title of Chinese rulers down to the end of the Jou (Chou^1) period.

WAYWUHBUH (WAI^4-WU^4-PU^4). The Chinese Ministry of Foreign Affairs. See also TZOONGLII YAMEN.

WUUDAY (WU^3-TAI^4). Literally, the Five Dynasties. The name is traditionally given to the period A.D. 907–60 when, between the end of the Tarng (T'ang^2) and the establishment of the Sonq (Sung^4), the emperors of five short-lived dynasties succeeded one another as rulers of north China. See List of dynasties and rulers, p. 209.

YAMEN (YA^{2}-MÊN^{2}). The official or private residence of mandarin; a public office.

YUAN (YÜAN^{2}). The Chinese dollar: from the word's original meaning of 'round' or 'circular'.

YUANN (YÜAN^{4}). An organ of government, a bureau or board. The Boards of the Five-Power Constitution advocated by Suen Yihshian (Sun Yat-sen) are: (i) *Lihfaa yuann* (*Li*^{4}-*fa*^{3}), Legislative Board; (ii) *Syfaa yuann* (*Ssŭ*^{1}-*fa*^{3}), Judicial Board; (iii) *Shyngjenq yuann* (*Hsing*^{2}-*chêng*^{4}), Executive Board; (iv) *Kaoshyh yuann* (*K'ao*^{3}-*shih*^{4}), Examination Board; (v) *Jiannchar yuann* (*Chien*^{4}-*ch'a*^{2}), Censorship Board.

Further information will be found in the following works:

Balázs, S. 'Beiträge zur Wirtschaftsgeschichte der T'ang-Zeit (618–906). Anhang II: Das Mass- und Gewichtssystem', *Mittheilungen d. seminars f. orient. Sprachen*, xxxviii (1933), 207–10.

Couling, S. *The Encyclopedia Sinica*. Shanghai, 1917.

Giles, Herbert A. *A glossary of reference on subjects connected with the Far East*. 2nd revised ed., Hongkong, 1886.

Lokotsch, K. *Etymologisches Wörterbuch der europäischen Wörter orientalischen Ursprungs*. Heidelberg, 1927.

Milburn, W. *Oriental commerce; containing a geographical description of the principal places in the East Indies, China and Japan, with their produce, manufactures and trade* . . . 2 vols. London, 1813.

Morse, H. B. *The trade and administration of China*. 3rd edn. Shanghai, 1921 (1908).

Zi, Etienne. *Pratique des examens littéraires en Chine*. (Variétés sinologiques, no. 5.) Shanghai, 1894.

5. CALENDARS AND SYSTEMS OF DATING

(i) DATING BY 'YEAR-PERIODS'

In the very earliest period of Chinese history dates were indicated either by reference to the Sexagenary Cycle or by giving the year-of-reign of the ruler. The first method, which is of great antiquity, is traditionally ascribed to Hwangdih (Huang²-ti⁴), the legendary Yellow Emperor.[1] The second is what we would expect to find in a strictly annalistic literature. Writers commonly used both methods together. This applies down to and a little beyond the end of the spring and autumn period (722–468 B.C.)

Not until the 4th century B.C. do we find an example of a ruler (Huey (Hui⁴), king of Liang (Liang²), 370–318 B.C.) dividing his reign into two eras, distinguished as *chyan* (*ch'ien²*) and *how* (*hou⁴*)—former and latter. Dates in his reign would be given as 'Liang Huey wang chyan 3rd (or other) year' or 'Liang Huey wang how 2nd (or other) year', and so on.

The first emperor to introduce the system of 'year-periods' (*nianhaw, nien¹-hao⁴*) was Wuudih (Wu³-ti⁴) of the Former Hann (Han⁴) dynasty, who reigned from 140 to 86 B.C. Altogether he promulgated eleven nianhaw to mark the different 'eras' into which he chose to divide his reign. (This total was only twice exceeded in later times.) The year-period was in effect an auspicious formula, given to longer or shorter periods of an emperor's reign, and changed at intervals either to mark some important event, or else because it was believed that a new *nianhaw* would avert or terminate some natural calamity. For example, in the year 100 B.C. the empire was suffering from drought, and the nianhaw was changed to Tianhann (T'ien¹-han⁴) in the hope of inducing the heavens to rain. From 140 B.C. then, dates were reckoned from the year of adoption of a particular nianhaw, and not from the year of the ruler's accession.

With the beginning of the Ming (Ming²) dynasty (1368) a new rule was introduced, namely, that the nianhaw adopted at the commencement of a reign should be kept unchanged for the duration of that reign. This rule (it was broken only once, by the Ming emperor Ingtzong (Ying¹-tsung¹), reigned 1436–50 and 1457–65) means that dating by nianhaw now comes to the same thing as dating from the accession-year of the ruler, and simplifies matters considerably for the western historian, especially as the later Chinese emperors are often referred to simply by their nianhaw, which are used as if they were personal titles. (For example: the Dawguang (Tao⁴-kuang¹) Emperor, 1821–50. *Dawguang* was his year-period; *Min-ning* (*Min²-ning¹*) his given name.)

The usual way in which a Chinese historical text will indicate a particular year is by an expression like the following: 'Shi-ning chi nian jeayn' (Hsi¹-ning² ch'i¹ nien² chia³-yin²). The last two

[1] Cyclical terms were first used to date cycles of 60 days. Only beginning with the Hann (Han⁴) dynasty were years dated in this way.

characters (*jeayn*) give the year's place in the Sexagenary Cycle (see ii below) and from the *jea* we can already be certain that the corresponding western date will end in a four. The first two characters (*Shi-ning*) are the year-period. This particular nianhaw, with the literal meaning 'prosperous and peaceful', was adopted by the *Sonq* (*Sung*^{4}) emperor Sherntzong (Shên^{2}-tsung^{1}) on his accession in 1068. Sherntzong's predecessor Ingtzong (Ying^{1}-tsung^{1}) died in the first month of 1067, and it should be noted that a new reign was almost always dated from the beginning of the year after the one in which the former emperor had died. The seventh year (*chi* means seven and *nian* year) of the Shi-ning year-period is therefore 1074, which agrees with the indication given by the term jeayn. (Note that it is incorrect to take the first year of the year-period—in this example 1068—and add seven. One less than the indicated number must be added, since the first year must itself be included in the total.)

The characters shi-ning have, in fact, only been used once as a year-period—by the Sonq emperor mentioned above. But many nianhaw have done service at various times for the emperors of different dynasties. An alphabetical list of nianhaw, such as is given in Tchang's *Synchronismes chinois*, will normally have to be used in order to make certain of the special period within which falls the date one is checking.

(ii) DATING BY THE SEXAGENARY CYCLE

Dates are also expressed by using the terms of the Sexagenary Cycle. This cycle (of sixty two-character phrases) is obtained by combining the characters of the two series known as the Ten, or Celestial, Stems (*Shyrgan* or *Tiangan*, *Shih*^{2}*-kan*^{1} or *T'ien*^{1}*-kan*^{1}) and the Twelve, or Terrestrial, Branches (*Shyrelljy* or *Dihjy*, *Shih*^{2}*-êrh*^{4}*-chih*^{1} or *Ti*^{4}*-chih*^{1}).

The names of the Ten Stems and Twelve Branches are:

	Stems (*Gan*)		Branches (*Jy*)
1	Jea (Chia^{3})	I	Tzyy (Tzu^{3})
2	Yii (I^{3})	II	Choou (Ch'ou^{3})
3	Biing (Ping^{3})	III	Yn (Yin^{2})
4	Ding (Ting^{1})	IV	Mao (Mao^{3})
5	Wuh (Wu^{4})	V	Chern (Ch'ên^{2})
6	Jii (Chi^{3})	VI	Syh (Ssu^{4})
7	Geng (Kêng^{1})	VII	Wuu (Wu^{3})
8	Shin (Hsin^{1})	VIII	Wey (Wei^{4})
9	Ren (Jên^{2})	IX	Shen (Shên^{1})
10	Goei (Kuei^{3})	X	Yeou (Yu^{3})
		XI	Shiu (Hsü^{1})
		XII	Hay (Hai^{4})

The two series are combined in the following way: the Ten Stems are repeated six times, giving a total of sixty characters; and the Twelve Branches five times, giving the same number of characters. When the terms of the two extended lists of characters are paired off, each year of the Sexagenary Cycle is clearly distinguished by a two-character compound.

In the cyclical terms that mark the years, the Stem character is written first and the Branch character second. It is useful to note that, as the Ten Stems recur with the completion of each decade, each Stem character will correspond to a single last digit in the western date to which it refers. Since each of the Sexagenary Cycles begins in a year whose western date ends in 4, the following Stems and numbers will always correspond:

Western dates				
ending in	1	have	shin (hsin^1)	as first term of their cyclic designation
,,	2	,,	ren (jên^2)	,, ,, ,,
,,	3	,,	goei (kuei^3)	,, ,, ,,
,,	4	,,	jea (chia^3)	,, ,, ,,
,,	5	,,	yii (i^3)	,, ,, ,,
,,	6	,,	biing (ping^3)	,, ,, ,,
,,	7	,,	ding (ting^1)	,, ,, ,,
,,	8	,,	wuh (wu^4)	,, ,, ,,
,,	9	,,	jii (chi^3)	,, ,, ,,
,,	0	,,	geng (kêng^1)	,, ,, ,,

The table that follows demonstrates the method of pairing the Stem and Branch terms, and also illustrates the point made above. Western dates for both the 1864–1923 (the last) and 1924–83 (the current) cycles are shown.

TABLE

1 (1–I) jeatzyy 1864/1924	2 (2–II) yiichoou 1865/1925	3 (3–III) biingyn 1866/1926	4 (4–IV) dingmao 1867/1927	5 (5–V) wuhchern 1868/1928
6 (6–VI) jiisyh 1869/1929	7 (7–VII) gengwuu 1870/1930	8 (8–VIII) shinwey 1871/1931	9 (9–IX) renshen 1872/1932	10 (10–X) goeiyeou 1873/1933
11 (1–XI) jeashiu 1874/1934	12 (2–XII) yiihay 1875/1935	13 (3–I) biingtzyy 1876/1936	14 (4–II) dingchoou 1877/1937	15 (5–III) wuhyn 1878/1938
16 (6–IV) jiimao 1879/1939	17 (7–V) gengchern 1880/1940	18 (8–VI) shinsyh 1881/1941	19 (9–VII) renwuu 1882/1942	20 (10–VIII) goeiwey 1883/1943
21 (1–IX) jeashen 1884/1944	22 (2–X) yiiyeou 1885/1945	23 (3–XI) biingshiu 1886/1946	24 (4–XII) dinghay 1887/1947	25 (5–I) wuhtzyy 1888/1948
26 (6–II) jiichoou 1889/1949	27 (7–III) gengyn 1890/1950	28 (8–IV) shinmao 1891/1951	29 (9–V) renchern 1892/1952	30 (10–VI) goeisyh 1893/1953
31 (1–VII) jeawuu 1894/1954	32 (2–VIII) yiiwey 1895/1955	33 (3–IX) biingshen 1896/1956	34 (4–X) dingyeou 1897/1957	35 (5–XI) wuhshiu 1898/1958
36 (6–XII) jiihay 1899/1959	37 (7–I) gengtzyy 1900/1960	38 (8–II) shinchoou 1901/1961	39 (9–III) renyn 1902/1962	40 (10–IV) goeimao 1903/1963
41 (1–V) jeachern 1904/1964	42 (2–VI) yiisyh 1905/1965	43 (3–VII) biingwuu 1906/1966	44 (4–VIII) dingwey 1907/1967	45 (5–IX) wuhshen 1908/1968
46 (6–X) jiiyeou 1909/1969	47 (7–XI) gengshiu 1910/1970	48 (8–XII) shinhay 1911/1971	49 (9–I) rentzyy 1912/1972	50 (10–II) goeichoou 1913/1973
51 (1–III) jeayn 1914/1974	52 (2–IV) yiimao 1915/1975	53 (3–V) biingchern 1916/1976	54 (4–VI) dingsyh 1917/1977	55 (5–VII) wuhwuu 1918/1978
56 (6–VIII) jiiwey 1919/1979	57 (7–IX) gengshen 1920/1980	58 (8–X) shinyeou 1921/1981	59 (9–XI) renshiu 1922/1982	60 (10–XII) goeihay 1923/1983

(iii) DATING BY THE ANIMAL CYCLE

Corresponding to the Twelve Terrestrial Branches there is another duodenary cycle—the Animal Cycle. This is sometimes used to designate a particular year (e.g. by a person in giving the year of his birth), but its more common use is to mark the twelve 'hours' (each corresponding to two of our own) into which the Chinese divide the 24 of a single day and night.

Branch		*Animal*	*Chinese name*	*Hour*
I	Tzyy	Rat	Shuu (Shu³)	11 p.m.–1 a.m.
II	Choou	Ox	Niou (Niu²)	1–3 a.m.
III	Yn	Tiger	Huu (Hu³)	3–5 a.m.
IV	Mao	Hare	Tuh (T'u⁴)	5–7 a.m.
V	Chern	Dragon	Long (Lung²)	7–9 a.m.
VI	Syh	Snake	Sher (Shê²)	9–11 a.m.
VII	Wuu	Horse	Maa (Ma³)	11 a.m.–1 p.m.
VIII	Wey	Sheep	Yang (Yang²)	1–3 p.m.
IX	Shen	Monkey	Hour (Hou²)	3–5 p.m.
X	Yeou	Cock	Ji (Chi¹)	5–7 p.m.
XI	Shiu	Dog	Goou (Kou³)	7–9 p.m.
XII	Hay	Pig	Ju (Chu¹)	9–11 p.m.

(iv) DATING SINCE THE REPUBLIC

Since the 1911 Revolution and the inauguration of the Republic, dates are given in the form: 'year . . . of the Republic' (Mingwo . . . nian, Min²-kuo² . . . nien²). The western date is reckoned by adding eleven to the year of the Republican era: e.g. Mingwo 37 nian = 1948.

(v) CHINESE CALENDARS

There are, if we include the Gregorian calendar which was officially introduced by the Republican Government in 1912, three different calendars now in use in China. Of the older traditional calendars, one is lunar and the other solar.

In the lunar calendar, the year is made up of 12 lunar months of 29 or 30 days each. Nineteen of these years will contain, therefore, 228 months, which is seven short of the 235 lunations occurring in 19 solar years of 365·25 days each. In order to bring about an equivalence between the lunar and solar calendars seven intercalary months (*ruennyueh, jun⁴-yüeh⁴*) must be inserted in each period of 19 years.

The intercalary month is not inserted at the end of the year (the 1st, 11th and 12th months may not be repeated) but is introduced between two other months, so that there may, for example, be two successive 'third' months in a given year.

The terms of the Sexagenary Cycle are also applied to the months of the lunar calendar, and the series repeats quinquennially (intercalary months do not upset the sequence as they carry the designation belonging to the month they duplicate). Cyclical terms for the months can easily be worked out if it is remembered that the first month in any jeatzyy year bears the designation biingyn.

The traditional solar calendar is primarily of importance for the peasant who has to accommodate himself to the rhythm of the seasons. The discrepancy between the lunar calendar and the seasonal cycle—a discrepancy which as we have seen is allowed to accumulate and is then abruptly rectified by the process of intercalation—makes the lunar calendar inadequate as a customary method of reckoning time for the farmer.

In the solar calendar, the year is divided into 24 sections or *jye* (*chieh*²). Their names and rough correspondence with the Chinese lunar and western calendars are set out in the table that follows.

TABLE

No.	*Jye*	*Translation*	*Chinese date*	*Western date*
1	Lihchuen (Li⁴-ch'un¹)	Spring begins	13th of 1st	5 Feb.
2	Yeushoei (Yü³-shui³)	Rain water	28th of 1st	20 Feb.
3	Jingjer (Ching¹-chê²)	Insects awaken	13th of 2nd	6 Mar.
4	Chuenfen (Ch'un¹-fên¹)	Spring Equinox	28th of 2nd	21 Mar.
5	Chingming (Ch'ing¹-ming²)	Pure and bright	14th of 3rd	5 April
6	Guuyeu (Ku³-yü³)	Grain rains	29th of 3rd	20 April
7	Lihshiah (Li⁴-hsia⁴)	Summer begins	16th of 3rd intercalary	6 May
8	Sheaumaan (Hsiao³-man³)	Grain forms	1st of 4th	21 May
9	Mangjoong (Mang²-chung³)	Grain in ear	17th of 4th	6 June
10	Shiahjyh (Hsia⁴-chih⁴)	Summer Solstice	3rd of 5th	21 June
11	Sheaushuu (Hsiao³-shu³)	Slight heat	19th of 5th	7 July
12	Dahshuu (Ta⁴-shu³)	Great heat	6th of 6th	23 July
13	Lihchiou (Li⁴-ch'iu¹)	Autumn begins	22nd of 6th	8 Aug.
14	Chuushuu (Ch'u³-shu³)	Heat stops	7th of 7th	23 Aug.
15	Bairluh (Pai²-lu⁴)	White dew	23rd of 7th	8 Sept.
16	Chioufen (Ch'iu¹-fên¹)	Autumn Equinox	8th of 8th	23 Sept.
17	Harnluh (Han²-lu⁴)	Cold dew	23rd of 8th	8 Oct.
18	Shuangjianq (Shuang¹-chiang⁴)	Frost falls	9th of 9th	23 Oct.
19	Lihdong (Li⁴-tung¹)	Winter begins	24th of 9th	7 Nov.
20	Sheausheue (Hsiao³-hsüeh³)	Slight snow	9th of 10th	22 Nov.
21	Dahsheue (Ta⁴-hsüeh³)	Heavy snow	24th of 10th	7 Dec.
22	Dongjyh (Tung¹-chih⁴)	Winter Solstice	9th of 11th	22 Dec.
23	Sheauharn (Hsiao³-han²)	Slight cold	24th of 11th	6 Jan.
24	Dahharn (Ta⁴-han²)	Great cold	8th of 12th	20 Jan.

(vi) BIBLIOGRAPHICAL REFERENCES

Chen, Yuan. *A comparative daily calendar for Chinese, European and Mohammedan history* [*Jong-Shi-Hwei shyy ryhlih*]. Five fascicles. Peking, 1926.

Havret, H., and others. *Mélanges sur la chronologie chinoise.* (*Variétés sinologiques, no. 52.*) Shanghai, 1920.

Hoang, Pierre. *Concordance des chronologies néoméniques chinoise et européenne.* (*Variétés sinologiques, no. 29.*) Shanghai, 1910.

Tchang, Mathias. *Synchronismes chinois. Chronologie complète et concordance avec l'ère chrétienne de toutes les dates concernant l'histoire de l'Extrême Orient (Chine, Japon, Corée, Annam, Mongolie, etc.). (2357 av. J.-C.—1904 apr. J.-C.)* (*Variétés sinologiques, no. 24.*) Shanghai, 1905.

6. DYNASTIES AND RULERS

(i) SHORT TABLE OF DYNASTIES

Roman numerals follow the names of those dynasties which are accepted as legitimate by traditional Chinese historiography, and indicate their sequence.

SHIAH (Hsia^{4}). I. 1989–1558 B.C.
SHANG (Shang^{1}) or IN (Yin^{1}). II. 1558–1051 B.C.
JOU (Chou^{1}). III. 1050–249 B.C.
CHYN (Ch'in^{2}). IV. 221–207 B.C.
Former HANN (Han^{4}). V. 206 B.C.–A.D. 8.
SHIN (Hsin^{1}). 9–23.
Later HANN (Han^{4}). V continued. 25–220.
Three Kingdoms: SAN GWO (San^{1} Kuo^{2}). 220–65.
JINN (Chin^{4}). VII. 265–420.
Sixteen Kingdoms: SHYRLIOW GWO (Shih^{2}-liu^{4} Kuo^{2}). 302–439.
WEY (Wei^{4}) and Succession States. 386–587.
Southern Dynasties: NAN CHAUR (Nan^{2} Ch'ao^{2}). 420–589.
SWEI (Sui^{2}). XII. 581–618.
TARNG (T'ang^{2}). XIII. 618–906.
Five Dynasties: WUU DAY (Wu^{3} Tai^{4}). 907–60.
Ten Minor Kingdoms. 901–79.
CHIHDAN (Ch'i^{4}-tan^{1}) LIAU (Liao^{2}). 907–1199.
SONQ (Sung^{4}). XIX. 960–1279.
SHIAH (Hsia^{4}) or Western SHIAH (Hsia^{4}). 1032–1227.
JIN (Chin^{1}). 1115–1234.
YUAN (Yüan^{2}). XX. 1206–1368.
MING (Ming^{2}). XXI. 1368–1644.
CHING (Ch'ing^{1}). XXII. 1644–1912.

(ii) TABLES OF RULERS

Notes.—(i) Names of persons and places are given first in GWOYEU ROMATZYH and following (in brackets) either in Wade (with superior numbers for the tones) or in a conventionally accepted romanization (without superior numbers) when this is more commonly met with than the Wade. Example: GOANGJOU (Kuang^{3}-chou^{1}) or (Canton)

(ii) CHYAN (Ch'ien^{2}) and How (Hou^{4}), i.e. Former and Later, have been translated. Example: Former HANN, instead of CHYAN HANN. Similarly with DONG (Tung^{1}) and SHI (Hsi^{1}), BEEI (Pei^{3}) and NAN (Nan^{2}), East, West, North and South. Example: Southern SONQ, instead of NAN SONQ.

(iii) In the dates given for reigns, the first is always that of the ruler's accession. If this date is given without an asterisk, it is also the year traditionally reckoned as the 'first' of his reign (i.e. that to which his NIANHAW or year-period is first applied). It was customary for a newly-enthroned emperor to continue the use of his predecessor's year-period to the end of the current year, and to proclaim his own year-period only at the beginning of the following year. When this happens, the date of accession is given with an asterisk. Thus SONQ TAYTZONG ascended the throne, and also began the use of his own year-period, in 976: this date is accordingly given without an asterisk. His successor JENTZONG, ascending the throne in 997, the third month, retained his predecessor's year-period during the remainder of that year, and began using his own only in 998: his accession date is therefore given as 997*.

(iv) The following abbreviations have been used: ad. s., adopted son; br., brother; gs., grandson; m., mother; n., nephew; s., son; u., uncle.

Shiah (Hsia^4). 1989–1558 B.C. Accepted as the First of the Official Dynasties by traditional Chinese historiography.

The historicity of the Shiah (Hsia^4) dynasty is more than doubtful. Its traditional dates are 2205–1766, but the chronology of the Bamboo Annals (Jwushu Jihnian, Chu^2-shu^1 Chi^4-nien^2) given above is to be preferred. The legendary Great Yeu (Yü^3) is regarded as its founder. Its last capital is thought to have been Yangshiah (Yang^2-hsia^4) (modern Taykang Shiann, T'ai^4-k'ang^1 hsien^4).

Shang (Shang^1). 1558–1051 B.C. The Second of the Official Dynasties.

This dynasty was also, until recently, regarded as legendary, but the oracle-bone finds from Anyang (An^1-yang^2) in northern Hernan (Honan) have fully established its historicity. The traditional dates of the dynasty are 1766–1123; the dates given above are de Saussure's emended chronology for the period (the dates given by the Bamboo Annals are 1558–1102). Founder: Tang (T'ang^1) the Victorious. (Note: the name In (Yin^1) was probably not applied by the Shang people themselves either to their kingdom or to their capital city.) In all, the Shang occupied seven different capitals (for notes on their probable location, see E. Chavannes, *Mémoires historiques*, i. 176–98).

Jou (Chou^1). 1050–249 B.C. The Third of the Official Dynasties.

The traditional dates are 1122–249. Founder: Fa (Fa^1), known as Wuu Wang (Wu^3 wang^2). Capitals: (i) Haw (Hao^4) in the Wey (Wei^4) valley, to 771; (ii) Wangcherng (Wang^2-ch'êng^2), slightly to the west of Luohyang (Lo^4-yang^2, modern Honan), from 770 to *c.* 509; (iii) Cherngjou (Ch'êng^2-chou^1) or 'Old Luohyang', about 13 miles north-east of modern Honan, from *c.* 509. The movement of the capital divides the Jou into Western Jou (1050–771) and Eastern Jou (770–249).

Chyn (Ch'in^2). 221–207 B.C. Fourth of the Official Dynasties.

The first ruler of the Chyn (Ch'in^2) Kingdom was Feitzyy (Fei^1-tzŭ^3), 897–858. King Jenq (Chêng^4), the 36th ruler (from 246), accomplished the unification of all China, and proclaimed himself first emperor in 221. Capital: Shyanyang (Hsien^2-yang^2) near Shi-an (Sian) in Shaanshi (Shensi).

Shyy Hwangdih (Shih^3 Huang^2-ti^4)	221–210
Ellshyh Hwangdih (Êrh^4-shih^4 Huang^2-ti^4), son of Shyy Hwangdih	209–207

Former or Western Hann (Han^4). 206 B.C.–A.D. 8. Fifth of the Official Dynasties.

Founder: Liou Bang (Liu^2 Pang^1), 247–195. Successful in the civil wars that followed the collapse of the Chyn (Ch'in^2), he took the title (206) of Hann Wang (Han^4 wang^2). Proclaimed emperor in 202. Capital (up to A.D. 25): Charngan (Ch'ang^2-an^1) near Shi-an (Sian) in Shaanshi (Shensi).

Gautzuu (Kao^1-tsu^3)	206–195
Hueydih (Hui^4-ti^4), s. of Gautzuu	195*–188
Gauhow (Kao^1-hou^4), m. of Hueydih	188*–180
Wendih (Wên^2-ti^4), s. of Gautzuu	180*–157

JIINGDIH (Ching^3-ti^4), s. of Wendih	157*–141
SHIAWWUUDIH (Hsiao^4-wu^3-ti^4)	141*–87
SHIAWJAUDIH (Hsiao^4-chao^1-ti^4)	87*–74
SHIAWSHIUANDIH (Hsiao^4-hsüan^1-ti^4)	74*–49
SHIAWYUANDIH (Hsiao^4-yüan^2-ti^4), s. of Shiuandih	49*–33
SHIAWCHERNGDIH (Hsiao^4-ch'êng^2-ti^4), s. of Yuandih	33*–7
SHIAWAIDIH (Hsiao^4-ai^1-ti^4), n. of Cherngdih	7*–1
SHIAWPYNGDIH (Hsiao^4-p'ing^2-ti^4)	1 B.C.*–A.D. 5
RUTZYY ING (Ju^2-tzŭ^3 Ying^1)	6–8

SHIN (Hsin^1). 9–23.

The WANG (Wang^2) family rose to power through the Lady Wang (b. 71 B.C.), Yuandih's empress, and empress-dowager during the reign of Cherngdih. WANG MAANG (Wang^2 Mang^3) attained high office in 8 B.C. and on the death of Pyngdih became surrogate emperor (JEAHWANGDIH, Chia^3-huang^2-ti^4). In A.D. 9 he deposed the last emperor of the Western Hann and himself ascended the throne. His reign is traditionally regarded as an usurpation.

WANG MAANG (Wang^2 Mang^3)	9–23

Later or Eastern HANN (Han^4). A.D. 25–220. Traditionally accepted as a continuation of the Fifth of the Official Dynasties.

Founder: LIOU SHIOW (Liu^2 Hsiu^4). Capital: LUOHYANG (Lo^4-yang^2) (modern Honan) in HERNAN (Honan).

GUANGWUUDIH (Kuang^1-wu^3-ti^4)	25–57
SHIAWMINGDIH (Hsiao^4-ming^2-ti^4)	57*–75
SHIAWJANGDIH (Hsiao^4-chang^1-ti^4)	75*–88
SHIAWHERDIH (Hsiao^4-hê^2-ti^4)	88*–105
SHIAWSHANGDIH (Hsiao^4-shang^1-ti^4)	105*–6
SHIAWANDIH (Hsiao^4-an^1-ti^4)	106*–25
SHAWDIH (Shao^4-ti^4), n. of Andih	125
SHIAWSHUENNDIH (Hsiao^4-shun^4-ti^4), s. of Andih	125*–44
SHIAWCHONGDIH (Hsiao^4-ch'ung^1-ti^4)	145
SHIAWJYRDIH (Hsiao^4-chih^2-ti^4), s. of Chongdih	145*–6
SHIAWHWANDIH (Hsiao^4-huan^2-ti^4)	146*–67
SHIAWLINGDIH (Hsiao^4-ling^2-ti^4), a descendant in the fifth generation from Jangdih	168–89
SHAWDIH (Shao^4-ti^4), s. of Lingdih	189
SHIANNDIH (Hsien^4-ti^4), br. of Shawdih	189*–220

SAN GWO (San^1 Kuo^2). Three Kingdoms. 220–65.

The collapse of the Later or Eastern HANN (Han^4) was followed by the 'Three Kingdoms' or SAN GWO (San^1 Kuo^2) period (220–65), when different dynasties ruled over the three HANN Succession States SHUU (Shu^3), WEY (Wei^4) and WU (Wu^2). SHUU or SHUU-HANN is traditionally accepted as the legitimate successor of the Later HANN.

(*a*) SHUU-HANN (Shu^3-Han^4). 221–63. Sixth of the Official Dynasties.

Founder: LIOU BEY (Liu^2 Pei^4), a prince of the HANN imperial family. Capital: YIHJOU (I^4-chou^1) (modern CHERNGDU, Chengtu) in SYHCHUAN (Szechwan). Ended by WEY (Wei^4) conquest.

JAULIEHDIH (Chao^1-lieh^4-ti^4)	221–23
HOWDIH (Hou^4-ti^4), s. of Jauliehdih	223–63

(*b*) WEY (Wei^4). 220–65.

Founder: TSAUR PEI (Ts'ao^2 P'ei^1), 188–226, s. of TSAUR TSAU

(Ts'ao² Ts'ao¹), a general of the Later HANN. Capital : LUOHYANG (Lo⁴-yang²) (modern Honan). Ended by JINN (Chin⁴) conquest.

WENDIH (Wên²-ti⁴) 220–26
MINGDIH (Ming²-ti⁴). 226*–39
FEYDIH (Fei⁴-ti⁴), s. of Mingdih 239*–54
SHAWDIH (Shao⁴-ti⁴), gs. of Wendih 254–60
YUANDIH HUANN (Yüan²-ti⁴ Huan⁴), gs. of Mingdih . . . 260–5

(c) WU (Wu²). 222–80.

Founder : SUEN CHYUAN (Sun¹ ch'üan²), 181–252, a general of the Later HANN. Capital : JIANNYEH (Chien⁴-yeh⁴) (modern Nanking). Ended by JINN (Chin⁴) conquest.

DAHDIH (Ta⁴-ti⁴) 222–52
FEYDIH (Fei⁴-ti⁴), s. of Dahdih 252–8
JIINGDIH (Ching³-ti⁴), br. of Feydih 258–64
MOHDIH (Mo⁴-ti⁴), n. of Jiingdih 264–80

JINN (Chin⁴). 265–420. Seventh of the Official Dynasties. (SHI JINN, 265–316 : DONG JINN, 317–420.)

The unity of China was re-established by the JINN dynasty. Founder : SYMAA YAN (Ssŭ¹-ma³ Yen²), s. of SYMAA JAU (Ssŭ¹-ma³ Chao¹), chief minister of WEY. Capitals : (i) LUOHYANG (Lo⁴-yang²) to 311 ; (ii) CHARNGAN (Ch'ang²-an¹) to 316 (both places were captured by the SHIONGNU JAW : see under Former JAW, 304–29) ; (iii) JIANNYEH (Chien⁴-yeh⁴) (modern Nanking), 317–420. The JINN of LUOHYANG are known as the Western (SHI, Hsi¹) JINN : those of Nanking as the Eastern (DONG, Tung¹) JINN. Ended by LIOU YUH (Liu² Yü⁴), founder of the (LIOU) SONQ dynasty, 420–79.

(a) Western JINN. 265–316.

WUUDIH (Wu³-ti⁴) 265–90
HUEYDIH (Hui⁴-ti⁴), s. of Wuudih 290–306
HWAIDIH (Huai²-ti⁴), br. of Hueydih 306*–11
MIINDIH (Min³-ti⁴), gs. of Wuudih 313–16

(b) Eastern JINN. 317–420.

YUANDIH (Yüan²-ti⁴) 317–22
MINGDIH (Ming²-ti⁴), s. of Yuandih. 322*–5
CHERNGDIH (Ch'êng²-ti⁴), s. of Mingdih 325*–42
KANGDIH (K'ang¹-ti⁴), br. of Cherngdih 342*–4
MUHDIH (Mu⁴-ti⁴), s. of Kangdih 344*–61
AIDIH (Ai¹-ti⁴), s. of Cherngdih 361*–5
HAESHI Gong (Hai³-hsi¹- kung¹), br. of Aidih . . . 365*–71
JEANWENDIH (Chien³-wên²-ti⁴), s. of Yuandih . . . 371–2
SHIAWWUUDIH (Hsiao⁴-wu³-ti⁴), s. of Jeanwendih . . 372*–96
ANDIH (An¹-ti⁴), s. of Shiawwuudih 396*–418
GONGDIH (Kung¹-ti⁴), br. of Andih 418*–20

SHYRLIOW GWO (Shih²-liu⁴ Kuo²). The Sixteen Kingdoms. 4th and early 5th centuries.

(1) CHERNG (Ch'êng²) or SHUU (Shu³). 302–47.
     In SYHCHUAN (Szechwan). Capital : CHERNGDU (Chengtu). Name of ruling family : LII (Li³). 7 rulers. Ended by JINN (Chin⁴) conquest.
(2) Former JAW (Chao⁴) or Northern HANN (Han⁴). 304–29.
     In SHANSHI (Shansi). Capital : JINNYANG (Chin⁴-yang²)

(modern TAYYUAN, Taiyuan). Founded by Southern SHIONGNU (Hsiung^1-nu^2). Name of ruling family (adopted): LIOU (Liu^2). 4 rulers. Ended by the adventurer SHYR LEH (Shih^2 Lê^4), founder of the Later JAW (Chao^4).

(3) Former LIANG (Liang^2). 313–76.
In SHANSHI (Shansi). Capital: HERSHI (Ho^2-hsi^1). Name of ruling family: JANG (Chang^1). 8 rulers. Ended by Former CHŶN (Ch'in^2) conquest.

(4) Later JAW (Chao^4). 319–52.
In HERBEEI (Hopeh). Capital: SHIANGGWO (Hsiang^1-kuo^2) (modern SHUENNDER, Shunteh). Name of ruling family: SHYR (Shih^2). 8 rulers. Ended by internal disorder and Former IAN (Yen^1) conquest.

(5) Former IAN (Yen^1). 349–70.
In HERBEEI (Hopeh). Capital: IAN (Yen^1). Name of ruling family: MUHRONG (Mu^4-jung^2). 2 rulers. Ended by Former CHYN (Ch'in^2) conquest.

(6) Former CHYN (Ch'in^2). 351–94.
In SHAANSHI (Shensi). Capital: CHARNGAN (Ch'ang^2-an^1). Founded by the DII (Ti^3) tribes of Southern Mongols. Name of ruling family: FWU (Fu^2). 6 rulers. Ended by Western CHYN (Ch'in^2) conquest.

(7*a*) Western IAN (Yen^1). 384–96.
In SHANSHI (Shansi). Capital: CHERNGTZYY (Ch'êng^2-tzŭ^3). Name of ruling family: MUHRONG (Mu^4-jung^2). 7 rulers. Ended by Later IAN (Yen^1) conquest. (The Later and Western IAN Kingdoms are usually counted together as one.)

(7*b*) Later IAN (Yen^1). 384–408.
In HERBEEI (Hopeh). Capital: JONGSHAN (Chung^1-shan^1) (modern DINQJOU, Ting^4-chou^1). Name of ruling family: MUHRONG (Mu^4-jung^2). 5 rulers. Ended by Northern IAN (Yen^1) conquest.

(8) Later CHYN (Ch'in^2). 384–417.
In SHAANSHI (Shensi). Capital: CHARNGAN (Ch'ang^2-an^1). Name of ruling family: YAU (Yao^2). 3 rulers. Ended by LIOU YUH (Liu^2 Yü^4), general of JINN ANDIH (Chin^4 An^1-ti^4) and later founder of the (LIOU) SONQ dynasty.

(9) Western CHYN (Ch'in^2). 385–431. (Subject to Later CHYN, 400–9.)
In GANSUH (Kansu). Capital: BAWHAAN (Pao^4-han^3) (modern HERJOU, Ho^2-chou^1, near LANJOU, Lanchow). Founded by SHIANBI (Hsien^1-pi^1) Mongols. Name of ruling family: CHIIFWU (Ch'i^3-fu^2). 4 rulers. Ended by SHIAH (Hsia^4) conquest.

(10) Later LIANG (Liang^2). 386–403.
In GANSUH (Kansu). Capital: GUTZANG (Ku^1-tsang^1) (modern WUU-UEI, Wu^3-wei^1). Founded by Western tribes of the DII (Ti^3) Southern Mongols. Name of ruling family: LEU (Lü^3). 4 rulers. Ended by JINN (Chin^4) conquest.

(11) Southern LIANG (Liang^2). 397–414. (Subject to Later CHYN, 404–8.)
In GANSUH (Kansu). Founded by the SHIANBI (Hsien^1-pi^1)

chieftain TUFAA UGU (Tu¹-fa³ Wu¹-gu¹). 3 rulers. Ended by Western CHYN (Ch'in²) conquest.

(12) Northern LIANG (Liang²). 397–439.
In GANSUH (Kansu). Capital: GUTZANG (Ku¹-tsang¹) (modern WUU-UEI, Wu³-wei¹). 3 rulers. Ended by WEY (Wei⁴) conquest.

(13) Southern IAN (Yen¹). 398–410.
In SHANDONG (Shantung). Capital: GOANGGUH (Kuang³-ku⁴) (west of modern CHINGJOU, Ch'ing¹-chou¹). Name of ruling family: MUHRONG (Mu⁴-jung²). 2 rulers. Ended by LIOU YUH (Liu² Yü⁴), founder of the (LIOU) SONQ dynasty.

(14) Western LIANG (Liang²). 401–421.
In GANSUH (Kansu). Capital: DUENHWANG (Tun¹-huang²) (modern ANSHI, An¹-hsi¹). Name of ruling family: LII (Li³). 3 rulers. Ended by Northern LIANG (Liang²) conquest. Note: LII IUAN (Li³ Yüan¹), the first emperor of the TARNG (T'ang²) in 618, was a descendant in the 7th generation of LII SHIN (Hsin¹), the second ruler of the Western LIANG.

(15) SHIAH (Hsia⁴). 407–431.
In SHAANSHI (Shensi). Capital: SHUOHFANG (Shuo⁴-fang¹) (near modern YULIN, Yü²-lin²). A SHIONGNU (Hsiung¹-nu²) kingdom. Name of ruling family: HEHLIAN (Hê⁴-lien²). 3 rulers. Ended by Tibetan conquest.

(16) Northern IAN (Yen¹). 409–436.
In northern HERBEEI (Hopeh) and LIAUNING (Liaoning). Name of ruling family: FERNG (Fêng²). 2 rulers. Ended by WEY (Wei⁴) conquest.

WEY (Wei⁴) and Succession States. 386–587.

WEY was the kingdom of the TUOHBAR (T'o⁴-pa²), a proto-Mongol or perhaps Turkish people, originally from eastern Mongolia. Founder: TUOHBAR GUEI (Kuei¹). From 436, after the completion of the WEY conquest of north China, the country was divided between two empires, that of the WEY north of the YANGTZYY (Yangtse) and that ruled (from Nanking) by successive Chinese dynasties in central and south China. In 496 the WEY changed their dynastic title to YUAN (Yüan). After 534 the TUOHBAR kingdom divided into two branches: Eastern WEY, 534–50, continued by Northern CHYI (Ch'i²), 550–7; and Western WEY, 535–57, continued by Northern JOU (Chou¹), 556–81. To this list may be added the minor kingdom of Later LIANG (Liang²), 555–87. In north China. Capitals: WEY: (i) PYNGCHERNG (P'ing²-ch'êng²) (east of modern DAHTORNG, Tatung), 386–494; (ii) LUOHYANG (Lo⁴-yang²) (modern Honan), 495–534. Eastern WEY: WEYYIIN (Wei⁴-yin³), 534–50. Western WEY: CHARNGAN (Ch'ang²-an¹), 535–57. Northern CHYI and Northern JOU retained the capitals of Eastern and Western WEY respectively. Later LIANG: JIANGLING (Chiang¹-ling²), 555–87.

(*a*) WEY or YUAN WEY (Wei⁴ or Yüan² Wei⁴). 386–534.

TAYTZUU DAWWUUDIH (T'ai⁴-tsu³ Tao⁴-wu³-ti⁴)	386–409
TAYTZONG MINGYUANDIH (T'ai⁴-tsung¹ Ming²-yüan²-ti⁴)	409–23
SHYHTZUU TAYWUUDIH (Shih⁴-tsu³ T'ai⁴-wu³-ti⁴)	423*–52

NAN-AN Wang (Nan^{2}-an^{1} wang^{2})	452
GAUTZONG WENCHERNGDIH (Kao^{1}-tsung^{1} Wên^{2}-ch'êng^{2}-ti^{4}), gs. of Taywuudih	452–65
SHEANTZUU SHIANNWENDIH (Hsien^{3}-tsu^{3} Hsien^{4}-wên^{2}-ti^{4}), s. of Wencherngdih	465*–71
GAUTZUU SHIAWWENDIH (Kao^{1}-tsu^{3} Hsiao^{4}-wên^{2}-ti^{4}), s. of Shiannwendih	471–99
SHIUANWUUDIH (Hsüan^{1}-wu^{3}-ti^{4})	499*–515
SUHTZONG SHIAWMINGDIH (Su^{4}-tsung^{1} Hsiao^{4}-ming^{2}-ti^{4})	515*–28
JINQTZONG SHIAWJUANGDIH (Ching^{4}-tsung^{1} Hsiao^{4}-chuang^{1}-ti^{4})	528–30
JINQDIH or DONGHAE Wang (Ching^{4}-ti^{4} or Tung^{1}-hai^{3} wang^{2})	530
JYEMIINDIH (Chieh^{2}-min^{3}-ti^{4})	531
CHUDIH or ANDINQ Wang (Ch'u^{1}-ti^{4} or An^{1}-ting^{4} wang^{2})	531–2
SHIAWWUUDIH (Hsiao^{4}-wu^{3}-ti^{4})	532–4

(*b*) Eastern WEY (Wei^{4}). 534–50.

SHIAWJINQDIH (Hsiao^{4}-ching^{4}-ti^{4})	534–50

(*c*) Western WEY (Wei^{4}). 535–56.

WENDIH (Wên^{2}-ti^{4})	535–51
FEYDIH (Fei^{4}-ti^{4})	551*–4
GONGDIH (Kung^{1}-ti^{4}), s. of Chudih	554–6

(*d*) Northern CHYI (Ch'i^{2}).
Six rulers from 550 to 577. Ended by Northern JOU (Chou^{1}) conquest.

(*e*) Northern JOU (Chou^{1}).
Six rulers from 556 to 581. Name of ruling family: YEUWEN (Yü^{3}-wên^{2}). Ended by SWEI (Sui^{2}) conquest.

(*f*) Later LIANG (Liang^{2}).
In HWUBEEI (Hupeh). Three rulers from 555 to 587. Name of ruling family: SHIAU (Hsiao^{1}). Ended by SWEI (Sui^{2}) conquest.

NAN CHAUR (Nan^{2} Ch'ao^{2}). Southern Dynasties. 420–589.

(*a*) Southern (or LIOU, Liu^{2}) SONQ (Sung^{4}). 420–79. Eighth of the Official Dynasties.
Founder: LIOU YUH (Liu^{2} Yü^{4}), a general of the JINN (Chin^{4}).
Capital: JIANNKANG (Chien^{4}-k'ang^{1}) (modern Nanking).

WUUDIH (Wu^{3}-ti^{4})	420–2
SHAWDIH (Shao^{4}-ti^{4}), s. of Wuudih	422*–4
WENDIH (Wên^{2}-ti^{4}), br. of Shawdih	424–53
SHIAWWUUDIH (Hsiao^{4}-wu^{3}-ti^{4})	453*–64
CHYAN (Ch'ien^{2}, Earlier) FEYDIH (Fei^{4}-ti^{4}), s. of Shiawwuudih	464*–5
MINGDIH (Ming^{2}-ti^{4}), br. of Chyan Feydih	465–72
HOW (Hou^{4}, Later) FEYDIH (Fei^{4}-ti^{4}), s. of Mingdih	472*–7
SHUENNDIH (Shun^{4}-ti^{4}), br. of How Feydih	477–9

(*b*) Southern CHYI (Ch'i^{2}). 479–502. Ninth of the Official Dynasties.
Founder: SHIAU DAWCHERNG (Hsiao^{1} Tao^{4}-ch'êng^{2}).
Capital: JIANNKANG (Chien^{4}-k'ang^{1}).

GAUDIH (Kao^{1}-ti^{4})	479–82
WUUDIH (Wu^{3}-ti^{4}), s. of Gaudih	482*–93
YUHLIN Wang (Yü^{4}-lin^{2} wang^{2}), gs. of Wuudih	493*–4
HAELING Wang (Hai^{3}-ling^{2} wang^{2}), br. of Yuhlin Wang	494
MINGDIH (Ming^{2}-ti^{4}), n. of Gaudih	494–8
DONGHUEN Hour (Tung^{1}-hun^{1} hou^{2}), s. of Mingdih	498*–501
HERDIH (Hê^{2}-ti^{4})	501–2

(c) Southern LIANG (Liang²). 502–57. Tenth of the Official Dynasties.

Founder: SHIAU YEAN (Hsiao¹ Yen³). Capital: JIANNKANG (Chien⁴-k'ang¹).

WUUDIH (Wu³-ti⁴)	502–49
JEANWENDIH (Chien³-wên²-ti⁴)	549*–51
YUHJANG Wang (Yü⁴-chang¹ wang²)	551–2
YUANDIH (Yüan²-ti⁴)	552–4
JENYANG Hour (Chên¹-yang² hou²)	555
JINQDIH (Ching⁴-ti⁴)	555–7

(d) Southern CHERN (Ch'ên²). 557–89. Eleventh of the Official Dynasties.

Founder: CHERN BAHSHIAN (Ch'ên² Pa⁴-hsien¹). Capital: JIANNKANG (Chien⁴-k'ang¹).

WUUDIH (Wu³-ti⁴)	557–9
WENDIH (Wên²-ti⁴), n. of Wuudih	559*–66
FEYDIH (Fei⁴-ti⁴), s. of Wendih	566–8
SHIUANDIH (Hsüan¹-ti⁴), u. of Feydih	568*–82
HOWJUU (Hou⁴-chu³), s. of Shiuandih	582*–9

SWEI (Sui²). 581–618. Twelfth of the Official Dynasties.

By his conquest of Northern JOU (Chou¹) in 581, YANG JIAN (Yang² Chien¹), founder of the SWEI, made himself master of north China. The conquest of Southern CHERN (Ch'ên²) in 589 re-established the unity of China under a single dynasty. Capital: CHARNGAN (Ch'ang²-an¹).

GAUTZUU WENDIH (Kao¹-tsu³ Wên²-ti⁴)	581(590)–604
YANGDIH (Yang²-ti⁴), s. of Wendih	604*–18
GONGDIH (Kung¹-ti⁴), gs. of Yangdih	617–18

TARNG (T'ang²). 618–906. Thirteenth of the Official Dynasties.

When the SWEI empire collapsed, the successful contender for power was LII IUAN (Li³ Yüan¹), duke of TARNG, the GAUTZUU of the new dynasty. The real founder of the dynasty was his son, LII SHYHMIN (Li³ Shih⁴-min²) (TARNG TAYTZONG). Capital: CHARNGAN (Ch'ang²-an¹).

GAUTZUU (Kao¹-tsu³)	618–26
TAYTZONG (T'ai⁴-tsung¹), s. of Gautzuu	626*–49
GAUTZONG (Kao¹-tsung¹), s. of Taytzong	649*–83
JONGTZONG (Chung¹-tsung¹), s. of Gautzong	683*–4
RUEYTZONG (Jui⁴-tsung¹), br. of Jongtzong	684
WUUHOW (TZERTIAN) (Wu³-hou⁴, Tsê²-t'ien¹), wife of Gautzong: a usurping reign	684–705
JONGTZONG (Chung¹-tsung¹) (restored)	705–10
RUEYTZONG (Jui⁴-tsung¹) (restored)	710–12
SHYUANTZONG (Hsüan²-tsung¹)	712–54
SUHTZONG (Su⁴-tsung¹), s. of Shyuantzong	756–62
DAYTZONG (Tai⁴-tsung¹), s. of Suhtzong	762–79
DERTZONG (Tê²-tsung¹), s. of Daytzong	779*–805
SHUENNTZONG (Shun⁴-tsung¹), s. of Dertzong	805
SHIANNTZONG (Hsien⁴-tsung¹), s. of Shuenntzong	805*–20
MUHTZONG (Mu⁴-tsung¹), s. of Shianntzong	820*–4
JINQTZONG (Ching⁴-tsung¹), s. of Muhtzong	824*–6
WENTZONG (Wên²-tsung¹)	826*–40
WUUTZONG (Wu³-tsung¹), br. of Wentzong	840*–6
SHIUANTZONG (Hsüan¹-tsung¹), u. of Wuutzong	846*–59
YIHTZONG (I⁴-tsung¹), s. of Shiuantzong	859*–73
SHITZONG (Hsi¹-tsung¹), s. of Yihtzong	873*–88
JAUTZONG (Chao¹-tsung¹)	888*–904
JAUSHIUANDIH (Chao¹-hsüan¹-ti⁴), br. of Jautzong	904–7

WUUDAY (Wu^{3} Tai^{4}). 907–60. The Five Dynasties.

With the fall of the TARNG the empire was again fragmented. In the North five dynasties ruled in succession (the 14th to the 18th of the Official Dynasties—hence the name WUUDAY), while the South was divided between a number of minor kingdoms. The LIAU (Liao^{1}) dynasty of the CHIHDAN (Ch'i^{4}-tan^{1}) began in this period, ruling the extreme north-east of China, and continued almost until the end of the Northern SONQ (Sung^{4}).

(*a*) Later LIANG (Liang^{2}). 907–23. Fourteenth of the Official Dynasties.

Founder: JU UEN (Chu^{1} Wên^{1}). Capital: BIANN (Pien^{4}) (modern KAIFENG).

TAYTZUU (T'ai^{4}-tsu^{3})	907–12
YIING Wang (Ying^{3} wang^{2}), s. of Taytzuu: a usurping reign	912*–13
MOHDIH (Mo^{4}-ti^{4}), br. of Yiing wang	913*–23

(*b*) Later TARNG (T'ang^{2}). 923–36. Fifteenth of the Official Dynasties.

Founder: LII TSWENSHIUH (Li^{3} Ts'un^{2}-hsü^{4}). Capital: LUOHYANG (Lo^{4}-yang^{2}) (modern Honan).

JUANGTZONG (Chuang^{1}-tsung^{1})	923–6
MINGTZONG (Ming^{2}-tsung^{1}), ad. s. of Juangtzong	926–33
MIINDIH (Min^{3}-ti^{4}), s. of Mingtzong	933*–4
MOHDIH or FEYDIH (Mo^{4}-ti^{4} or Fei^{4}-ti^{4}), br. of Miindih	934–6

(*c*) Later JINN (Chin^{4}). 936–46. Sixteenth of the Official Dynasties.

Founder: SHYR JINQTARNG (Shih^{2} Ching^{4}-t'ang^{2}). Capitals: (i) LUOHYANG (Lo^{4}-yang^{2}) in 936; (ii) BIANN (Pien^{4}) (modern KAIFENG), from 937.

GAUTZUU (Kao^{1}-tsu^{3})	936–42
CHUDIH (Ch'u^{1}-ti^{4})	942–6

(*d*) Later HANN (Han^{4}). 947–50. Seventeenth of the Official Dynasties.

Founder: LIOU JYYEUAN (Liu^{2} Chih^{1}-yüan^{3}). Capital: BIANN (Pien^{4}) (modern KAIFENG).

GAUTZUU (Kao^{1}-tsu^{3})	947–8
YIINDIH (Yin^{3}-ti^{4}), s. of Gautzuu	948–50

(*e*) Later JOU (Chou^{1}). 951–60. Eighteenth of the Official Dynasties.

Founder: GUO UEI (Kuo^{1} Wei^{1}). Capital: BIANN (Pien^{4}) (modern KAIFENG).

TAYTZUU (T'ai^{4}-tsu^{3})	951–4
SHYHTZONG (Shih^{4}-tsung^{1}), s. of Taytzuu	954–9
GONGDIH (Kung^{1}-ti^{4}), s. of Shyhtzong	959–60

Ten Minor Kingdoms. 10th century.

(1) Former SHUU (Shu^{3}). 901–25.

In SYHCHUAN (Szechwan). Capital: CHERNGDU (Chengtu). Name of ruling family: WANG (Wang^{2}). 2 rulers. Ended by Later TARNG (T'ang^{2}) conquest.

(2) WU (Wu^{2}) or HWAINAN (Huai^{2}-nan^{2}). 902–37.

In JIANGSU (Kiangsu). Capital: YANGJOU (Yang^{2}-chou^{1}).

Name of ruling family: YANG (Yang²). 4 rulers. Ended by Southern TARNG (T'ang²) conquest.

(3) WU-YUEH (Wu²-Yüeh⁴). 908–78.
In JEHJIANG (Chekiang). Capital: HARNGJOU (Hangchow). Name of ruling family: CHYAN (Ch'ien²). 5 rulers. Ended by SONQ (Sung⁴) conquest.

(4) MIN (Min²). 909–44.
In FWUJIANN (Fukien). Capital: FWUJOU (Foochow). Name of ruling family: WANG (Wang²). 6 rulers. Ended by Southern TARNG (T'ang²) conquest.

(5) Southern HANN (Han⁴). 917–71.
In GOANGDONG (Kwangtung). Capital: GOANGJOU (Canton). Name of ruling family: LIOU (Liu²). 4 rulers. Ended by SONQ (Sung⁴) conquest.

(6) NANPYNG or JINGNAN (Nan²-p'ing² or Ching¹-nan²). 925–63.
In HWUBEEI (Hupeh). Capital: JINGJOU (Ching¹-chou¹). Name of ruling family: GAU (Kao¹). 5 rulers. Ended by SONQ (Sung⁴) conquest.

(7) CHUU (Ch'u³). 927–52.
In HWUNAN (Hunan). Capital: CHARNGSHA (Ch'ang²-sha¹). Name of ruling family: MAA (Ma³). 6 rulers. Ended by Southern TARNG (T'ang²) conquest.

(8) Later SHUU (Shu³). 934–65.
In SYHCHUAN (Szechwan). Capital: CHERNGDU (Chengtu). Name of ruling family: MENQ (Mêng⁴). 2 rulers. Ended by SONQ (Sung⁴) conquest.

(9) Southern TARNG (T'ang²). 937–75.
In JIANGSU (Kiangsu). Capital: JIANGNING (Chiang¹-ning²) (modern Nanking). Name of ruling family: LII (Li³). 5 rulers. Ended by SONQ (Sung⁴) conquest.

(10) Eastern or Northern HANN (Han⁴). 951–79.
In SHANSHI (Shansi). Capital: PYNGYANG (P'ing²-yang²) (modern TAYYUAN, Taiyuan). Name of ruling family: LIOU (Liu²). 4 rulers. Ended by SONQ (Sung⁴) conquest.

CHIHDAN (Ch'i⁴-tan¹) LIAU (Liao²). 907–1199.

The anarchy of the Five Dynasties period (907–960) enabled the CHIHDAN (Ch'i⁴-dan¹) Tartars, a Mongol horde from south-east Mongolia who had established themselves in southern Manchuria at the beginning of the 10th century, to conquer the northern marches of the empire. The founder (temple name: TAYTZUU) of the dynasty was YELIUH AHBAOJI (Yeh²-lü⁴ A⁴-pao³-chi¹). The CHIHDAN adopted the dynastic name LIAU in 947. Between 1116 and 1123 the RUUJEN (see under JIN dynasty, 1115–1234) conquered the LIAU empire, a small CHIHDAN group led by YELIUH DAHSHYR (Ta⁴-shih²) or DERTZONG (Tê²-tsung¹) escaping into central Asia to continue the line as the Western LIAU or Kara-khitai (1124–99). Capitals (to the time of the RUUJEN conquest): (i) principal: LINHUANG (Lin²-huang¹); (ii) central: DAHDINQ (Ta⁴-ting⁴); (iii) western: DAHTORNG (Ta⁴-t'ung²); (iv) eastern: LIAUYANG (Liao²-yang²); (v) southern: SHIJIN (Hsi¹-chin¹) (modern Peking). Capital of Western LIAU: Balāsāgūn.

(*a*) Chihdan Liau. 907–1125.

Taytzuu (T'ai^4-tsu^3)	907–26
Taytzong (T'ai^4-tsung^1), s. of Taytzuu	926–47
Shyhtzong (Shih^4-tsung^1), n. of Taytzong	947–51
Muhtzong (Mu^4-tsung^1), s. of Shyhtzong	951–69
Jiingtzong (Ching^3-tsung^1), s. of Muhtzong	969–82
Shenqtzong (Shêng^4-tsung^1), s. of Jiingtzong	982*–1031
Shingtzong (Hsing^1-tsung^1), s. of Shenqtzong	1031–55
Dawtzong (Tao^4-tsung^1), s. of Shingtzong	1055–1101
Tiantzuohdih (T'ien^1-tso^4-ti^4), gs. of Dawtzong	1101–25

(*b*) Western Liau or Kara-khitai. 1124–99.

Dertzong (Tê^2-tsung^1)	1124–35
Gaantian How (Kan^3-t'ien^1 hou^4), wife of Dertzong	1136–41
Rentzong (Jên^2-tsung^1), s. of Dertzong	1142–54
Cherngtian How (Ch'êng^2-t'ien^1 hou^4), sister of Rentzong	1154–67
Mohjuu (Mo^4-chu^3), s. of Cherngtian	1168–99

Sonq (Sung^4). 960–1279. Nineteenth of the Official Dynasties.

Founded by Jaw Kuangyinn (Chao^4 K'uang^1-yin^4), regent for the child emperor Gong (Kung^1), the last ruler of the Later Jou (*q.v.*). Gongdih was forced to abdicate in 960, and Kuangyinn in the same year ascended the throne as the first emperor of the Sonq. The six survivors of the Ten Minor Kingdoms (*q.v.*) were defeated and annexed (963–979) and the whole empire (except for the northern marches held by the Chihdan) was again united under a Chinese dynasty. An invasion of the Ruujen (see under Jin) in which the capital was sacked and the emperor taken prisoner (1127–35) led to the transfer of the court to south of the Yangtzyy (Yangtse), where the dynasty maintained itself, though ruling over a much limited territory. The earlier period is therefore known as the Northern Sonq, and the later as the Southern Sonq. Capitals: Northern Sonq: Biannliang (Pien^4-liang^2) (modern Kaifeng); Southern Sonq: Lin-an (Lin^2-an^1) (modern Hangchow).

(*a*) Northern Sonq (Sung^4). 960–1127.

Taytzuu (T'ai^4-tsu^3)	960–76
Taytzong (T'ai^4-tsung^1), br. of Taytzuu	976–97
Jentzong (Chên^1-tsung^1), s. of Taytzong	997*–1022
Rentzong (Jên^2-tsung^1), s. of Jentzong	1022*–63
Ingtzong (Ying^1-tsung^1), ad. s. of Rentzong	1063*–7
Sherntzong (Shên^2-tsung^1), s. of Ingtzong	1067*–85
Jertzong (Chê^2-tsung^1), s. of Sherntzong	1085*–1100
Hueitzong (Hui^1-tsung^1)	1100*–25
Chintzong (Ch'in^1-tsung^1)	1125*–7

(*b*) Southern Sonq (Sung^4). 1127–1279.

Gautzong (Kao^1-tsung^1), s. of Hueitzong	1127–62
Shiawtzong (Hsiao^4-tsung^1), ad. s. of Gautzong	1162*–89
Guangtzong (Kuang^1-tsung^1), s. of Shiawtzong	1189*–94
Ningtzong (Ning^2-tsung^1), s. of Guangtzong	1194*–1224
Liitzong (Li^3-tsung^1), ad. s. of Ningtzong	1224*–64
Duhtzong (Tu^4-tsung^1), ad. s. of Liitzong	1264*–74
Gongtzong (Kung^1-tsung^1), s. of Duhtzong	1274*–6
Duantzong (Tuan^1-tsung^1), br. of Gongtzong	1276–8
Dihbiing (Ti^4-ping^3), br. of Duantzong	1278–9

Shiah (Hsia^4) or Western Shiah (Hsia^4). 1032–1227.

The Shiah kingdom was founded in north-west China by the

Tangut, a 'semi-oasis' (part-nomad, part-sedentary) Tibetan people descended from the TUOHBAR (see under WEY, 386–587). Name (adopted) of ruling family: LII (Li^{3}). They were recognized by the CHIHDAN (Ch'i^{4}-tan^{1}) court in 990 as the legitimate rulers of a part of GANSUH (Kansu), and in 1032 proclaimed their domain an empire. LII SHIANN (Li^{3} Hsien^{4}), the last SHIAH ruler, was taken prisoner and executed by the Mongols. Capital: SHINGCHINQ (Hsing^{1}-ch'ing^{4}) (modern NINGSHIAH, Ning^{2}-hsia^{4}).

JIINGTZONG (Ching^{3}-tsung^{1})	1032–48
YIHTZONG (I^{4}-tsung^{1})	1048*–67
HUEYTZONG (Hui^{4}-tsung^{1}), s. of Yihtzong	1069–86
CHORNGTZONG (Ch'ung^{2}-tsung^{1})	1086*–1139
RENTZONG (Jên^{2}-tsung^{1}), s. of Chorngtzong	1139–94
HWANTZONG (Huan^{2}-tsung^{1})	1194–1206
SHIANGTZONG (Hsiang^{1}-tsung^{1})	1206–11
SHERNTZONG (Shên^{2}-tsung^{1})	1211–23
SHIANNTZONG (Hsien^{4}-tsung^{1}), s. of Sherntzong	1223–6
LII SHIANN (Li^{3} Hsien^{4}), br. of Shianntzong	1226–7

JIN (Chin^{1}). 1115–1234.

The RUUJEN (Ju^{3}-chên^{1}), founders of the JIN kingdom, were a Tungusic people, originally from the forests of north Manchuria, and vassals of the CHIHDAN. In 1114 their leader, AHGUUDAA (A^{4}-ku^{3}-ta^{3}), of the ruling WANYAN (Wan^{2}-yen^{2}) clan, threw off CHIHDAN suzerainty and succeeded (1116–23) in destroying the LIAU empire. Establishing themselves as a new ruling dynasty in north China, the RUUJEN adopted the dynastic title JIN (Chin^{1}). They were finally destroyed by the Mongols. Capitals: HUEYNING (Hui^{4}-ning^{2}) (modern KAIYUAN, K'ai^{1}-yüan^{2}) and (from 1152) DAHSHING (Ta^{4}-hsing^{1}) (modern Peking).

TAYTZUU (T'ai^{4}-tsu^{3})	1115–23
TAYTZONG (T'ai^{4}-tsung^{1}), br. of Taytzuu	1123–35
SHITZONG (Hsi^{1}-tsung^{1}), gs. of Taytzuu	1135–49
HAELING Wang (Hai^{3}-ling^{2} wang^{2})	1149–61
SHYHTZONG (Shih^{4}-tsung^{1}), gs. of Taytzuu	1161–89
JANGTZONG (Chang^{1}-tsung^{1}), gs. of Shyhtzong	1189*–1208
WEYSHAW Wang (Wei^{4}-shao^{4} wang^{2}), s. of Shyhtzong	1208*–13
SHIUANTZONG (Hsüan^{1}-tsung^{1}), gs. of Shyhtzong	1213–23
AITZONG (Ai^{1}-tsung^{1}), s. of Shiuantzong	1223*–34

YUAN (Yüan^{2}). 1206–1368. Twentieth of the Official Dynasties (from 1280).

Činggis-Qan, the founder (TAYTZUU) of the Mongol dynasty, first uniting the many Mongol tribes, succeeded in making himself master of the whole of Mongolia by 1204. In 1206 his sovereignty was confirmed by the tribal diet: the Mongols therefore dated their dynasty from that year. The dynastic title was changed from Mongol (MENGGUU, Mêng^{2}-ku^{3}) to YUAN (Yüan^{2}) in 1271. Although the SHIAH and JIN kingdoms were overrun and destroyed (1227 and 1234 respectively), the SONQ continued to rule in south China until 1279. For this reason the YUAN is only accepted as the Twentieth Official Dynasty (by traditional Chinese historiography) from the year 1280. Capitals: Qaraqorum (Chinese: HERLIN, Hê^{2}-lin^{2}) founded 1235; TAYDU (T'ai^{4}-tu^{1}), the Great Capital, also known as Qanbaliq (the Cambaluc of Marco Polo), the Khan's city, from 1267. The Upper or Summer Capital was at SHANQDU (Shang^{4}-tu^{1})

(modern Kaipyng, K'ai^1-p'ing^2) in Chahar (the Ciandu of Marco Polo).

Taytzuu (T'ai^4-tsu^3) (Činggis)	1206–27
Regency of Tolui (s. of Činggis)	1227–9
Taytzong (T'ai^4-tsung^1) (Ogödäi), s. of Činggis	1229–41
Regency of Turakina (wife of Ogödäi)	1241–6
Dinqtzong (Ting^4-tsung^1) (Güyük), s. of Ogödäi	1246–8
Regency of Oġul Ġaimiš (wife of Güyük)	1249–51
Shianntzong (Hsien^4-tsung^1) (Mongkä), gs. of Činggis	1251–9
Shyhtzong (Shih^4-tsung^1) (Qubilai), br. of Mongkä	1260–94
Cherngtzong (Ch'êng^2-tsung^1), gs. of Qubilai	1294*–1307
Wuutzong (Wu^3-tsung^1), br. of Cherngtzong	1307*–11
Rentzong (Jên^2-tsung^1), br. of Wuutzong	1311*–20
Ingtzong (Ying^1-tsung^1), s. of Rentzong	1320*–3
Taydinqdih (T'ai^4-ting^4-ti^4)	1323*–8
Wentzong (Wên^2-tsung^1)	1328–9
Mingtzong (Ming^2-tsung^1), s. of Wuutzong	1329
Wentzong (Wên^2-tsung^1) (restored)	1329–32
Ningtzong (Ning^2-tsung^1), s. of Wentzong	1332
Shuenndih (Shun^4-ti^4) or Hueytzong (Hui^4-tsung^1), br. of Ningtzong	1333–68

Ming (Ming^2). 1368–1644. Twenty-first of the Official Dynasties.

The gradual collapse of Mongol authority in south China in the 1350's was accompanied by the appearance of numerous 'rebel' contenders for the supremacy. The victor, and founder of the Chinese Ming (Ming^2) dynasty, was Ju Yuanjang (Chu^1 Yüan^2-chang^1), temple name Taytzuu (T'ai^4-tsu^3). The dynastic capital was at first Jiangning (Chiang^1-ning^2) (modern Nanking), but in 1409 the court moved to Beeijing (Peking) and the latter place became the official capital from 1421. (Note: with the Ming dynasty the custom began of retaining a single year-period for the whole of a reign, and Ming rulers are often referred to in historical writings by their year-period alone: e.g. the Horngwuu (Hung^2-wu^3) emperor for Taytzuu (T'ai^4-tsu^3). The year-periods are therefore given as the final entry for each reign.)

Taytzuu (T'ai^4-tsu^3) (Horngwuu, Hung^2-wu^3)	1368–98
Hueydih (Hui^4-ti^4), gs. of Taytzuu. (Jiannwen, Chien^4-wên^2)	1398*–1402
Cherngtzuu (Ch'êng^2-tsu^3), u. of Hueydih, s. of Taytzuu. (Yeongleh, Yung^3-lo^4)	1402*–24
Rentzong (Jên^2-tsung^1), s. of Cherngtzuu. (Horngshi, Hung^2-hsi^1)	1424*–5
Shiuantzong (Hsüan^1-tsung^1), s. of Rentzong. (Shiuander, Hsüan^1-tê^2)	1425*–35
Ingtzong (Ying^1-tsung^1). (Jenqtoong, Chêng^4-t'ung^3)	1435*–49
Daytzong (Tai^4-tsung^1) or Jiingdih (Ching^3-ti^4), br. of Ingtzong. (Jiingtay, Ching^3-t'ai^4)	1449*–57
Ingtzong (Ying^1-tsung^1) (restored). (Tianshuenn, T'ien^1-shun^4)	1457–64
Shianntzong (Hsien^4-tsung^1), s. of Ingtzong. (Chernghuah, Ch'êng^2-hua^4)	1464*–87
Shiawtzong (Hsiao^4-tsung^1), s. of Shianntzong. (Horngjyh, Hung^2-chih^4)	1487*–1505
Wuutzong (Wu^3-tsung^1). (Jenqder, Chêng^4-tê^2)	1505*–21
Shyhtzong (Shih^4-tsung^1), cousin of Wuutzong. (Jiajinq, Chia^1-ching^4)	1521*–66
Muhtzong (Mu^4-tsung^1), s. of Shyhtzong. (Longchinq, Lung^2-ch'ing^4)	1566*–72
Sherntzong (Shên^2-tsung^1), s. of Muhtzong. (Wannlih, Wan^4-li^4)	1572*–1620

GUANGTZONG (Kuang^{1}-tsung^{1}), s. of Sherntzong. (TAYCHANG, T'ai^{4}-ch'ang^{1}) 1620

SHITZONG (Hsi^{1}-tsung^{1}), s. of Guangtzong. (TIANCHII, T'ien^{1}-ch'i^{3}) 1620*–7

JUANGLIEHDIH (Chuang^{1}-lieh^{4}-ti^{4}). (CHORNGJEN, Ch'ung^{2}-chên^{1}) 1627*–44

CHING (Ch'ing^{1}). 1616–1912. Twenty-second of the Official Dynasties (from 1644).

The Manchus (MAANJOU, Man^{3}-chou^{1}) were descendants of the RUUJEN (see JIN dynasty, 1115–1234) of north Manchuria, who under Nurḫači (1559–1626, Chinese transcription NUU-ERL-HA-CHYH, Nu^{3}-êrh^{2}-ha^{1}-ch'ih^{4}, temple name TAYTZUU) were united into a single Khanate (*c.* 1606). The name MAANJOU (Manchu) was adopted in 1616. Nurḫači and his successor Abaḫai (temple name TAYTZONG) extended the Manchu power into south Manchuria (LIAUDONG, Liaotung) and Mongolia. BEEIJING (Peking) fell to the Manchus in 1644, and Nurḫači's grandson (temple name SHYHTZUU, Shih^{4}-tsu^{2}) became the first CHING emperor in that year. The dynastic title, at first JIN (Chin^{1}), had been changed to CHING (Ch'ing^{1}) in 1636. Capitals: SHEENYANG (Shên^{3}-yang^{2}) (Manchu name Mukden), from 1625; BEEIJING (Peking), from 1644.

(Note: the CHING dynasty continued the custom of retaining a single year-period for the whole of a reign, and CHING rulers are often referred to by their year-period: e.g. the KANGSHI (K'ang^{1}-hsi^{1}) emperor for SHENQTZUU (Shêng^{4}-tsu^{3}) or Emperor REN (Jên^{2}). Year-periods are therefore given as the final entry for each reign.)

TAYTZUU or GAUHWANGDIH (T'ai^{4}-tsu^{3} or Kao^{1}-huang^{2}-ti^{4}). (TIANMINQ, T'ien^{1}-ming^{4}) 1616–26

TAYTZONG or WENHWANGDIH (T'ai^{4}-tsung^{1} or Wên^{2}-huang^{2}-ti^{4}), s. of Taytzuu. (TIANTSONG, T'ien^{1}-ts'ung^{1}) 1626*–43

SHYHTZUU or JANGHWANGDIH (Shih^{4}-tsu^{3} or Chang^{1}-huang^{2}-ti^{4}), s. of Taytzong. (SHUENNJYH, Shun^{4}-chih^{4}) 1643*–61

SHENQTZUU or RENHWANGDIH (Shêng^{4}-tsu^{3} or Jên^{2}-huang^{2}-ti^{4}), s. of Shyhtzuu. (KANGSHI, K'ang^{1}-hsi^{1}) 1661*–1722

SHYHTZONG or SHIANNHWANGDIH (Shih^{4}-tsung^{1} or Hsien^{4}-huang^{2}-ti^{4}), s. of Shenqtzuu. (IONGJENQ, Yung^{1}-cheng^{4}) . . . 1722*–35

GAUTZONG or CHWENHWANGDIH (Kao^{1}-tsung^{1} or Ch'un^{2}-huang^{2} ti^{4}), s. of Shyhtzong. (CHYANLONG, Ch'ien^{2}-lung^{2}) . . . 1735*–96

RENTZONG or RUEYHWANGDIH (Jên^{2}-tsung^{1} or Jui^{4}-huang^{2}-ti^{4}), s. of Gautzong. (JIACHINQ, Chia^{1}-ch'ing^{4}) 1796–1820

SHIUANTZONG or CHERNGHWANGDIH (Hsüan^{1}-tsung^{1} or Ch'êng^{2}-huang^{2}-ti^{4}), s. of Rentzong. (DAWGUANG, Tao^{4}-kuang^{1}) . 1820*–50

WENTZONG or SHEANHWANGDIH (Wên^{2}-tsung^{1} or Hsien^{3}-huang^{2}-ti^{4}), s. of Shiuantzong. (SHYANFENG, Hsien^{2}-fêng^{1}) . 1850*–61

MUHTZONG or YIHHWANGDIH (Mu^{4}-tsung^{1} or I^{4}-huang^{2}-ti^{4}, s. of Wentzong. (TORNGJYH, T'ung^{2}-chih^{4}) 1861*–74

DERTZONG (Tê^{2}-tsung^{1}), cousin of Muhtzong. (GUANGSHIUH, Kuang^{1}-hsü^{4}) 1874*–1908

MOHDIH (Mo^{4}-ti^{4}). (SHIUANTOONG, Hsüan^{1}-t'ung^{3}) . . 1908*–12

SECTION V

JAPAN

1. The romanization of Japanese words.
2. Names and titles :
   (i) Family and personal names. (ii) Titles.
3. Place-names and geographical terms.
4. Select glossary.
5. Calendars and systems of dating.
6. Dynasties and rulers.
   (i) List of emperors. (ii) List of *syoogun* and administrators.

I. THE ROMANIZATION OF JAPANESE WORDS

The Japanese language can be written both in ideographs (*kanzi*), which were adopted from China, and by means of a syllabary (*kana*). Since *kana* are used to express the sounds of the Sino-Japanese characters, it is this syllabary which is the basis of romanization. The syllabary consists of fifty symbols (*go-zyuu-on*), each of which, when romanized, is represented by a vowel alone or by a syllable consisting of one or two consonants followed by a vowel. In addition, there is one symbol equivalent to the Roman *n*. A further twenty-five symbols (sonants and half-sonants) are formed by adding two dots (¨) or a small circle (°) to the top right-hand corner of certain of the *go-zyuu-on*: these symbols, when romanized, start with the consonants, *g*, *z*, *d*, *b*, and *p* (see Table A on p. 219). The total of seventy-six thus obtained is reduced in practice to seventy-three, as three of the symbols each appear twice in the syllabary.

The *kana* symbols, as is shown in Table A, are usually arranged in lines of five, each line being based on the vowel sounds *a*, *i*, *u*, *e*, *o*: when romanized, each line consists of vowels alone or of syllables having a common initial consonant. This is the accepted pattern, but all lines do not conform exactly, and it is from the irregularities that most of the problems of romanization have arisen. For instance, what one can call the *k* line is regular, and hence can be both written and pronounced as *ka*, *ki*, *ku*, *ke*, *ko*. The *t* line, however, is irregular in pronunciation. One would expect it to be *ta*, *ti*, *tu*, *te*, *to*, but it is in fact pronounced *ta*, *chi*, *tsu*, *te*, *to*. In these and similar instances we are forced to choose between the orthographic forms *ti* and *tu*, which give no guide to pronunciation, and the more nearly phonetic *chi* and *tsu*.

Some symbols have identical pronunciation, though differing in the written *kana*. For instance, the sonants formed from the symbols *tu* (*tsu*) and *su* are both pronounced *zu* and, if phonetic representation is the important criterion, can thus be romanized. On the other hand, the two different *kana* are not used indiscriminately in Japanese, and have their origin in early differences of pronunciation. Hence there is a case for distinguishing them as *du* (or *dzu*) and *zu*. A similar choice must be made where compound syllables, formed by elision, make use of these 'irregular' *kana*.

Long vowel sounds are a special form of elision which can be formed by a number of different *kana* combinations. They are usually represented either by placing a stroke over the vowel (*kō*) or by doubling the vowel (*koo*).

Other problems arise from euphonic changes which take place in the spoken language. For instance, *n* is usually pronounced *m* when followed by *b*, *p*, or *m*. As no such change occurs in the written *kana*, in romanization we have to choose between the written and the spoken form. Sonants may be used euphonically instead of the 'pure' *kana* from which they are formed, and such a change is usually common to both spoken and written forms. Where doubt exists, however, variants may be found in which *g* is used for *k*, *z* for *s*, *d* for *t*, *b* or *p* for *h*. Finally, there is in Japanese a kind of glottal stop which is almost always represented by doubled consonants.

It can be seen from this that a large number of systems of romanization are possible. The Jesuits in the 16th century and the Dutch traders of the 17th and 18th centuries devised their own. In modern times romanization has varied not only with the nationality but with the purpose of the writer. However, we shall consider here only the three systems most often found in works on Japanese history.

(*a*) HEPBURN

The system of romanization devised by Dr. Hepburn was the earliest and most popular of the modern era. In intention it was phonetic, and it used transcriptions which represented as nearly as possible the standard pronunciation. Thus *chi* was preferred to *ti* and *tsu* to *tu*. Since they reproduced sounds still in use in certain dialects, such syllables as *kwa* and *dzu* (for *ka* and *zu*) were also used. Long vowels were indicated by placing a stroke over the vowel (*kō*), and stopped syllables by a doubled consonant.

In 1884 the *Roomazikai* was formed to investigate problems of romanization, and accepted the Hepburn system with certain modifications. It was made more phonetic by dropping such exceptional syllables as *dzu*, while *y* was substituted for *i* in some syllables representing combinations of *kana* (e.g. *kyo*, *kyō* instead of *kio*, *kiō*). As so modified, the system has been used by many Japanese and most non-Japanese writers to the present day.

(*b*) *NIPPONSIKI*

This system was originally proposed by Professor Terao to the *Roomazikai*, but was rejected in favour of Hepburn. More orthographic than Hepburn, *kana* were so transliterated as to indicate the line of the syllabary to which each belonged. Thus *si*, *ti*, *tu* were preferred to the Hepburn *shi*, *chi*, *tsu*. The sonants of *su* and *tu* were written *zu* and *du* respectively, whereas Hepburn, as modified by the *Roomazikai*, used *zu* for both. Similar modifications were made in compound syllables. Long vowels could be shown either by use of a circumflex (*kô*) or by doubling the consonant (*koo*). Though not generally accepted, the system was widely used and contributed much to the more recent National *roomazi*.

(*c*) NATIONAL

In 1937 the Japanese Government decided to adopt an official system of romanization, now known as National *roomazi*, which combined elements of both the Hepburn and *Nipponsiki* systems. It followed *Nipponsiki* in basing itself closely on the lines of the syllabary, for example in preferring *si*, *ti*, *tu* to the Hepburn *shi*, *chi* and *tsu*. On the other hand, no attempt was made to distinguish between different *kana* of the same pronunciation—the sonants of *su* and *tu* were both rendered *zu*. Long vowels were to be marked as in Hepburn (*kō*), but recently the *Nipponsiki* double vowel (*koo*) has often been used. The *kana* corresponding to *n* was always to be transliterated as such, though Hepburn had followed the usage of speech in substituting *m* before the consonants *b*, *p* and *m* (e.g. *kampaku* was now to be written *kanpaku*).

Hepburn *roomazi* is the easiest for foreigners to pronounce and has been the system most widely used in English-language works. However, National *roomazi* has been officially adopted, and will probably be widely used in future; it is therefore chosen for use here, and for convenience long vowels are indicated by doubling the vowel (*koo*). Table A gives the complete syllabary of the National *roomazi*, those syllables which are differently rendered in other systems being printed in italics. Table B lists the points of difference between the three main systems, the variants of each being shown in parentheses.

TABLE A: NATIONAL *ROOMAZI*

Single *kana*					*Kana* compounds		
Go-zyuu-on							
a	i	u	e	o			
ka	ki	ku	ke	ko	kya	kyu	kyo
sa	*si*	su	se	so	*sya*	*syu*	*syo*
ta	*ti*	*tu*	te	to	*tya*	*tyu*	*tyo*
na	ni	nu	ne	no	nya	nyu	nyo
ha	hi	*hu*	he	ho	hya	hyu	hyo
ma	mi	mu	me	mo	mya	myu	myo
ya	i	yu	*e*	yo			
ra	ri	ru	re	ro	rya	ryu	ryo
wa	i	u	e	*o*			
n							
Sonants							
ga	gi	gu	ge	go	gya	gyu	gyo
za	*zi*	zu	ze	zo	*zya*	*zyu*	*zyo*
da	*zi*	*zu*	de	do	*zya*	*zyu*	*zyo*
ba	bi	bu	be	bo	bya	byu	byo
Half-sonants							
pa	pi	pu	pe	po	pya	pyu	pyo

Note: syllables printed in italics are differently rendered in other systems of romanization.

NOTE ON PRONUNCIATION

1. Japanese vowels are pronounced approximately as follows:

a as in *arm*
i as the *e* in *evil*
u as in *lute*
e as in *end*
o as in *lord*

Long vowels (e.g. *ō* or *oo*) are pronounced by prolonging the vowel sound.

Two consecutive different vowels are pronounced separately, except

ai as in *aisle*
ei as in *reign*

2. Consonants are generally pronounced as romanized by the Hepburn system, *g* always being hard. For equivalents in other systems, see Table B.

Double consonants are pronounced separately (e.g. *sep-puku*).

3. Generally there are no stressed syllables. However, *u*, especially in *su, tu,* is often elided or omitted in speech, e.g. Yokosuka is pronounced Yokos'ka.

TABLE B: DIFFERENCES BETWEEN *NIPPONSIKI*, HEPBURN AND NATIONAL *ROOMAZI*

National	Hepburn	*Nipponsiki*
e	e (ye)	e (ye)
ga	ga (gwa)	ga, gwa
hu	fu	hu
ka	ka (kwa)	ka, kwa
o	o (wo)	o (wo)
si	shi	si
sya	sha	sya
syo	sho	syo
syu	shu	syu
ti	chi	ti
tu	tsu	tu
tya	cha	tya
tyo	cho	tyo
tyu	chu	tyu
zi	ji	zi, di
zu	zu (dzu)	zu, du
zya	ja	zya, dya
zyo	jo	zyo, dyo
zyu	ju	zyu, dyu
also in compounds kyo kyu etc.	kyo (kio) kyu (kiu) etc.	kyo kyu etc.

2. NAMES AND TITLES

(i) FAMILY AND PERSONAL NAMES

Since the Meizi Restoration (1868), it has been obligatory for all Japanese to have a family name (*myoozi*) and one given name (*zokumyoo* or *nanori*). They are usually written in that order, e.g. Itoo Hirobumi, where Itoo is the family name. Owing to western influence, they are sometimes found reversed, especially after Mr. or a title, e.g. Prince Hirobumi Itoo. In written works referring to this modern period, where the full name is not given, the family name is used alone or with a title.

Before the Meizi Restoration the military and court families alone had two names, other classes having given names only. In writing of the feudal and earlier periods, the Japanese order of family name followed by given name is most often used. When the full name is not quoted, it is usual to find the given name alone, especially for *syoogun* and great administrators. For example, Oda Nobunaga is known simply as Nobunaga and Toyotomi Hideyosi as Hideyosi.

It will often be found that different names are used of the same man at different stages of his career. Until a boy came of age at fifteen he used his boyhood name (*yoomyoo*). Thereafter he took his adult name, and this he might well change at any crisis in his affairs. For example, the first of the Tokugawa *syoogun* used the *yoomyoo* of Taketiyo until the age of fifteen, when he became Matudaira Motonobu; in 1569 he took the name of Tokugawa Ieyasu after one of his Minamoto ancestors, and eventually became *syoogun* under that name. Men who became priests changed their names in the same way. Those who entered another family by marriage or adoption changed their family names by that act, and this can still happen in modern Japan.

Emperors and some great men are known historically by the names which were bestowed on them posthumously (*okuri-na*). These might be chosen from the name of a residence, temple or burial-place, after a previous emperor (prefixed by the syllable *Go-*), or as the era-name (*nengoo*) longest used during the reign. For instance, the emperor Meizi was given this posthumous name after the *nengoo* which was used throughout his reign. The correct reading of the characters forming these names is often in doubt, and the variants found may cause confusion.

The whole problem of Japanese names is complicated by the practice whereby scholars, artists, craftsmen and others regularly adopted pseudonyms and professional names (*goo* and *azana*). These names were changed at will, and could be transmitted in whole or in part to a favoured pupil to enhance his reputation or increase his chances of success. Artists, authors and scholars are usually known historically by these names.

The following list summarizes the types of names which may be found in works on Japanese history.

(i) Family name (*myoozi*). Originated either from the old clans and titles (*uzi* and *kabane*), e.g. Huziwara, or from place-names, e.g. Tokugawa.

(ii) Common name (*zokumyoo* or *tuusyoo*). One of the two types of given name: frequently records order of birth with such endings as *-taroo, -ziroo, -saburoo* (first, second and third child).

(iii) True name (*nanori* or *zitumyoo*). Second form of given name, originally of more formal significance than the *zokumyoo,* though the two have assimilated. Frequently named after desirable qualities, e.g. Yositune (fortune and constancy).

(iv) Boyhood name (*yoomyoo*). Used before assuming adult names at age of fifteen.

(v) Posthumous name (*okuri-na*). Used principally of emperors, and chosen usually from the name of a place or era.

(vi) Special and scholarly names (*goo* and *azana*). The *azana* was often adopted by a boy at school and retained thereafter, especially by Confucianists. The *goo* in general applies to writers, painters, craftsmen, etc. It has several sub-divisions, such as *gagoo,* used by painters, and *geimyoo,* used by dancers and actors.

(ii) TITLES

Japanese titles in the period before the introduction of Chinese legal and administrative ideas present many problems of nomenclature and definition. In this period, sometimes known as the Age of the Clans and Titles (*Uzi* and *Kabane*), the gradations of nobility corresponded generally with the administrative hierarchy. The more important official designations were:

Oo-omi: Great *Omi*.
Oo-murazi: Great *Murazi*.
Omi: Heads of the clans of Imperial Descent (*Koobetu*).
Murazi: Heads of the clans of Divine Descent (*Sinbetu*).
Kuni no miyatuko: District chieftains.
Tomo no miyatuko: Heads of corporations.

Most of these names, at one time, represented both a rank and an office. However, in many cases they were retained as a rank, or even as a surname, after the office had been transferred or abolished. It is difficult, therefore, to distinguish when they should properly be termed titles.

During the 7th century A.D., Japanese practice was strongly influenced by Chinese administrative methods, and this led to the creation of a court hierarchy on the Chinese model. In 605 the emperor established a number of court ranks named after six virtues and distinguished by coloured caps. The names and insignia were often changed during the next hundred years, but in the Yooroo period (717–23), a new system was introduced which persisted with little change until the 19th century. In this there were eight numbered ranks arranged in numerical order, the first rank being the highest. Each was divided into two classes, senior and junior, and some of the middle ranks were further subdivided into an upper and lower grade of each class. Below the fifth rank there were two kinds of titles—inner, for those residing in or near the capital; outer, for the provincial nobility

In addition to these ranks, there were a large number of court offices, originally administrative, but tending in time to become no more than honorary titles. They are too numerous to be listed separately. After the military dictatorship was established late in the 12th century, the functions of government were carried out by the *Bakuhu* and its subordinate offices. The titles of such offices are often found untranslated, and the most important of these are included in the glossary. So also are the few imperial titles (e.g. *mikado* and *tennoo*) likely to be used in books by western writers.

Many of the feudal lords held court titles but are not generally known by them. They were usually designated according to the size of their domains by such terms as *daimyoo*, but the names of clan and fief are the usual methods of designation, e.g. Simazu of Satuma, or Simazu, *daimyoo* of Satuma. These cannot be regarded as geographical titles in the European sense.

In 1884 a new peerage (*Kazoku*) was created, assimilating the former court and feudal titles. It consisted of five degrees—duke (or prince), marquis, count, viscount and baron. They are almost always translated in books in European languages, and are then followed by either the full name or family name of the holder. The titles are not geographical.

In the modern period it is also customary for the Japanese to use courtesy titles, roughly equivalent to the English Mr. or Esquire. They are, in descending order of politeness, *dono* or *sama*, *san* and *kun*. *San* and *kun* usually follow the family name used alone, but are often translated, e.g. Yamamoto *San* or Mr. Yamamoto. *Dono* and *sama* may also be used as a polite suffix to a title or the name of an office. This can be likened to the use in English of such formal phrases as 'The Rt. Honourable' or 'His Excellency'.

Further information on Japanese names and titles may be found in:

A. J. Koop and H. Inada, *Japanese names and how to read them.* London, 1923.

B. H. Chamberlain, *Things Japanese.* Reprint of 5th edn. London, 1927.

3. PLACE-NAMES AND GEOGRAPHICAL TERMS

Among the most difficult problems facing the reader of Japanese history are the changes undergone by place-names. Before the Meizi era, Japan was divided into large administrative areas called *kuni* (provinces), whose names were of ancient origin. In 1871 the country was reorganized into *ken* (prefectures) and *gun* (counties) with entirely different names. The old names are still sometimes used of modern Japan and, of course, are often found in histories.

The names of some cities have also been changed. Kyooto (Kyoto) was originally known as Heian (-kyoo) or Miyako and Tookyoo (Tokyo) as Edo (Yedo); these changes were due to the transfer of the imperial court. Other apparent changes are due to the growth of some little-known village, which has eventually engulfed an older town near by and given its own name to the new city so formed. In this way the old city of Sakai became a suburb of its newer neighbour Oosaka (Osaka).

A number of Japanese geographical terms may be found in use untranslated, e.g. Huzi *San* or (incorrectly) Huzi *Yama* for Mt. Huzi. In Japanese, such terms always follow the name of the physical feature they describe, e.g. Lake Biwa is Biwa *Ko*. Some of these geographical terms are used as terminal components in place-names, and may give an indication of terrain. Endings of this kind should be used with care, however, for such terms, especially *sima* (island), are often used without geographical significance; Hirosima and Kagosima are both coastal cities, while Kirisima is an inland resort.

Despite this, the following list of geographical terms may be found useful.

dake	mountain
daki	waterfall
gawa	river
hama	beach
hantoo	peninsula
heiya	plain
kai	sea
kaikyoo	strait
kawa	river
ko	lake
minato	harbour
misaki	cape
nada	sea, roadstead
numa	lake
oka	hill
saki	cape
sanmyaku	mountain range
san	mountain
sima	island
suidoo	channel
take	mountain
taki	waterfall
tooge	mountain pass
ura	beach, lake, bay
wan	bay
yama	mountain
zaki	cape
zan	mountain
zima	island

The following non-geographical endings are also found:

den	palace
dera	temple
dono	palace
guu	shrine, palace
in	temple, palace
miya	palace, shrine
mon	gate
tera	temple
zi	temple
zinguu	shrine
zinzya	shrine
zyoo	fortress, castle

4. SELECT GLOSSARY

Introductory notes.

(*a*) Words in the glossary are given in National *roomazi*, romanization by other systems being shown in brackets. Where the first syllable differs in the Hepburn or *Nipponsiki* forms, this is also given in its correct alphabetical order.

(*b*) Alternative readings of the characters or different words of the same meaning are preceded by the word 'also'.

(*c*) English words are listed when they have been adopted from Japanese or are used in a special sense in Japan. Terms, especially commercial terms, which were generally used on the China coast, will be found in the section on China.

(*d*) Bibliographical note

The following works may be found useful to supplement this glossary:

F. Brinkley, *An unabridged Japanese-English dictionary.* 10th edn. Tookyoo, 1904.

B. H. Chamberlain, *Things Japanese.* Reprint of 5th edn. London, 1927.

H. A. Giles, *A glossary of reference on subjects connected with the Far East.* 3rd edn. Shanghai, 1900.

E. Honzyoo, *Social and economic history of Japan.* Kyooto, 1935.

E. H. Norman, *Japan's emergence as a modern state.* I.P.R. Inquiry Series. New York, 1940.

E. Papinot, *Historical and geographical dictionary of Japan.* Tookyoo, 1909.

AMIDA. Amitabha Buddha.

ASIKAGA PERIOD. See ZIDAI.

BAKUHU (BAKUFU). 'Tent Government'; Shogunate, the term used to describe the government of the *syoogun* (*q.v.*) during the feudal period (1192–1867).

BON, also O-BON. Festival of the dead, celebrated 13–15 July.

BONZE. See BOOZU.

BOOZU (BŌZU). A bonze; a Buddhist monk. See S.E. Asia Glossary, p. 113.

BU. See WEIGHTS AND MEASURES.

BUGYOO (BUGYŌ). High-ranking officials of the *bakuhu*, including the governors of Edo.

BUKE. The military class of feudal Japan.

BUKKYOO (BUKKYŌ). Buddhism.

BUSI (BUSHI). Warrior or *samurai* class.

BUSIDOO (BUSHI-, -DŌ). 'The way of the *samurai*'; the warrior code of Japan, combining elements of Buddhism, Confucianism and *Sintoo*, and emphasizing the qualities of loyalty, courage and endurance.

BUTUDAN (BUTSUDAN). Household Buddhist shrine.

CHA-. See TYA-.

CHŌ-. See TYOO-.

CHŪ-. See TYUU-.

CURRENCY. A copper coin, the *mon*, was minted in Japan in the 9th and 10th centuries, but thereafter, for 600 years, Chinese copper coins were imported. Late in the 16th century coins came into widespread use, and the coinage was standardized by Tokugawa Ieyasu. The gold *ryoo* was made the unit of currency, and the *koban* established as a gold coin of one *ryoo* value. Originally a little less than two English sovereigns by weight and with a gold content of 86 per cent., the *koban* was often debased or reduced in weight by the *syoogun*.

Silver and copper coins existed in great variety, being minted both officially and privately. They were normally exchanged by weight against gold, the original ratio being about 50 *monme* of silver or 4 *kanme* of copper to 1 gold *ryoo*. This ratio, too, was subject to considerable fluctuation.

In 1771 the *en* (*yen*), divided into 100 *sen*, was adopted as the unit of currency. It was defined in terms of gold, but the silver *en* (equivalent in bullion content to the Mexican dollar) was legal tender in the treaty ports. After some variation, it was fixed at about 2*s*. 0½*d*. (at par), until the period 1934–9, when it was stabilized at 1*s*. 2*d*.

DAIHON-EI. Imperial Supreme Headquarters; the headquarters of the emperor as Commander-in-Chief.

DAIMYOO (DAIMYŌ). 'Great Name'; feudal lord whose fief was rated at more than 10,000 *koku* of rice a year.

DAIZIN (DAIJIN). Minister of State; Cabinet Minister.

DAZYOOKAN (DAZYŌ-, DAJŌ-, -KWAN). The Council of State, superseded in 1885 by the Cabinet (*Naikaku*).

EDO (YEDO). The capital of the Tokugawa *syoogun*; became the capital of Japan and was renamed Tookyoo (Tokyo) after the Meizi Restoration of 1868.

EDO PERIOD. See ZIDAI.

E-HUMI (E-FUMI). Test instituted as part of the Tokugawa persecution of Christianity; suspected converts were invited to trample on the Cross to prove that they were not Christians.

EMISI (EMISHI), also EZO (YEZO). Barbarian; the Ainu.

EN (YEN). See CURRENCY.

ETA. Outcasts; the lowest class of Japanese society.

EXTRATERRITORIALITY. The principle whereby foreigners were exempt from the jurisdiction of Japanese courts of law, and subject only to their own consular courts. It was embodied in the treaties negotiated with the western powers in 1858–9, and not abolished until after 1894. See China Glossary, p. 181.

EZO (YEZO). 1. Old name of Hokkaidoo.
2. See also EMISI.

FU-. See HU-.

GAIMUSYOO (GWAIMU-, -SYŌ, -SHŌ). The Japanese Foreign Office.

GENROO (GENRŌ). Elder Statesman; member of the *Genroo-in*.

GENROO-IN (GENRŌ-IN). Council of Elder Statesmen; extra-constitutional body of personal advisers to Emperor Meizi.

GO-KAMON. See KAMON.

GOKENIN. Feudal vassal of low status.

GO-SANKE. See SANKE.

GOYOOKIN (GOYŌKIN). Benevolence or forced loan of the feudal and early Meizi eras.

GUMBATSU. See GUNBATU.

GUN. A county; subdivision of a *kuni* (province) before 1871, subdivision of a *ken* (prefecture) thereafter.

GUNBATU (GUNBATSU, GUMBATSU). Service circles; military cliques.

GWAI-. See GAI-.

HAN. A term usually translated 'clan' which, in the feudal period, denoted the fief and vassals, including the *samurai*, of a *daimyoo*.

HARAKIRI. See SEPPUKU.

HATAMOTO. 'Banner warriors'; direct feudal vassals of the Tokugawa, whose fiefs were too small to qualify them for the status of *hudai-daimyoo*.

HEIAN PERIOD. See ZIDAI.

HEIMIN. Commoners; after the Meizi Restoration, those who did not belong to the noble or former military classes.

HININ. A beggar; a pariah.

HU (FU). An urban prefecture; an urban area with somewhat greater local powers than the English county borough. See China Glossary under FUU (p. 181).

HUDAI-DAIMYOO (FUDAI-, -DAIMYŌ). A *daimyoo* who was an hereditary vassal of the Tokugawa family.

HUZIWARA (FUJIWARA) PERIOD. See ZIDAI.

HYAKUSYOO (-SYŌ, -SHŌ). A farmer; a peasant.

INKYO. Abdication; retirement from a position of authority or responsibility.

JI-. See ZI-.

JUN-. See ZYUN-.

KABANE. Status or title; clan or family.

KABUKI. The popular drama of Japan, which developed in the early Tokugawa period. *Kabuki* was the entertainment of the commoners while *noo* (*q.v.*) was that of the *samurai*.

KAISINTOO (KAISHIN-, -TŌ). See POLITICAL PARTIES.

KAMAKURA PERIOD. See ZIDAI.

KAMI. 1. A *Sintoo* deity, of whom there are many.
2. Also used as 'Lord' in a number of titles, e.g. *Hizen no Kami* for Lord of Hizen.

KAMIDANA. The household 'god-shelf', at which *Sintoo* rites are performed.

KAMME (KWAMME). See KAN.

KAMON, also GO-KAMON. 'Related Houses' of the Tokugawa family, not in the line of succession to *syoogun*.

KAMPAKU (KWAMPAKU). See KANPAKU.

KAN (KWAN), also KANME, K(W)AMME. See WEIGHTS AND MEASURES.

KANPAKU (K(W)AMPAKU, K(W)AMBAKU). Regent to an adult emperor; originally the highest office of government, but later, under the *bakuhu*, a largely honorary title. Can be translated 'Mayor of the Palace'.

KANSAI (KWANSAI). Originally the main island of Japan west of the Hakone Pass; now usually confined to the district west of Gihu (Gifu), including Kyooto (Kyoto), Koobe (Kobe) and Oosaka (Osaka).

KANTOO (K(W)ANTŌ). Originally the main island of Japan east of the Hakone Pass. Now primarily the plain or district surrounding the bays of Tookyoo (Tokyo) and Sagami, but also used for the whole district between *Kansai* and *Toohoku*.

KARAHUTO (KARAFUTO). Saghalien (Sakhalin).

KAROO (KARŌ). Steward; the principal official serving a *daimyoo*.

KAZOKU (KWAZOKU). The modern peerage of Japan, established in 1884, and consisting mostly of former *daimyoo* and *kuge*.

KEMPEITAI. See KENPEITAI.

KEN. 1. Prefecture; major administrative unit of modern Japan, introduced in 1871.
2. Measure of length. See WEIGHTS AND MEASURES.

KENPEITAI (KEMPEITAI). Gendarmerie; a police force under army administration chiefly employed in colonial or occupied territory; in Japan proper principally concerned with cases of espionage.

KIGENSETU (-SETSU). *Sintoo* festival of 11 February, celebrating the accession of the first emperor, Zinmu *Tennoo*, and the foundation of the Japanese Empire (supposedly 660 B.C.).

KIN. See WEIGHTS AND MEASURES.

KIRISUTE-GOMEN. 'Permission to cut down and leave'; the privilege of the *samurai* to cut down a commoner with impunity.

KŌ-. See KOO.

KOBAN (KOBANG, KOPANG). See CURRENCY.

KOKU. Measure of capacity, used particularly for rating feudal fiefs by their rice income. See WEIGHTS AND MEASURES.

KOKUGAKUSYA (-SHA), also WAGAKUSYA (-SHA). The nationalist Tokugawa scholars who acclaimed the value of the native cultural heritage as opposed to the Chinese influences then dominant.

KOOBETU (KŌ-, BETSU). 'Imperial descent'; the clans and families of early Japan who claimed descent from the gods through the imperial line (cf. SINBETU).

KOODOO (KŌDŌ). 'The Imperial Way'; a modern *Sintoo*-nationalist slogan, associated with a vague dogma imitated from the Confucian doctrine of *Wangdaw* (Kingly Way), inculcating loyalty to the emperor and national aggrandisement.

KOZIKI (KOJIKI). One of the two earliest chronicles of Japanese history, compiled early in the 8th century A.D. It begins with the mythical cosmogony, and recounts legends and some history to about A.D. 500. It is valuable as an historical source, despite its entirely unreliable chronology. See also NIHONGI.

KUGE. The court nobles (as opposed to the feudal *daimyoo*).

KUNI. 1. A country.
2. Province; the major divisions of Japan before the regrouping into *ken* in 1871.

KWA-. See KA-.

LACQUER. Lacquer, as used in China and Japan, is a natural product, the sap of the lacquer tree, which is indigenous to China but was introduced to Japan in or before the 6th century A.D. The production of lacquer-ware is a long and complicated process. A wood form is usually used, to which are applied many coats of lacquer, each being allowed to dry before the next is applied. Japanese craftsmen are particularly famous for gold lacquer-ware, in which gold-dust or small pieces of gold are used with the lacquer.

MABIKI. 'Thinning'; a term for infanticide.

MATI (MACHI). Town or subdivision of a city; an administrative unit intermediate between *mura* (township) and *si* (city).

MEIZI-ISIN (MEIDI-, MEIJI-, -ISHIN). The Meizi Restoration, 1867–8, as a result of which the *de facto* rule of the emperor was supposedly restored after the fall of the *bakuhu*.

METUKE (METSUKE). Censor; an official of the *bakuhu*, whose duty it was to report on the activities of local administrators; hence sometimes rendered 'spy'.

MIKADO. The emperor; the term is often used by westerners.

MINSEITOO (-TŌ). See POLITICAL PARTIES.

MIYAKO. Capital city; generally used for Kyooto (Kyoto), the former capital.

MOMME. See MONME.

MON. See CURRENCY.

MONME (MOMME). See WEIGHTS AND MEASURES.

MONTO SECT. See SIN SECT.

MURA. Township; usually a group of rural settlements.

MUROMATI (MUROMACHI) PERIOD. See ZIDAI.

NAIKAKU. The Cabinet, established in 1885 (cf. DAZYOOKAN).

NANBANZIN (NAMBANJIN). 'Southern Barbarians', the term used to describe westerners in the period of early contacts.

NARA PERIOD. See ZIDAI.

NENGOO (NENGŌ). Era-name. See subsection on methods of dating, p. 235.

NEW YEAR. Festival now celebrated during the first five days of January, and an occasion for expressions of loyalty and patriotism. Before the adoption of the Gregorian calendar in 1873, it was celebrated in the first three days of the first month of the lunar calendar, i.e. late January or early February by western calendars.

NIHON. Japan.

NIHONGI. The second of the early Japanese chronicles (see also KOZIKI), dating from the 8th century A.D. Like the *Koziki*, it begins with the mythical period, but carries the narrative to A.D. 697. After the 5th century, its account is more or less historical, but the chronology is unreliable in detail.

NIPPON. Japan.

NITIREN (NICHIREN) SECT. A Buddhist sect founded by the priest Nitiren (1222–82), which identifies religion closely with national life and has always been noted for its aggressiveness and intolerance. It opposes the worship of Amida (Amitabha Buddha) observed by the Zyoodo and Sin sects, and substitutes worship of Sakyamuni (*O-syaka-sama*), based on the Lotus Sutra.

NOO (NŌ, NOH). Classical Japanese drama, dating from the Asikaga period; patronized chiefly by *samurai* and, later, the professional classes (cf. KABUKI).

O-BON. See BON.

ODA PERIOD. See ZIDAI.

OO-METUKE (Ō-, METSUKE). Senior Censor; a chief *metuke* (*q.v.*) concerned principally with *daimyoo*.

OOTYOO (ŌTYŌ, ŌCHŌ). Dynasty. By the *ootyoo* period is meant the period of imperial rule before the *bakuhu* was established.

O-SYAKA-SAMA (-SHAKA-). See SYAKA.

POLITICAL PARTIES. The names of Japanese political parties are misleading in that they give little indication of policy or politics. The *Ziyuutoo* ('Liberal Party'), founded by Count Itagaki in 1881, has been characterized by Japanese writers as Radical, and derived much of its political thought from France. It was reorganized under the influence of Prince Itoo and renamed the *Seiyuukai* ('Society of Political Friends', often translated 'Conservative Party'). It became for a time virtually a government organ, and continued to show strong conservative and bureaucratic tendencies.

The *Kaisintoo* ('Progressive Party') was founded by Marquis Ookuma in 1882 to oppose the 'extreme' *Ziyuutoo*, and based its ideas on English political thought. It later proved unable to hold its own against the newly-formed *Seiyuukai*, and broke up into a number of groups which were eventually succeeded by the more conservative *Minseitoo* ('Democratic Party'). There were few differences in political outlook between the *Seiyuukai* and the *Minseitoo*, though the latter showed at times a tendency towards Liberalism. Both parties broke up during the late nineteen-thirties, and were followed during the Second World War by a succession of patriotic associations.

RANGAKU. 'Dutch studies', the name given in the Tokugawa period to the study of western science and learning introduced by the Dutch.

RI. See WEIGHTS AND MEASURES.

ROONIN (RŌNIN). Vagrant swordsman; *samurai* who no longer owed fealty to a lord.

ROOZYUU (RŌ-, ZYŪ-, -DYŪ, -JŪ). The Council of State of the Tokugawa *bakuhu*.

RYOO (RYŌ). See CURRENCY.

SAMURAI. Feudal warrior (cf. ROONIN); also used for the warrior class as a whole.

SANKE, also GO-SANKE. The most important branch families of the Tokugawa (those of Owari, Kii and Mito), to whom the succession to the *bakuhu* could pass if the direct line failed to produce a suitable heir.

SANKIN-KOOTAI (-KŌTAI). The system whereby, under the Tokugawa *bakuhu*, *daimyoo* were compelled to reside alternately for periods of a year or six months in their own fiefs and in Edo; instituted in order to minimize intrigue against the Tokugawa.

SE. See WEIGHTS AND MEASURES.

SEI-I-TAI SYOOGUN (-SYŌGUN, -SHŌGUN). 'Barbarian-subduing Generalissimo', the full title of the *syoogun* (*q.v.*).

SEIYUUKAI (SEIYŪKAI). See POLITICAL PARTIES.

SEN. See CURRENCY.

SEPPUKU, also HARAKIRI. Ceremonial suicide (literally by cutting open one's belly, though in normal cases it was beheading by an assistant, immediately after the ceremonial cut, which brought death).

SHA-. See SYA-.

SHI-. See SI-.

SHŌ-. See SYOO-.

SHOGUNATE. Translation of BAKUHU (*q.v.*).

SI (SHI). City.

SIN (SHIN) SECT, also known as ZYOODO SINSYUU or MONTO SECT. A Buddhist sect founded by Sinran (1173–1262), a disciple of Hoonen (see ZYOODO SECT). Its doctrine is similar to Zyoodo, but simpler, and with even greater emphasis on justification by faith in Amida alone. It observes no ascetic practices and allows its priests to marry.

SINBETU (SHINBETSU). Divine descent; clans and families claiming descent from the gods, but not through the imperial line (cf. KOOBETU).

SINGON (SHINGON) SECT. A Buddhist sect introduced into Japan from China by the priest Kuukai, or Kooboo Daisi (774–835). It is an esoteric philosophy with a complex symbolism, but none the less has wide popular appeal.

SINTOO (SINTŌ, SHINTŌ). Shinto-ism; originally a primitive nature- and (perhaps) ancestor-worship, which was evolving into a State religion at the beginning of Japanese history, but early became combined with Buddhism. This 'contamination' was rejected after the Meizi Restoration, and *Sintoo* was established as a nationalist State cult with the emperor, as a living deity and high priest, at its head: the same period also saw the growth of popular sects distinct from this State Sintoo.

SIZOKU (SHIZOKU). The military class or gentry; the term applied after the Meizi Restoration to the former *samurai*.

SOOROBAN (SŌROBAN). The abacus. See China Glossary, under SWANPAN, p. 191.

SYAKA (SHAKA), also O-SYAKA-SAMA. Sakyamuni Buddha.

SYAKU (SHAKU). See WEIGHTS AND MEASURES.

SYOOGUN (SYŌGUN, SHŌGUN). Generalissimo; the title, an abbreviation of *Sei-i-tai syoogun*, taken by the feudal military dictators who were *de facto* rulers of Japan from about 1192 to 1867. The succession was vested traditionally in the Minamoto clan, by whom the office was founded, and from whom most later *syoogun* traced their descent.

TAIKOO (TAIKŌ). Title taken by a retired *kanpaku* (*q.v.*); most often used of Toyotomi Hideyosi, who took the title in 1592.

TAIKUN, also TYCOON. 'Great Prince', one title of the *syoogun*; often used by foreigners in anglicized form, Tycoon.

TAIROO (TAIRŌ). 'Great Elder' or Chancellor, a member of the *Roozyuu* (*q.v.*) selected as chief adviser to the *syoogun*.

TAIWAN. Formosa.

TAN. See WEIGHTS AND MEASURES.

TENDAI SECT. A Buddhist sect introduced into Japan from China by the priest Saityoo, or Dengyoo Daisi (767–822). It maintains that all forms of Buddhism are aspects of true doctrine, but emphasizes the importance of the Lotus Sutra.

TENNOO (TENNŌ). The sovereign of Japan; used after the personal name, e.g. Meizi *Tennoo* is Emperor Meizi.

TO. See WEIGHTS AND MEASURES.

TOKUGAWA PERIOD. See ZIDAI.

TOOHOKU (TŌHOKU). The north-east part of the main island of Japan.

TOYOTOMI PERIOD. See ZIDAI.

TOZAMA-DAIMYOO (-DAIMYŌ). Outside feudatory; a *daimyoo* who was not a vassal of the Tokugawa.

TREATY PORTS. Those Japanese ports opened to foreign trade by the earlier treaties with western powers. At these ports all foreign trade was to be conducted, and foreign merchants were confined to the ports and their immediate neighbourhood. In 1854 the Japanese agreed to open Simoda and Hakodate, and in 1859 added Kanagawa (Yokohama), Nagasaki, Niigata and Hyoogo (Koobe). Hyoogo (Koobe) was the last to be opened (in 1868). See China Glossary, p. 193.

TUBO (TSUBO). See WEIGHTS AND MEASURES.

TYA-NO-YU (CHA-NO-YU). Tea ceremony; the ceremonial drinking of tea to assist repose and meditation, a cult peculiar to Japan.

TYCOON. See TAIKUN.

TYOO (TYŌ, CHŌ). See WEIGHTS AND MEASURES.

TYOOBU (TYŌBU, CHŌBU). See WEIGHTS AND MEASURES.

TYOONIN (TYŌNIN, CHŌNIN). Merchants and artisans; city-dwellers.

TYOOSEN (TYŌSEN, CHŌSEN). Korea.

TYUUBU (TYŪBU, CHŪBU). The central mountainous part of the main island of Japan.

TYUUGOKU (TYŪGOKU, CHŪGOKU). The south-west part of the main island of Japan.

UZI (UJI). The clans or clan-names of early Japan.

WAGAKUSYA (-SHA). See KOKUGAKUSYA.

WEIGHTS AND MEASURES. The metric system has been used in Japan since 1893, and was adopted in 1924 as the official system of weights and measures. However, the old standards are still used, and are given below.

Weights.

1 *kan* = 1,000 *monme*	=	8·267 lbs. Av. 10·047 lbs. Tr.	= 3·75 kilograms
1 *kin* = 160 *monme*	=	1·322 lbs. Av. 1·607 lbs. Tr.	= 0·60 kilograms
1 *monme*	=	0·132 oz. Av. 0·120 oz. Tr.	= 3·75 grams

Length.

1 *ri* = 36 *tyoo* = 2,160 *ken* = 2·44 mls. = 3·927 km.
1 *ken* = 6 *syaku* = 5·965 ft. = 1·813 metres
1 *syaku* = 0·994 ft. = 0·303 metre
1 *syaku* (cloth measure) = 1·25 *syaku*
1 *tan* (roll of cloth) = 28 *syaku* (cloth measure)

Area.

1 *tyoo* (*tyoobu*) = 10 *tan* = 2·45 acres = 99·17 ares
1 *tan* = 10 *se* = 9·9 ares
1 *se* = 30 *tubo* = 119 sq. yds. = 0·99 are
1 *tubo* (1 *bu*) = 3·95 sq. yds. = 3·305 centiares

Capacity.

$$1\ \textit{koku} = 10\ \textit{to} = \left\{\begin{array}{l} 4{\cdot}96 \text{ Eng. bushels} \\ 5{\cdot}11 \text{ Amer. bushels} \\ 39{\cdot}68 \text{ Eng. gallons} \\ 47{\cdot}95 \text{ Amer. gallons} \end{array}\right\} = 1{\cdot}8 \text{ hectolitres}$$

[These standards have varied slightly at different periods. See the notes of Kurt Singer to Tsuchiya Takao, *An economic history of Japan*, Trans. Asiat. Soc. Japan, Second Ser. XV, Tokyo, 1937.]

YAMATO. 1. Old name for Japan, still sometimes used.
2. One of the provinces (*kuni*) of pre-Meizi Japan.

YAMATO AGE. See ZIDAI.

YAMATO-DAMASII (-DAMASHII). The Japanese spirit; the traditional virtues of the Japanese, especially that of loyalty to the emperor.

YE-. See E-.

ZAIBATU (ZAIBATSU). Financial circles; the great commercial and industrial firms, especially those of Mitui, Mitubisi, Sumitomo and Yasuda.

ZEN SECT. A Buddhist sect introduced into Japan from China by the priests Eisai (1141–1215) and Doogen (1200–53). It rejects scripture as a medium of revelation of the truth, and prescribes meditation and an austere discipline, bodily and mental. It consequently attracted many adherents among the *samurai*, and played an important part in the development of *busidoo*. It has exerted a powerful influence on Japanese art and poetry.

ZIDAI (JIDAI). Era or period (see also section on methods of dating). A number of periods in Japanese history have been given names, the commonest being:

Yamato	660 B.C. to A.D. 551
Nara	A.D. 707 to 781
Heian	781 to 833 (or 1185)
Huziwara	889 to 1185
Kamakura	1185 to 1335
Asikaga or Muromati	1335 to 1569
Oda	1569 to 1582
Toyotomi	1582 to 1600
Tokugawa or Edo	1600 to 1867

ZIYUUTOO (ZIYŪTŌ, JIYŪTŌ). See POLITICAL PARTIES.

ZYOODO (JŌDO) SECT. A Buddhist sect founded by Hoonen (1133–1212) and largely Chinese in origin. It teaches that salvation lies not in works, but in absolute faith in Amida (Amitabha Buddha). Strongly influenced the Zyoodo Sinsyuu or Sin sect (*q.v.*)

ZYUNSI (JUNSHI). Suicide on the death of one's lord.

5. CALENDARS AND SYSTEMS OF DATING

The Japanese have made use of a number of systems of dating, and several different ones are still used. Originally dates were indicated by reference to the reigns of emperors, but this method has long been abandoned, and records based on it are often unreliable. Early in the 7th century A.D. the Chinese calendar was adopted, and thereafter years were computed according to the sexagenary cycle. Shortly after, under the emperor Kootoku, it was decided to identify periods as in China, by giving them era-names (*nengoo*). Each of these remained in use until some great event gave occasion for a change. Accordingly the number of years in a period was never constant, periods varying in length from a few months to over forty years. Under this system a date was normally fixed by citing the era-name, followed by the number of the year within that period, e.g. A.D. 1594 was Bunroku 3. Sometimes a reference to the sexagenary cycle was given in addition to, or instead of, the number.

Both methods of dating remained in use almost without change until after the Meizi Restoration of 1868. On 1 January 1873 the Gregorian calendar was brought into force in Japan, and thereafter the lunar calendar and the sexagenary cycle went out of general use. Meanwhile the growth of nationalist feeling during the 19th century had led to the adoption of a national calendar, based on the supposed date of accession of the first emperor, Zinmu *Tennoo* (660 B.C.). There are thus three methods of computing dates which are widely used in modern Japan—the Christian calendar, the National Calendar and *nengoo*. The following notes give a more detailed account of the systems mentioned above.

(*a*) THE LUNAR CALENDAR

This calendar, adopted from China in the 7th century, was based on the true movements of sun and moon. The year began when the sun entered the sign of the Fishes—that is, between 20 January and 19 February by the Gregorian calendar. It consisted normally of twelve lunar months, a total of 354 or 355 days. A thirteenth (intercalary) month was added about every third year, whenever the New Year would otherwise have fallen one whole moon too early.

Each month was divided into three periods of about ten days, called *zyoozyun* (first period), *tyuuzyun* (second period) and *gezyun* (last period). These terms are still used. In addition to this, the year was divided into periods of approximately fifteen days, named after the characteristics of the climate, season, etc.

(*b*) THE SEXAGENARY CYCLE

The sexagenary cycle was adopted at the same time as the lunar calendar, and was normally used with it. The cycle consisted of sixty years, each of which was given a name formed by taking a character from each of two separate series.

The first series, the ten Calendar Signs, consisted of five pairs, each pair being dedicated to one of the five elements : *ki* (wood), *hi* (fire), *tuti* (earth), *ka* (metal) and *mizu* (water). Each pair consisted of an elder brother (*e*) and a younger brother (*to*). Thus the ten signs (*zikkan*), in their correct order, were *kinoe, kinoto, hinoe, hinoto, tutinoe, tutinoto, kanoe, kanoto, mizunoe, mizunoto.*

The second series consisted of twelve characters (*zyuu-ni-si*) corresponding roughly to our signs of the zodiac. They were, in order, *ne* (rat), *usi* (ox), *tora* (tiger), *u* (hare), *tatu* (dragon), *mi* (snake), *uma* (horse), *hituzi* (sheep), *saru* (monkey), *tori* (bird), *inu* (dog), *i* (hog).

One sign from each series was taken in consecutive order to build up the cycle of sixty years, in which each of the *zikkan* was used six times and each of the *zyuu-ni-si* five times. Thus the first year of the cycle was *kinoe-ne* and the last *mizunoto-i.* The year 1924 was *kinoe-ne*, which will also be the designation of the years 1984, 2044, etc. The cycle was also applied to the naming of days.

(*c*) *NENGOO* (ERA- OR YEAR-NAMES)

Under the emperor Kootoku it was decided to adopt the Chinese practice of using names (*nengoo*) to identify periods of years, and the first year of his reign, A.D. 645, was declared to be the first year of Taika. After his death in 655 the practice was discontinued until reintroduced by the emperor Tenmu in 672. Since that date the custom has been followed without a break until the present day.

Normal practice is for the year to be identified by quoting the *nengoo* followed by the consecutive number of the year within that period, e.g. Syoowa 22 for the twenty-second year of the Syoowa era. However, *nengoo* have been used in conjunction with the sexagenary cycle, and are often used alone to identify a period, as in the phrase 'the Meizi era'.

Usually a new *nengoo* was adopted at the beginning of each reign, but it might be changed during the reign on the occasion of any great event. In fact, there were two occasions when eight different *nengoo* were used in a single reign, and in several there were six or more. At the end of the Meizi era in 1912 it was decided that thereafter the same era-name was to be used throughout any one reign.

Nengoo, on whatever day and month they are introduced, are always changed at the New Year. Chronological lists will give the date of the first year of a *nengoo*. When calculating the western equivalent for later years of a period, add to this date *not* the consecutive number of the year, but that number *minus one.* Thus the equivalent of Meizi 15 is correctly 1882 (1868 plus 14) *not* 1883 (1868 plus 15).

(*d*) THE NATIONAL CALENDAR

The use of this system of dating is a comparatively recent development. However, since it recommends itself on nationalist grounds as purely Japanese, it has been much used in modern Japan. It is based on the date of accession of the first emperor, Zinmu *Tennoo*, supposedly 660 B.C., which has been made the year 1 of the National Calendar. Thus A.D. 1940 was the year 2600 of the Japanese or National Calendar.

(e) *ZIDAI*

In addition to their use with a number to designate single years, *nengoo* are often used alone to describe the whole period (*zidai*) during which they were in force. Most of the important ones so used will be found in Table C below, p. 236.

Japanese history is also commonly divided into a number of longer *zidai*, usually named after the family or residence of the rulers (*de facto* or *de jure*). Historians differ in their choice of names and dates for these periods, but those most often found are given in the glossary under the heading *zidai*.

Additional information on calendars and dating can be found in

A. J. Koop and H. Inada, *Japanese names and how to read them*, (London, 1923), Chap. iv.

William Bramsen, 'Japanese Chronological Tables', *Trans. Asiatic Soc. Japan*, xxxvii (Yokohama, 1910), Suppl. 1–127. Gives western equivalents for Japanese days, months and years of the lunar calendar.

TABLE C. *NENGOO*

Nengoo	Date A.D.	*Nengoo*	Date A.D.
Tenbun (Tenmon)	1532	Kanpoo	1741
Koozi	1555	Enkyoo	1744
Eiroku	1558	Kan-en	1748
Genki	1570	Hooreki (Hooryaku)	1751
Tensyoo	1573	Meiwa	1764
Bunroku	1592	An-ei	1772
Keityoo (Kyootyoo)	1596	Tenmei	1781
Genwa	1615	Kansei	1789
Kan-ei	1624	Kyoowa	1801
Syooho	1644	Bunka	1804
Kei-an	1648	Bunsei	1818
Syoo-oo (Zyoo-oo)	1652	Tenpoo	1830
Meireki (Meiryaku)	1655	Kooka	1844
Manzi	1658	Ka-ei	1848
Kanbun	1661	Ansei	1854
Enpoo	1673	Man-en	1860
Tenwa	1681	Bunkyuu	1861
Zyookyoo (Teikyoo)	1684	Genzi (Ganzi)	1864
Genroku	1688	Kei-oo	1865
Hoo-ei	1704	Meizi	1868
Syootoku	1711	Taisyoo	1912
Kyoohoo	1716	Syoowa	1926
Genbun	1736		

6. DYNASTIES AND RULERS

In the following lists, names are given in National *roomazi*. Alternative readings of the characters are given in brackets. Posthumous names (*okuri-na*) are given for all emperors, except the present emperor, who is referred to as such. The names of reigning empresses are printed in italics.

There has been only one imperial dynasty, and the emperors consequently have no family name. For one brief period there were two rival courts, northern and southern. Although a court in exile, the southern court retained the imperial regalia, and is hence regarded as the legitimate line. The emperors of the northern court are listed separately.

The dates given indicate the official beginning of a reign. In many cases the emperor's actual accession took place in the previous year. There are difficulties in fixing dates for many reigns, especially the earlier ones. The traditional view puts the accession of Zinmu at 660 B.C., and the so-called National Calendar is based on this assumption. Modern research, however, while able only to give approximate dates for the earliest reigns, has shown them to be much later. The discrepancy is most marked in the first twenty-six reigns, and for convenience both series of dates are given here.

(i) LIST OF EMPERORS

No.	Name	Date	
		Probable	*Traditional*
		B.C.	B.C.
1	Zinmu	c. 40	660
2	Suisei	c. 10	581
		A.D.	
3	Annei	c. 20	549
4	Itoku	c. 50	510
5	Koosyoo	c. 80	475
6	Koo-an	c. 110	392
7	Koorei	c. 140	290
8	Koogen	c. 170	214
9	Kaika	c. 200	157
10	Suzin	c. 230	97
11	Suinin	259	29
			A.D.
12	Keikoo	291	71
13	Seimu	323	131
14	Tyuu-ai	356	192
	Zingoo Koogoo (Regent)	363	201
15	Oozin	380	270
16	Nintoku	395	313
17	Rityuu	428	400
18	Hansei (Hansyoo)	433	406
19	Inkyoo	438	412
20	Ankoo	455	454
21	Yuuryaku	457	457
22	Seinei	490	480
23	Kensoo	495	485
24	Ninken	498	488
25	Buretu (Muretu)	504	499
26	Keitai	510	507

(i) LIST OF EMPERORS (*continued*)

No.	Name	Date	No.	Name	Date
27	Ankan	534	80	Takakura	1169
28	Senka	536	81	Antoku	1181
29	Kinmei	540	82	Go-Toba	1184
30	Bidatu	572	83	Tuti-Mikado	1199
31	Yoomei	586	84	Zyuntoku	1211
32	Suzyun	588	85	Tyuukyoo (Kyuukyoo)	1221
33	*Suiko*	593	86	Go-Horikawa	1222
34	Zyomei	629	87	Sizyoo	1233
35	*Kookyoku*	642	88	Go-Saga	1243
36	Kootoku	645	89	Go-Hukakusa	1247
37	Saimei	655	90	Kameyama	1260
38	Tenti	662	91	Go-Uda	1275
39	Koobun	672	92	Husimi	1288
40	Tenmu	673	93	Go-Husimi	1299
41	*Zitoo*	686	94	Go-Nizyoo	1302
42	Monmu	697	95	Hanazono	1309
43	*Genmyoo* (*Genmei*)	708			
44	*Gensyoo*	715		*The Southern Court*	
45	Syoomu	724	96	Go-Daigo	1319
46	*Kooken*	749	97	Go-Murakami	1339
47	Zyunnin	759	98	Tyookei[1]	1368
48	*Syootoku*	765	99	Go-Kameyama	1373
49	Koonin	770		*The Northern Court*	
50	Kanmu	782		Koogen	1331
51	Heizyoo (Heizei)	806		Koomyoo	1336
52	Saga	810		Sukoo	1349
53	Zyunna	824		Go-Koogen	1352
54	Ninmyoo	834		Go-Enyuu	1372
55	Montoku (Buntoku)	851	100	Go-Komatu	1384
56	Seiwa	859	101	Syookoo	1413
57	Yoozei	877	102	Go-Hanazono	1429
58	Kookoo	885	103	Go-Tuti-Mikado	1465
59	Uda	889	104	Go-Kasiwabara	1501
60	Daigo	898	105	Go-Nara	1527
61	Syuzyaku	931	106	Oogimati	1558
62	Murakami	947	107	Go-Yoozei	1587
63	Reizei	968	108	Go-Mizu-no-o	1612
64	Enyuu	970	109	*Myoosyoo* (*Meisyoo*)	1630
65	Kazan	985	110	Go-Koomyoo	1644
66	Itizyoo	987	111	Go-Sai (Go-Sai-In)	1655
67	Sanzyoo	1012	112	Reigen	1663
68	Go-Itizyoo	1017	113	Higasiyama	1687
69	Go-Syuzyaku	1037	114	Naka-no-Mikado	1710
70	Go-Reizei	1046	115	Sakuramati	1736
71	Go-Sanzyoo	1069	116	Momozono	1748
72	Sirakawa	1073	117	Go-Sakuramati	1763
73	Horikawa	1087	118	Go-Momozono	1771
74	Toba	1108	119	Kookaku	1780
75	Sutoku	1124	120	Ninkoo	1817
76	Konoe	1142	121	Koomei	1847
77	Go-Sirakawa	1156	122	Meizi	1867
78	Nizyoo	1159	123	Taisyoo	1912
79	Rokuzyoo	1166	124	The present emperor	1926

[1] Tyookei is sometimes omitted, making the reign of Go-Kameyama the 98th, beginning in 1368. Subsequent emperors are then re-numbered accordingly.

(ii) LIST OF *SYOOGUN* AND ADMINISTRATORS

Syoogun	*Date*	*Administrators*	*Date*
	A.D.		A.D.
Minamoto family			
Yoritomo	1192	*Hoozyoo regents*	
Yori-ie	1199	Tokimasa	1199
Sanetomo	1203	Yositoki	1205
Huziwara family			
Yoritune	1226	Yasutoki	1225
Yoritugu	1244	Tunetoki	1242
		Tokiyori	1246
Imperial princes			
Munetaka	1251	Nagatoki	1256
Koreyasu	1266	Tokimune	1270
Hisa-akira	1289	Sadatoki	1284
Morikuni	1308	Moritoki	1300
		Takatoki	1315
Asikaga family			
Takauzi	1336		
Yosinori	1344		
Yosiaki	1358		
Yosimitu	1368		
Yosimoti	1394		
Yosikazu	1423		
Yosinori	1429		
Yosikatu	1441		
Yosimasa	1443		
Yosihisa	1473		
Yositane	1490		
Yosizumi	1494		
Yositane	1508		
Yosiharu	1521		
Yositeru	1547		
Yosihide	1567		
Yosiaki	1568	Oda Nobunaga	1573
		Toyotomi Hideyosi	1582
		Hideyori	1598
Tokugawa family			
Ieyasu	1603		
Hidetada	1605		
Iemitu	1623		
Ietuna	1651		
Tunayosi	1680		
Ienobu	1709		
Ietugu	1713		
Yosimune	1716		
Iesige	1745		
Ieharu	1761		
Ienari	1787		
Ieyosi	1838		
Iesada	1853		
Iemoti	1858		
Yosinobu (Keiki)	1866–1867		

ALPHABETICAL LIST OF DYNASTIES AND RULERS

NOTE. This list is *no more than* an index to the names of dynasties and rulers appearing in the five sections of this Handbook. Therefore to avoid confusing the readers for whom this work is primarily intended, we have not adjusted or made consistent in the index the various systems of transliteration necessarily used in the five sections. For convenience those Arabic names which are preceded by the Arabic article (see p. 5) are listed both with and without the article; identical names are distinguished by the addition in brackets of their dynasties; a ruler who has a well-known name which does not happen to be the first element in that name (e.g. Akbar) appears under both his well-known and full name; and lastly, names which have obtained an historical or popular fixity of spelling (e.g. Jenghis Khan) are duly entered in this list as well as their more precise forms.